Teaching Young Children at School and Home

Edythe Margolin

FLORIDA INTERNATIONAL UNIVERSITY

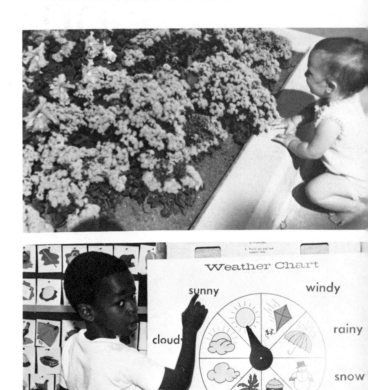

Teaching Young Children at School and Home

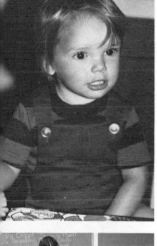

Macmillan Publishing Co., Inc.
NEW YORK

Collier Macmillan Publishers
LONDON

To Diane,
who gave us our first loving and exciting
experience as parents.

Macmillan Publishing Co., Inc.
866 Third Avenue, New York, New York 10022

Collier Macmillan Canada, Ltd.

Library of Congress Cataloging in Publication Data

Margolin, Edythe.
    Teaching young children at school and home.

    Including bibliographical references and index.
    1. Education, Preschool—Curricula. 2. Education,
Primary—Curricula. 3. Children—Management. 4. Parent
and child. I. Title.
LB1140.4.M37   372'.21   80-28606
ISBN 0-02-375980-1

Printing: 1 2 3 4 5 6 7 8   Year: 2 3 4 5 6 7 8

PREFACE

This book is planned for people who interact with or are responsible for young children on a somewhat regular or daily basis. It is also intended for the part-time parent (e.g., divorced, physically separated from the child, but still psychologically a parent), grandparent, aunt, uncle, or close friend who may see the child periodically and want information regarding decisions that have to be made for or with the child.

Each day society and life in complex situations seem to pose more problems related to choices that seriously affect how one may live. Scientific studies disclose the presence and dangers of carcinogens in food; ecological limitations and problems with oil-producing sources make people aware of habits that will need to be changed. Thus, not only do adults have difficulty at times deciding what they ought to do in terms of their own future goals, they have difficulty deciding for their children. Even though children may not accept their parents' decisions or suggestions, parents are nevertheless involved in responsibilities related to making "forced" choices.

Child rearing is perceived by many people as a great responsibility. Often, the more education an individual has, the more (s)he may be concerned about making the proper decisions (appropriate to his/her terms of analysis) in guiding the child. There are no absolute guidelines for the process except to say that the adult typically uses his/her own values in making choices. These decisions are consciously or subconsciously made. In any case, adults in contemporary society are exposed, through television programs and written forms of communication, to various explanations and analyses of human decision making. The decision-making process, especially among people who are introspective, analytical, and studying it through psychological techniques, can be complicated. Parents and teachers, discussing choices they have made for guiding children's behavior, often say that in one sense they feel selfish regarding a decision they have made, but in another sense they feel unselfish, indicating they were acting in the best interests of the child.

The societal context of any year in one's life affects choices for individual aspects of living, often to a greater degree than one is aware. Adults may often wonder what kind of society today's school children may live in as adults. This perspective makes many people more aware of their own vulnerability or helplessness in relation to knowing what the future will bring and how one ought to prepare for it.

Most teachers and parents are teaching children values and norms that are pertinent today and at the same time are anticipating what the children may need to know when they become adults in a society of their own future. Can anyone really prepare children to function in a society that will differ from the present one, one whose economy, political faction, and ecological patterns may be different? Can we know what the specific obligations or commitments might have to be?[1]

Our basic assumptions about the necessity for teaching children how to read, write, and compute rest on the fact that we expect those skills to be part of any adult's repertoire of behavior if (s)he is to function effectively in society. Thus, on the one hand, we are educating children for a world that we envision will be like the one we know today; on the other hand, we know that society will not stay the same. We are well aware that each generation grows in a societal context or social history somewhat different from the one we knew in our earlier developing years. This awareness carries with it an implication that we have to help parents, teachers, and children in emphasizing patterns of open-mindedness and attitudes in problem solving that will serve them well, not only now, but also in the future. This book is written with that orientation toward learning, problem solving, and decision making.

From the point of view of the author, as one individual among others who has taught university students in their pre- and in-service teaching courses, it has become increasingly clear how important it is for teachers to respect themselves for their own competency and personal characteristics if their work with children is to have the element of success in it. The way they treat children is often a reflection of, or is affected by, their own feelings toward themselves. Typically, the more a teacher is able to respect her/himself, the more (s)he is able to help the pupils cope with problems and to develop the self-respect needed for growth. The teacher may not always be successful in that effort, of course, but at least the effort is made. Compassion for the child's attempts in learning difficult concepts is evident in the classroom. Patience and an awareness of the child's need for support and encouragement are part of the teacher's interaction style for pupils in the classroom.

Because learning occurs, not in steady or consistent spurts, immediately soaring to the top of one's achievement capabilities, but in gradual (sometimes accelerated) paths to refinement, for the most part, children need steadiness in guidance. They need an adequate balance of nurturing, subject matter information, data on their own progress (e.g., awareness of improvement), and guidelines for further stages of development. This book hopes to sensitize teachers and parents to children's moods, temperaments, and needs for constant support. To those adults who are already sensitive

1. Hilda Taba, *Curriculum Development* (New York: Harcourt, Brace Jovanovich, Inc., 1962), p. 37. Taba indicated that although important changes used to occur in society over centuries or generations, significant changes have recently accelerated so that they are counted and observed almost every five or ten years. Those changes are often extremely difficult to predict.

to children's needs for learning and growth, this book can serve to rededicate energies in that direction. Helping the young not only enriches the teacher or parent, it also contributes to the strength of social goals in society. It affects both the individual and the collective, and can be done in the best positive sense.

The author is extremely grateful for the support of many people who allowed pictures of their children to be taken and to be published. Dr. Dave Felton, the principal of Shadowlawn Elementary School of Dade County Schools, and Mrs. Jean Felton, the kindergarten teacher allowed the pupils in the kindergarten to be photographed after permission from the parents was obtained. To the photographers, Gerald J. Margolin and Priscilla Margolin, for the time and energies expended, a debt of gratitude will always be remembered.

E. M.

CONTENTS

The Curriculum, Its Programs, and Underlying Philosophies   119

Priorities in Communication: Helping Children Express Themselves   153

Mathematics: Who Needs It and Why?   249

6

Science in Young Children's Lives   *291*

7

Social Studies and the Social Sciences: Finding Out About One's Society   *317*

The Arts: Their Potential in Children's Development   *360*

Index   *401*

LIST OF TABLES

LIST OF CONCEPT ILLUSTRATIONS

Societal Settings and Children's Development

Introduction

Teachers, like parents, are often heard discussing how certain children are progressing at school. As the early years of children's lives are spent in the informal and formal developmental processes of learning how to read, write, and compute (among other skills), it is understandable that these concerns are central to the thoughts of adults responsible for the well-being of children.

At times adults who want to help children progress at school or home become frustrated. They are not sure that their efforts are benefiting the children. Then, too, as educational processes change from generation to generation, parents who experienced a different system of instruction are often puzzled by the practices in today's schools. The burden of supporting or explaining the contemporary patterns of education often falls upon the teacher and administrator.

Not only does the society of today function differently from former societies, and have different value orientations, it also generates people of a nature different from those of the 1930s or 1940s, for example.[1] Research, popular literature, mass media, have provided evidence that one's efforts in shaping an effective life style, can be exerted in a variety of ways. The individual does not simply try to learn a language and the mores of a culture. The democratic system of education seeks to ensure equality of opportunity for each person. Although we are aware that this ideal is not, in fact, attained, at least the awareness of it has changed many forms of the educational system. Methods of teaching, teachers' attitudes, types of teaching equipment, use of school facilities have all been affected by the knowledge that not all children have been receiving sufficient intellectual or academic benefits from attending school. The inequalities of educational opportunities reside in the system of instruction as well as in other aspects of society.

Teacher training institutions have undergone changes in the last thirty years. Many of those changes are due to Civil Rights Movements, Head Start Programs for young children, and greater awareness of human variability and change as reflected in psychological measurement techniques. Human development, examined in life-cycle age spans, reveals greater plasticity in intellectual orientation than was known years ago.[2] Each individual is born with broad limitations in a biological sense as well as an intellectual one, but the view of intelligence held decades ago—as fixed and nonchanging no matter what differences in environmental circumstances might occur—is suspect today.

Even the methods of teaching young children are tested to the point of trying to focus on optimal teaching styles for working with three to five-year-old children.[3] Interest in the teacher's effectiveness has been manifested by teacher-education institutions as well as parents. Studies on the characteristics of the successful teacher sometimes focus on the children's test scores in order to find out whether the children learned more information with one teacher than another. Some researchers consider that the teacher's style of teaching should be the focus of investigation. Humanists want to see a teacher who is concerned about the pupils' feelings. Some writers suggest that more important than the information learned is whether children want to come to school, and consequently that the teacher has to be encouraging, supportive of and interested in the child's self-concept. With favorable attitudes toward school as a place for discovery of facts, new books, and an awareness of self-worth, children may acquire enduring patterns of desirable study habits. Thus, the various attitudes of educators, professors in teacher-education institutions, parents, and writers in popular forms of literature represent different perspectives on what constitutes the qualities of good teaching.

In the process of deciding what a good teacher does, educators take their cues from the societal context, a combination of one that they experienced when they were children and one that they think of as "today's" world. The impressions they formulate are not always as clear as one might think.[4] If yesterday's views and today's conflict in the teacher's mind, the behavior of the teacher as (s)he interacts with the child often manifests those uncertainties. This is not to suggest that the teacher is helplessly ambivalent. It also does not suggest that the teacher is constantly giving the children confusing directions. Human behavior, whether the teacher's or the child's, is not expected to be as consistent as many textbooks ideally prescribe. It is possible, however, to be sufficiently aware of internal inconsistencies so that one is not overwhelmed by them. With some awareness of human nature, an individual may attempt to reconcile contradictory internal struggling.

The issue of reconciling inconsistencies in the teacher with instruction of children in the classroom becomes a vital force in affecting what and how children learn. The next section presents data focusing on the sources of conflicting perceptions that influence the teacher who interacts with young children.

Society's "Messages" to the Teacher

We grow in a society, advised and cared for in various ways by certain people who are guided by specific norms, values, and habits. In that process of growth, we have an image of reality, our own microcosmic view of what society is like. We receive from various care-givers (e.g., parents, teachers, relatives) impressions as to what constitutes "good" and "bad" behavior. Sociologists refer to this process as *socialization,* or the manner in which "society" gets into our heads.[5]

Society, as an abstract concept, refers to a group of people who have similar understandings (in a broad sense), live in a particular region, and share expectations about roles and statuses. Although we receive information from outside the self, we bring those external impressions inside ourselves, and create our own impressions of what society is like. We act on those perceptions and assume that others have similar views.[6]

Society is perceived both on a broad, impersonal, or indirect level, and on a unique, personalized, or direct level. These interpretations of what are considered to be "society's views," are often mainly what our parents and relatives have told us *should be* our orientations to life. This level of meaning from the collective, to our parents and to ourselves, does not necessarily represent or match what the abstract concept of society may be to many people. It may be similar to the views of some groups of people. Yet, often we hear people say that "society" wants us to do a specific act or conduct ourselves in certain ways. In fact it may have been a parent or teacher who told us that we should do something that s(he) (not necessarily "society") desired.[7]

To further remind the teacher of the ways in which a societal context affects values and attitudes that function in the classroom, it is necessary to consider that social and parental mores affect even the infant at birth as well as prior conditions of prenatal development. Berger and Berger disagree with the notion, to which many subscribe, that infants are born with a mind that is a "clean slate," or *tabula rasa*.[8] Infants are influenced, to a great extent, by what happens after they are born, it is true, but they cannot be perceived as an inactive nonsubstance with nothing within them to respond in their own ways to the environment.

Teachers as individuals are also influenced, not only by their own families in one way or another, but also by the educational institutions of higher learning that present courses for the preparation of teaching in the elementary school. In that sphere of influence are the professors, who are themselves part of society outside the university and are also committed to specific ideologies regarding life's values, and what childhood should be on a broad, collective level as well as an individual level.[9] Professors are presenting both their own individualistic interpretations of society and an institutional perspective (in part).

These delicate patterns of intermeshing individual impressions with those of a broader cultural and socializing agency, such as a university or college, influence mainly at the start of the teacher-as-student's education at the institution of higher learning, the way the teacher will teach young children. The way this process occurs is very subtle, and therefore difficult to analyze.

University students preparing to teach may typically have a couple of years of lower-division work (of a total four-year period of higher educational preparation for a degree and a credential). They receive a concentration of courses that apply to educational instruction, techniques, and materials for children in the elementary school. Even though some students may have one course or more in the social foundations of education in society, they do not always have sufficient academic information about the structure and function of various institutions in society in the same way that sociologists examine these phenomena. What students understand of these mechanisms often comes mainly from personal experiences. This perspective is not adequate in the total concentration of what teaching is or can be. It also does not permit the teacher to have as much of a global standpoint on the children's backgrounds and development as an academic or systematic representation can create.

Resilience, flexibility, and accommodation in one's initial impressions can allow for perceiving children more in terms of what they are rather than how (perhaps in negative terms) they will be.[10] With a basic premise of this sort, the teacher may, even while being annoyed with a child and aware of this irritation within, still recognize that "natural" differences in children are to be expected. These differential effects in behavior, facial expressions, mannerisms, and the like are in part due to the children's backgrounds and experiences (e.g., personality development, genetic endowment, sociological factors of family, parents) and in part due to the teacher's own behavior and attitudes prevailing in relationships with the child. Anticipating differences among people as something that reflects among other things, simply a mode of perspectives that vary from the teacher's, can minimize the explosiveness or shock when the two come together as teacher and pupil. This view is not to oversimplify the process, but rather to enlarge on or amplify a perspective.

Differences between the teacher and pupil, then, should not always be perceived as mainly an occurrence that arises only on a basis of irritations with one another. The "natural" order of events when people interact with one another on a daily basis would appear to lean more toward disequilibrium than equilibrium, when deeply honest emotions emerge. In this sense, "honest emotions" are perceived as the gut-level reactions (unsocialized or presocialized, not socially conditioned anger) of a baby, with minimal self-control in an angry outburst.

There is a part of the social self that conflicts with the ideal self and the environment. When this conflict arises in the person-to-person interaction process in the classroom, it is bound to manifest itself. The teacher does, in fact, have the more compelling influence in the teacher-pupil relationship, in affecting the child's tendency or desire to submit. Generally, however, the children are vulnerable and dependent on their own trust and on the nurturance of their teachers, who are presumably expected to act in the best interests of their pupils, if the most ideal sense of a philosophy of teaching is to be taken seriously. Teachers, as people, have to be highly sensitive to and critical of some of their own predispositions to act and to think in certain ways, because many of those ways affect children's learning.

It seems clear through various media messages[11] about the nature of society, and the sociological data[12] presented by sociologists, that teachers, as individuals and as professionally prepared socializing agents of society, have to be alert and knowledgeable in their perceptions of their own processes of thinking and acting. The societal context in any given era of the total history of a country or society affects greatly the directions of a teacher's thinking. As a result, the teacher's behavior with children takes on a specific orientation. Since much of the process occurs almost without thought and is typically developed in the automatic or habitual responses of the individual, it is often not even subject to self-analysis. Many teachers, however, with whom the author has worked in university classroom sessions, have been interested in and intrigued by becoming introspective enough to re-examine their own childhood experiences, attitudes, or beliefs, when they became aware of the extent to which their earlier perceptions could shape interaction patterns with children in the classroom.

Society's Effects on Parental Roles and Behavior

One of the most difficult tasks in life is to be responsible for the development of an infant and the guidance that must necessarily follow in childhood and later years. Many parents want information, in view of a complicated society and conflicting value orientations, on what is best for their children. The problems arise, not only in the early years when many recommendations come to parents in the form of advice from their own elders, mass media, religious sources, and the like, but also when parents begin to consider deeply what they think are the ideal (or perhaps for them the best) ways to rear their young.[13] It is obvious that the redefinition of role gender itself and how males and females are expected to conduct themselves in various social task-orienting situations results in confusion of parental behavior. Maleness or femaleness is learned to some extent during one's childhood years. That learning does not instruct us, however, in what is required after one's maleness or femaleness creates a human being, of whichever gender.[14]

Societal contexts and dynamics affect parent behavior and roles in at least ten different ways.

1. Views of Earlier Generations

The first of these concerns the specific *ideas that a couple have accepted as valid from the views of their own generation and also the one prior to theirs.* The one prior to theirs is the generation that represents the views of parents and people who affected the ideas of children advancing through earlier years.

The newly mated couple bring with them to the plans they have for interacting with their own infant, the effects of their four parents (except in cases where they have not interacted with their own parents, for whatever reason) and some significant relatives or friends. It is difficult as parents, to analyze in some cases, whose points of view affected us more than others.

2. Patterns of Identification

The second quality of characteristics that the societal context affects in parent behavior is related to *patterns of identification* with a specific model or set of models in the parenthood role. Mothers may use their own mothers or other configurations represented in contemporary literature or women's magazines as a model to which they want to aspire or compare themselves. They want to judge themselves and their own behavior in terms of how it measures up to their self-selected models for emulation.

Fathers are interested in the success of their role. Awareness of their concerns for performing well as a father became publicized in the last decade. Lamb[15] indicates that, interestingly enough, research on the father's role acquired data not from the fathers themselves, but from other sources, until fairly recent works focused on other than mothers' information and concentrated on data received from the fathers directly. As recently as the middle of the 1960s, researchers were not interviewing fathers or observing them, even though their concern was mainly with the properties and elements in the role of fatherhood. Although fathers are interested in doing well in their own roles as parents, they often have to mediate that role in terms of the way their wives perceive tasks that need to be done by the fathers.

Patterns of identification that the mothers have for their own performance in that role, and *patterns of identification* that fathers may have for their performance as fathers, then, affect the self-concepts of parents. In a society that brings widespread attention to the skills and satisfaction of being a parent, the personality aspect of any parent in that role will be affected. If, for example, an individual feels that he does well in a particular situation as a father, he allows himself some self-esteem in that self-judgment. Thus, the model that an individual holds "out there" as a mirror to be used in self-reflection, affects the quality of self-approval that can be achieved.

Society, through mass media, literature, public lectures, religious, and educational institutions presents morally oriented images of how a "good" parent ought to act. Some perceptions that counteract or conflict with those views and confuse parents at times are those that involve intellectualization of the maternal role as part of a total personhood.[16] The contemporary emphasis on facing reality with honesty, with seeing life clearly instead of through romantic vision where marriage and its intricate dynamics are concerned, brings doubt and stress to some men and women. This urgency to seek truth in a sexual relationship, with some faith in commitment for each other as well as for a child, blurs *patterns of identification*. Tendencies toward uncertainty in one's own judgment prevent conceptualization of guidelines for behavior that one may use for one's self.[17] This does not mean that an individual cannot proceed with life in somewhat clear terms. It means that where one may be definitively clear about intentions for behavior, there is a greater likelihood that the individual knows what (s)he wants.

From time to time, a parent seeks, by looking around at her/his friends or groups with whom (s)he wants to identify, the qualities in the role of parent that should be emulated. All parents do not necessarily do this; those who are concerned about their own performance in the role or are perhaps uncertain about their own children's development may almost unconsciously check themselves.

3. Financial Status of Parents

The third way that a societal context affects the behavior of a parent involves the *location of the child-rearing adult and mate in the financial structure of society at any given time.* Parents in the early years of their marriage may be in economic straits as compared with the relative affluence of their later years. This affects the manner in which the children are cared for, fed, clothed, dressed, and perceived as dependent people.[18] Some mothers have wished to work, whether their household budget has needed it or not. Some mothers have had to work in order to give children even the bare necessities of child care.

For mothers who were able to pay someone else to care for their children while they were away from their homes, the child generally had the protection that was needed. For some researchers, however,[19] trends in the direction of other-than-parent care for children are worrisome. This does not mean that mothers should never work. It means that better ways should be found to ensure that the child has parental time and interaction. Bronfenbrenner speaks of the "fragmentation of the extended family, the separation of residential and business areas" . . . different social activities for age groups, and several other indicators of children's placement apart from mixed activities and functions of life, as they were known prior to a highly technological age or society.[20]

A parent's location in the stratification system in which financial adequacy affects education and the life style of the family creates attitudes toward constraints in patterns of child rearing. Whether an individual is on a higher educational stratum may affect access to the power stratum and the economic stratum.[21] Each of these dimensions relates to the way an individual or a family may live. Access to comfortable means of daily living determines in part the decisions one will make for children.

Some parents who are wealthy desire that their children experience manual labor of some kind. Their children are not lavished with money or excluded from doing what is needed to know that money does not come easily without providing a product or service for it. Children who live in large homes, however, still acquire a somewhat distorted view compared to the low-income laborer. But then, that perspective was not the intention of the parent.

Values of parents are often similar to those of the groups with which they themselves identify. If parents want their children to become like those of a specific group in society, they may orient their children's thinking and behavior in that direction. The children are encouraged to become proficient in skills or activities that are admired by a given social group. This is often referred to as *anticipatory socialization.* It prepares the individual for behavior that will be acceptable to an envisioned group with whom a child may become associated. We are reminded, however, that roles are changing rapidly in contemporary society, and that their future behavioral expectations may be different from impressions people have of them today.[22]

Parents in low-income groups are involved in acquiring adequate food, shelter, clothing, and the like for their children. They may not have as many choices for selection of their purchases, given the limitations of funds. They are interested in the quality of life, as are people in other income categories. Their specific desires, however, may differ. Here, too, we need to remember that discussions of individuals, conceptualized within a category, must include awareness that people differ in various ways.

4. Educational Level of Parents

A fourth way that the societal context affects a parent's orientation to a child is the *educational level* at any given time in the parent's background. A parent may have graduated from high school and continued educating him/herself by reading and learning other than pursuing a degree in higher education. Interest in *keeping one's self informed* of recent data and in preventing one's self from becoming stagnant, affects the parent's attitude toward the child. The parent who is somewhat open, flexible, and tending toward curiosity about societal dynamics may be inclined toward a self-awareness that facilitates interaction between parent and child.[23]

Parents' ideas about self-development were transmitted in some ways to their young. Studies indicated, in harmony with the psychiatric world view, that individuals would have to learn how to actualize their own personalities. The changing attitudes about how parents should talk to their children, rather than merely expecting obedience from them or being authoritarian toward them, reflected efforts to help their children know their own skills and resources. Self-knowledge, it was reasoned, could help the individual achieve what (s)he wanted. To expect social change through commitment to a society, rather than to one's own goals and efforts, was viewed as a lack of sophistication and unawareness in the thinking of individuals. Reissman and Miller suggested that a psychological mode of thinking prevented in part the development of a vocabulary for the means of social change.[24]

Although parents may keep themselves aware of current news and intellectual writings, it appears well warranted that they also view new ideas in terms of the societal context, when one considers its effects on social or self-development. Popular views of one era grow out of reactions to views of the preceding period. At times there appears to be an exaggeration of attitudes that do not appropriately respond to the behavior itself. This is seen in the attempt, too, to "become one's own" authority, so to speak.[25] When a parent feels that (s)he has been overcontrolled by some thing, person, idea, or institution, a strong reaction may occur. A parent who has shorn her/himself of strong feelings toward someone whom (s)he has respected and loved, regards the person once admired as hypercritical, dominating, "oppressively controlling . . . tyrannical and egocentric . . . rather than a loving and enabling mentor."[26] This view also affects the parent's behavior toward his/her own child, resulting in compensatory consideration or special efforts *not to be controlling* with his/her young. These efforts can become confusing to the parent struggling with his/her own views of self-development. Thus parents have to weigh in the balance their own personal views of how to rear their young, what the current societal context appears to be (with all its contradictions), and what traditional aspects are desirable to suit the individuals involved.

5. Parents' Attitudes Toward Work

The fifth element that the societal context affects in parental behavior toward the young is related to the *social ethic of attitudes toward work or industriousness*. Different periods in social history support religious and moral beliefs about work and its contribution to society and the individual's self-worth. To make useful contributions to one's society, whether through scientific ideas or inventions using the hands to create them, brings reflected self-praise. Religious principles glorified in the early development of the United States[27] influenced patterns of work and self-discipline. Whether work is currently viewed as part of a religious ethic, whether it motivates one to be self-actualizing and self-developing to higher levels of aspiration, or whether it is viewed as a means to an end affects the parents' attitudes toward the beliefs they instill in their young.

Some consider that because middle-class parents tend to have degrees of autonomy in their jobs, they try to raise their children to participate in the socialization process. The emphasis is not on obedience to others in superior positions, necessarily, but on understanding and being creative in their own socialization or development.[28] Parents who experience in their occupations the need to obey, conform, and cooperate with superiors, teach their children to do the same. This is considered to occur in occupations paying lower wages.

The view that virtue lies in work and self-discipline is not new to American society. Throughout the years, however, the manner in which some people have perceived a work "ethic" has been related to a sense of self-identity. Doing a job well, meeting a challenge in higher aspirations, and accomplishing ever greater skills has provided new self-awareness for those who were seeking fulfillment. During the various liberation movements, many women found in themselves new qualities and attributes that emerged in work activities.

Work is central to a way of regulating one's time. It is the means through which people support themselves, it is true. But the profession or occupation of men and women can also provide most of what they enjoy in their lives. They take pride in the productivity and skills that are evident in their own handiwork. If one's children acquire these impressions, it is not surprising. Contemporary society emphasizes that the quality of one's working life measure up to humane standards that work and its conditions are satisfying to individuals. Many people have left the market place for the quiet, less hectic, less pressured pace in country areas. Work, for them, has taken on a different meaning. They do not want work to interfere with human existence as they view it in the best sense of the concept. They may perceive such an environment as "closer to nature" than the steel buildings of the city, as representing a choice more congruent with human characteristics interacting with a less harsh world.

Work as a social ethic supporting industriousness and as an aspect of character in the individual has changed in the minds of some people. The focus is now on what work can do for the individual as an end in itself, rather than how it can help society. But virtuousness of work in relation to religious beliefs still exists today in the views of religious groups. Thus, on the one hand, there are those who consider work as an important part of the personality and identity, and those who think of it as a fact of life, religion, and depth of character in a spiritual sense. There are, of course, those who do not fall within either category, but reflect degrees of those tendencies.

6. Parents' Beliefs About Child Rearing

The sixth way in which the societal context affects a parent's behavior toward a child is reflected in the *belief of a given child-rearing perspective of the social era.* What the parent accepts as a "best" way to raise a child influences deliberate acts on the part of the parent, insisting on certain responses from the child. Parents from various income groups, as we have discussed, see the world in terms of their "digested meanings" of life. One's ideas emerge in the context of relationships with similar people, as well as in the context of dissimilar people. Social groups, however, strengthen the beliefs of individuals who frequent (through work, visiting, or neighborhood patterns) the same places at the same time, and are exposed to the same agreed-upon views. This does not suggest dogma or indoctrination but rather inclinations toward the acceptance of certain values related to ways of believing or conducting one's self in life.

Friends and neighbors indirectly affect the acceptance (or lack of it) of one's decisions regarding children's behavior. Parents may prevent their children from being with others considered undesirable. They can also be instrumental in planning for their children's interaction with others preferred by the parent. Neighborhood conversation provides up-dating, at times, of what may be happening at the children's or parents' levels. Even though neighborhoods differ in terms of the amount of time people spend in them, the cohesiveness of them, or the appearance of them,[29] they nevertheless affect in various ways, where we go, what we do, how we think, and how we plan our daily routines.

Various contradictions prevail in parents' minds, given what they would prefer to do and the limitations that prevent them from carrying out their ideas. Time, money, opportunity, or an accessibility to the means for implementing parental desires in behalf of their children can affect their beliefs one way or another. On the direct level of what is known from personal experiences, "close to home," and what is heard about or learned from less personal sources (e.g., television, magazines, books, newspapers), opinions are created that guide behavior. Even though books, magazines, and other consulting sources may not be equally distributed or accessible in the population, adults see and hear about the experiences of other people and may be affected by them, "middle-class" biases, notwithstanding.

Many writers have commented on changes in philosophies of child care.[30] They describe differences in behavioral restriction, some of which were demonstrated in attitudes toward a child's sense of autonomy and its development; some restrictions were obvious in attitudes toward children's handling of their own body parts or genitals; some restrictions were evident in the forms of feeding habits parents were advised to follow with their infants. One sociologist comments on changes in the advice given in governmental editions on *Infant Care* since 1914 as compared with today.[31] From resistance to what were perceived as a child's needs, to submitting to them has represented decades of time in attitude change in raising children. This does not mean that everyone agreed to these changes. It does mean, however, that contemporary views in general differ from those published in 1914, at least.

A unique view of children and their relationships to parents was introduced by Sigmund Freud, who emphasized the significance of childhood experiences and the quality of them.[32] These effects are still current today. They seemed to have led toward the work of Dr. Benjamin Spock, who advocated the kind of participatory socialization observed by noting the advice of child psychologists or developmentalists. As parents decide, first whether they want their children to assist in the decision-making process for their own development, and second, how they will implement that orientation of thought, they have some means of self-guidance in how they will interact with or raise their children.

Participatory or democratic decision making in a family is perceived mainly as a middle-class philosophy. It fosters an active attitude toward one's fate and goals. It embraces both the individualistic, expressive view of the personality and a view that is oriented toward the collective and toward activity perceived to be in the best interests of society as a whole, beyond one's own social stratum. The individual is expected not only to express concerns about him/herself and rational means of acquiring his/her goals, but also to be critically and constructively aware of social needs, problems, and solutions supporting social justice.[33]

Some of the views of parents in lower-income groups are affected by feelings of helplessness in regard to their own fate. They do not have easy access (financially or verbally—although this has changed to some extent through social programs of citizen advocacy) to what is needed to ameliorate their frustrating conditions. It takes a long time for them to attain what is taken for granted by those in higher-income groups. Articulation for their needs often occurs through people of higher-income groups who have grown up with varying degrees of commitment to a social order.

Although parents are affected, whether in lower- or higher-income groups by the child-rearing perspectives of professionals in any given era of a society's history, they are affected in different ways. Their access to those views differs, as does their concern for the justifiability of them.

7. Hero/Heroine Images

The seventh perspective taken from a societal context that influences a parent's manner of interaction with a child involves *hero/heroine images in a society at any given time*. This phrase refers to people in the arts, the sciences, or sports who excel in a variety of ways such that they are admired by broad segments of a population. Their behavior and activity become a model, in some ways, that lead parents to accept them for their own emulation.

Some women admire writers who skillfully discuss home life in dramatic but humorous ways and listen to the words or phrases they use, perhaps to use them themselves at an appropriate time. Some admire actresses who appear gracious, beautiful, and bright in the roles they play on the screen. Some parents think of being a reporter for television or other news teams—one who seems informed, intelligent, and successful in interviews with world leaders and other highly visible or powerful people.

Entertaining or well-known people who appear on the screen, stage, or television become the embodiment of values that are held in high esteem by many members of a society. Magazines and newspapers often describe the phenomenon of fashion, jewelry, or other accessories worn by people in the limelight (Washington, New York, or Hollywood—the film capital in California) becoming the focus of popular appeal. Hats worn by the "first lady" or president's wife are purchased by thousands of women who have seen her wear a hat of a specific style.

Items of children's apparel become copies of clothing seen on teen-age idols or famous people's children. Sweatshirts, jogging clothes, running shoes, are made in all qualities and at various prices. When certain styles are seen as preferred (or advertised as desired) by attractive athletes, tennis stars, acrobatic, and skating competition winners, people note the clothing and find it satisfying to buy similar types to wear themselves. A psychological association or personal identification with the image of the person or star is an indirect result for some people.

With greater numbers of children performing on the screen, stage, and athletic field now than there used to be decades ago, younger children are observing others their own age who have characteristics and skills that are appealing to them. In this sense, children are, in some adaptive ways, acquiring habits related to nutrition improvement, development of skills, self-discipline, and body care. When hero/heroine idolization is associated with people that do not (for some) epitomize favorable qualities of a society (e.g., "bad," malevolent characters portrayed in plays involving criminals or "parasitic" bully types), children may imitate them, as well. Parents have to be aware of their children's preferences and of activities that appear to represent an "acting-out" of those choices.

Children's love of baseball, football, and basketball stars and other athletic "champions" reflects the need to look up to someone who demonstrates qualities of prowess, self-management, and persistence in pursuing what needs to be done in order to succeed.[34] The helplessness and dependence of children in the overpowering perspective of their interaction with the world are transcended in the favored symbolism of the champion, who, at least in the view of the child, represents strength in one's self rather than dependence on others.

Positive and negative effects of hero/heroine worship in society are the prerogative of all to utilize as they will. What children gain from it, or what detracts them from a pursuit of healthy and effective living, are there in the society from which they select or identify for purposes of their own needs. This is not necessarily a deliberate or conscious, logically thought-out process that persuades people to imitate people they like. It often occurs in complex and subtle ways, difficult to measure in scientific terms.[35]

Again, it is obvious that "society" is out there as well as "in here," in ourselves, as we choose and select what we like and want to internalize and accept as part of our own personality development. Parents are selecting for their children, and the children are selecting for themselves what they see around them and choose to take on for their own identities. It is true that children will act in ways that are similar to the ways of their friends, but the discussion here is focused on how the parents are affected by societal contexts of any given era in relation to the visible, popular, hero/heroines in the activity of various fields cherished by many people in a society.

Fathers' impressions about outstanding people who are unusually talented and competent in sports, the arts, or the academic spheres are affecting their interaction with children. Some men formulate an image, as do women, of how they want to appear in their children's eyes or perceptions. They manifest these hopes, implicitly, in their activity with children. Many fathers inhibit or facilitate certain tendencies or skills and mannerisms in themselves and their children that they feel are inappropriate or appropriate to the male role. Impressions of good or bad, relative to the way a "properly behaving" male or female would act, are evident in the direction a parent gives his child. These views are often associated, in part, with someone who may be a social hero/heroine at the time.[36]

Just as tendencies toward virtuous and nonvirtuous behavior are evident in society, so are they observable in people. That does not mean that people are totally bad or good.[37] We are reminded to conceptualize human beings as manifesting and thinking of both good and evil—to recognize this phenomenon in one's nature is to know one's self better than one would by thinking that only someone else (who thinks differently) is evil, mean, foolish, etc. To place evil or violence as a reality only in others rather than to realize that each of us has feelings in that direction as well as feelings in the direction of kindness and consideration, is to falsify the world, to some extent.[38]

Heroes, seeking better self-images, presenting ourselves to the world and to people who are important to us, occupy a great deal of our time and energies. This is not wrong. But to be unaware of what we are doing and how we are doing it can mislead us. It is necessary to become aware. To enjoy playing *at* a different hero/heroine type role, with the knowledge that it is a temporary role, not one's "true" self (however one might want to define this), can be amusing, experimental, and appealing. Benson's concern is that people ought to separate themselves in their own minds from some of the hero/heroine images, even though the embodiment of admired qualities of a society may be evident in guiding their own forms of self-expression.[39]

Parents will be affected by the ideas and characteristics that heroes/heroines of society in any given time advertise in their public acceptance. It is to the advantage and disadvantage of children's development in terms of how the parents perceive the images they want their children to accept. The images themselves are not what we need to be worried about, but rather how they are adapted, perceived, and implemented by people in any society.

8. The Medical Technology

The eighth aspect of the societal context that affects parental interaction with children is one that is more formally and systematically introduced to family life than some of the elements mentioned prior to this one. The *medical technology in any societal context and how it is put to use by and among members of a society* can change attitudes and patterns of behavior of parents with their young. This does not mean that medical, scientific, logical, or statistical knowledge is received in a nonsubjective manner by individuals. Intellectual thought is affected by emotions and how we view the content of new ideas. Technology influences what is available to people. This does not mean that everyone uses it.

The medical technology that has affected lowered percentages in the last fifty years of the incidence of diseases, of deaths, of various restricting or crippling effects in the human body, has changed, affording parents of today, who are fortunate enough to have access to it when needed, a means for improved care-giving for children. The accessibility, although limited in terms of the numbers who need them, of organ transplants, kidney dialysis machines, respirators, and other complicated, expensive human aids for staying alive have helped parents know what can be done for children. Encouragement for greater chances of amelioration when a parent is faced with ill health or birth defects of a child can be assured. Genetic information can educate parents about the chances of certain problems occurring in an unborn child, thereby giving them the opportunity to make certain decisions before the birth of a baby, and affecting the life situation for the infant.

The strides made in the investigation of foods have made it possible to know which foods should be avoided for children (and adults as well). Chemical additives, artificial sugars, salt, and dyes in food are unhealthful. Food cooked in specific ways can be harmful, too. Consumer protection units, both private and public (Food and Drug Administration), provide data frequently on "errors" in baby foods among others. Products are whisked from the shelves, in some cases, at least, when legal agencies mandate a ruling.

Research that reveals problems of pollution in the air or certain toxic wastes from industrial processing plants, is made public, thereby warning people of certain risks that are prevalent in some parts of the country. The data are available; people hear about ways of protecting themselves; medical researchers are ever seeking solutions to problems that threaten the health of the population.

Psychological probing and the investigation of human nature and how people respond to various situations in their lives have benefited many who are learning to know themselves and their predispositions better than was possible decades ago, owing to the depth of research, knowledge, and technical machinery now available to measure people's responses in studies.[40] Parents are learning through distributed books, materials, and mass media how to understand parent-child relationships. The information that is dispersed has typically been processed through formal research patterns that scientific techniques control in objective modes. This may not always be true, but the materials prepared on the basis of monitored, systematic, and controlled research screen through "opinion" and minimize personal biases, that is, if the study has been done in accordance with a scientifically based design. Researchers have to be aware of their own personal biases, conduct their studies dispassionately, and be willing to interpret the data as indicated whether they are in agreement or not with what they find. Even though we are aware that errors are part of studies, we nevertheless try to avoid pitfalls in research techniques that allow personal opinion to skew the data or produce spurious results.

Computers, too, have facilitated the quality and quantity of medical services that can be supplied to a large population. Information kept in memory banks that can quickly supply doctors with data they need to help a patient (or to participate in research), have accelerated some patterns of assistance to the ill.

With the advance of some of these ideas come also, as with other things, the negative aspects of their use. More information on and about drugs, for example, has in some cases resulted in drug abuse. In part, it may be owing to ignorance, too, that drugs or pharmaceuticals are misused. Extensive programs have been used to inform, and to rehabilitate, children, youth, and adults to the end that they may understand what they are doing and how the unwise use of drugs can interfere with health and effectively functioning life.[41]

Volumes could be written about this topic alone, that is, how medical technology has affected and will continue to affect parent-child relationships. Hospitals, doctors' offices, and documentaries to inform the public all attest to the fact. With more choices, the individual has a greater responsibility to decide what is best for him/herself and the family. The phenomenon of groups collectively helping an individual decide on his/her own action on a problem is evident in contemporary society.[42] Choices, how one will view others who make certain decisions, whether the individual will be accepted by people who are important to him/her, are central to the formulation and popularity of consciousness-raising gatherings. When people become deeply confused about "good decisions" or "the right ones" they often turn to groups that can provide concurrence (in various levels of reflective thinking) and the emotional support needed for self-esteem. Broom and Selznick indicate that sometimes concurrence seeking is done at the expense of critical thinking.[43] This does not mean that any group experience is indicted, or that none help individuals. Broom and Selznick were discussing the purposes that groupthinks seem to serve and how they give individuals a sense of protection, the need to act in certain ways in order to remain in the high esteem of group members, and a greater sense of assurance. Again, as with other modes or social codes of thinking and acting that come from one's societal context, various advantages and disadvantages can result. Too great dependence on groupthinks can deter an individual from developing his/her own perspective and sustaining self-respect for that perspective in spite of differing from a group consensus.

Parents attempting to solve dilemmas regarding a wise or moral choice for the guidance of their young face challenges that often depress them. They seek answers in every conceivable source. Medical technology with its specific information can help to a point, in some cases in which physical problems are at a peak. Psychological problems, however, are diffuse, more difficult to pinpoint in relation to a direct cause, and more difficult to define in regard to the best approaches needed for their ultimate solutions. The scientific language (or lexicon) that researchers use in discussing concepts with their colleagues, eventually, however, reaches the lay public for use, either as individuals or as part of a group strategy implementation. Thus, an informal use of psychological technologies developed by research and investigations of scientists, becomes part of the public domain.

9. Law and the Political Setting

A ninth way in which the societal context of any given social era affects parents' interaction with children involves *law and the political settings of the local, state, regional, national and international areas of which parents are a part.* Again, it must be remembered that the parent is not a direct "receiver" of influence, in many cases, of what happens on a broader, societal level. Yet someone, for example, who works in the diplomatic service, residing temporarily in another country, may be directly affected. Children whose parents are in the service units of army, navy, air corps, etc., may live for a while in countries other than those of their birth. They may live in different parts of the world for relatively brief periods at a time during their childhood years, and may be influenced by what some may consider "international" effects.

Studies on the quality of care given to children and its effects on children's health, economic support, and cognitive development have been conducted in the United States, and in these studies social policy changes are sought.[44] New laws can emerge as a result of an examination of broad injustices created in part by social forms or procedures. Years of struggle typically have to occur in order to get the attention of those who have the power to make changes for families and children. This involves the energies of people at various levels of society. Professionals can become the means through which the articulation of those injustices in society can be examined, assessed, and formulated into recommended policies or laws affecting children. Many say that respect for children has been lacking in the public forum.

Writers indicate that they do not see the professional person as the one to substitute for or supplant the parent's place with the child in the family, but hold, rather, that the professional should initiate the voice for and help the parent him/herself in directly providing the child with what is needed.[45] The suggestions are that parents can be helped when they have information, awareness of how to transmit or translate it into their own personal perspectives of their children's needs, and a social policy that validates such views.

Laws related to an improved set of conditions for children, protection from harm, or from inadequate shelter and food have been part of societal contexts for many years. Contemporary life, however, with its complexities and contradictory activities that both hinder and facilitate children's lives to the extent that they do, poses different problems involving more people, as a result, and needing more effective ideas for improved solutions.

Almost every moral, ethical, or life/death issue is associated in some way to law or religious perspectives and beliefs by people in a society. At the point that people are confused and indignant about an issue that is moral and ethical, they will find that they want to exercise a measure of control over the events that occur in connection with such issues. A law that will punish, in some measure, the behavior of those who do not comply with it, can have the power to force people to change their attitudes to some extent. This does not mean that people will change their thinking, necessarily, or their feelings about a given issue. They will, however, be forced to constrain impulses to act in certain ways that would bring punishment to them through enforcement of the law.

Parent-child relationships are private, to a point. What people do in their homes can be evident, however, in what they or their children say to others outside the home. Thus, while privacy used to be protected by some laws, the intricate responsibility of parent, teacher, doctor, and other adults who are jointly concerned about the child has encroached, to a degree, into the privacy of the home. Patterns of raising one's child, are made up in part of the energies of others who come in contact with family members. The openness of today's orientation toward even the most private or intimate matters has affected relationships between parents and children. Privacy, laws, intimate patterns of interaction with one's family, are deeply felt and central to how people direct their own daily lives. For that reason, the conduct of such relationships becomes important to the broader societal context as well. If people are expected to oversee the well-being of their own social context, that context, in turn, also has to provide some rationality to them. Social dynamics indirectly reflect the fact, in American society, that the exercise of choice is highly valued. Laws become the instrument to warn people when that freedom of choice is endangering the lives or well-being of the human species in a given social context or era.

Thus, the issue of whether law hinders or facilitates the health and progress of a country in a given time of history leans on the individual's preference. At times the law is perceived as "working" in behalf of justice to an individual; at times it is viewed as not. When the problems focus on what is best for children, and an adult or several of them have to make significant decisions that seriously affect the future (sometimes life or death), then it behooves all of us to at least give serious thought to the examination of children's environments.[46]

10. Atypical Events and Stresses

The tenth aspect in the societal context that affects parents and their relationships to children, is *the occurrence of unique or atypical events such as ecological stresses, assassination of leaders, governmental scandals, and other sudden or overwhelming incidents that symbolize severe violations of deeply held values among members of a society.* A society that advocates self-expression of ideas is incensed, appalled, by an event that snuffs out the life of an individual who is trying to lead and advance ideas for certain groups.

Although it must be remembered that society does not act as an individual with a single mind, but rather is constituted by many kinds of people, a large proportion of the country and world, deeply shaken in the aftermath of an event, does affect its next adult generation or children who are currently in the care of parents. The national mourning for a president, religious leader, or widely loved individual presents visible evidence of the depth of shared feelings that prevail among millions of people who do not know each other. The phenomenon of collective behavior in the study of sociology and social psychology describes the effects on a nation of people's demonstrations of grief and the need for implementation of a therapeutic means for channeling those energies in socially approved forms. [47]

An interesting result of two assassinations in 1968 was that one very large national retail store whisked from its shelves all its toy guns one Christmas season and ordered its 815 stores to stop "advertising guns and similar toys of violence." [48] Citizens' groups asked for a toy disarmament. [49]

From toys, to books, to procedures in schools, the population and its children are affected by unusual events that almost call things to a halt in the way they attract universal attention. The societal context constitutes the backdrop; the people are the dynamics in that backdrop, and are greatly affected by the spirit, the *zeitgeist*, and general emotional contagion that pervade in a highlight of that *zeitgeist* (or trend of the times in a society).

Parental relationships to children are in part the result of the parents' efforts to sort out some meaning from certain events. The parents may talk with their own friends, parents, relatives, and teachers reflecting on the events that recently occurred "shaking everybody's life" to some extent. The shock, the suddenness of an event, plus a deeply held feeling that it could never happen in one's society, combine to bring great impact on people. Children sense that something is going on and watch their parents for clues. They listen for bits of information as they usually do when comments or discussion take place over their heads, in a sense. Their views are not typically sought, nor are they included at that first initial impact when their parents hear about the tragic or dramatic event and are trying to make sense in their own minds out of what actually happened.

Newspaper headlines announcing "doomsday" kinds of reports are bound to have their effects on a population. The aftermath of those events and how they change the lives of people, are the unplanned results of any impact. Announcement of a draft program for a specific age group to be inducted into one of the service units of a country triggers serious plans for an immediate set of decisions for individuals. Plans for marriage, children, buying a home, may either be shelved or postponed or placed into top, immediate priority, depending on the couple's philosophy or emotions.

People are typically held to certain norms learned in the process of growing from infancy to their adult years. When the routines they had used to guide them in their daily lives, to a point of expecting a wholeness or meaning for them, become shattered by an unexpected tragedy it requires time to process the event in their own minds so that the world does not seem to have collapsed. Tragic events that seem to symbolize a lack of control or foresight in society lead people to a sense of panic. They wonder how something such as an assassination, for example, could have happened in a society that appears to have the most sophisticated people, machinery, and techniques monitoring the functions and activities of highly visible leaders of a country. Thus, moral and ethical disappointments in one's system create fears and doubts in people for their own safety as well as the security of their society and country.

People begin to question the meaning of justice or how it happens when they see the ravages of war, starvation of children in various countries, or a gunshot stilling the life of a significant leader. They wonder whether guiding their children to do what they perceive to be morally right will bring the personal and psychologically satisfying rewards one expects by living according to a social code of integrity, honesty, and concern for the well-being of others.

One has a sense of belief in an equation: if one lives in an "honorable way," then it follows that things will turn out well.[50] Unusual or dramatic events that seem to create and sustain chaotic conditions run counter to expectations of the "good" society. Such events shake the moral fiber and the predictability of behavior that typically guide people in mutual concern for the good will and progress of their social groups. They feel somewhat betrayed and frightened. They look for someone to blame. They seek stability and a trusted foundation that they believe somehow escaped them.

Unusual phenomena such as men's flights to the moon, inquiry into outer space and other planets, and new technological break-throughs affect people in various ways. What the society gains from those events in further development of knowledge, the people learn about too. The scientific view in American culture is that almost anything can be conquered, if human beings focus on the problem.[51] For example, diseases can be controlled or wiped out; the suppression of ideas by unfair means—means other than intellect or wit—can be protested and prevented; almost unbelievable tasks can be accomplished if their performance is facilitated by machinery. It is that view of energy and brain power that engenders people's expectations of an all-powerful social group.

Impact of atypical and dramatic events that attract the attention of the world, whether attention is perceived negatively or positively, has an effect on individual's lives. Parents utilize these events in ways that make sense to them and fit into their own value systems. They tell their children about them and may justify or denigrate such phenomena when the parent wishes to use them as an object lesson of some sort. Societal contexts, however, encroach and penetrate, at various levels and degrees, the hopes and expectations of people.[52] Ginsburg, as one writer among others, warns that people need, for their own mental health, a concept of social reality that includes both the destructive and the "pampering overprotective reality as well."[53] Where parents are concerned, their mental health will transmit itself in some way to how the children perceive what is expected of them.

Although ten ways in which societal contexts of parents in any era of the history of a society affect parent and child relationships have been delineated in this section, there are other subtle ways in which parents are affected. The economics of labor markets, availability of reasonable purchasing power as reflected in an employment or Wall Street system, translation of one's skills at any given time to financial exchange by a society, laws that affect one's compulsory leave from the job market, and other social, economic, scientific, and legal phenomena of an unusual, sudden, or dramatic nature affect parents' thoughts and their actions toward their children. Thus, planned or not, deliberate or not, the societal context of one's psychological world of meaning constitutes a reality that parents transmit in one way or another to their children.

Society, As Represented in the Minds and Activities of Children

As more books are written on how to represent children's best interests in the market place or social welfare areas, advocacy of children's rights or privileges becomes more elaborate, more complex, and more analytical.[54] The family is an integral part of the total social system and in that sense, children's development is seriously affected when parents function in a fashion too-isolated from wholesome perspectives that could help them. Several writers recommend ways to help the parents, making their lives less stressful, and providing more support than they have had to this point rather than intervening and taking their children from them to a place where professionals give children what the state thinks they need.

Children view the world through the screen of their parents' eyes. They acquire values and habits that parents inculcate and for which the parents have reward-and-punishment systems to ensure that the children internalize or accept those values. Thus, when one speaks of the world or society as they are perceived by children, it is obvious that a highly complicated intellectual and interaction system is at work in that function of perceptual development. Half the time people are aware of the mechanisms, and half the time the process seems so natural (or automatic), that people are not critically aware of influences that exert pressures resulting in what we think are the total proddings of our own personalities.

As shown in previous discussions on ways that parents are affected by a contemporary societal context during the process of guiding a child's growth, as well as the context in which their own personality was developed prior to becoming a parent, children are receiving images, words, gestures, all of which shade their feelings and attitudes as presented to them by their parents. As Piaget indicates, however, children do have a way of responding to the world that is qualitatively different from that of their parents.[55]

The world is conceptualized through children's sensations and physiological receptors as well as through the information they receive from their parents, who comment on the world. Associations described or defined about the world, and the feelings through which a child knows the world, differ from the associations that adults have with their words. It is understandable, then, that children will not actually experience the world in the same way as do adults, but they may name experiences in similar ways. Meaning differs, but the words may be the same, thus, the adult thinks that the child understands the same perspective as the adult's.[56]

Piaget indicates that up to the ages of seven or eight the child's mind is filled with contradictions of ideas, words, thoughts, and meanings. He says that children are not able to reason logically about those contradictions in their own minds until after they are about seven or eight years old. About that time, they become conscious of a definition of concepts that they are accepting or using, and that they obtain an ability to examine their "own mental experiments."[57] Between the years of seven and eight, to about eleven and twelve, children begin to be more conscious of discrepancies of thought that arise from their awareness of their own mental operations, and not purely from the children's observation (or action upon) nature, whether this observation may be actual or imaginary.[58]

Children begin to evaluate what truth is when they are able to reason. They do not accept only what they touch, see, taste, smell, or hear. When the element of mental reasoning begins to take on several ways of looking at an object or event, children begin to perceive how things can happen from the point of view of others. An awareness of one's mental operations takes on greater complexity for the child.

Taking on the perspective of others toward a given idea is an intellectual development that involves awareness of mental juxtaposition of thought and separation of the self from that thought. This is not the same kind of outward response that a child demonstrates when (s)he quickly hides something that mother or father has forbidden to the child. Automatic responses which indicate that a child has internalized a proscription of "thou shalt not" differ from the reasoning and the ability to change a theme of thought in one's mind and to respond to such mental operation instigated by one's own thinking.

The societal context of a child's world affects the child's life directly or indirectly, and depending on the age of the child, mixtures and various combinations of both, the levels or skills of maturity *and* societal contexts. If an infant is born when new kinds of diapers are accessible to parents, the infant will be the recipient, perhaps, of diapers other than the cloth ones used by parents decades ago. If available choices in household appliances allow the mothers to spend less time in cleaning, this affects the infant indirectly.

Time with the parent, attitudes of the parent toward the child, and general readiness of the parent's aptitudes and desires to play with the child and explain the world to the child, and the extent of societal endorsement of such parental attitudes all affect how the child will perceive his/her world.

When children attend school, they are, of course, going to be affected by another adult (the teacher) as well as by other children and their points of view. This experience is an example, par excellence, of a need to juggle what one thinks relative to what others say is right. The truth as perceived by others, impressions of that truth, and the need to influence others by saying what one *wants*, rather than what represents truth, opinion, fallacy in points of view, or incorrect reporting of an event, exert power and energy on children to achieve equilibrium of some sort when they interact with others.

Wanting to get along with others, children may subordinate their own judgment in order to do as others ask. They may not stop to be critical of something they have been taught was not permissible. Personal desires become the overpowering influence in favor of putting aside one's better judgment.

Children view society through a television set, children's literature, cartoons in the newspapers, and other societal means or contrivances, planned or not, to attract their attention. Some things succeed in attracting their attention; others do not. Human beings selectively listen and focus on things in their environment. It would be humanly impossible to attend to and make sense of everything that surrounds the individual. What society focuses on, however, by means of special reward and punishment sanctions, exercises great power over the minds of individuals. These sanctions are emphasized by the socializing agents with whom the children are involved.

We cannot here take the time or space warranted for the analysis of specific things, events, and societal clusters of techniques that affect children's view of the world, nor can these subjects be amplified. The age of children, whether they are in their infancy, whether they are in preschool, in kindergarten, or the primary grades, greatly affects their perceptions of life. The way they approach any attempts to understand the world around them is, of course, affected not only by the substance and content of the world in a certain time in societal history, but also by the way they formulate thought or reasoning in terms of their intellectual capacities.

Noting Table 1-1, it can be seen how the interweaving of experiences that are direct, formal, and informal produces a blend of influences on the perceptions of children. The most intricate plans for teaching them how to conceptualize could not be as specific in description as they are in the way they happen. Subtle effects of many elements that occur in the child's life make it difficult to arrest the timing mechanisms and the dynamics of learning about one's world, to the point of microscopic design. Generally, however, children seek, they listen selectively, and they formulate conclusions, contradictory or not, within a classification of thought of their creation, about the things they see around them. Contradictory thinking may occur at any time in the minds of adults as well. Children, however, need to be learning from adults who are cognizant of confusion as it can occur in the

Table 1–1 The Child's Perceptions of the World in a Particular Societal Context Affecting Learning Processes

Interpretation of Direct Experiences	⟷	Informal Knowledge Obtained at Home, in the Neighborhood, and at School	⟷	Formalized Knowledge Obtained at School
Direct experience with such things as rain, snow, hail, mud, paint		Parent attitudes Sibling attitudes Peer attitudes		Teacher–child relationships in discussion and formalized lessons

⟷ means "affects and is affected by" the experiences or content.

"logical thought" processes, particularly when the children are just beginning to become aware of their own levels of thinking. Discussion needs to be clear.

The fact that children, especially before the age of eleven or twelve, perceive ideas in qualitatively different ways than do adults has implications for parents and teachers. When children use the words indicating that they understand a specific issue, parents and teachers may begin to become more sensitive to the various levels of understanding or intellectualizing that children may actually be able to reach. Such sensitivity requires empathy, patience, and analytic listening on the adult's part. Children want to please others; they want to understand and to be considered intelligent. They will respond to those ends, if and when they are able. It is unfair to chide them when they cannot comply.

Later chapters will involve discussion on the interrelationships between specific content presented at school and children's technical processes in attempting to conceptualize content at school and at home. Teachers are instructed at universities, even though the instruction differs, on how they should adapt activities for children in order to help children be successful in mastering academic content at school. Ideas can be presented in simpler forms, though still accurate and less complicated, to reflect an instructional awareness of the way children think. To present highly abstract content to children, before they even understand the most rudimentary of basic foundations needed for the underpinnings of abstract thought, is to invite confusion and frustration in the child, and in the teacher as well.

Societal contexts that have introduced gender-role definitions differing from those of the past will have their effects in children's books, games, and activities. Girls are shown in a broader selection of sports activities than ever before. Curriculum development (activities or books) in the schools also reflect substantial differences between today's women and yesterday's and in their roles at home, in industry, and in the professions. Family development, amplification of the father's role in children's development, and the way people spend their time at home and in recreational activities are influencing children's impressions of society as they find those ideas described in their schoolbooks.

The societal context provides a way of looking at the self. Children learn about this definition and apply it to their own perspectives (depending on their own ages). Authenticity of personality has been prized by many in the societies of the 1960s and 1970s and is still prized in the 1980s. Psychiatrists and psychologists, as well as parents with their children, motivate individuals toward that goal. The plastic personality (somewhat superficial) is not to be confused with a personality that can change itself, express itself "honestly," and consequently be perceived as an honest one (to the self and others). Benson states that often when people say they want to do their own things, they may "in fact, be doing someone else's thing," if they are doing it to please someone else rather than acting in accordance with their own code of behavior.[59] He indicates that it is necessary to one's mental health to know the difference between one's own thing and someone else's.

Children will define themselves, not only in terms of their particular societal context in the history of a society, but also in terms of the attitudes of others toward them. Teachers, parents, relatives, peers, and others who represent "society out there," a concept which children are expected to internalize and accept as their "own thing," present definitions that will always be important to children as they comprehend their world and themselves in relation to it.

SUMMARY

This chapter involved the presentation of a backdrop for the rest of the book in that it demonstrated ways that the societal context in one's time strongly affect one's value orientation. Teachers, parents, and children are greatly influenced by the society in which they live in any given era of social history. Clothing, values, food, technology, medicine, forms of shelter, and social protection vary in terms of a specific social era in history.

Teachers' beliefs are influenced by their own family backgrounds as they have grown from childhood. They are also learning to accept or reject certain philosophies to which they are exposed at various institutions of higher learning. Teaching techniques, psychological theories, and attitudes toward the way children should be taught are not the same among universities preparing students for teaching. Thus teachers, as people entering a profession, have certain attitudes and beliefs about what ought to be happening in that profession, but also develop ideas on how their conceptions of teaching should be implemented in the classroom with the pupils.

Teachers as well as parents are influenced by a spirit of the times, or zeitgeist, which creates responses, pro or con, in their behavior with children. Between the years of late teens and late forties and early fifties, when parents may be responsible for young children, many personality orientations are affected by contemporary trends. Teachers may retain a traditional approach or they may try to update themselves in current attitudes. They may hold to past perceptions because the current society's are not congruent with formerly valued (and evidently, by them, still valued) larger philosophical frameworks that had guided and still do shape their lives. Whatever they choose, however, they are affected in their activities and their choices influence modes of instruction they use with children. This can be perceived as positive or negative in the eyes of any observer, even the teacher him/herself. Some teachers may have a career that includes a period of life from their late teens to their sixties, and this makes a difference in the way they teach. This is not to suggest that older teachers or experienced ones, using what may be considered traditional techniques, are not effective teachers. These views relate to how teachers are perceived by their supervisors and the public and by parents and children.

Parents are affected by the societal context in at least ten different ways. Parents of young children in the 1970s were learning different proscriptions of behavior for parent-child interaction than those of the 1940s, 50s and 60s. Their own behavior experienced in recollection of their own childhood, acts as an impetus to affect what they may do with their own children. They may, with their own children, overcompensate in protective or other kinds of behavior, for the responses they felt they missed from their own parents.

The technological and economic bases of society in a given social era, as well as the political and legal bases, act upon what may or may not happen in the lives of individual members of the society. Parents make their decisions on the basis of those opportunities or restrictions.

Children formulate their views of what represents "society," through the eyes and interpretations of their parents. They also, depending on their age at any given time, are influenced by intellectual capacities for thought, for understanding, and for reasoning that prevail at various levels of growth.

TOPICS FOR DISCUSSION

1. Why and how do the societal contexts of people as parents or teachers affect the transmission of values to children? What has gone into the growth and development of adults that has influenced their perceptions of the way they feel "life should be lived"?
2. Comment on the ten ways that the societal context of a parent affects judgments or decisions made in relationships with children. Add to those ten ways that were discussed in the chapter.
3. How has society changed between the years of 1940 and 1980 where parental attitudes are concerned? How have these attitudes affected children's activities at school in terms of what parents seem to want for their children?
4. Is teaching considered a position of high status? Does contemporary American society respect teachers? Justify your point of view in any case. Is the American view representative of the way other societies think? How so or not so?
5. What mediates children's understanding of the environment in terms of parental explanations of society or the way people are? Are children's verbal expressions the same in meanings and childlike associations as are the adults'? How does Piaget perceive these ideas?

NOTES

1. Leonard Broom and Philip Selznick, *Sociology: A Text with Adapted Readings*, Sixth Edition (New York: Harper, 1977), pp. 360–367. The authors indicate that during the first decades of the twentieth century immigrants came to this country and tried to learn the language and social mores in order to acquire jobs. Their children tried to become "American" through educational skills. Many inequalities were discovered, however, in the structure of the educational system as reported by the Coleman Report, as one among many others. (See pp. 362–366.)

2. Herbert Ginsburg and Sylvia Opper, *Piaget's Theory of Intellectual Development*, 2nd ed. (Englewood Cliffs, N.J.: Prentice-Hall, 1979), pp. 23–24. The explanations of Piaget's renowned works are helpful to teachers. Ginsburg and Opper describe Piaget's theory in which the development of one's intellectual structures reflects the interactive nature of the individual and various environmental situations throughout life. Intelligence is not perceived as fixed nor nonadaptable. It is developmental, even with certain broad biological limits.

3. Carolyn L. Thomson, Margaret Cooper Holmberg, and Donald M. Baer, *An Experimental Analysis of Some Procedures to Teach Priming and Reinforcement Skills to Preschool Teachers*, Monograph of the Society for Research in Child Development, Vol. 43 No. 4 (Chicago: U. of Chicago, 1978), pp. 40–44. The authors discuss their study of five teaching styles in five different settings involving 42 teachers in all. They indicate that effective teacher behavior can be measured by observing the child's responses to which the teacher's behavior had directed the child. They describe various styles of feedback to the teacher. The one in which the teacher is given frequent information and an opportunity physically to record behavior or changes seems to create the best effect for teacher and child-learning success.

4. Norman K. Denzin, "Children and Their Caretakers," pp. 38–51 in *Socialization and the Life Cycle*, edited by Peter I. Rose (New York: St. Martin's, 1979), p. 38. Denzin comments on the view that children in themselves do not carry meaning as social entities, when an individual tries to define them or childhood. Rather, he says that they are defined differently with each generation and social group. Children discover that they are interpreted in contradictory ways as they encounter different people and situations. This confusion between the child's own perceptions of self and what childhood is "supposed to be" arises again and again in the educational process, as Denzin views it.

5. John A. Clausen, "Introduction," pp. 3–17 in *Socialization and Society*, edited by John A. Clausen (Boston: Little, Brown, 1968), p. 3. Clausen offers a definition, as one among others, of socialization as a process which involves an ongoing interaction between an individual and others who seek to influence him. Edward Zigler and Irvin L. Child, "Socialization," pp. 450–589 in *The Handbook of Social Psychology*, Vol. III, 2nd ed., edited by Gardner Lindzey and Elliot Aronson (Reading, Mass.: Addison-Wesley, 1969), p. 474. Zigler and Child refer to the broad process of socialization as a total process of the individual's development of certain patterns of "socially relevant behavior and experience." These socially relevant patterns are learned through interaction with others.

6. Broom and Selznick, op. cit., p. 4. Although individuals have their own unique histories in terms of private experiences of happiness, joy, grief, etc., sociologists note that people who are involved in similar life experiences observe reality as it is common to a particular social group. Peter L. Berger and Brigitte Berger, "Becoming a Member of Society," pp. 4–20 in *Socialization and the Life Cycle*, edited by Peter I. Rose (New York: St. Martin's, 1979), p. 14. Berger and Berger describe the process of internalizing the culture of society. They say that through a complicated process of reflection, of reciprocity in the context of interaction with others, the individual takes into his/her own consciousness the constraints of the external social world. This effect is unique to his/her own makeup of character.

7. Alex Inkeles, "Society, Social Structure, and Child Socialization," pp. 73–129 in *Socialization and Society*, edited by John A. Clausen (Boston: Little, Brown, 1968), p. 84. Inkeles states that to think of "society as demanding" something, is to erroneously personify society or to assume that a population speaks as one voice. Individuals may demand, not society.

8. Berger and Berger, op. cit., p. 2. Berger and Berger note that no individual is born without some predispositions or "inheritance" of behaviors all of which add up to anything but a blank mind, ready for imprinting. They suggest that beyond the "natural" or genetic endowments that one inherits from parents (and by which one is thereby shaped as an individual), there is an inheritance that comes with the norms, values, and attitudes that prevail in the groups of which the parents are a part in any given society. Prenatal care of the mother, diet, exercise, and the like are effects of advice and thinking of parents in certain social groups. Thus children are not only born with biological genes but social ones as well, by virtue of their parents and family. These influence a specific cluster of attributes existing in the infant from the moment of birth.

SOCIETY, AS REPRESENTED IN THE MINDS AND ACTIVITIES OF CHILDREN 27

9. Norman Goodman and Gary T. Marx, *Society Today*, 3rd ed. (New York: Random, 1978), p. 83. Institutions may be defined, in part, as "a relatively stable configuration of values, norms, statuses, roles, groups, and organizations that provides" structures for the way people may interact with each other on a relatively frequent basis. Goodman and Marx indicate that institutions may be relatively stable, as part of a culture, but that they are also a mechanism for social control, or a way of affecting people's behavior. They suggest that culture and social control are linked and often difficult to separate in an analysis of the two.

10. D. Stanley Eitzen, *In Conflict and Order* (Boston: Allyn, 1978), p. 17. Eitzen says that it is difficult for any one of us to be free of stereotypes or value-free in making assumptions about people or society and the behavior we will expect from them before we even meet or interact with them. He suggests that our own experiences are too limited and idiosyncratic in nature. This is not abnormal, but must be recognized as a legitimate fact of life.

11. Eitzen, op. cit., p. 17. Eitzen indicates that the media provide another source which people use to discover "authoritative" information about what life is, or should be. In fact, however, much of the information can be overdramatized or distorted representations of reality in some way, thus individuals need to be critical of what they see or hear.

12. Ibid., p. 545. The difficulties that face some individuals when they have a "surfeit" of choices as to how they may live often become translated into confusion, immobility, and various reactionary attitudes.

13. Alice S. Rossi, "Transition to Parenthood," pp. 132–145 in *Socialization and the Life Cycle*, edited by Peter I. Rose (New York: St. Martin's, 1979), p. 136. Rossi mentions that research on the transition experiences from preparenthood to being a parent reflects great difficulties of parents and child-rearing patterns. Also she indicates that research on what it is to be a parent used to focus more on the infant and child than it has more recently, when it has been emphasizing what the parent does or should do.

14. Goodman and Marx, op. cit., p. 141. They refer to gender role as a particular cluster of behaviors related to activity, other than sexual reproduction, considered essential for members of each sex in a given society. They indicate too, that even though we learn as we grow in a society, how intimacy, morality, obedience, aggressiveness are to be perceived and expressed in our behavior, the number of people involved in teaching us these lessons is so mixed, varied, and unclear, that it is no small wonder we are not sure exactly of what we have learned, from whom, and how, or why. These gender-related perceptions as described in American society have undergone many changes in the last twenty-five years. Where the parent role is involved, and how the father or mother should be expected to fulfill a role is still subject to discussion and disagreement in the light of contemporary demands.

15. Michael E. Lamb, "The Father's Role in the Infant's Social World," pp. 87–108, *Mother/Child, Father/Child Relationships*, edited by Joseph H. Stevens, Jr., and Marilyn Mathews (Washington, D.C.: National Assoc. for the Education of Young Children, 1978), p. 87.

16. Elaine Heffner, *Mothering* (Garden City, N.Y.: Doubleday, 1978), p. 19. "Women do not have to sacrifice personhood if they are mothers." Heffner is concerned about women's feelings as mothers. She fears that they are persuaded that they are less than full persons just because they want to nurture their children and fulfill their needs at home. Heffner does not see mothers as being exploited in their role of nurturing a family.

17. Goodman and Marx, op. cit., p. 346. "Love, marriage, and sex are three different behavioral systems." Even though the interrelationships of the three systems are defined in some way by all societies, they do not view the three systems as one. Marriage in America is idealized as one system including the other two as an integral part, and not to be separated. Parenthood is added on to that entity, completing the total impression of family life.

18. Jessie Bernard, "Changing Family Life Styles: One Role, Two Roles, Shared Roles," pp. 235–246, in *The Future of the Family*, edited by Louise Kapp Howe (New York: Simon & Schuster, 1972), p. 238. The way was opened in the American social context so that women who wished to work outside the home were less uncomfortable about whether they were serving their children well by being absent. Social images were less punitive on that subject than they had been.

19. Urie Bronfenbrenner, "Who Cares for America's Children?" pp. 139–150 in *The Future*

of the Family, edited by Louise Kapp Howe (New York: Simon & Schuster, 1972), p. 142. Bronfenbrenner expresses deep concern for the isolation of children from adults who can interact lovingly with them as well as their own parents can.

20. There are exceptions to this, of course, in situations where groups of people (communes, large low-income families) share their worldly goods, so to speak.

21. Broom and Selznick, op. cit., p. 159. Although the major elements of stratification in a society are "power, prestige, and wealth," any resource or reward can be perceived as an element in stratification of people in society.

22. Goodman and Marx, op. cit., p. 150. Anticipatory socialization may be outdated in the role behaviors one envisions will be appropriate in the future. The "unprecedented rate" of change in American society forewarns us of this tendency which can lead to inaccuracies in behavioral expectations of people in various roles.

23. Frank Reissman and S. M. Miller, "Social Change Versus the 'Psychiatric World View,' " pp. 64–76 in Mental Health and Social Change, edited by Milton F. Shore and Fortune V. Mannino (New York: American Orthopsychiatric Assoc., AMS Press, 1975), p. 66. Reissman and Miller point out how important it is to know the intellectual context(s) of a given period in social history. They comment on the "psychiatric world view" that motivated intellectual thought in the 1940s. It was a reaction to a sense of disappointment in social change on a broad trend-setting mode. If people were to learn how to control themselves and their own egos so that they could be more creative and self-actualizing, it was reasoned that society might go forward.

24. Reissman and Miller, op. cit., p. 75.

25. Daniel J. Levinson, Charlotte M. Darrow, Edward B. Klein, Maria H. Levinson, and Braxton McKee, "Stages of Adulthood," pp. 279–293 in Socialization and the Life Cycle, edited by Peter I. Rose (New York: St. Martin's, 1979), p. 287.

26. Ibid., p. 287.

27. Broom and Selznick, op. cit., p. 397. Individual initiative was encouraged by the assurance that work, self-discipline, avoidance of "worldly pleasures," could bring one to the good graces of one's God. The Calvinist doctrine led the individual toward constant striving and productivity.

28. Eitzen, op. cit., p. 368. Strict modes of socialization are described by Eitzen as "repressive," demanding conformity and obedience to parental demands. Less repressive forms of parent-child relationships allow the child to explore ideas and behavior for him/herself, thereby discovering more about his/her own potential.

29. Peter L. Berger and Richard John Neuhaus, To Empower People Washington, D.C.: American Enterprise Institute for Public Policy Research, 1977), p. 8 Berger and Neuhaus state that people have different feelings about their neighborhood, and "It may not be the place where we are entirely at home, but it is the place where we are least homeless."

30. John A. Clausen, Editor Socialization and Society (Boston, Mass.: Little, Brown, 1968), 400 pp.; Urie Bronfenbrenner, "Socialization and Social Class through Time and Space," pp. 400–425 in Readings in Social Psychology, 3rd ed., edited by Eleanor E. Maccoby, Theodore Newcomb, and Eugene Hartley (New York: Holt, 1958); Daniel R. Miller and Guy E. Swanson, The Changing American Parent (New York: Wiley, 1958), pp. 3–60.

31. Eitzen, op. cit., pp. 368–369. He indicates that in 1914 the views of a psychologist, John B. Watson, influenced child care. Mothers were instructed not to rock their babies, to prevent thumb-sucking, to "begin toilet-training by the third month."

32. Ibid. Eitzen traces the Freudian effects in children's development and parental views of what their own behavior was causing in their children's personality development to contemporary attitudes resulting from reading Baby and Child Care, by Dr. Benjamin Spock.

33. Caution needs to be advised here that one not be led to believe that a simple one-to-one (cause and effect) relationship exists. To assume that a child who is reared in the manner discussed will always be defending causes of social justice, would be an erroneous oversimplification of a long-term process.

34. Even though persistence and self-management may be part of an adult's view of what one needs for winning games, competitions, and the like, children value the all-powerful and independent inferential qualities.

35. Otis Dudley Duncan, Howard Schuman, and Beverly Duncan, Social Change in a Met-

ropolitan Community (New York: Russell Sage, 1973), p. 123. The researchers of the study indicate that their ethical responsibility affects their need to refrain from making broad interpretations of their work. They indicate how subtle the interplay is among what people say and what they do, and which "factors" or events in society may have contributed to their perspectives and activities.

36. Lou Benson, *Images, Heroes, and Self-Perceptions* (Englewood Cliffs, N.J.: Prentice-Hall, 1974), p. 27. Although all of us doubt our own skills and abilities at times, we need to see that someone is able to accomplish in the way we would like. We compare ourselves to certain people in society whom we think others admire too. It is often that projected image that keeps us busy in supporting an ego, rather than feeling more comfortable with what we actually are.

37. Ibid., p. 106.

38. Ibid. He suggests that to delude ourselves by not accepting the fact that we are human, with all the attendant characteristics of admired and nonadmired behavior, is to deny a part of our recognition of the fact that we are human. This denial can interfere with perceiving the world clearly and with less apprehension about what we can find in ourselves (the parts of ourselves that we have been socialized to think are unspeakable and would reveal to everyone how unworthy we are of being loved).

39. Ibid., p. 28.

40. This is not to suggest that people, years ago, did not know themselves in relation to the demands made on them in their social context of the time. Contemporary psychology and medicine, however, are closely related, and have the advantage today of intricate research techniques and machines that enhance methods.

41. Benson, op. cit., pp. 318–326.

42. Broom and Selznick, op. cit., p. 150. They discuss a "psychology of groupthink," and at least eight symptoms noted in records of history that promote the conditions of "groupthinks." Shared feelings ease the pain of frustration during personal experiences that seemed to have no satisfying answer for the individual. A mutual effort among members of the group to elevate self-esteem provides support against the nongroup world or people who are "responsible" for the members' feelings of vulnerability.

43. Ibid., p. 151.

44. Kenneth Keniston and The Carnegie Council on Children, *All Our Children* (New York: Harcourt, 1977), p. xiii. The team of researchers point out that our nation's view of children often hinders our awareness of an " 'ecology of childhood'—the overall social and economic system that exerts a crucial influence on what happens to parents and children." Patricia A. Vardin and Ilene N. Brody, Editors, *Children's Rights: Contemporary Perspectives* (New York: Teachers College, 1979), p. xv. The advocacy perspective for children is discussed here, reflecting an urgent request for change in attitudes toward children and their rights as individuals.

45. Keniston et al, op. cit., p. 23. The researchers suggest that parents be criticized less, and that the societal context be examined more, in the way that the institutions sap energy and self-esteem from parents. Peter L. Berger and Richard John Neuhaus, *To Empower People* (Washington, D.C.: American Institute for Public Policy Research, 1977), p. 21. They say that the parent is "way ahead of the expert in sheer knowledge of the child's character." It is urged that the social structure allow parents as knowledgeable persons to make their own choices in interaction with children, and that it can support the parents through providing policies that facilitate family strengths and decisions. The family is perceived as a mediating structure between government and the child.

46. James P. Spradley and David W. McCurdy, *The Cultural Experience. Ethnography in Complex Society* (Chicago: Sci. Res. Assoc., 1972), p. 15. The writers indicate that the objective study of any society is difficult because our personal experiences shut out some things from view . . . "like a pair of blinders." We virtually do not see certain things in the environment because of past association with proscriptions or contraints, making an observation of those taboos (in our own mind) painful and difficult to judge.

47. Broom and Selznick, op. cit., p. 226. Crowds observing an event that is dramatic for people in a society are highly charged with emotion at times; visibility of people's emotions affects contagion in a group and engenders feelings of not knowing what to expect next. Extended unstructuredness in events is a characteristic that people find uncomfortable; for this reason crowd behavior is unpredictable.

48. *Time Capsules, 1968.* (Time-Life, 1969), p. 240.
49. Ibid.
50. Belief in fate as a phenomenon that metes out favors or punishment—in ways somewhat random at times or more focused at others—to members of a society is in part a philosophy, in part a religious association. The automatic prize of only "good" happening to people who live according to their own convictions of "goodness" or virtue does not materialize in the way many people think. Societal events are not pure distillations of personal or individualized goals, even though they may be indirectly involved.
51. Robin M. Williams, Jr., "Individual and Group Values," *The Annals of the American Academy of Political and Social Science*, Vol. I. Social Goals and Indicators for Society, Vol. 371 (May 1967), pp. 20–37. Williams indicates after an intensive study, that a general theme among others running through the fifteen belief clusterings among American people's views, is "an emphasis on active mastery rather than passive acceptance of events," p. 33. He mentions also that many people trust rationalism rather than traditionalism in a perspective of society and for their own guidance.
52. Sol W. Ginsburg, "Mental Health and Social Issues of Our Times," pp. 21–34 in *Mental Health and Social Change*, edited by Milton F. Shore and Fortune V. Mannino (New York: American Orthopsychiatric Association, AMS Press Inc., 1975), p. 24.
53. Ibid.
54. See Vardin and Brody's *Children's Rights*, discussed in earlier pages; also Berger and Neuhaus' *To Empower People* quoted before; and the report of The Carnegie Council on Children, chaired by Kenneth Keniston, from which comments were noted. These are only a few among others that emphasize the need for professionals, lawyers, educators, and others to articulate what children must have if society is to flourish and if people are really to believe that children's well-being is important to contemporary directions.
55. Jean Piaget, *The Child's Conception of the World*, translated by Joan and Andrew Tomlinson (Paterson, N.J.: Littlefield, Adams, 1960). Piaget states that the child does not know "the nature of thought, even at the stage when he is being influenced by adult talk concerning the 'mind,' 'brain,' 'intelligence.' " p. 37. He says that compared with adults, the child experiences much less the "sensation of the thinking self within him, the feeling of being independent of the external world," p. 37. Even in the child's use of words, the associations are different than those of adults, where meaning to the child is concerned.
56. Ibid., p. 28. It is suggested that some children will accept totally what is told to them, and some will not. The child's world of thought, and the world to which the child adapts combine to accept or not accept what the adult tells him/her.
57. Jean Piaget, *Judgment and Reasoning in the Child*, translated by Marjorie Warden (Paterson, N.J.: Littlefield, Adams, 1959), p. 243.
58. Ibid.
59. Benson, op. cit., p. 5.

SELECTED REFERENCES

BENSON, LOU. *Images, Heroes, and Self-Perceptions.* Englewood Cliffs, N.J.: Prentice-Hall, Inc., 1974. 434 pp.
BERGER, PETER L., and BRIGITTE BERGER. "Becoming a Member of Society," pp. 4–20 in *Socialization and the Life Cycle*, edited by Peter I. Rose. New York: St. Martin's Press, Inc., 1979 412 pp.
———, and RICHARD JOHN NEUHAUS. *To Empower People.* Washington, D.C.: American Enterprise Institute for Public Policy Research, 1977. 45 pp.
BERNARD, JESSIE. "Changing Family Life Styles" One Role, Two Roles, Shared Roles," in *The Future of the Family*, edited by Louise Kapp Howe, New York: Simon & Schuster, Inc., 1972. 378 pp.
BRONFENBRENNER, URIE. "Socialization and Social Class through Time and Space," pp. 400–425 in *Readings in Social Psychology*, 3rd ed., edited by Eleanor E. Maccoby, Theo-

dore M. Newcomb, and Eugene L. Hartley. New York: Holt, Rinehart and Winston, 1958. 674 pp.

———. "Who Cares for America's Children?" pp. 139–150 in *The Future of the Family*, edited by Louise Kapp Howe. New York: Simon & Schuster, Inc., 1972. 378 pp.

BROOM, LEONARD, and PHILIP SELZNICK. *Sociology: A Text with Adapted Readings*. New York: Harper & Row, Publishers, 1977. 619 pp.

CLAUSEN, JOHN A., Editor. *Socialization and Society*. Boston: Little, Brown and Company, 1968. 400 pp.

Denzin, Norman K. "Children and Their Caretakers," pp. 38–51 in *Socialization and the Life Cycle*, edited by Peter I. Rose. New York: St. Martin's Press, Inc., 1977. 412 pp.

DUNCAN, OTIS DUDLEY, HOWARD SCHUMAN, and BEVERLY DUNCAN. *Social Change in a Metropolitan Community*. New York: Russell Sage Foundation, 1973. 126 pp.

EITZEN, D. STANLEY. *In Conflict and Order*. Boston: Allyn & Bacon, Inc., 1978. 598 pp.

GINSBURG, HERBERT., and SYLVIA OPPER. *Piaget's Theory of Intellectual Development*, Second Edition. Englewood Cliffs, N.J.: Prentice-Hall, Inc., 1979. 253 pp.

GINSBURG, SOL W. "Mental Health and Social Issues of Our Times," pp. 21–34 in *Mental Health and Social Change*, edited by Milton F. Shore and Fortune V. Mannino. New York: American Orthopsychiatric Association, AMS Press, Inc., 1975. 330 pp.

GOODMAN, NORMAN, and GARY T. MARX. *Society Today*, Third Edition. New York: Random House, Inc., 1978. 592 pp.

HEFFNER, ELAINE. *Mothering*. Garden City, N.Y.: Doubleday & Company, Inc., 1978. 177 pp.

INKELES, ALEX. "Society, Social Structure, and Child Socialization," p. 73–129 in *Socialization and Society*, edited by John A. Clausen. Boston: Little, Brown and Company, 1968). 400 pp.

KENISTON, KENNETH, and the Cargnegie Council on Children. *All Our Children*. New York: Harcourt Brace Jovanovich, Inc., 1977. 255 pp.

LAMB, MICHAEL E. "The Father's Role in the Infant's Social World," pp. 87–108 in *Mother/Child, Father/Child Relationships*, edited by Joseph H. Stevens, Jr., and Marilyn Mathews. Washington, D.C.: National Association for the Education of Young Children, 1978. 258 pp.

LEVINSON, DANIEL J., CHARLOTTE M. DARROW, EDWARD B. KLEIN, MARIA H. LEVINSON, and BRAXTON MCKEE. "Stages of Adulthood," pp. 279–293 in *Socialization and the Life Cycle*, edited by Peter I. Rose. New York: St. Martin's Press, Inc., 1979. 412 pp.

MACCOBY, E. ELEANOR, THEODORE M. NEWCOMB, and EUGENE L. HARTLEY, Editors. *Readings in Social Psychology*, New York: Holt, Rinehart and Winston, 1958. 674 pp.

MILLER, DANIEL R., and GUY E. SWANSON. *The Changing American Parent*. New York: John Wiley & Sons, Inc., 1958. 302 pp.

PIAGET, JEAN. *The Child's Conception of the World*, translated by Joan and Andrew Tomlinson. Paterson, N.J.: Littlefield, Adams and Company, 1960. 397 pp.

———. *Judgment and Reasoning in the Child*, translated by Marjorie Warden. Paterson, N.J.: Littlefield, Adams and Company, 1959. 260 pp.

REISSMAN, FRANK, and S. M. MILLER. "Social Change Versus the 'Psychiatric World View,'" pp. 64–76, in *Mental Health and Social Change*, edited by Milton F. Shore and Fortune V. Mannino. New York: American Orthopsychiatric Association, Inc., AMS Press, Inc., 1975. 330 pp.

ROSSI, ALICE S. "Transition to Parenthood," pp. 132–145 in *Socialization and the Life Cycle*, edited by Peter I. Rose. New York: St. Martin's Press, Inc., 1979. 412 pp.

SPRADLEY, JAMES P., and DAVID W. MCCURDY. *The Cultural Experience*. Chicago: Science Research Associates Inc., 1972. 246 pp.

THOMSON, CAROLYN L., MARGARET COOPER HOLMBERG, and DONALD M. BAER. *An Experimental Analysis of Some Procedures to Teach Priming and Reinforcement Skills to Preschool Teachers*. Monograph of the Society for Research in Child Development, Vol. 43, No. 4. Chicago: U. Chicago, 1978. 86 pp.

Time Capsules/1945. New York: Time/Life Books, 1968.

Time Capsules/1968. New York: Time/Life Books, 1969.

VARDIN, PATRICIA A., and ILENE N. BRODY, Editors. *Children's Rights: Contemporary Perspectives*. New York: Teachers College Press, 1979. 182 pp.

WILLIAMS, ROBIN M., JR. "Individual and Group Values," *The Annals of The American Acad-*

emy of Political and Social Science, Social Goals and Indicators for American Society, Vol. I., Volume 371 (May 1967), 20–37.

ZIGLER, EDWARD, and IRVIN L. CHILD. "Socialization," pp. 450–589 in *The Handbook of Social Psychology*, 2nd ed., Vol. Three, edited by Gardner Lindzey and Elliot Aronson. Reading, Mass.: Addison-Wesley Publishing Co., Inc., 1969. 978 pp.

Children's Potential and Growth Characteristics

Chronological Age Groups and Variability

Teachers see children after several years of growth and interaction with parents have already begun to formulate their personalities. It would be interesting to see how teachers might be affected by receiving a total album and perspective of each child, including photographs, anecdotes, and excerpts of the child's statements at various times of life in the years between birth and four years old. This range of information, representing dramatic changes in growth during early childhood years, would add greatly to the teacher's insight on a child's development. It would help the teacher acquire a broader perspective, as well, and one that the parents take for granted in the daily responsibility for the child. This does not suggest that the parent does not appreciate the child's growth during the first four years of life; it means that given the responsibility involved in caring for the child's needs and the like, it is often not possible fully to appreciate, from another perspective, the remarkable changes that the human infant goes through during the first year and those following.

Early childhood education begins at home with parents and older siblings, if there are any in the family, giving each child a beginning repertoire of behaviors in the educational process. Whether this is done deliberately or not, extensively or not, reflectively or not, the care-givers of the child are educating him/her. As babies and young children acquire the habits and patterns of interacting with family members are preferred by the care-givers, education takes place whether negatively or positively perceived (by an onlooker or parents themselves), where certain qualities are concerned in the child's behavioral responses. The variability of this process depends on the ages of the infants or children as well as the tendencies inherent in the biological genetic, emotional, intellectual, physical, and social characteristics.

Ages, Stages, and Developmental Trends

The following sections on growth of infants and children are divided into descriptions of the physical, motor, intellectual, emotional, and social developmental characteristics of children as they relate to the children's ages. The first category involves descriptions of the period from birth to twelve months; the second one is on the child's development between one and three years old; the third category deals with the child's development from three to five years old; the next is on the child from five to seven, and the last is on the child from seven to nine.

The Child from Birth to Twelve Months

Even though a developmental pattern of growth has already begun in the infant, from the moment of conception to birth, and an introduction to the world outside the mother's womb, the incredible growth activity that is yet to take place in the first twelve months is impressive. Human infants have been perceived differently throughout history. Attitudes toward them, and what they are able to do at various age levels, change about every fifty years. With recent technological tools, however, and with various psychological perspectives, greater numbers of contributions and ideas have been included in perceptions about infants' growth and intellectual capacities. These ideas have accelerated and expanded, to a great extent, the field of growth and development of children.

Although some may argue about the legal, medical, or philosophical moment that life begins for an infant, whether at the time of birth, at twenty-eight weeks prior to birth, or at the moment of conception when the egg of the mother and the sperm of the father unite and begin the fertilization process, an intricate *growth system begins* at the moment the male sperm penetrates the ovum or egg of the female. As the eggs of the female travel through the Fallopian tube of the female at mid-cycle of her menstrual period, one from among about five million sperm of the male may penetrate one of the ova of the female. A few hours after the egg cell and the sperm cell have joined, they begin to multiply themselves within one entity. This complicated, but systematic, process of cell growth marks the beginning of the differentiated and integrated system of a human being.[1] All the ingredients, in a sense, that are needed to begin the creation of a human being are given their start in the early process of fertilization.

Within the sperm cell and the egg cell are *chromosomes,* which have joined together in pairs. There are forty-six chromosomes (twenty-three pairs). Each pair involves a contribution from the male and one from the female. The hereditary characteristics, such as hair color, eyes, sex determination, facial features, and the sequence of chemical processes are in the chromosomes and are called, *genes.* When someone refers to the genetic constitution of an individual, in discussing his/her specific characteristics or potential, it typically refers to this unique set of "blueprints," which go into the constitutional or biological substance of the person's appearance, potential for intellectual capacity, for musical skills, for language abilities to an extent, and a number of other qualities that individuals use when they think, when they express themselves in various ways, physically, mentally, emotionally, and the like. These characteristics are developed through the genetic "beginnings" in an individual. They do not automatically provide an individual with a developed talent or skill. Growth of a skill and its refinement toward greater competence are assisted by people and resources in one's environment.

After about two weeks, when the cell division and chromosome reproduction have taken place in the newly joined egg and sperm, this embryo attaches itself to the wall of the uterus of the mother. In about eight weeks, the embryo has grown to about an inch in length, taking on the appearance of a human baby, having the major organs and systems within the body, such as the heart, lungs, kidneys, and intestines as well as the shaping of the eyes, ears, nose, fingers, and toes. This miraculous human system is referred to as the *fetus* in its further development within the uterus or womb of the mother's body.

The enrichment of the fetus within the uterus is accomplished through the placenta, an outer membranous protection surrounding the unborn child. This placenta provides nutrients, chemicals, for hormone-producing glands in the fetus, and helps the functions of the heart, liver, kidneys, and intestines prior to the infant's birth.[2]

When one considers the functions in the human system prior to an individual's birth, and compares these mechanisms with what happens after birth, it is reasonable to expect the unexpected in an individual's personality development and interaction with other people. Children are capable of many things; they can grow with the help and understanding of others. The birthright they inherit from parents is tempered with what happens with and to their parents at every level of life. Their own futures are affected by that outside world for which the intrauterine life had developed them. Teachers and parents have a responsibility, as do other socializing agents who come in contact with them (siblings, relatives, doctors, and so on), toward facilitating children's growth.

PHYSICAL DEVELOPMENT FROM BIRTH TO TWELVE MONTHS

At birth, many phenomena occur that affect stages of development. These stages are not affected to the extent that many might think, however, in the sense of showing an indelible and permanent effect throughout an individual's life. Too many other experiences later in life have crucial and long-range effects, depending on decisions an individual makes for him/herself. Scientists cannot predict those effects with any precision. Birth patterns, combined with several other factors or elements in a child's life, can set the stage for many other things that happen to a child after that date of emergence from the mother's womb. Attitudes of the mother toward the infant, for example, and the father's as well, whether he is participating in the birth process and/or preparation for it,[3] how many of the parents' relatives or the infant's grandparents are waiting at the hospital (or home) for the infant's birth, and the emotional atmosphere, all affect the event of the birth itself.

Whatever the emotional atmosphere that comes with the arrival of the new infant, there are certain aspects of normal growth that can be expected and that have been validated by scientific work.[4] Infants' growth proceeds in a *cephalocaudal* and a *proximodistal* direction. The *cephalocaudal* direction means that the infant develops in a head-to-lower back (or toe) direction. The head is larger in proportion than the rest of the body. The torso and extremities become larger in the first year. The *proximodistal* direction of growth refers to development from the spinal cord and central nervous system tending outward toward the extremities. A neurological unfolding seems to take place, in a sense.[5] Greater control and coordination occur in the central part of the body, affecting the function and activity of the extremities.

Typically, when babies are born, their weight ranges from about 6 to 9 pounds, with boys being slightly heavier than girls. Nutritional differences in the prenatal period can result in smaller or larger weights and heights at birth. The average for the weights of boys is about 7½ pounds, and for the girls about 7 pounds.[6] An infant of about 5 pounds or less is considered premature and is given special care at birth.

The average height of infants at birth is about 20 inches. In fact, the baby's head constitutes about 22 per cent of his/her body's length or height. One of the most significant changes during the first year of an infant's life is the lengthening of the torso and extremities in proportion to the head at birth. In the first year of growth, a child's body can become more than one third taller than it was at birth[7] (or 9 to 10 inches)[8].

The weight of babies in the first year of growth may triple itself so that by the end of the year, a baby that weighed 7 pounds at birth, may weigh about 20 pounds, more or less. These figures are averages, thus it must be considered that the differences can vary widely above or below those given here. Body weight consists of about 23 per cent of muscle[9]; males have a greater proportion of muscle in body make-up. "Different muscle groups grow at different rates,"[10] not only among individuals but also within individuals at various times of their lives.

The baby's bones are soft, and although one might think that their plasticity is an advantage (regarding a break in any bone structure), it is significant that they can be easily deformed, if handled improperly or roughly pulled by anyone. Babies need to have a proper diet that can fortify the growth of bones so that their skeletal structure can support the growth that must occur during the first year.

The infant's metabolic functions are in part regulated by the thyroid gland, which develops greatly during the first four months[11] and doubles in size by the time an individual reaches early adulthood, about age twenty. This gland also affects the individual's energy levels. Nutrition, mood, and temperament affect energy levels, too, as does the nervous system itself. Adrenalin, blood sugar, and heart rate influence movement and activity in the body. Glandular functions, respiration rate, and chemical changes all affect activity levels of the child's performance.

At the top of the infant's head, one may notice a soft place, or anterior fontanelle, that can be felt between two harder parts of the skull. (There are six soft areas in the baby's skull.) This softness or connective tissue will become harder and turn into bone (a process referred to as, ossification) becoming a smoothly joined part of the rest of the skull by the time the baby is about 18 months old.

Facial features of the infant change greatly throughout the first year. This change has something to do with the bone structure that is calcifying, as well as the teeth that are erupting from within the jaw and up through the gums. Even though the baby has the potential structure for all the teeth that are to erupt for several years, the first few teeth that will be visible typically come through in the first year—at different times for different babies. A large number of babies have, by the time they are about six months old, gone through the process of the lower central incisors cutting through the gums and becoming visible. At about 7 months, the lower lateral incisors (one on each side of the central incisors) push through the lower jaw.[12]

By about seven and one half months old, the baby's upper two front central incisors are visible; and at about nine months, on either side of those central incisors, the lateral ones may appear through the gums. It is suggested that children's teeth be cared for early, that just because all of them are not visible does not mean they are not there in the child's jaw. Since the roots of the temporary teeth and the permanent teeth lie beneath the teeth that erupt, it is very important that sweet foods, or a bottle filled with milk, not be left in the child's mouth when (s)he is put down for a nap or to sleep at any time. The food or milk chemicals can damage the teeth beneath the gums as well as those that have cut through the gums. Caplan suggests that children between two and three years old be taken to the dentist. A survey recently disclosed that about 50 per cent of children at about age two have decayed teeth.[13]

The quality and condition of the teeth greatly affect a child's physical appearance and smile, as well as the health of the total body. Starting a young child out with wise dental care is an insurance policy reflecting readiness to protect one's self.

The growth of one's body, muscle structure, weight, height, teeth, and glandular activity all affect the way one will move and coordinate one's self in various activities. Infants and their movements through the crawling, rocking, walking processes used to be simply enjoyed for those aspects of infancy, but these stages are now taken more seriously and considered as signs of perceptual motor development. The next section touches on the stages of motor development in the child's first twelve months and how those stages affect the child's personality and the way others respond to the child.

MOTOR DEVELOPMENT FROM BIRTH TO TWELVE MONTHS

Most normal infants enjoy movement, especially when they learn that they themselves have control over their own activity. They enjoy moving about in their own cribs, looking around, responding to sounds and people in the environment. In fact, interaction with others is very important to the child's healthy development. Many babies are able to sit up, with support, by the time they are about four months. At seven or eight months, they are able to do so without support.

Between the skills and muscle coordination required for moving around in the crib to the period of being able to sit up unsupported a great deal of growth has occurred. Typically, the baby and parents have had an enjoyable time watching this happen. If, of course, other elements intervene, as in a crowded home in a lower-income family, where illness, inadequate food and the like characterize the infant's environment, sitting around and observing the baby's competencies in each stage of development may not occur very conveniently. This does not mean the parents do not care; it

Sitting at the age of six months and sensing further mobility than only one's crib is enjoyable as shown by Michael's look of expectancy. (Photo by Priscilla Margolin.)

means that life takes their attention to high-priority functions such as earning a living and protecting themselves from harm and hunger, as part of their responsibility for the family.

When children move, they often have their eyes on something or someone they want to touch, reach, or simply to be near; they may also hurry to get away from something. In any case, however, a healthy baby's world expands when crawling and larger locomotor movements are achieved. Some babies are crawling around when they are about seven months old, although crawling movements have occurred earlier in smaller circumferential areas, that is, a kind of self-propelling by using the knees or arms while on the stomach serves the purpose of crawling.

With abilities in crawling, comes the beginning of the infant's wanting to hold on to something and pull him/herself up to a standing position. Depending on the infant's age and strength and muscle structures will the baby be able to stand for a few seconds. Later as the child becomes stronger, (s)he will be able to stand for a longer time. Typically, this period represents proximity to the walking stage.

The walking stage involves its uncertain, tottering beginnings when the baby makes attempts, even inside the crib, to hold on to its sides and walk along. Balancing in walking is achieved by the arms fanning out as one moves one's legs in a hesitant, jerky fashion. By about a year old, babies have tried to walk and are practicing various stepping patterns in order to "stay up there" longer. By fourteen or fifteen months, many babies are able to sustain themselves while walking independently.

Discussion about feeding, intricate differences among children, and the various levels of their development in relation to age cannot take place here. Space does not permit. Most child development references present data on research that has been done in contemporary contexts. Today, more information than ever has been focused on adult-child relationships

Michael enjoys a special place for him to eat. At six months old, a child is beginning to expand all experiences even those that relate to routines such as eating. Perspectives are broadening because of the growth of physical skills as well as intellectual. (Photo by Priscilla Margolin.)

and how they affect individual children's growth or at least the facilitation of their tendencies toward growth.[14] Some studies have focused on intellectual development as it occurs in the sensorimotor activities of babies.[15] In the coming years, more books and articles in journals will be available for teachers and parents and others who are responsible for the well-being of infants and young children. The reader need only to avail him/herself of those materials. They are helpful and insightful.

Because of the focus on motor development as an influence on how the baby learns to understand and relate to things and people in the environment, teachers are learning more in their courses at the universities that prepare them for teaching young children. The necessity for babies to taste, touch, sense, things that are safe in the environment is viewed as a precursor to the framework in an infant's intellectual thinking modes-of-action. The infant's sucking, feeling, receiving, and "knowing experientially," impressions from the outside world of things and people provide him/her with a personal structure of thought.[16] In a sense, what the individual cannot sense or feel, the individual cannot add to a personal intellectual framework of thought. Two or three factors in an experience that become organized into a relationship type pattern represent what Piaget calls *schema*. It is a "repeatable psychological unit of intellectual behavior or its prerequisites."[17] *Schemata*, in Piaget's theory, refer to an intellectual product that can be applied to a category of understanding.[18]

It is also through imitation, play, and emotions that the infant in the first twelve months after birth builds on the cognitive development gained by sensorimotor activity. Repeated experiences provide for the child a repertoire of information. This becomes in part a nucleus to which more ideas can be added. "Towards the end of the child's first year, he has refined his capacity to generalize and to differentiate to the degree that specific experiential episodes are generalized into classes of experience."[19]

The first twelve months of an infant's life have been an active, productive, and variegated process when one considers the amount of information that has been acquired and the amount of growth that has taken place. The infant, as a totally integrated organism, is affected by all parts of him/herself. Each part affects the whole. As the child's intellectual structure grows, so does the perceptual-motor development. As the child recognizes more opportunities that are available to him/her in the environment, so does the brain activity "tell" the motor system what to do.

In the next section, the intellectual development of the infant will be continued as it is affected by other aspects of the child's system.

INTELLECTUAL DEVELOPMENT FROM BIRTH TO TWELVE MONTHS

The child's cognitive development, how the infant thinks and associates patterns of thought with objects perceived in the environment, was not examined in the same way in earlier history as it is in contemporary thought. If one traces this development of infant-thinking patterns, many, other than pediatricians, would not describe or measure intelligence per se. In fact, as one examines the historical trends in various societies, it becomes obvious that children were considered more as custodial trusts, rather than human beings with great potential in readiness for development by caring adults.

The work of deMause,[20] like that of other writers in sociology who trace historical effects of social thought, indicates that societal contexts provide backdrops for parents, and others as well, for the understanding of ways to conceptualize attitudes toward children and modes of child rearing. The "psychogenic theory of history," however, as deMause discusses it, suggests that it is not technology or economics that affects changes in history, but rather "the psychogenic changes in personality occurring because of successive generations of parent-child interactions."[21] This view promulgates an attitude on the part of parents that will put them in the frame of mind of the child, so that they try to accompany the child through his/her childhood experiences and work out various problems. He says that the contemporary pressures for "psychic change" are a result of "the adult's need to regress and . . . the child's striving for relationship," and this need occurs "independent of social and technological changes."[22]

Sociologists do not see human thought as occurring separately at times from the societal context, although deMause does. The psychoanalytic approach as was discussed by Reissman and Miller in Chapter 1 of this text, is represented as a world view that gears people toward expectations of a certain kind.[23] They say that people conceptualize the world in terms of certain themes and norms of any given era. In any case, however, deMause's point is, in part, that as one traces the history of childhood from its earliest ideas to those of today, one notes that parents' and children's psychic distance seems to be diminishing. He feels that, in that sense, the psychogenic orientation in child-rearing, that is, a form of the adult's acquiring the frame of reference of his/her child, does create anxiety. "The reduction of this adult anxiety is the main source of the child-rearing practices of each age."[24]

If parents are trying to empathize with children and if they are trying to understand them with fresh eyes for the world as the parent is presenting it, then those parents are raising the level of respect they are prepared to give the child. Becoming the child's peer, in a sense, suggests that at least for a few moments the adult is experiencing (or attempting to experience) the helplessness, but intelligence, of the child at his/her level. This perspective is promising. It provides a type of readiness on the parent's part to take on the child's point of view, and in that sense the parent must be open and nonjudgmental in behalf of the child's best interests.

It becomes increasingly clear that not only does the child's development at any growth cycle affect his/her intellectual processes of thought, but also the attitudes of parents and siblings. In the first year, the amount of time, energy, and attention the adults spend with the infant affects the child's intelligence. Their patience with the child, interaction, and games played with the infant provide the stimulus that is needed for the substance of intelligence.

The degree to which infants show interest in objects and follow them with their eyes or hands reflects to some extent an awareness of objects and events in the environment. A baby's responses to people, imitating sounds, and watching the faces and eyes of those nearby, are signs of learning. Between four to eight months, manipulation of objects becomes the means through which intellectual activity is obtained. Sitting up, crawling, standing in many cases before the end of the year, add stimuli to the baby's experiences at home and outdoors so that (s)he begins to do some things with ease. Practice or repetition at play with toys, or in eating and drinking, all of which involve manipulation of objects, bringing them to the mouth, moving them in a coordinated manner, are the intellectual work of the infant.

Language development, a significant aspect of intellectual skills, is a form of expression that has begun with the baby's sounds. Then, in the latter part of the twelve-month period, the child is becoming more aware of certain words that refer to people and objects. "Where's Mommy?" may affect a turn of the head toward the child's major care-giver, if the child has been accustomed to hearing "Mommy." Children understand more than they can indicate with speech.

Many mothers and fathers talk to their babies in the first few weeks of life, establishing a loving, soothing relationship with words, and generally satisfying interaction patterns. Even though babies do not understand words, they sense a great deal of pleasure from the adult's intonation and pleasing sounds. This interaction is effective and begins significant relationships between care-givers, siblings, and infants. Babies of just a few months old often make sounds that give the impression of attempts to respond to adults who are cooing and talking softly to them.

Because the normal healthy baby is curious and will examine objects by placing them in the mouth, the home has to be well protected from sharp objects, broken ones, or toxic materials that can be placed in an infant's mouth. Intelligence involves curiosity. The mother is not always there when a child is probing, crawling off from the spot at which (s)he was placed. The child has no way of knowing what is dangerous. The environment may appear totally safe. The healthy infant is quick, too. Tiny objects that may escape an adult's eye, are not missed by the infant's.

Sensitivity to stimuli in the environment is measured in various ways. When children attend, concentrate, touch, examine objects and people's faces, this is an expression of one aspect of intelligence. This is also a form of curiosity. The measurement, however, of various abilities (visual, auditory) of infants in their perceptual skills is difficult. The manner in which the infant is to respond is part of the problem.[25] What children see, hear, smell, feel, however, are involved in early cognitive development. Infants are born with a readiness to receive information about their world and to assess it. They have perceptual abilities that permit them to perceive size constancy and depth when exposed to experiments testing their awareness. Each normal child has "an extensive number of basic perceptual competencies which it makes use of to form a broader, comprehensive, and mature knowledge of the world."[26]

Sense perceptions, whether inborn or facilitated by experiences, have been underestimated in their contributions to an infant's cognitive development. Piaget, as noted earlier, became aware of this and based his theory of language development on this phenomenon. The research that has been conducted on babies and their ability to discriminate among size, shape, depth, and even among sounds and smells, provides evidence that attests to their wide range of responses that direct thought. Scientists used to think these responses were automatic and mechanistic. Many researchers today view reactions to stimuli in the environment as developmental and in part due to experience and judgment made by the infant, the organism itself. The inborn readiness to respond is like an initial program design within the child. When responses are observed coming from the child, they represent an enlargement on the process of growth. Qualitative development builds on the child's interaction with the environment, and the way the child incorporates what (s)he sees, thinks, and feels in that environment. Changes in the individual, in turn, affect the way the world will look to that individual. Learning is less an automatic reaction than it is reflective and responsive. Thinking is different from the automatic eye-blink.

By the end of the baby's first year his/her cognitive development regarding thought and action includes an awareness of ways to achieve what (s)he desires. Ideas learned prior to this period become integrated into more complicated systems of thought. This *accommodation* of incorporating into the system what is observed in the environment and using that information in terms of other ideas that are already known and integrating it, in *assimilatory* terms, as Piaget has written, are part of a cause-and-effect system that the infant uses.[27]

Intelligence is part of the total system of the individual, and in that sense is affected by the sensory characteristics, biologically and psychologically.

Judgment of the environment has to involve a give-and-take in the internal functioning process. How an individual feels, the emotional aspect or state of agitation, excitement, tension, influences thought and action. The next section will present information on the child's emotional development. Personality development, intelligence, behavior, relationships to others, perceptions of the world, and the skills one brings to one's world are bound into the individual's emotional levels and range of expression. Cultural expectations facilitate or inhibit certain emotional responses of an extreme nature. Proscriptions for expression of emotions are learned through the socialization process. Babies in the first twelve months are permitted to cry in relation to the parents' feelings about what that crying represents. Nurturing, holding, coddling, and helping the baby are also parental qualities that provide the infant with an emotional base. It will be discussed next.

EMOTIONAL DEVELOPMENT FROM BIRTH TO TWELVE MONTHS

The human organism has a potential for a wide expression of emotion, and the predisposition of this expression is within the infant before it is born. Pleasure of parents or care-givers in the child, demonstrated by smiles, holding, loving, and the like, give impressions as to which emotions, and the extent of their expression, are acceptable. The baby repeats what is pleasurable and what is approved by the parent in the process of interaction.

Emotion may be perceived as a level of excitation or arousal, expressed at various levels of intensity, from minimal to extreme, in the child. Expressions and limitations of emotions are both externally and internally controlled. Children watch for reactions to their feelings (physical or psychological affects) and modify to some extent their own expression of them.

Babies' expressions of fear, anger, and elation can be observed by parents who learn to understand their infants' responses. Physical pain is expressed by a sharp cry, and various levels of discomfort may be detected by significantly loud cries for help. Research on the expression of emotions is difficult, especially with infants. As they cannot verbally express their feelings, researchers have to infer them from the baby's response and to interpret the meaning of it.

Personality development is greatly affected by the individual's emotions and the way (s)he responds to events or people in the environment. The individual perceives danger in some way when (s)he becomes frightened, angry, or hostile. Babies respond physiologically to the environment. Thus, their cries are a form of letting care-givers know what is needed; this is a mode of self-protection that fortunately is present at birth.

Emotional expression is greatly shaped by the responses of people around the child. Before an infant is born, parents have specific predispositions toward the way they will treat the baby. Noting Concept Illustration 2–1, one can conceptualize some of the elements that contribute to the parents' attitudes toward the infant. These impressions are not necessarily at surface levels of the parents' consciousness, but they are nevertheless

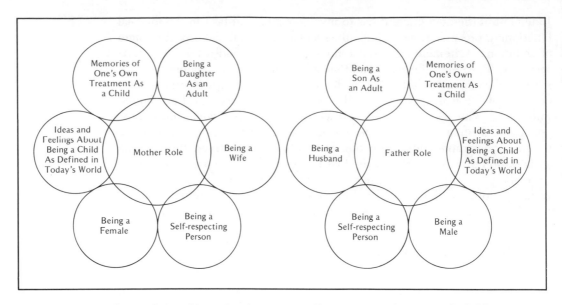

Concept Illustration 2–1

Interrelationships of Role Images Affecting Attitudes Toward Child.

present in people. They contribute to the conflicts, satisfactions, dilemmas, and "conquests" that parents may feel when they interact with their infants.

Similar to feelings that parents try to reconcile within themselves are their attitudes that stem from inconsistencies in thought related to their own parents, to their siblings, and to current child-rearing recommendations. These attitudes, as well as other psychoanalytically defined traits and characteristics that they feel are present or absent in themselves and may want to instill in their infants, shape their own behavior in various situations with their children.

The smile may be one of the first responses of emotional exchange between human beings. When it occurs in the infant, however, the interpretation of what it means varies among pediatricians and psychologists. Bower indicates that smiling of a sort can be noted a few hours after birth, but that it is not regarded as the smile adults recognize later as registering pleasure at some level.[28] Stroking the skin on the cheek or face can evoke a smiling response in the first week.

Most psychologists and pediatricians consider that a smile occurs because of physical reasons. It also may occur when a baby sees an object with light and dark spots on it.[29] In any case, the response of an adult with emotional cooing and loving embraces often reinforces (or creates tendencies in the baby to repeat) the child's smile. Researchers discuss vigorous smiling, half-way smiling, nonsocial smiling, mouth-but-not-eyes smiling. This in a sense dissuades some parents from thinking that the infant is actually smiling lovingly at the parent. Salk suggests that parents be allowed and encouraged to believe that the child is smiling.[30] He and Bower do not agree with comments that the child smiles from the effects of gas after feeding.

Fear, anger, rage, pleasure, hostility, and creative behaviors are channeled differently by people depending on what they are taught by parents and other care-givers. As value associations (or external judgments) are made with given responses, the individual continues to demonstrate them or is discouraged from doing so. Confusion among people and care-givers as to what constitutes appropriate responses to given stimuli stems in part from uncertainty about limits for expression or boundaries that are set for acceptable (nonpunishable) behavior. Permissiveness, strictness, and democratic forms of parental behavior toward the child evoke a range of emotional responses. Thus, a child learns early how much (s)he must control and how much (s)he may release or express openly.

Even though emotional development is central to the individual's personality and to what makes the human being distinctively different from other animals, it is difficult to study, in babies especially. It is less difficult, although not completely understood, as it occurs in adults. The diffuseness of the cause and effect in emotional expression makes it difficult to specify exactly what causes occur to precipitate certain behaviors prior to certain expressions of emotion.

As a child develops and adults give certain labels to his/her behavior (e.g., "stubborn, lazy, mean, nice, good") and attach reasons to be ashamed or proud of it, the child begins to struggle with desires to express or withhold certain feelings in order to comply (or not comply) with parental preferences or demands. The rest of one's life is a series of struggles between what to do or say, when, where, and with whom. How much it is necessary to subordinate one's own feelings in deference to another's becomes a never-ending quest for appropriate answers, depending on what is desired as an end reward in given situations with people.

Emotional behavior or its socially acquired development, relative to how it appears to or is acceptable by adults, represents a wide range of moral orientations, value judgments, and the question of what constitutes pleasing personality characteristics. The interaction between what seems best in the child's interests and what will bring the support or love that is desired from others is, in part, an emotional tug of war that is central to family life. This is not intended to mean that the total of the child's or parents' existence is unpleasant in the context of whose needs will be satisfied in these struggles. It does say, however, that the struggle occurs and to have it occur is a normal part of people's development. Each family has its own way of defining these issues.

Emotions protect the individual. The organism, after all, has to communicate to the environment what its own problems are. Thus, emotions are to be valued, to be recognized, to be defined for the individual's maximal levels of understanding and for self-management of them as is decided best for one's own growth. To understand them, and to decide how to use them to the best advantage (however one may define this) or not, is part of the human condition. It is not new to the current society to be engrossed in this process; what is new is the way people have learned to define feelings in the context of a new technical system of words and concepts in a psychic sense, described by deMause and others (earlier in this chapter).

Emotions arise from and cause anxiety, concerns about interaction with others, and accelerated needs that appear to be unmet for the individual.

The context of social interaction adds to emotional development in the experiences it provides and the new labels and qualifiers it extends to the child. The next section will show how social interaction creates and responds to complicated mechanisms in the individual.

SOCIAL DEVELOPMENT FROM BIRTH TO TWELVE MONTHS

What is true of other aspects of development within the child is true of social development. A readiness to respond exists in the child; the environment affects responses in terms of the adults and children in it.

An infant's observation and fixed gaze on the mother's face can mark the beginnings of attraction to others. In the ordinary routines of caring for the child, much time is spent very close to the infant. Games played with the baby during the feeding, bathing, dressing, bedtime hours nourish the playful enjoyment of mother, and father, and child. These early attachments to people provide a foundation for patterns that can be repeated later with other people. Some writers indicate that the baby's needs in the first six months could be satisfied by care given to him/her from someone other than the mother, provided it is done well, of course. At seven months, however, the baby is able to discriminate the mother from other people, or at least the individual who provides care most of the time.[31] It is suggested that what the infant seeks is stimulation and an answer to needs, rather than the mother specifically. By about ten months, many infants have strong attachments to their mother and are distressed when she leaves the room.[32]

As the infant develops a familiarity with those who fulfill needs, a trust begins to build with those adults from the infant's perspective, but not with others who are not actively involved in the infant's life. Fear of strangers that may have developed for some babies between eight and ten months, can begin to subside by the end of the year if the child begins to see other people and becomes accustomed to them.

Bower indicates that imitation skills are present in very young babies, and that they are an aspect of sociability.[33] An infant is able to imitate an adult who has opened his/her hand or mouth, or even protruded the

The wide smile of Michael, at four and a half months old, gives evidence of social interaction in settings other than his crib. The couch is used by older children and adults. He accepts happily and eagerly this form of growth. (Photo by Priscilla Margolin.)

tongue.[34] Within only a few hours after the infant is born, an interaction pattern may be observed between the infant and its parents. Bower suggests that this interactional synchrony is something like the interaction of two people who move together in concert and that the infant can show this synchronization with the mother very soon, just a few hours, after its birth. "The behavior is specifically human; it can be elicited only by human speech and no other auditory stimulus."[35] This, in effect, gives the infant an ability in being social, in being responsive, and in acquiring an identity with (rather than being isolated from) its own kind, as Bower interprets the imitative behavior.

Social development in almost a "natural" form of playfulness is a powerful mode of learning. The infant and young children are playful by nature. They are ready to test, to pursue, to explore, and not to take this seriously. It is reality to them, but at the same time, it produces surprises as well. They engage easily in humorously teasing interplay. This gives them some sources and foundation for a sense of humor. It is there unless it is stifled by grim, unfriendly people in their environment.

Social development continues throughout the individual's life cycle. Interaction with human beings changes. It seems to be, for some, one of the most difficult aspects of life. Its effectiveness for an individual influences emotional stability, a philosophy of life, and conditions of mental health.

Babies are affected by the interchange with parents, who are in turn being influenced by the responses of the child. Some babies who are with mothers who talk a great deal to them do not, at an early age, respond in kind.[36] They may become accustomed to the stimulation, or they may have a limit that moderates their interest and their will to respond.[37]

The behavior of mothers changes with each baby they have. The time of life for the mother, conditions of marriage, maturity, physical aspects of the mother's development, other siblings in the home with the baby, father's work and time out and in the home, and other subtle factors affect parents' interaction with children. These elements bring social behavior into a focus that differs from that of earlier relationships with children born prior to the most recent one. Birth order affects the treatment of an infant. First-borns have more attention from the parents, typically, than those that follow. A first girl, born to a family of three boys, will receive treatment different from a third boy born to a family of boys. This is not suggesting positive or negative attitudes; the treatment differs because the characteristics of the environment and of the mother at a different time of life differ.

Social relationships change with circumstances and with the child's development. Early attachment behaviors do not provide assurance that the relationship "will be a happy one . . . [and] are controlled by interactional events as well as by the physical-maturational status of each participant in the relationship."[38] Plasticity is a quality of the formulation of social relationships; for this reason as well as others, they are not anchored in a secure base that can be identified as a cluster of responsive "feelers" functioning in the same way all the time, once nurtured at birth.

The remarkable qualities of an individual's body and the process of growth, or its potential, in the individual, emphasize the adaptability of human beings. This tendency toward change in growth and in attitude toward the external environment, as well as toward one's self, affects new attachments and new relationships with others. "Social adaptation and its byproduct, attachment behavior, reflect processes that continue throughout life. Simply because a social preference is established early in life does not ensure that it will remain functional or primary."[39]

The infant's need in early stages of life to be nurtured in order to survive is often regarded as the same psychologically preferred need that one individual may have for another later in life. But adult preferences are based on choices among individuals and are not the same in basis as infant attachment that occurs in the first year of life. The infant's needs at birth are given no choices; satisfaction of them *is* the infant's need, not necessarily a personal choice that has been made from among several people who were interested in performing that function. This does not take away from the fact that a mother's and father's love for the infant can provide the "best" instinctual and psychologically energized care for the infant. Babies benefit from the care of people who are intimately concerned about their well-being. Caring parents have the highest stake in the child's health. Change, adaptation, and various events in learning in the infant, however, predispose one to new feelings and new attachments at different times of life.

Social behavior is a part of cognitive, linguistic, motor, and emotional development in children. It is understandable, then, that the amount and quality of stimulus a child receives from the environment will affect various patterns of exchange that occur between the infant and parents as well as between the infant and siblings or others who are frequently in the environment. Relationships made at that time are not totally unchangeable. They may set the emphasis or beginning approaches in behavioral attachments, so that subsequent behavior is affected, although not permanently. They do not represent a closed system reaching an apex of some sort or completion unto itself.

The difficulty of conducting longitudinal research on the development of individuals from infancy throughout a life cycle is obvious. Studies have been made on children and their development up to the age of early adulthood, but the expense and conditions for carefully controlled scientific work introduce subtle compromises that often have to be made for valid reasons. With high-quality studies, it might be possible to determine the degree to which life in the first year of an infant's development carries through to adult life.

Social relationships depend on self-perceptions acquired by the individual from people in the environment. These are diffuse the first year of life, compared to their status and understanding in the years following the first twelve months. Selfhood, identity, individuation of self from others, are concepts that apply to processing of thought in the child in early stages of life as well as those following throughout the life cycle. In the first year of life, however, identity does not mean the same in conceptualization of thought as it will mean in the second, third, and following years of life.

Differences between the parents' childhood experiences and those desired for their own infant (and which may often reflect the child-rearing views of the times) often create confusion. This confusion may result in anxiety in the child who receives permissive treatment at some times, and strictness at others.[40] These concerns on the part of the parent may transmit mixed messages to the child, who eventually formulates his/her own social interaction patterns based on what is considered feasible at the time. Identity, selfhood, and other aspects of knowledge of one's own personality "equipment," or freedom to act, combine to affect social interaction between the child and others.

One obtains impressions as to how difficult the measurement of social behavior can be relative to what one measures, how it is measured, and what is considered desirable in the context of the researcher's theoretical orientation in a given cultural group.[41] These variations in point of view of the researcher and those who apply the ideas of the research findings lead to considerable disagreement.[42] In any case, a great deal happens to an infant *after* the first year of life to affect personality development and subsequent interaction patterns with other people.

Caution needs to be taken that one not consider unimportant what does in fact happen in the first year of life to an infant. Just because research indicates that early behavior may not be perpetuated in all ways after the first year of life does not mean that what happens at the time is not important. This would be a false conclusion or assumption, and could surely do much harm to an infant's care. Each year of life is important.

The best attention possible should *always* be given an infant, whatever the period or age. Infants and young children are helpless in their dependence on their care-givers. Permanence of behavioral traits, however, is not the crucial issue of concern that should affect the kind of care an infant receives. Taking thoughtful, wise care of babies is extremely important to their well-being, whether their responses or habits are "welded into permanency" or not.

Just as the intra-uterine processes of growth set a stage of readiness in the infant to respond to the outside world, so does the first year become a precursor affecting in varying degrees what happens to the child in the next year and the year after that. New developments combined with growth of locomotor and intellectual skills in the child bring many new energies to bear upon the external world even though no one knows how one might respond in future experiences. The next sections focus on the child's development between one and three years old.

The Child from One to Three Years

With all the skills that a child has developed in learning to walk, talk, relate to others, in a somewhat limited sense compared to later experiences, the period between one and three years old will be exciting for a child's growth. This period will also take more energy from parents and others around the child, who needs to be protected from unsafe or dangerous objects in the environment. Watching the one-year-old become more competent in standing, walking, reaching, and concentrating on objects and people, an adult senses the self-pleasure derived by the child who is "conquering larger and larger worlds" in the home and close surroundings.

As physical development affects, to a great extent, the child's locomotor skills and the space that can be covered in crawling around, the next section will deal with aspects of the toddler's physical development.

PHYSICAL DEVELOPMENT FROM ONE TO THREE YEARS

Genetic qualities in a child's growth and body patterns affect his/her direction and maturation. They impose limits to some extent and offer great potential in another way. What happens at a given time in a child's life (e.g., accident) can affect a spurt or a limitation and deceleration of growth in his/her first years. These levels of growth and their extensions are influenced by both the genetic qualities and the environmental elements in his/her life.[43]

Nutritional advantages of good food, proper dietetic balance, adequate rest, nurturing, cleanliness, and the chemical growth hormones contribute to the physical gains and/or losses in the child's physical development. Readiness to utilize the food that goes into the infant's body is in part influenced by the chemical inheritance; the environmental experiences answer to or create new needs in food consumption and body functions. Strength, energy levels, and motivation can be affected by chemical digestive patterns and the body's integration of minerals or other contents of food.

Children in the first two to three years of life typically experience their most rapid growth rate. By the time they are two, some children are about 36 or 37 inches tall. Almost twice as much growth occurs between one and three years old as between three and five.[44] At three, the height range among children is about 35 to 39 or 40 inches tall.

The weight gain of children between one and three is rapid and represents greater development in muscle tissue, skeletal growth, height, and fat. Children at two years old may weigh about 24 to 35 pounds. Exceptions to these figures are found in unusual cases of genetic differences or nutritional effects/deficiencies.[45]

Body types affect to an extent the motor development, movement and coordination of young children, as well as their weight and height, and their environmental opportunities to experience various interactions with objects and people. The next section will involve information on children's activities in moving, extending, reaching, walking, and other gross and fine motor discriminations and performances.

MOTOR DEVELOPMENT FROM ONE TO THREE YEARS

Sitting, walking, running, and generally beginning to control one's own movement occur over several years of learning. At about sixteen months old, a child can walk, unaided, and is beginning to refine the skill increasingly every day, given normal circumstances (exceptions may be due to illness, disease, unexpected disruptions in growth, or some tragic event).

Large muscle development in a child's activity is referred to as a gross motor skill. Finer coordinated activity in the use of smaller muscle involvement refers to fine motor skills. Walking involves gross motor development first.[46] After children learn to walk, they can do several other activities,

With her feet wide apart and arms fanning out, Sarah sustains stability and balance as she pursues her goal of staying up in the process of walking. Her facial expression reflects the pleasure of success. (Photo by Gerald J. Margolin.)

such as jumping, running, climbing, and managing themselves up and down the steps.

Maturation, which refers to a condition in the child that occurs with genetically determined growth changes,[47] affects the child's ability to succeed in a given skill. If the child's neuromuscular development does not support his/her activity or beginning efforts in a skill, it is best to wait before urging too soon what the child is not yet able to do.[48]

A principle that can be used is this: *Encourage the child, but do not force him/her. Motivate, love, show support for the child, but do not be disappointed if the child does not do something when urged. Be patient. Guide, be kind, smile in success or nonsuccess.* Consider the skills that individuals attempt to master at adult levels of development: driving a car, for instance, or learning to play golf or tennis. Apply this concept to the child who is doing something that may appear simple to an adult, but is not simple to the child. Children are learning for the first time, minimizing defeat, and continuing in good nature. When they become frustrated they need adult support all the more.

Adults' unawareness of this principle of readiness often leads to child

Michael, at one-and-a-half years old, enjoys a rocking horse at Christmas time. Motor development strengthens the fun that one is able to have in the many opportunities that are available in life. (Photo by Priscilla Margolin.)

At about a year old, Diane seems to be reaching for the doll's eyes in examination of how they work. Curiosity, manipulation, and experimentation leads to finding out about one's world. This is serious work for young children. (Photo by Gerald J. Margolin.)

abuse. When adults are expecting young children to do what they are asked and it involves a skill of some kind, adults often perceive the child's inability to perform (or comply) as unreasonable or stubborn or deliberately defiant. This absurd expectation, when it is counter to human possibility at certain age levels, is often a serious source of continued maltreatment of the child. The repeated pressures in this regard aggravate rather than improve the child's progress in a given skill.

Physical coordination develops in several ways from one to three years old. Eating, playing with blocks, being able to control and manipulate physically what is needed, the child finds that the environment is a place that yields to one's touch. Along with sensorimotor perceptions that help the child in knowing how things feel to the touch (hot or cold, soft or hard, brittle or smooth) come other ideas about how the child can control those things.

Children enjoy pulling toys behind them, pushing objects and other items that can be subordinated to their manipulation. These activities are important to the children's educational development, as well as to the motoric aspects of growth. Children between two and three are also handling books and crayons, and their own clothing at minimal levels of dressing. Parents need to be ready to assist when needed, but need to allow a fair amount of time for the child to manage things independently.

Children's energies and physical development shape to some extent what they will enjoy. They are curious, however, and will try many things with objects that move, that can be stacked inside each other, with a little wagon that can carry things around the house, and which they can sit in if it is big enough for them. Safety, anticipation of any kind of unexpected

Keith is proud of doing the puzzle by himself. (Photo by Gerald J. Margolin.)

break in a toy or in household item that is attractive to them, needs to be under constant surveillance of the care-givers.

Hand-eye coordination becomes a significant factor when children learn to read, to recognize shapes, forms, and letters. Although this is, at times, considered part of motor development in the process of coordination skills, it involves the perceptions to a great extent. Perceptual-motor development is related to artistic skills, musical ability, handcraft, and sports, among other things. Intellectual, academic, sports, and musical ability, in their relationships to motor skills, are described variously by different authors. Some will categorize perceptual motor skills under motor development; some will discuss them as cognition. It is difficult, however, to separate motor development completely from brain coordination and skills related to the academic.

The next section will go into the intellectual development of children between one and three years old and will include more information on the sensorimotor perception and interrelated skills that are crucial in the total development of children.

INTELLECTUAL DEVELOPMENT FROM ONE TO THREE YEARS

Children's perceptions of the world result in part through the quality of interaction they have with other people and in part from their own genetic levels or potential for thought, language, movement, judgment, and assessment of what other things or people represent to them. Children have to interpret through their own systems the effects of the language of people, the associations made with language, and the people's attitudes toward the child's understanding. Attitudes toward the child are screened through a cognitive base in the child's mind, as well as an emotional base. Together they process ideas or concepts in the child's mind and feelings, so that cognition and impressions of the world begin to formulate themselves in the growing child.

According to Piaget, as was mentioned earlier, an individual's intelligence is affected by the way that individual organizes and adapts to the information received from the environment.[49] This is common to all species, as a biological means of responding to the surroundings. "While organization and adaptation are inherited, they are not structures (like reflexes) but *tendencies*."[50] A human being inherits, according to Piaget, "few particular intellectual reactions; rather, he inherits a tendency to organize his intellectual processes, and to develop particular adaptations to his environment."[51] *Assimilation* and *accommodation* are the terms Piaget uses to describe the organization and adaptation modes of intellectual processes used by human beings.

Between one and three years old, children are gaining a great deal from the environment, because it is what they see, touch, feel emotionally, hear, and smell that provides the substance for intellectual processing. As White suggests in his concern for the toddler's curiosity and searches for stimulation throughout the house in the first three years, a safe area must be available.[52] Young children are not aware, until they try to find out, what is dangerous and what is not. As they have a tendency to taste, smell,

Sarah, at about two years old, is pleased that her Daddy has given her the opportunity to feed the dolphins. She is learning about ways of interacting with her environment while having the physical and psychological support of her father, who is also fond of dolphins. (Photo by Gerald J. Margolin.)

Sarah, at about two years old, enjoys seeing a large and unusually colored fish close at hand as she is held by her father, who is explaining distinctive elements about the fish to her. Many experiences of this kind provide the intellectual development that comes from exposure to images and explanations of an exciting world out there! (Photo by Gerald J. Margolin.)

eat, and the like, and this is adding to their intellectual functioning, caregivers need to see that endangering products (e.g., liquids, toys that are toxic in any way, and sharp edges) are kept out of the child's environment. To prevent children from tasting deprives them of learning. Their learning, however, should not result in illness, disease, or a rush to the emergency room of a hospital.

With each new item of information the child brings in to join other data, which become part of a total network of thought, further assimilation and accommodation are made. This internalization of the "pictures of the world around the child" creates a reservoir of knowledge that is carried around in one's head to maturity. Some of the information may change to adapt to the challenge of later thinking and reasoning; some may not, unless it is brought to conscious re-examination when contradictory concepts or evidence are encountered. Many psychoanalysts, of course, deal with these subconscious, or deeply accepted but unexamined, ideas acquired in childhood.

By the age of two, the child is able to "juggle" mental images in the

Michael, at about thirteen months old, is contemplating the ocean, sky, and sand as he gazes from his place on a large rock at a California beach. (Photo by Gerald J. Margolin.)

mind. Mental manipulation of objects can be made without having to act on them in the immediate environment. "Toward the end of the second year, the child begins to develop novel *cognitive*, or mental processes."[53] This is termed *semiotic function*, which means that between two and four years old, a child can make a mental symbol, word, or object represent something else.[54] It implies that the child recalls something from past experience and applies it to the present. An object, such as a spoon, can represent something else that can become useful as a toy.

As children begin to process words in their own minds and begin to endow them with meanings in terms of their own personal experiences, they establish a framework of meaning in the context of certain situations. The frustration that often results from the child's inability to express what is desired can be played out by the child in symbolic play activities. For example, when a child becomes angry because it is obvious that his re-

If children's curiosity is encouraged even at a very early age, they can remain interested in various phenomena (things that move, that flit from place to place, that crawl slowly) even while feeling odd on one's arm or body. Diane was patient and still while observing the butterfly that flew away and re-alighted on her arm. (Photos by Gerald J. Margolin.)

quests for something are not being met, (s)he may scream, break something, kick the furniture or perhaps even the person who does not seem to understand what the child's message is intended to convey. A parent may become angry. When, however, a child reprimands a toy, hits it, or throws it a short distance, a parent may not comment about this manifestation of frustration, irritation, or hostility, realizing that the child is upset about his/her own ability to deal with his/her needs.

Meaning, conflict, indecision, and childlike purposes struggle for clarity. Between the ages of two and four, the child is able more safely to express anger and aggression with his/her toys rather than with people. The degree to which this expression is permitted affects the child's ability to mediate problems with the environment. A child needs some margin (or psychological space) for venting feelings. The child's frustration does *not* need punishment, but rather needs understanding.

Children are developing language rapidly between one and three years old. They may not have the appropriate word, of course, each time they want to convey an idea. They can only use what they have heard around them, and it requires time and experience to associate the meaning with the word itself. In any case, this early period of a toddler's life brings many exciting learning events for the development of knowledge and ways to approach one's world.

Imagination, play, imitation of what is seen by the child, all contribute to intelligence needed for functioning effectively in one's environment. The child who is observing, using skills, developing words and meaning, is learning to adapt all the resources needed for acquiring control over the environment.

Recent studies on hemispheric laterality of the brain involve researchers' concerns with the right half, which presumably has been neglected in educational development. *Laterality* refers to the localization of an area or part of the brain that performs certain functions for the body. Cerebral dominance, as reflected in skills that are facilitated by one half or the other of the brain, has been studied with people who have had brain injuries. Although these studies provide information in a provocative, heuristic sense, they are "suspect because of the difficulty of determining with certainty what structures or nerve systems in the brain were damaged."[55] Injuries to the left hemisphere affect language. The right hemisphere of the brain seems to process spatial integration, aesthetics, and musical abilities. Researchers are seeking more sensitive measurements for work to determine how the left and right hemispheres function, and which half facilitates which skills and abilities in the human being.

Writers indicate that although most language features such as "syntax, abstract words, and concepts are represented in the left hemisphere—for all right-handed people and for most left-handed people, . . . we should not assume that all language functions are located in the left hemisphere."[56] Some mechanistic type functions are guided by the right hemisphere; learning the names of objects, which is done earlier in life, indicates an active right hemispheric function.

Interestingly enough, noting that the right hemisphere is presumed to be functioning to a greater extent earlier in life,[57] and diminishes later as "the left hemisphere of the brain begins to dominate,"[58] the work of Edwards is relevant.[59] She suggests, with documenting research reports, that the right brain is dominated by the critical, logical functions of the left because the left half processes things differently. The right half as well as the left uses "high-level cognitive modes which, though different, involve thinking, reasoning, and complex functioning."[60] The right half of the brain can use metaphors, dream, and create new ideas. This creativity is often inhibited by the left hemisphere because it "analyzes, abstracts, verbalizes, counts, marks time, plans step-by-step procedures, verbalizes, makes rational statements based on logic."[61]

The young child's tendencies toward the characteristics ascribed to the mode of processing of the right hemisphere are worthy of reflection. It is as if the right side of the brain, less hampered by logical sequencing of thought and critical analyses (of one's own thought as well as the concepts of others), retains a freedom of vision and intuition that is valuable for creative activity.

Edwards indicates that the right side of the brain of adults is not so good at sequencing, categorizing, caring about the passage of time, analyzing, or being logical.[62] These are the same characteristics of thought that Piaget notes are not developed in children between two and four. With limited knowledge of language and logical reasoning, a mode of processing information similar to that ascribed to the right hemisphere of the brain is used by young children. They also use imagination with less constraint than they may later at school. It seems that the development of creativity and perceptiveness cannot be urged by talking or trying to help children accelerate logical thought. That orientation evidently does not coincide with the processing mode of the right hemisphere. Rather than encouraging children to *be* creative, we may need to give them more opportunities to use exploratory, imaginative, undirected, multiple paths (rather than sequential) approaches to experiences at school. These are typically aesthetic, self-expressive, and original thinking activities offered in art, music, rhythms, creating poetry and stories, or nonsense syllables.

The next section, which involves data on the emotional development of children between one and three years old, indicates the many ways that their emotions are affected by the environment, people, and events and the manner in which children perceive those elements in relation to their own personalities. Cognition, thinking, adaptiveness, energy levels, language facility, and other factors in the child's physical and mental make-up affect his/her emotions. This aspect of children's development is influenced by the meanings that are attached to incidents and how the children regard them, that is, as "good" or "bad," in terms of parental perspectives or admonitions.

EMOTIONAL DEVELOPMENT FROM ONE TO THREE YEARS

Emotions are one of the most difficult characteristics to assess in scientific research. The term refers to a physiological arousal in the individual that affects his/her internal and external form of response to the environment. The classification of causes for children's responses to various incidents in their environment is not totally satisfactory because it separates in analysis what is not separated in the human emotional act. A cluster of variables typically have to be considered in evaluating an emotional response.

Pain, anger, hostility, aggressiveness, and fear can be noted in the child. When a child draws back upon seeing an animal, hearing a loud noise, or seeing a stranger, it is obvious that elements of fear are at work. Experiments reveal, too, that heartbeat rate changes, visceral tension increases, adrenalin flow accelerates. A sudden reaction, focused on responses to specific objects, can be observed and judged in terms of the classification of an emotion, more so than it can in nonlaboratory experimental settings, which have not prelocalized a given set of stimuli to determine whether an individual's feelings will be affected. Testing an individual's reactions to known objects requires different means of judgment and measurement than discovering what caused an emotional arousal in a young child.

Causes leading to an outburst from a child, when a teacher or a parent has not been present to see the antecedent or precipitous qualities of the moment, are more difficult to ascertain by the adult care-giver. Thus, while a researcher may attribute certain causes to the environmental properties as having elicited certain emotional responses from a child, this is different from the adult care-giver's judgment in trying to guess what happened.

A young child's limitation of a vocabulary for self-expression may inhibit sufficient knowledge provided to the care-giver in order to determine what has upset a child. Simpler judgments of fear of an animal, it is true, do not involve as much "detective work" on the part of a care-giver as do judgments of other and more unusual environmental elements. It is in the more complex judgments related to several dimensions arising in people's interactions that more difficulty exists in defining the causes of an emotional response.

Children between one and three years old are having a far greater number of experiences with others, and a great variety of experiences as well, than they did in their first twelve months. This fact suggests, in itself, that many kinds of emotional responses are generated. The attitudes of others toward young children provide, in part, some idea to the children as to how they should feel about themselves. These attitudes reflect cultural values. They also represent people's interpretations of values. Children observe their care-givers' behavior in relation to specific events. With those

Keith enjoys doing new things with his parents, who go slowly in order to have the child experience various activities with them. (Photo by Gerald J. Margolin.)

views, they begin to classify their own acts in terms of whether they may bring pleasure or irritation to the adults.

Activities such as birthday parties, playing games with children one's own age, washing the car with one's parent, talking on the telephone even briefly, introduce sets of new experiences. These bring greater and more complicated emotional responses involving more people and reactions to one's self than had occurred earlier in the child's life.

Emotional development in the child is unique. Each one responds to people and the environment differently. The manner in which a child interprets what is happening affects personality development. Whether the child views the world as a safe place that holds a promise of satisfying things, or whether a child perceives the world as a place to fear and as a punitive source, will influence the personality characteristics of that child. *Personality* refers to a readiness of response that becomes habitual in different situations. An individual, because of a beginning point of view, perceives comments and behavior of people as punitive or as pleasant, with gradations between them.

Emotional readiness in the individual to react to people in terms of fear or pleasure builds a predisposition to act in a manner that perpetuates or reinforces the original response. It sets into motion a circular process (of original fulfillment) that prevents the individual from seeing the possibility of pleasure when it may actually be ready to occur. The individual's behavior brings about the exact behavior in others that (s)he wishes would not happen or has already feared would happen.

The emotions, and means of showing or inhibiting them, affect the individual's outlook as well as how that perception is integrated into the individual's behavior. The disclosure of one's emotional levels, for example, influences others, who may, in turn, respond in kind or be disconcerted by them and not respond in an understandable manner.

My friend congratulates me on my birthday! (Photo by Gerald J. Margolin.)

Keith shows his father how much he loves him. "I love you this much!" (Photo by Gerald J. Margolin.)

Young children are learning patterns of response from adults who are giving commands, cues, support (or lack of support) for various characteristics of the children's behavior. Language expression, understanding, and vocabulary extensiveness becomes a larger part of emotional development and interpretation as the child becomes older. When children are between one and three years old, however, most of the disapproval and approval mechanisms of adults in responding to the behavior of children necessarily limit lengthy explanations and the use of language because of children's limited comprehension.

The next section, which deals with the social development of young children between one and three years old, indicates how cognitive impressions, attitudes of others toward the self, meanings and interpretations of facial expressions of others, and circularity of behavior in the interaction process affect growth in social interaction.

SOCIAL DEVELOPMENT FROM ONE TO THREE YEARS

Interaction with others begins at birth. In this sense, social interaction, rather than "socialized" interaction occurs immediately. The style or patterns of interaction change as the child matures, as do other forms of behavior that will be adapted by the child at later stages.

Michael at about one year old is ready to go as he sits in his car seat, safely bound in, and notes that his parents are as pleased as he is, looking forward to a family outing. There is much to see out there! (Photo by Gerald J. Margolin.)

Social interaction involves reciprocal behavior, that is, one individual affects the other in the process and the way it goes. Behavior, response to it, leading to reciprocity of responses back and forth to each other in a social interaction process involves a complexity of characteristics on the part of both individuals. This cluster of qualities is difficult to study. One can, however, understand why it is of interest to researchers. It affects greatly the way children's and adults' behavior can be interpreted.

Social development is recognized as involving internal mechanisms of reasoning, reflecting, emotional constraints, and visceral functions. It involves negative and positive behavior, which is valued or nonvalued by adults responsible for a child's well-being. In the process of learning what

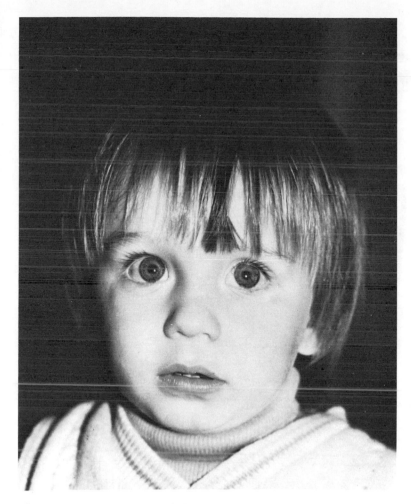

The expression on Michael's face, at thirteen months old, reflects thought. While taking in images and activity of the people around him, he also is attempting to sort out the meanings. Social interaction is significant and necessary to the child's development. (Photo by Gerald J. Margolin.)

those positive and negative sanctions are, a child adapts certain qualities, and internalizes them as his/her own.

Moral orientations, conscience, and fear of reprisal begin to integrate themselves into a child's personality and reasoning processes.[63] These effects build on each other, layer by layer, one's thoughts and feelings about how one ought to interact with other people. Although children are able to differentiate among the expectations of their behavior that adults and children have for them, they nevertheless affiliate many proscriptions of their parents to be those that represent "the world."[64] In fact, from the child's point of view, those proscriptions become so universally attributed that they create an ethnocentric view of how people "ought to" function if they

Social interaction at one's party involves in part being aware of and enjoying the attention that one receives and managing it without being frustrated by some of the unexpected pressures to respond in certain ways. Westry, at age three, was in control, not thrown by the excitement of an enjoyable function planned for her. (Photo by Gerald J. Margolin.)

are to avoid punishment or blame. An ethnocentric view assumes that all people should govern their behavior by the same proscriptions one learned from parents when value orientations were inculcated. Standards used for the self to determine "goodness" or "badness" are perceived as a universal set of criteria in the ethnocentric orientation of thought. This view can interfere with various forms of social development at levels of impeding understanding of others.

It is not reasonable to expect, of course, that a child between one and three years old can understand all the subtleties that are involved in developing the reflection and reasoning of social development. They should not, therefore, be punished for a lack of such understanding. The sophisticated interpretations of certain values at the adult level should not be expected as a biological process unfolding itself in the child. It requires time, maturity, and several other aspects of intellectual and emotional adaptations.[65]

Sharing, empathizing, sympathizing, and other forms of behavior that involve the ability to take the point of view of others and sense the hurt or pain experienced by others occur in processes of interaction. Meanings that are interpreted when those processes arise become the substance upon which higher developmental social understandings are built. Timing, judgment, and verbal associations or cognition are intricate combinations that have to mesh at appropriate times if effective social interaction is to result.

Even though cultural trends in any given period of history may affect to some extent how a parent will perceive social prerequisites, there are some that transcend the passage of time. Such characteristics as sharing, degrees of selfishness or unselfishness, and emotional outbursts at various times and places are greatly affected by any given set of parental preferences in that regard. Leniency or strictness with the child in terms of violation in any direction depend in part on how the parent perceives such behavior and the effects it may have for the future personality development of the child.

Big sister Sarah holds Michael at thirteen months old. Sarah has been involved in taking care of Michael from the moment of his arrival into the family. Brother and sister bonds can begin early. (Photo by Gerald J. Margolin.)

It is in this focus that parents can become emotionally committed to certain value orientations in their children such that the boundaries of human frailties are forgotten. When a parent becomes emotionally involved to an extreme degree with the way a child will respond to any given direction, abuse of the child can often occur. Unreasonable expectations of children at any given age can incur in the parent an unreasonable response mechanism.

Social development in the context of people outside the home involves not only the parents' expectations for the child's behavior, and the child's awareness of what is expected, but also the *assumed* expectations perceived by the parents that other people may have for one's own child. A third force of judgment comes to bear, not at all clear, as to what is expected of the child by all in the situation, when combinations of thought are assessed. Parents may know, the child may know, but what the impressions of the outside observer should be, ought to be, or are, may not be validated. The mixture of impressions among parent, child, and observer may involve embarrassment, shame, guilt, perhaps pride, uncertain or not. One may note the parental reactions when a child refuses to obey a parent engaged in an argumentative posture at the supermarket, shopping mall, or any other public place, to see an example of this complexity of parent, child, and imagined impressions of observers regarding the child's behavior.

In current concerns for expression of children's feelings, parents become confused about being permissive or controlling. They are not sure when they are going to either extreme in their supervision of children. This is an individualistic judgment greatly related to the parents' feelings about authority, dependence, emotionalism, self-gratification, aggressiveness, hostility, courtesy, moral orientation, and many other characteristics they want to discourage or encourage in their children. Various models on parenting behavior can be consulted.[66] Here, too, one cannot assume that any given mode will be comfortable for a parent. Attitudes toward children, however, can be developed so that the parent realizes that an interplay between what appears sensible and what appears manageable for a child at any given period should be considered. Each parent has to devise his/her own most effective model within the framework of thoughtful parental child-rearing practices in social development.

Interestingly enough, current intelligence testing among children includes not only cognitive skills and knowledge (a traditional mode in testing), but also the social skills related to ways of coping, and "knowing when to be assertive and when not to."[67] Concepts referring to themes of assertiveness or nonassertiveness reflect contemporary values that have grown out of a reaction based on impressions that a stultification or inhibition of personality results from social conformity at various levels. Such views on a singular style or on an expectation of homogeneity of a population grew from a contrasocietal backlash, in a sense, by people who felt that social constraints were forcing people to be overconforming.

It was felt that if individuals were not permitted to be more directed toward the self (e.g., their own feelings, views, and needs), they would not

Parents know the importance of sharing experiences with children. Sarah, at about two, is not sure of the feel of the swing apparatus, but with parents at her side she is willing to try a ride. (Photo by Gerald J. Margolin.)

be creatively productive and their unique individuality would be lost in deference to a collective perspective of some kind. Anti-establishment and antibureaucratic feelings emphasized individualistic rather than societal directions in value orientations. Paradoxically, nothing that occurs within society is a characteristic of a nonsociety concept. This antisocietal view was an ambiguous perception, meaning different things to different people at different times; consequently, it, too, needed group validity and conformity to test its "workability."

It is not difficult to understand why and how parents may have experienced some confusion as to what they wanted in their own children's per-

Westry at three has older children at her party and does not appear to feel overpowered by her guest. (Photo by Gerald J. Margolin.)

sonality development and social orientations, considering their adult years in an era that vacillated between the benefits of a social self or a more inwardly directed self. Between the ages of one and three, the decisions may be less difficult and less complicated in nature than they will be later on as the child matures. With maturity and competence in vocabulary usage and reasoning that can be used against parental requests for the child's obedience or conformity to household "rules," come concomitant struggles and strategies that may challenge the parents' expectations and authority.

Maturity, competence in varieties of skills, language development, social knowledge in coping, compromising, and asserting, are all on the child's side in helping him/her to achieve what is desired even against the parent's wishes. These become the substance of future challenge to the parent who tries to exercise "leadership" in the child's life.

The next section presents information on modes of maturity in the child between three and five years old and how these modes are used by the child to enhance an identity of self.

The Child from Three to Five Years

Many children in this age range have begun to widen their circles of familiarity with a world outside the home. Some attend nursery school or are in a preschool program three or four times a week. Many by the time they are over four years old (in some states, four years and nine months), attend a public or private kindergarten every day. Personality development in this period is impressive. Children's awareness of their own abilities and some interaction skills with others assist in a knowledge that the environment can be controlled by them in varying degrees and at varying times.

Children in this age range are often with people other than their own parents. In part, this is a result of interacting with neighborhood friends, visiting relatives, and being in places that are part of an everyday function of living in a community. Schools, recreation areas, and community agencies become service facilities for families, and in them children begin to interact with people different from their own parents and siblings.

The next section provides information on the physical development of children between three and five, and how these gains in strength and capabilities affect growth as an individual entity.

PHYSICAL DEVELOPMENT FROM THREE TO FIVE YEARS

By the age of three, a child may be about 3 feet tall, and will gain about 6 inches in height by the time (s)he is five years old. The weight of a three-year-old can be about 30 pounds or more and the child may be expected to weigh about 40 pounds at the age of five. Variations in height and weight are a result of genetic differences, nutritional effects, and various factors in the early growth history of the child. Boys are usually taller and heavier than girls of the same age, but even this difference depends on individual children's care and growth tendencies.

Body proportions change between three and five years old as children's legs lengthen and their abdomens become less prominent. This period of life manifests an emergence from the baby years with this period emphasizing a preparation for firm early childhood feats and endeavors. Children are acquiring strength in muscles, firmer tissues and cartilage. "In the preschool child's growing skeleton, cartilage turns into bone and existing bones grow larger and harder."[68]

Writers indicate that by the time a child is five the brain has developed to 75 per cent of its adult weight,[69] but this does not necessarily indicate that *knowledge* has accrued in the same percentage. Physical growth changes can enhance and facilitate the possibilities of new achievement levels. The changes do not in themselves, of course, advance their own potential. Environmental influences are significant in affecting new patterns of integration in the child's growth after the age of five regardless of brain weight at five.

Most children of five have all twenty of their baby teeth, which will be replaced at a later stage of their development by permanent teeth. The growth and placement of teeth in the child's gums affect the shape of the jaw, and vice versa, as well as the mouth, and the general form of facial features and appearance. Contemporary information on the proper care of teeth can aid greatly on retaining the permanent teeth when they erupt. Proper cleansing, nutrition, and dental care can assist in strengthening the condition of children's teeth so that in later years and adulthood they may have and retain healthy teeth. Teeth also affect one's willingness to smile in the knowledge that one's appearance is enhanced.

Just as one's health is affected by teeth and other aspects of bodily growth and structure, so it is that one's motor development is enhanced by physical health and growth. The next section treats the ways that children's motor development occurs.

MOTOR DEVELOPMENT FROM THREE TO FIVE YEARS

Motor development in children of this age range, involves not only walking, running, hopping, riding a tricycle, throwing, pushing, pulling, turning, and many hand-eye coordinating activities, it also involves drawing, painting, scribbling, and other controlled, and self-guided activities in which children participate. Skills are developing at a rapid rate for children in this age period.

As children become more at ease and practiced in the motor skills, they move easily and in a more coordinated fashion than they did at earlier stages of their development. Their equilibrium and balance improve. They are able to run with their arms closer to their bodies. They try many different activities, having greater confidence in their own skills.

Children can manipulate small objects such as puzzle pieces in an inlaid puzzle background form. They are able to play with blocks of various sizes and shapes, to pile them on top of each other, and to make designs of their choosing.

Since children between three and five like to imitate the activities of other children, they can often do things that are done by their age mates and also by older children. Challenge, curiosity, and desire can motivate children to perform tasks that they would ordinarily not think of doing. Good health, precautions for safety, adequate rest and exercise, provide some of the essentials that go into motor development.

Children like to climb in and out of large boxes, under tables, and to run and hide from or with someone. The activity involved in the pursuit of a ball, toy, or person energizes motor development. By the time a child is five years old, many games and functions have involved motor skills. For this reason, the play of the child gives a myriad of opportunities for growth that is physical at the same time that it is mental.

Four-year-old children are engaged in many motor activities at prekindergarten levels. They play games that involve large groups, such as "Ring-Around-the-Rosy" games, "Pop, Goes the Weasel," a directional group game, and several other forms that involve them in running, stooping, hopping, and jumping up and down. Between four and five, children's motor coordination and related skills increase in competence. The children can be asked to do several tasks, such as pouring, holding, putting something together, and taking it apart. They do them well. They need to be told that they are doing well in order to continue efforts in difficult situations.

Children's enjoyment of movement is a self-motivating energy. They do not like to sit for long periods of time unless they are ill and do not have the energy levels needed for involving them in play. Competitive games are not appropriate for children in this age range. They should not be placed in a position of failure through unfair challenging or teasing in a race or game. Because their own pleasure in movement motivates them for running, swinging, hanging, jumping, riding a tricycle, and managing themselves on equipment of various types, they like to practice those skills for their own sake. It is unfair to expect them to go beyond their own abilities by placing them in a situation that may set them up for failure.

Acrobatic feats, swimming, and other forms of organized activities for children are typically instructed by people who know young children's capabilities. At least, parents who offer those forms to children should be sure that people who teach those classes to their children are familiar with the temperament, personalities, and physical capabilities typically expected of young children. Parents observing teachers of those classes can usually ascertain whether the instruction will be beneficial to the child or not. These activities are often recommended for children who appear to have endless periods of energy. Channeling or directing children's energies is important to their development. If their energies are not geared to socially approved outlets of expression, they are easily "dissipated" in other ways. This is not to suggest that parents always need to have a formalized program for children's motor activities. It does recommend, however, that parents observe how their children use their energies, and not be upset by what appears to be aimless behavior.

Differences between guiding behavior and allowing children to express themselves through play or their own inclinations are often obscure. What matters is that children's motor development be respected for what it does for the child. Even though play may seem purposeless to the parental eye, it is not when it involves practice, repetition of acts, increasing mastery over small and large motor skills, and an absorption with an object or skill that even precludes hearing when someone is calling the child. Experimentalism is close to discovery, which is also akin to creativity. These characteristics are desirable in children and should be allowed to develop.

As organized motor activity begins to occur and develop in many games and coordinated tasks required of children in preschools, it is not necessary to be concerned about formalizing motor skills at home. Practicing, choosing, and persisting in motor skills that are selected by the child (and are determined as safe by the parent) can follow nonsystematic lines. Children will be involved in many formalized activities at school. Their own choices at home can prepare them for moving into the more coordinated and planned school tasks.

The next section points up the interrelationships between motor activity and intellectual approaches to tasks for children between three and five years old. Children cannot learn by sitting in chairs and hearing about various phenomena and how things work. They have to experience what they are expected to learn. They have to touch, rearrange, build on, and affect the things in their own surroundings, if their environment is to affect their development.

INTELLECTUAL/ACADEMIC DEVELOPMENT FROM THREE TO FIVE YEARS

Children from three to five continue as they did earlier in their development, interacting with others as well as with things and events in their environment. They are judging, perceiving, and retaining images and ideas through sensory (firsthand) experiences and intellectual functioning. Their intellectual capacities are strengthened in terms of what they receive or are exposed to in their environment at home and in nonhome events. These experiences are informal. At school, however, plans for children's involvement are more formalized than they are at home. In that sense, academic development refers to knowledge and experiences that are more organized than the open and nonstructured experiences of children at home. It also refers to the structure of subject matter, or discipline, that is unique to any given field of study.

Academic disciplines, such as mathematics, social studies, physical or natural sciences, all have an internal structure as part of the organization of their facts. This aspect of organization is part of what children need to learn in the academic context of a subject. Facts, techniques, logical order or development of certain ideas about the world as depicted in a given subject matter area, are categorized into disciplines or studies that children investigate. In this sense, the knowledge itself is more organized for teaching than the information that children were learning about earlier in their intellectual development.

Even though parents may not be instructing children at home in the more formal manner that occurs with groups of children at school, they are nevertheless teaching. Information about objects, their names and their functions, represent data that are needed for the child's framework of the intellectual structure that forms a significant basis for the child's interplay series among processes of thought, language, interpretation of concepts, facts, and generalizations.

Between three and five the child's observation of things, names given for them, and direct sensory contact provide intellectual and academic bases. The older the child becomes, of course, the more (s)he is able to deal with concepts, complicated functions in objects, and a means of filing away in the mind information obtained in the sensory contact.

Piaget's work on children's thinking suggests that between three and five the child is in what he terms a preoperational period in the process of cognitive development.[70] The child is able to think of things and their function even when the object is not presently at hand. Mental images are related to an object with which a child has had previous experience. A child can remember playing with a ball, what it does, how it acts, and where one may play with it.

Cognitive development, play, and language development are interrelated. Children in this age range are adding to their knowledge repertoire. They are also learning new cognitive skills. Studies conducted to ascertain the elements of play and their contribution to children's intellectual development indicate that higher levels of thought are involved in play than most adults with children realize.[71]

The imaginative qualities that facilitate thinking for language, play, or words and symbolic representations contribute to the developmental advancement of children between three and five. A playful attitude toward an object or experience can yield more information and lead to more answers for a curious and searching mind at times than an attitude of direct simple cause and effect. Language, then, can be binding or releasing depending on how it is understood, how it is used, and what rules one uses to integrate meanings.

These views should not be considered as negating the use of facts in learning about the more formalized disciplines at school. Exploratory behavior in investigating or adaptating to one's environment is *not* debilitating to the development of intelligence or academic depth. It can enhance curiosity. It can also broaden the child's knowledge of techniques for the assessment of facts that are learned as part of an academic pursuit.

The interplay between cognitive development and qualities of play behavior suggests that skills are exercised in the process. Meanings are transferable as the child wishes for the moment. Representations of thought are implemented by specific activity created by the child. Mastery of thought is accomplished for a brief time. Cognitive information builds in the activity of experimentation.[72]

Children's expression of language has been developing with their abilities to master pronunciation, sounds, intonation of words. According to Vygotsky, until the child is about two years old, speech and thought have been developing in a parallel sense. When this joining occurs, the child "becomes curious about words and begins naming everything within sight, touch, and hearing. . . . The child seems conscious of the symbolic property and power of language. The two lines are now inextricable. Thought becomes verbal, speech becomes rational."[73]

A blend of different types of speech and thought occur in an *inner speech*, which assists in reasoning and which is difficult to measure in the young child; there is also *verbal thought* similar to the presentations in a formal debate; *concept development* involves words that show how a child classifies his/her own systems of meaning about objects in the environment; and also in *pure meaning* when an individual is "engaged in making sense of experience and life. . . ."[74]

Various psychological patterns in the development of the child affect the kind of language s(he) will develop; the intonation, the dynamics, the general patterns of speech and meanings that may be derived from what is heard are influenced by cultural elements, adults who guide the child, and experiences the child has at home and school relative to language and speech. Psychologists indicate that identification patterns selected by the child, that is, who and what the child will choose to model for his/her own behavioral expression, affect language and speech and thought.

The scene is set for children between three and five years old as a significant period of growth in mental skills and capacities. Children need opportunities to exercise those skills and elements that are growing within them. Adding knowledge to one's repertoire of information requires changing, re-integrating, questioning, taking in new ideas which, in turn, may create different concepts. These concepts as well become, in part, an additional element in the structure of thought and language.

Thus it seems that not only formalized language emerging from the structure of disciplines that children are exposed to at school contributes to children's intellectual and academic development, but also the thought that arises in imagery, in symbolization, and in the child's manipulation of things and events in the process of playful engagement with his/her environment adds to intellectual growth. Discursive thought is described as different from imagery in that imagery is spatial in conceptualization, and discursive thought is linear and sequential.[75] These styles must be retained in children's learning.

Although direct correspondence of truth may not exist between content [of imagery] and the sequential organization of thought,"[76] it nevertheless has a significant contribution to the thinking in a child's development. Spatial organization of thought differs from discursive, logical, and sequential lines of thought. Spatial perceptions, however, do not depart from truth. They represent another way of seeing or responding to one's environment.

Truth as a concept is often associated with logic and objective examination of things or events and people. Objectivity, however, does not preclude impressions that can be compared by spatial conceptualizations. *Eidetic imagery,* which represents spatial organization of thought impressions, takes in whole patterns of ideas, much like a *gestalt* in which the total impression is greater than the sum of its parts. A glorious sunset, for example, is viewed in its entirety; one does not separate its elements in linear discussion and thought. Diffusiveness, images, color, shapes, forms, impressionistic ideas that present an aura of a feeling, all are useful modes for communicating certain thought patterns one has in mind. These should not be lost or minimized in the name of precision or fact that is necessary in logical or discursive lines of thought.

Mathematical learning proceeds from clearly distinct counting processes and manipulation of objects placed in order of some kind. Children learn about counting, placing similar objects together in a single category of classification, and about various systems of order that are unique to the mathematical process and that help people master a variety of complex functions and operations. Children have typically had many experiences at home with objects that are used at school in implementing the mathematical rules and system of classification.

Comprehension of counting, of rearranging objects that add up to different amounts, subtracting objects and dividing them into groups, engender new meanings for children when concepts are associated with specific action performed with items, objects, and individuals. The abstract system of mathematics ultimately can be understood when countless experiences with numbers, functions, operations, classifications, and other forms of creating order within a given system of thought are introduced to children. These activities continue as part of an abstract system.

The nature of the mathematical system becomes less abstract when children are able to handle the counting objects and to see how the performances relate to figures symbolizing those objects and operations. With more frequent opportunities to be in control of changing, adding, subtracting, moving about in classificatory groups, the objects that represent symbols in the mathematical system, children are able to make the system more a part of their own (internally structured) knowledge.

As one adapts to functional necessities related to an understanding of a classfication of the world and elements important to humankind, one also develops greater capacity for feelings about the world and its people. The next section reflects children's concerns about internal feelings that both puzzle them and, at times, make them uncertain about their own behavior.

EMOTIONAL DEVELOPMENT FROM THREE TO FIVE YEARS

Descriptions of one's own emotions require experiences in which names have been given for certain behavior. Children observe various levels of excitation representing emotional responses in others as well as in themselves. Even though emotional responses may, at times, be direct, impulsive, and loud, they are nevertheless complex. Children learn through various admonitions and encouraging words what should make them feel better or worse about themselves.

Emotions build on self-awareness at various levels. They build on self-image. Self-image provides layers of remembered successes and the lack of them. Children will adapt to the self-images that their parents affect and will incorporate parental views as "real" or authentic and permanent qualities in their self-concepts. Some of these attitudes toward the self may change; some may lie dormant; and some may remain at subconscious levels.

Between three and five years old, children are still greatly dependent on their parents and other adults who are responsible for the well-being of the young. They have fears, anxieties, and hostilities in relation to obtaining what they want when they want it. They search for various cues that will help them accomplish goals related to their needs.

Genetic characteristics may be involved in the physiological expressions of fear, anger, and other forms of emotion. They do not, however, override other aspects of the cultural setting that influence the manner in which emotions may be expressed, to what extent, and when. Children's emotions have often been measured by physiological stress counts. This is only part of the information that is needed to ascertain emotional development.

The reciprocal process involved in interaction, that is, the parent's behavior toward the child, may influence a certain response from the child. The parent responds to the behavior of the child. Often this circular process sets up changes in condition and in the manner in which a parent may ultimately respond to the child at the moment and at later times. The child modifies the parent's behavior toward him/her. Difficulties encountered in experiences with a child can wear down or minimize the parent's expectations and willingness to persist in requesting certain behavior. It may drain the energies of the parent more than the attainment of a given value performance on the part of the child may be worth to the parent.

Children select certain behaviors for their own internalization at different times. They may pattern certain mannerisms and voice levels and intonations of a parent. Selection, discrimination of models, and integration of those behaviors and choices combine to set a stage for emotional responses that children learn from those around them. To the degree that the perceptions of others toward the child are congruent with the child's perceptions, emotional dissonance may or may not occur. If others treat the child as the child wishes to have them respond, things may go along rather smoothly. When too much conflict arises between the child's expectations and what actually happens when people respond or react to the child, emotions may become more intense. They represent protest and anger at the environmental influences that stand between their own self-regard and the attitudes of others toward their own feelings about a self-image.

Emotions constitute in part a personality, its temperament, its degree of volatility, complacence, compliance, and other qualities of interaction with others. They also affect the development of strength in skills related to speech, aesthetics, handwriting, reading, and other school experiences.

Teachers' and parents' attitudes toward the child's attempts in acquiring any skills affect further development. Whether a child will stop trying or not is affected by adults' or other care-givers' reactions to the child. Emotions are part of a process involving an integration of the responses of others into one's own system of behavior imbuing them with feeling. Thus, children's attempts at growing can be affected, facilitated, or inhibited by adults' comments about the children's products.

Children sense the attitudes of their teachers when trust and confidence are transmitted through a feeling tone. A teacher who hears a child describing a number of objects (and has given an incorrect response in regard to the number of objects pictured) "recognizes the exaggerated perception of the number of apples as a more accurate indicator of affect than of number, and feels that to deal with it as number would be psychologically irrelevant."[77] This feeling represents empathy and an understanding on the teacher's part. (S)He remembers to note future answers of the child in relation to number responses, so that awareness of the child's understanding of number may be noted. The teacher does not cut into an idea expressed by a child in deference to exactitude, which can be checked later on when specific work on number is explored.

Teachers who are cognizant of the emotional development in a child, and its place in supporting or denying his/her skills, are careful to provide the child with substance for self-esteem. This does not mean that it is done in any dishonest form. The judgment of the teacher and the major orientation of a curriculum can represent respect for the learner's self-esteem. This direction is an enduring source of support for the child.

As emotional development builds on meanings, not only in regard to one's environment but in association with one's cultural setting, it is conceivable that young children's development increases, for the most part, with maturity of experience and thought. There are some elements in the emotional process, however, that do not undergo great change throughout the life cycle. Feelings of self-worth, being needed by someone, being considered with respect and expecting others to pay attention to one's concerns or complaints, remain in the emotional cluster related to the ego structure. How one construes those reactions from the environment toward the self, however, becomes a more complicated judgment as one matures.

The emotional repertoire developed by an individual often arises in the context of situations with others. Social development is an essential component in this regard. The next section involves discussion on that variable.

SOCIAL DEVELOPMENT FROM THREE TO FIVE YEARS

Interest in the social development of children has fortunately provided more research and writing on the subject in recent years. Children's development in that complicated process of interpersonal relationships, self-regard in that context, confusion between what is or is not expected in given situations, parental or adult concerns for their children's development in moral orientation or conscience growth, all affect how children will learn what is valued in their behavior and in their society or family.

Researchers have attempted to study role perceptions of children, perceptions of the intentions of others toward themselves, and the effects that various forms of language expression have on children. Cognitive-developmental theory is represented in three new directions: "These are its integration with the more general approaches of cognitive psychology, the new life that it has provided for symbolic interactional approaches to social behavior, and basic advances that have been made in the conceptualization of intentionality and motivation."[78]

Memory studies that have focused on children's organization of memory and their use of it in relation to certain concepts and classes of events indicate a diffuseness in children's recall and in the way they apply what they remember. This finding suggests that social relationships can change and be remodified as the child becomes older, and without violating former views.

Sociologists have been interested in symbolic interaction studies for many years. They were interested in the circularity of interpersonal relationships and the way in which language affected the behavior of people in the interaction process. Emphasis was placed on the process of interaction rather than what happened with individuals, even though one affects the other in any social exchange.

Within the processes of interaction, individuals impute a great deal of intentionality to each other. Disagreements arise when behavior seems totally incongruent with expectations that each has for the other. Inkeles suggests that sociologists need to consider psychological variables in situations as well as the sociological ones.[79]

Inkeles cites instances that raise questions as to whether social change occurs in the production of personality adaptation to change, or whether certain personality types are taking advantage of prevailing conditions in a society at any given time. He suggests that "Probably both processes are at work in a complex interaction of personality mode and social structure, producing changes both in the sociocultural system and in the type and distribution of the personalities generated in the community."[80]

Inkeles notes that sociologists should be doing work in studies on child-rearing processes; he focuses on the fact that parental patterns of child-rearing are affected by the life situations of the parents and by various pressures that they experience in those contingencies. In that recognition of the ways in which the social structure affects parents in rearing their young, it appears that psychological elements in the personality are influenced by social and environmental impact.[81] He also suggests that an important clue has been neglected, that of studying the child-rearing practices of each generation, as the "means whereby social stress in one generation leads to social change in the next."[82]

Symbolic interaction is part of a significant process that allows the individual personality to interact with people of one's own age, family, social groups, and the components of society or professional and occupational categories. This process intermeshes the individual with the social system and its structure. Young children slowly learn this and begin to respond accordingly in given situations as significant people in those situations seem to indicate.

Children perceive others in the environment in a given situation. If they think the teacher expects them to conform to a certain kind of behavior (such as sitting still to listen to a story), they may comply. Some children are more concerned about conformity than are others. In any case, however, they do perceive some kind of pattern or expectation, and children sense what the intentions of others are for their own behavior. This is one aspect of social cognition. The ability of the children to perceive what others may expect of or intend for their behavioral performance does not necessarily mean that they will comply with such expectations.

With a current view that children's perceptions be respectfully listened to and examined, and that children, generally, be taken more seriously in the way they think or conceptualize, there is a greater chance that they will be understood as individuals in the process of developing. Researchers are human and are adults. It is difficult to retain an adult perspective at the same time that one is trying to adopt the child's frame of reference. This does not mean that the effort should not be made; it does mean, however, that perspectives of adults reporting children's views be scrupulously analyzed for misimpressions or misapplications.

Given the choice, children will veer toward situations and people that provide the most satisfaction for internal needs. Social interaction often determines those choices. Parents have to observe the elements of social interchange that motivate their children's behavior. Friendship choices are made on those bases. Attraction of groups for any child is in part due to the groups' qualities that satisfy various needs in the child.

Qualities that lead to competitive behavior, aggressiveness in sports, and leadership in groups are encouraged in various situations that children experience. Cultural settings encourage some aggressive behaviors and discourage others.[83] The degree of competitiveness is suggested as related to the degree of complexity in techno-economic systems. Under certain conditions in societies that stimulate desires to have more, seek more, and to work for more things available in the society, individuals seem to be more competitive. Some researchers view this direction of human behavior as a "natural concomitant of surplus economic systems. In this view, then, to behave competitively in the urban-industrial setting is to behave adaptively."[84]

Adaptability to one's cultural values as encouraged by parents and other significant adults responsible for children becomes one among several other qualities that children have to learn. Mass media provide various models for children's adaptation to specific behavior.[85] These grapple with and conflict in personal ways with what one's parents expect one to do. In any case, however, the broadening vistas of children's social horizons and the expectations of a world "out there" provide choices, dilemmas, and ultimate decisions as to how one will guide one's behavior in social contexts.[86] It is suggested that children need order and have to discover ways of getting along with other children. They know that they must learn to wait their turn, not to pick their noses, spit, or soil their underwear. These concerns for order and almost ritualistic processes, as indicated by the Sutton-Smiths, lead toward an appreciation of "fairy tales, cartoons, and stories, which help to convince them that success and victory are possible."[87] Social constraints can appear overwhelming.

Social development continues throughout life. People adapt to elements in events as they perceive those elements to be affecting their own life and goals. Young children, therefore, are just beginning to adapt to mature forms of social interaction. Between three and five, they are largely under the protection, with certain exceptions, of adult or older sibling supervision. Life at school presents new situations for which children may not be prepared. These have to be worked out by using some of their own principles or "rules" for self-guidance and efforts to manage the environment in some way in order to sustain independence of some sort.

Developmental patterns of growth that gradually bring children to greater responsibility and maturity to use in their own behalf lead this discussion into the next section, which deals with children's development from five to seven years old.

The Child from Five to Seven Years Old

The age range five to seven represents for many children their attendance at school. Kindergarten is typically attended by five-year-olds; first grade consists of six-year-old children; and second grade at school has mainly seven-year-old children, either at the early or latter part of seven years. Academic growth, as well as physical and social, is significant at this time of a child's life. A greater proportion of these children's lives is spent with people other than their own family compared to the time spent mainly at home in the earlier years of their lives.

Children in this age range are doing many things that evolve from their own thinking. As their parents are not in the environment of the school or of their friends' homes, children are thinking and acting in terms of their own decisions and judgments.

The children are increasingly acquiring a sense of their own strengths and weaknesses, physically, psychologically, emotionally, and socially. The amount of information that they need to learn between five and seven in the formalized context (in an organizational sense) is impressive. Physical growth affects the children's appearance and the skills they acquire. It also influences various social and emotional fluctuations in the children's lives. The next section is on physical development of children between five and seven years old, a crucial school time in their lives.

PHYSICAL DEVELOPMENT FROM FIVE TO SEVEN YEARS

Nutrition, rest, adequate care, and observance of general daily routines affect the growth and physical appearance of children from five to seven, as well as their good health. The active schedules that children in this age range typically experience need the undergirding of a wise health regime. Bones that are growing, internal organs that are developing, energies that are expended in the pursuit of active engagement at school or at play in the neighborhood, all depend on a good condition of the child's body.

Children at about five years old may be about 44 inches tall, and weigh about 43 pounds. At six years old, they may be about 46 inches tall and about 48 pounds in weight. At seven years old, they may be about 49 to 50 inches in height and about 49 to 50 pounds in weight. A few inches are achieved each year, as well as a few pounds.

Children in this age range are losing some of the baby fat they had in earlier years, and they are losing temporary, or deciduous, teeth, and obtaining their permanent teeth. Children in the early primary grades are typically showing gaps in their front teeth and are preoccupied with their falling out and new ones coming in. They often compare with one another the progress of their teeth; they need to be reassured that taking wise care of them will help them have strong teeth and an attractive smile.

Excess sweets, food additives, and the manner in which food is cooked can often contribute to poor health of the body as well as of the teeth. Cleaning the teeth is essential to preventing the decay that occurs when food particles remain in the mouth and between the teeth, causing plaque, a hard substance that erodes the teeth. Although children do not like to be reminded of cleanliness and habits that can support better health and growth, they need assistance in ensuring that their bodies do receive the best health care that is possible. This information is given to them at school, and various incentives for approval from teachers can obtain their cooperation.

Parents do not give their children as many sweet snacks as they did years ago. Many will send the child to school with carrot sticks, celery, raisins or other natural fruit forms and vegetables. Teachers can explain to children why candy, cookies, and an excess of nonnutritional foods are not recommended for consumption. Young children can be taught to understand what the contents of food can create in one's body and how it can affect future development or perhaps cause pain, such as a stomach ache.

Physical appearance influences in the child a self-concept, feelings of inferiority or confidence, and sheer levels of good health. Children who are able to feel good in their approach to activities and have a sense of control over the environment stand taller, psychologically as well as physically. They take pride in what they are and do not mind if everyone sees them. For these reasons, physical appearance in children should not be minimized as an egotistical element in growth. It is significant for them and the way their personalities develop.

The next section is on motor development, which is closely related to physical growth and coordination.

MOTOR DEVELOPMENT FROM FIVE TO SEVEN YEARS

With height and weight gains in proportion to one's years of growth, come greater strides in motor development for normally growing children. Between five and seven years old, the child can manipulate skillfully, balance him/herself, and run faster than was possible earlier in life. These skills of running, balancing, skipping, throwing, catching, hanging, all contribute to competence among one's peers. School groups are a form of audience; children are watching each other. They know who can do what, and when they can do it. Friendships are often acquired on the basis of physical skills.

Sarah was pleased to receive this gym set for her sixth birthday. She enjoyed the proximity of opportunities for swinging, pumping faster and higher on the swing, sliding, pushing, stretching, and doing other acrobatic feats. When children are at school or in public places, they do not always have enough opportunity to use the equipment because of many other children having to share it. (Photo by Gerald J. Margolin.)

Sports activities, aesthetics, such as painting, drawing, dancing, manipulation of objects in crafts involving cutting, pasting, managing scissors, hammers, string, yarn, and the like, are affected by the child's motor development and skills. Coordination of muscles, large and small, with vision and other components of the mind involve the child in a myriad of events at school and in neighborhood areas. For the child who is not well coordinated and does not move well, life with other children is not much fun. A self-concept carrying a message that one is not liked, valued, or sought by other children is not helpful in one's development. Motor skills are essential in some form to help a child acquire what is his/her birthright.

With increased motor development, there are, of course, possibilities for accidents. Care, awareness, and general visual and auditory acuity can help children in being normally cautious about accident prevention. It is understandable that the more one expands one's horizons and activities, and the broader one's scope is in trying various skills, the more one is vulnerable to normal events or accidents that may arise with others. Unanticipated events call for quick thinking and action. Children can be taught how to protect themselves to a certain extent.

The child who moves well is often asked by the teacher and others to carry out small tasks. Impressions about a child are made in terms of how much facility a child seems to have in moving around and coordinating him/herself. Agility, vitality, and general eagerness or enthusiasm to perform various functions in a classroom or for one's parents are easy to observe; in some situations at school or home certain children are asked repeatedly where others are ignored. This occurs often without deliberate thought. A teacher who is aware of this oversight in not asking children who seem less well coordinated or eager to do small tasks for him/her has often deliberately requested the less-chosen ones.

Motor development is related to the acquisition of skills, and often the variety of skills that are sought for greater achievement become part of one's intellectual functioning. Learning how to play tennis, to swim, to play basketball, or any other sport that involves mind and body coordination, associates itself with intellectual skills as well. The next section presents data on the development of intellectual and academic skills of the child between five and seven years old.

INTELLECTUAL/ACADEMIC DEVELOPMENT FROM FIVE TO SEVEN YEARS

The focus for children in the age range of five to seven is to a great extent the academic and intellectual world. These children are faced in every direction by people, things, books, materials in the forms of kits, at times, toys, that are geared toward helping them learn.

Children become more conscious in this period of life of the necessity for knowing, naming, conceptualizing, and generally becoming responsible for intellectual skills. Those skills may be perceived in different ways by different people and by the children themselves. In any case, most children at this age become aware that it is important to know answers to questions that may not necessarily be related to routine, personal living.

Beyond one's own knowledge of self is a multiplicity of things, ideas, and facts that must be sorted out in the child's mind and that (s)he can be expected to recall at the appropriate time in order to demonstrate that (s)he has knowledge.

Researchers have conducted investigations on children's skills and their acquisition of knowledge in the years between five and seven. They find evidence of observable changes, but do not agree on how those changes have occurred.[88] Some indicate that changes occur in the growth and development of the brain to cause differences in the child's behavior; some suggest that large units of behavior encompassing children's abilities to take a perspective other than their own in the use of language bring about change in the children's behavior; and still others attribute changes in behavior to a form of the stimulus-response view of psychologists.

The physical growth of the brain, as well as parts of it becoming more mature in function, affects the way children will perceive the world. A particular part of the brain makes connections between feelings and symbols, as well as sounds. It is affected by language development of the child. In this period of life, between five and seven, a great number of words, ideas, concepts, and symbolic representations are observed and mentally recorded both through experience and understanding, to influence the child's development of the brain. The information that is processed across each hemisphere of the brain provides connections between sight and symbolization of what is seen. Someone mentioning an eye can evoke an image in one's mind of what an eye is.

Dominance of the right or left hemisphere of the brain is still a subject of research. Adults can be studied to determine which skills in the brain have been interrupted in functioning. Children, however, are still in the process of growth and some studies indicate that brain dominance of left or right is less determined than can be established in later years.[89]

Children's interaction with objects, books, and various tools for learning is intimately bound up with their impressions of people around them. How children regard their own skills or performance in tasks will affect their willingness to persist in acquiring improved performance. Challenges abound. It is up to them to decide whether it is worth the effort and energies, plus the possibility of not doing well, to concentrate on a given task. Intelligence, however, involves attempts, involvement, persistence, trial-and-error techniques.

Forms of speech with intent to communicate may be different in quality from speech that is used for one's own inner-reasoning processes. Children who are learning to express themselves to others are expected to do this more at school than they had been expected to do it at home. What they know will be measured by what they say they know. Interaction with others, then, and the way one uses language, will greatly affect one's acquisition of knowledge and techniques for enlarging upon it.

Children's continued situations of testing at school, in one way or another, make the formalized aspects of language become more significant. Different from telling someone what one is thinking in a nonsequential sense, and different from generalizing rather than being precise as one should be in stating a mathematical sentence, is that mode of thought and language that must be honed to a fine point by the child when taking a test. The testing, questioning, and sometimes elaborate forms of thought (prompted by the teacher) that occur when a child is trying to arrive at an understanding of facts or concepts represent a great stride in the child's intellectual development.

The child, in trying to assess what the teacher is expecting him/her to know, tries different paths of understanding. Various forms of language are attempted in this proces. Drawings, the placement of various objects in juxtaposition, writing, and other processes intended to assist the child in learning, and in turn, letting the teacher know what has been understood, are needed particularly for young children.

Vocabularies are in process of development.[90] Meanings, as well, are growing. Children learn that words can have many meanings. The word *bed* may conjure up an image of one's own bed; a bed of flowers evokes another idea; the bed of a truck creates still another thought. The value of education lies, in part, in the development of many meanings and the myriad ways that ideas or concepts are integrated to formulate still more. Past associations become linked into new ones, based on the broader scope one meets at school and in the context of interaction with others of similar age and older or younger.

Concepts of space and time in an abstract sense are difficult for young children to learn. It requires time and repeated experiences associated with appropriateness of time and activity (lunch time, breakfast time, time to go to school, etc.) for children to assimilate why one needs to understand that time is passing and to read the figures on a clock.

Spatial concepts are difficult to learn in their application to mental impressions having no frame of reference. Children can assemble pieces of a puzzle when they see relationships among spaces and puzzle pieces. Varied experiences with space, fitting parts together, noting proportions of large and small gradually acquire meaning for the child. Many adults still have difficulty in understanding relationships between space and size. Trying to remember while at a store whether a piece of furniture, such as a lamp, chair, or table will fit into a specific space near one's window at home, one can appreciate the difficulties involved in shifting ideas and sizes in one's head.

Intellectual activity continues in one form or another when one notes what happens around the child. Each individual knows it is an advantage to have information. Whether this information is used in deviant ways, counter to cultural interests, or whether it is used to advance one's society or social group and one's self at the same time, depends on the individual. Information, fact-gathering, concept-judging, and assessing what one learns in constructively critical fashion are all part of the intellectual pursuit. It is exciting and satisfying in a variety of ways to different people who are involved in it.

The next section involves concepts that contribute to an understanding of the emotional development of young children between five and seven years old. This emotional aspect of the child affects greatly the way his/her personality is perceived, and in turn, affects the child's perceptions of the self.

EMOTIONAL DEVELOPMENT FROM FIVE TO SEVEN YEARS

Since the child from five to seven is in contact with wider circles of people in school and in the nonhome environment, (s)he is becoming more adept at interpreting feelings. As people talk about each other, what they like and dislike, children retain some ideas about feelings and labels affiliated with those feelings. They begin to apply those notions to vague inner reactions and soon have names for internal arousal, whether that arousal is related to joy, sadness, fear, anger, or whatever.

The venting of emotions becomes a point of conflict between parents and children. Self-control is valued as an attribute that approaches growth and sophistication, different from an emphasis on immediate self-gratification. When one sees that unfair treatment by someone has occurred, anger, resentment, and hostility develop. The way one mediates or reconciles these feelings within one's self at any given time is part of the process of control.

Sarah's smile shows satisfaction with events occurring around her. Emotional development is reflected in one's smile. (Photo by Gerald J. Margolin.)

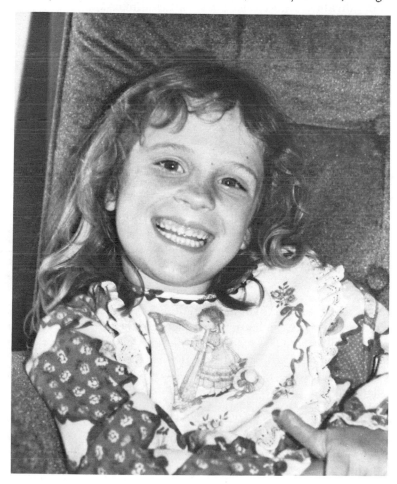

Emotional health consists of an adaptive system that is able to balance self-satisfaction with new knowledge needed to help one grow. An individual must be able to withstand negative comments from others so that the self is not disintegrated. What may appear to be disapproval from others may be evidence that others want more of the individual's time and stronger responses from him/her.

The emotional balance of children is developing (or should be) continually. Because of schooling experiences and the nature of large groups of children interacting simultaneously, more happens in interpersonal relationships among children than the teacher is able to observe close at hand.

Strength in each child to understand and classify in his/her own mind the meaning of those relationships becomes the core around which emotional health clings. Qualities of caring, concern for others, and empathy with others are present in varying degrees in children. The degree to which those characteristics can function depends on the child's capacities for feeling and understanding. The particular combination of emotional sensitivity and intellectual identification with other people results, for many, in an ability to care about the problems of others. The ability to understand the problems of others can extend to an emotional range of feeling in an individual. An expansiveness of this dimension in someone's personality begins to create a foundation of human awareness and social consciousness that is one of the most treasured traits in human beings. This can vary among cultures and societies, of course.[91]

A delicate balance of self-awareness and other-awareness, combined with sound judgment of what seems to be fair in the flux of human interrelationships, can sustain healthy emotional growth. The teacher, however, must be a wise model and guide in the process. This area is extremely significant in children's total development.

Teachers and parents need to be fair in their expectations of what children can control and what they cannot. They are only just beginning to be aware of their own emotions as being different at certain times from those of others, and interfering with the wishes of others. Understanding one's self is a lifetime process. The child, however, who must depend on the empathy and concern that caring adults have for the feelings and anxieties that loom very large for him/her, learns to adapt in a variety of situations. Children learn, too, that certain expectations are made of them by some people, and that those expectations differ from the expectations made by others.

Many young children fear their own emotions, as do adults. They are afraid that what they think can harm people because they think the thought can turn itself into an act of some kind. Children's anger and fears cause them anguish. They are fearful about telling what they think if they know it is not socially acceptable to think in certain ways. Fear of punishment is strong, understandably so.

Emotional development that relates to feelings of guilt, shame, embarrassment, and other forms of self-punishment is mixed with what children have heard is wrong to do, what they should be ashamed of doing, or thinking or feeling. Wishing ill of someone else can bring feelings of shame or guilt. Hating someone, or having feelings of anger toward someone whom one depends on as a source of love, can be extremely upsetting. The American culture builds children's attitudes of compliance in the concept of love—receiving it or losing it. It is a strong motivating source, and at times becomes very confusing to a child.

An individual's emotions "involve the *higher* brain centers, . . . the *lower* or phylogentically *older* portions of the brain stem, and the autonomic nervous system."[92] Both cognition and emotion are physiologically regulated, "but they differ physiologically."[93] In this sense, one may compare cognitive behavior as something that can be assessed, perhaps objectively; where emotional behavior is concerned, however, there is no right or wrong answer. When people discuss what they expect from a child, or are annoyed with a demonstration of emotional release, they are referring to their own assessment of appropriate expectations within themselves. This does not necessarily endow the impression with rightness or wrongness in the judgement of a child or the child's behavioral reaction to an incident.

Children should not be chided for babyish behavior as some might refer to it. Emotions are always real and not age-graded. A child cannot help but say or do what prompts that child from within, creating strong pressures to vent inner stress.

Children also need help in learning to value their own emotions as providing them personal messages of some kind. Indecisiveness, irritation, boredom, and restlessness can, if guided properly, lead toward constructive thought.

Emotions are extremely significant resources for helping individuals know what their feelings are. Boredom, restlessness, oversensitive reactions to what people say to the individual can be a sign that the individual is not meeting greater needs for the self. Taking action or new directions as a result of an awareness of dissatisfaction with the way one's life is going, is often the result of emotional disequilibrium that the individual has been able to acknowledge in the self. Children can be helped in knowing how to use their emotions so that constructive energies are channeled. For this reason emotions should not be denied in self-awareness. Teachers can help children know themselves better as human beings who can affect and direct their lives with greater satisfaction when they know how to use their emotions, rather than to step away from or deny them.

From five to seven years old, emotional development occurs not only in the context of the home, but also, outside and in school. Situations encountered by the children can often be difficult. When the child comes home from school, certain incidents take on a larger perspective that can be very upsetting. It is not easy for the child to describe what happened when the parent questions various facets of the disconcerting event. These years, then, add another perspective to one's awareness that parents have to be observant of their children's changes of behavior.

Several new aspects of emotional qualities may be approached in school. Teachers are often discussing problems or issues that arise in classroom interaction. Characteristics such as cooperation, sharing, helping, waiting one's turn to do something, all involve deferred gratification or subordination of certain feelings. Discussion of events calling for these qualities can be helpful in showing the child how certain emotions can be perceived or interpreted, ultimately clarifying reasons for not being devastated by them. Personal satisfaction can be gained either from the knowledge that one is thoughtful of others or that one is learning how to manage one's feelings in a way that is conducive toward and constructive in growth.

The next section, closely related to emotional development in the individual, is on social development. This area of knowledge in which interpersonal skills are essential to understanding others, at least in part, is relevant not only to the child in this age range of five to seven, but also continuously throughout life. Entering further into one's emotional development are concepts of identity, one's worthiness where other people's impressions are concerned, and gender-related questions that are significant at this stage of development.

SOCIAL DEVELOPMENT FROM FIVE TO SEVEN YEARS

Participating in games with children and being chosen for groups at play are in part the ingredients of social development for children from five to seven. Children's self-consciousness at this stage reflects their heightened awareness of differences between their own characteristics and the questions/comments of age mates who infer deficiencies in people generally.

Studies indicate that children select friends on the basis of preferences in given situations.[94] Where they may prefer one friend for one activity, the same friend may not be sought for participation in another. At five, children's friendships are fluid. They have "best friend" attachments which are not sustained for lengthy periods of time.

A theme of responsiveness and reactivity seems to set itself in motion when children interact with each other. The tone is set within the interchange. Although some expectations may be involved in the individuals who interact, there are times when younger children do not have expectations and the content of the interchange occurs when they meet.

Children do not necessarily use the same interpersonal behavioral adaptations in different settings. And much like pupils who have a substitute teacher in the classroom when their own teacher is ill, they act differently with the temporary individual. A general feeling of knowing more than (s)he does about classroom routines makes them feel justified in telling the teacher what to do, rather than waiting to hear what (s)he wants them to do. Thus, even in the same classroom, children's behavior can take on a different quality when the other component involved in the interchange of behavior is different.

Between five and seven years old, children are interested in gender-related differences as they see the variety of classmates at school divided into "lines for the boys," and "lines for the girls." At this period, children of the same sex may enjoy being with each other. According to Freud's view of the *libido* and attachments of psychological preferences made to others,[95] it is in the latency period (about five and six to twelve years old) that children begin to choose being with others of the same sex. One cannot be sure whether this is culturally influenced, or whether other reasons may be attributed to it.

Social, outgoing behavior at five years and five months shows Sarah's attraction to other people. (Photo by Priscilla Margolin.)

Some writers suggest that Freud's interpretation of personality development, with its combinational causes of biological and environmental factors during the first few years of life, is predeterministic. He suggested that an infantile instinct affected personality and was stabilized throughout life. Social and cultural factors that can affect changes in an individual's life cycle were not considered to the extent that some writers consider them today. Many middle-class parents who read Freud's work, with its implications that certain stages through which a child was going could be damaging if not treated properly, became very anxious and tried to avoid repressing the child's presumed wishes for certain objects, people, or feelings.[96] According to one group of writers,[97] however, Freud had expected parents to use their mature judgment and to set limits in the child's development, not to let the child have the wide range of impulsive expression that parents interpreted Freud as advocating.

Certain stimuli in an environment can evoke specific behavior in individuals. When children at school are involved in activities that they enjoy they respond and interact effectively with other children. Social development is greatly affected by the environment, the situation, and how it is interpreted. It appears that children's behavioral tendencies are not as fixed or as unchanging and predetermined as has been suggested in early studies of human development.

In kindergarten and first grade, children play in groups involving both sexes. Depending on the way the teacher arranges the environment and discusses instruction, the children accept in matter-of-fact terms what is presented to them.

Repressiveness in the classroom exists in a variety of ways. It is not, however, intended to squelch children's expression of ideas and feelings at all times. Effective teachers attempt to help children channel feelings in several ways through individualized activities, games, song, and selection of choices so that pupils do not feel anonymous. Organization of classroom functions assists in facilitating the number of things that have to be accomplished in the classroom. These efforts can be implemented, however, in ways that do not insensitively restrict children's desires to express their feelings and ideas.

Social development occurs in a variety of settings in the classroom and at school. Not only does it take place in academic contexts when children are learning how to improve their cognitive skills, it also arises in the less formalized classroom settings in which aesthetic functions (such as painting,

Neighborhood friends are important. One can just talk to them through a hole in the fence. This facilitates great friendships. (Photo by Gerald J. Margolin.)

Sarah, at six and a half, is reflective, in part shy, as she looks at her mother who is taking her picture. Children at this age are acquiring broader horizons outside the home. They are bringing into the home, in a sense, some of the outside world and in that context are becoming more expansive in personality development. (Photo by Priscilla Margolin.)

music, games involving running, skipping, jumping, tossing objects) are offered to children.

Children's sense of themselves as human beings with a number of different facets to their personalities is learned in one-to-one relationships with individual friends, with children in small groups, and in larger ones, too, as well as in crowds watching the same parade. A sense of self arises in the context of enjoying the same things with people of varying ages. An expansion of the self occurs, too, when one is with others who like the same things. Discussing what has been seen or appreciated becomes a shared event in still another perspective. Such discussion nurtures experiences and one's understanding of other people as well as of one's self.

Important, too, in the child's social development is the way parents and teachers interpret the behavior of others to the child. Motivation attributed to others in relation to a given experience can affect the way a child will generalize about people's behavior. The parents' interpretation may reflect an identification with the well-intended actions of others, or it may reveal a feeling of mistrust of others. Children base their expectations and reasoning of others in terms of explanations they hear from their parents. They also note gestures and implausible inconsistencies that lead to uncertainties or misunderstandings.

As children's language skills increase in abilities to specify shades of meanings and graphic descriptions of events, the children are better able to interpret interpersonal relationships. They may also become more skillful in describing what they thought or felt about given instances of activities among people. Their groups of friends at school and home further provide impressions that may coincide with their own or add a different perspective to their judgments. These considerations are all a part of social development and provide a repertoire of thought and judgment about a wide range of interpersonal relationships and their settings.

The period between five and seven is significant in its beginning point for the school life of the child. It also brings various experiences to parents that are unique as kindergarten and the primary grades introduce elements into the child's life and create great changes in his/her personality and cognitive skills. Life is different for one's child than the experiences the parent had when (s)he was in kindergarten and the primary grades. Different parents, different setting, different orientations of parents other than one's own, affect qualities of an unknown quantity. Parents may anticipate the child's experiences, but only up to a point. The child's knowledge of school life will be different from that of the parents.'

The next section will mark the beginning of a childhood period that goes beyond early childhood and not typically included in an early childhood text. It is however a significant time for the child in that it precedes an approaching adolescent stage, which involves observing older children with great interest and wishes for maturity. In that sense of young children's observations of preadolescent models, characterizations of children from seven to nine are included in this text.

The Child from Seven to Nine Years

From the second grade to the fourth, the child matures rapidly in various ways. So much is being learned from the schooling processes and the dynamics of interrelating to others during these years which the child will bring to the preadolescent period of development that the creation of foundational ideas strengthens. Physical growth in this period is holding its own, occurring gradually just prior to the adolescent spurt of sexual and bodily growth.

Children in this age range have enough of a background to equip them for asking questions that pierce the heart of problems. They are in a period of maturity of their childhood and are able to perceive sensitive issues occurring among people around them. They are also able to consider the perspectives of others and attempt to be fair in the way they interact with others. Friendship circles are broadening in some cases, as well as extensions in meeting many other people through one's classroom acquaintances (not formally, but incidentally, through a variety of activities). Sports activities, skating rinks, birthday parties, after-school activities, involve contact in various ways with people other than those the child meets in the neighborhood, at school, or in relatives' homes.

Typically, children of this age are impulsive, sensitive, and judgmental. They are not sure of themselves in their growing skills and are constantly comparing themselves to others in either a disparaging or a boastful way. They are, however, enjoyable in the way they show capacities for understanding. They need support and reassurance from those who are significant in the development of their well-being.

Physical development of the seven- to nine-year-old child introduces many changes—in personality, social interaction, cognition, and awareness of the varieties among people and situations that create different experiences for the self. The next section is on physical development of this age group.

PHYSICAL DEVELOPMENT FROM SEVEN TO NINE YEARS

The height of children from seven to nine years old does not increase as rapidly as it will in the adolescent years to come, nor as it did in earlier years. Between seven and nine years old, some children may show a gain in height of about 4 inches, with variations in either direction depending upon genetic and environmental qualities and their effects. A child of about seven may be about 49 inches, more or less, in height. By the age of nine, the child may be about 53 inches tall. There is great variation among body builds, muscular structure, and body fat. Although many children thin out and grow taller in this period the change is only a precursor to what will come later in preadolescent growth.

As a race, human beings have been growing taller and heavier through the years. More knowledge about nutrition, exercise, and muscular strength now available to the public has influenced diet, rest, and various forms of exercise that people have implemented to their advantage.

Heavier and larger children may begin puberty at about eight or nine years old; many start their spurt of growth when they are about eleven. This means that children in elementary school in latter grades (after nine years old) are already beginning the adolescent period of development. Evidence of this shows in small beginnings of changes in sexual characteristics. Peak periods of growth are attained by about the thirteenth year for many girls and by about the fourteenth year and one half for boys. These years mark for children several changes in body sensations and functions. It is small wonder that they become more sensitive to people, things, events, perceptions, and the like. Internal functions are affecting new ideas, concepts, and a broadening scope of what is available to and expected from them. These variations, furthermore, are different in specific groups, in their families, and among those whom they do not even know.

The heart's development between four and ten years old is slow. Competitive sports during those years can be hard on the heart and respiratory system. Children between seven and nine are pressured to become successful in games. They need to have other outlets so that they do not feel forced to compete more than they are physically able.

Contours of the body change, as well as the internal structure, for the child between seven and nine. The entire body system is in readiness by age nine to move to the period of preadolescence. In this sense, teachers can do children a service by being aware, as much as possible, of contemporary information and research on children's internal development at this time.[98]

Facial changes take place, and bottom jaw, forehead, and eyes take on different proportions as the body grows in height. Girls can become more graceful appearing in this process; boys become more masculine looking in the muscular and body proportions of the physique.

The strength that is increasing through growth in the child sensitizes him/her to internal states at various times. Children may tease or taunt each other about body proportions and physical appearance. This tendency toward teasing, comparing, daring, or staring can be mediated by thoughtful adults who can empathize at any time with victims receiving the brunt of a childhood form of behavior.

The physical growth of children between seven and nine years old affects motor development as well as formulating ideas about identity, self-esteem, and gender-related views about the self. The next section involves information on motor development, a significant element for children in this age range.

MOTOR DEVELOPMENT FROM SEVEN TO NINE YEARS

The skills acquired by children in this age range vary from time to time. At one time in this seven-to-nine-year period, muscular development permits competent performances in rhythmic movement, cable- (or rope)-jumping, controlled hopping, and stunts of various kinds that challenge legs, arms, and torso coordination. Later in the period, one is able to reach farther, run farther, and perform stunts with the agility of more than a novice.

Books on the physical education of elementary school children give extensive information on how children perform, at which ages, and how the sexes do surpass each other at times. With the various contemporary viewpoints on male and female roles, the sexes are now encouraged in equal fashion to do well in physical skills related to sports. Some delineate differences between contact sports, considered dangerous for women in some cases because of heavy or strong impact of bodies upon each other, as observed in football, and other sports such as swimming, tennis, golf, and others that do not involve contact.

With practice and encouragement, children become competent, given certain conditions, in several areas of acrobatics, some team games, and a variety of self-testing skills that utilize energy, strength, bodily coordination, and motivation to excel in one's own repertoire of abilities. The friends one chooses, the preferences one has for the way one wishes to perceive one's self, and various social or cultural conditions at any given time can affect the time and energy one permits for motor development (beyond walking, running, throwing balls, hitting them with a bat, swimming, and other typical activities engaged in by many children).

Because of their growing skills and broadening circles of friendship, children in this age range need to be helped to recognize dangers. They are involved in accidents, such as breaking an arm or leg, falling from a tree into which one of them has ventured to a very high, but weak, branch. Dangerous weapons, often used for hunting or starting a fire, or other camping equipment that may be used incorrectly, should be stored in a place that is not accessible to a child. Even though one's own child may be aware that those things are not to be touched, a friend, or several friends, can exert enough pressure and leverage so that the child submits. Wanting the approval of one's friends can be a strong source of urgency that results in forgetting or ignoring what one's parents have admonished one against doing. Accidents are common in this age range. Children need to know what precautions are necessary to protect themselves from their growing motor skills and from the curiosity that challenges them in self-testing as well as testing the environment and other people.

Motor skills and their development can have gender-related overtones. A girl may not want to climb fences or trees if she has heard that "tomboys" do it. The term *sissy* affects what boys will be willing to do. They want a bicycle made for boys; they want accelerated speed vehicles and equipment that looks tough. In fact, these preferences or the lack of them toward skills and activities that have been culturally labeled as for male or female affect children's willingness to participate in them, as well as in subject matter areas, such as mathematics, ballet, painting (in some cases), if parents and other people comment in a derogatory way about these as being classified specifically for boys or for girls.

Research has indicated that motor development affects perceptual development and cognition as well as other qualities in the individual's intellectual growth.[99] The next section demonstrates how many influences from the external environment of the individual, as well as internal changes and functioning, combine to accelerate certain ideas that children in this age range of seven to nine will accept or question.

INTELLECTUAL/ACADEMIC DEVELOPMENT FROM SEVEN TO NINE YEARS

Many American educators and psychologists recognize and use Piaget's contributions to apply to the way children develop an intellectual structure. He views the child between seven and nine years old as being in the *concrete operations* period. That term refers to children's abilities mentally, to manipulate objects in front of them without having to act on the objects themselves. Children are able to construct in their own minds actions or operations that can be taken to change objects in a row in front of them.

These children, according to Piaget, are beginning to manage thought processes that will develop to abstract levels after the children are eleven years old.[100] Children's responses to experiments conducted by Piaget indicated that "from seven to eight until eleven to twelve there is a consistent effort on the part of thought to become more and more conscious of itself."[101] He also suggests that up to the age of seven and eight a "child begins to distinguish thought from things, and logical justification from causal explanation."[102] At this point, in terms of Piaget's perspective, the child has become conscious of his/her reasoning processes, or at least of their unfolding. At about this age, too, the child becomes aware of argument as a situation in which one point of view differs from another. The child is also motivated to make his/her own point of view known to the other as well as to understand the other person's view.[103] Before this point, argument consisted of repeated affirmations without understanding or motivation toward that end.

Piaget indicates that many adults still persist in egocentric thought. They are not able to distance themselves from certain ideas that they strongly cherish. He says that rather than their being more introspective and knowing themselves better than others who are able to take the perspective of another person, "they seem to be immersed in an inner life that is all the more intense."[104] He goes on to say that "this way of living in oneself . . . develops a great wealth of inexpressible feelings, of personal images and schemas, while at the same time it impoverishes analysis and consciousness of self."[105]

Knowing how to reason and to be aware of one's processes of thought, or going back over a particular line of thinking in order to assess where one differs with another's logic or reasoning, varies with content. The correctness of one point of view or another that emerges from value judgments of some kind cannot be considered, necessarily, in the same light that one expects two individuals to agree that one penny and another one are equal to two pennies, to put it in its most simple form. Often, however, these emotional perspectives are called on to test statements such as, "If you loved me, you would, etc.") in an attempt to inject a logic that does not necessarily follow in such syllogistic thought.

Children's skills in reading and expressing their views on what they know strengthens in this age range as does the ability to judge their own logical thought and remarks. Classroom performances, techniques used in grappling with a problem, using several perspectives in attempting to understand a given statement, fact, or concept, can all contribute to greater skills in intellectual functioning.

The period between seven and nine involves increasing uncertainties as well as an awareness of greater facilities that one may have in academic or intellectual skills. Children need to be given reasons for various cause-and-effect phenomena (as in science, for example, or in mathematics). They need firm foundations of knowledge and facts on which to build understandings that will be used in logical discourse with others in several age-level categories. They need valid information upon which they can place their trust. Although children's points of view may be expressed differently from those of adults (in childlike language, perhaps), the children can, nevertheless be in possession of the facts needed to defend a position or to give information of some kind to another individual. Children need the support of teachers and parents who can provide them with what they need to know in order to communicate effectively and factually with others.

Respectful disagreement with parts of the concepts that Piaget demonstrates in describing his work has increased among several psychologists and learning theorists. This disagreement can affect how intelligence testing will occur and how children's intellectual development will be perceived. The idea that a "structured whole—an interrelated set of operations—at least as it is reflected in the concrete operational stage . . ."[106] is an accurate way to conceptualize the means by which children acquire certain skills and abilities, is suspect to other researchers. Some view intelligence as consisting of figurative knowledge that can be described as the ability to recall ideas, words, and meanings, sharpness of the senses in determining differences, similarities, and detail in what is seen or understood, and abilities to note shape, form, size, etc. of figures.[107]

Researchers are concerned that Piaget's tests with children involve a manipulation of the physical in the real world and that eventually those operations result in a transformation of words or other symbols that represent the physical, real world. Memory, recall, ability to recognize similarities and differences among words, do not seem relevant in Piaget's framework. "In Piaget's view figurative knowledge, makes little substantive contribution to the intellect. Yet it is precisely this knowledge that is highlighted in the standard intelligence test, particularly in its verbal portion: definitions, number heard and recalled, facts and figures about the world."[108]

As figurative skills are involved in a large proportion of information dealt with in the schools, some researchers are concerned about ways to reconcile some of these discrepancies between one way to conceptualize the acquisition of knowledge (physical) and another way to comprehend or develop abstract meanings, memory, and recall, among other things. It is suggested that children from seven to nine years old are able to note "specific details and static properties—the so-called figurative knowledge probed by intelligence tests."[109] It is also of concern to researchers that these skills are neglected in Piaget's work: "the ability to express oneself clearly; the skills involved in reading and in remembering what one reads; the capacity to relate appropriately to works of art; and a sensitivity to social and emotional cues in interpersonal situations."[110]

Learning theorists typically view a stage, such as a concrete operational stage, as consisting of several components and abilities and would rather break down into parts and skills what a child is able to do at a so-called given stage of development. Psychologists who have perspectives that differ from Piaget's do not consider his cognitive-structural approach satisfactory for their definitions of intelligence and its measurement. For them, "There are no [nor should there be] stages, no regular sequences, no structured wholes. Instead, there exist a number of discrete mental abilities—and perhaps one all-important *general* mental aptitude—that individuals possess to a greater or lesser extent."[111] It is suggested, too, that despite various shortcomings, some intelligence tests provide some data indicating rough estimates of relative abilities in linguistic, memory, and problem-solving skills that are prized, whether they should be or not, in the educational system.

Alternative modes of testing in performance, such as arranging pictures in order, or putting a puzzle together, provide for information on another response system related to mental skills. Their use indicates, in part, an attempt to tap various modes of answering and various skills related to intellectual capacity.

Scientific attitudes are such that examination, investigation, and consciousness of one's own cultural biases (or personal prejudgments as to what one expects or hopes to find) have to be governed in the conduct of further research. Intelligence tests often reflect what a culture values. Problem solving, reasoning processes, understanding of and facility in the various levels of meanings of words and appropriate levels of usage, as well, are valued in the American context. In a sense, certain assumptions are made about what constitutes intelligence or academic gain.

Psychologists will continue to study these assumptions as will learning theorists and environmentalists. Schools, however, in some way, have to help children so that they can function effectively as youngsters and later as adults in their society. Curriculum theorists, too, have their conflicts, issues, and trends in "deciding" what is most significant for learning. Educators have to attend to the various controversies that scientists articulate. All can benefit from this kind of interchange. And, the children, we hope, can ultimately benefit.

Evaluation of what individuals know, of what children ought to know, and the means through which one may discover this information has been difficult and complex (as well as not very satisfactory) for many years. With greater sophistication in technology and scientific sensitivity to rigorously conducted (nonbiased) and carefully controlled research, more information is disclosed. Typically researchers report that as many questions were answered in their research there were almost as many or more (fortunately for science) that emerged. This attests to the open-mindedness of researchers at times, who refuse to accept too easily what they would like to see in the results of their work. Critical self-analysis in one's conduct of the study is one element that operates to elevate the quality of it. Those who know the most and have studied in areas of measurement and human intelligence are the most critical of various forms of testing that have been accepted for use. Total satisfaction seems difficult. Compromises arise, never to everyone's satisfaction.

Just as many scientists are aware of human frailties in themselves as well as others, and know that it is difficult to be totally objective or nonsubjective in what one perceives and studies or interprets, so are they equally aware that relative progress must be perceived in a developmental sense, bits and pieces, and sometimes chunks, of data at a time leading to greater insight and deeper understanding of a problem.

Children's intellectual development between seven and nine is guided by what the schools perceive as important for learning. Schools, in turn, affect parents' points of view and what they seek in their children's development.

Language development, as indicated in its significance in intelligence tests, is an essential part of the curriculum devoted to language arts, reading, self-expression, vocabulary, and varieties of meanings at several levels of usage. Even though societal trends may affect changes in the orientation of some things that happen at school, some conservatism is evident. An emphasis on language development will probably continue as it has been, particularly since the 1960s, as a result of studies related to the unique introduction of Head Start programs for young children.

Reading and writing will continue to be a major part of instruction at school. Mathematical qualities and symbols will be stressed, too. Creativity and problem solving are valued in a democratically based society, and those skills are also needed for scientific productivity. Children's drives toward achieving higher levels of competence are derived from various sources, both internal and external. Emotional development can be related to energy levels allocated to achievement. Friends, significant people, teachers, or parents can often be perceived by the child as persons worthy of pleasing, whether or not some consider this an appropriate motivation.

The next section deals with the emotions of children between seven and nine. Many changes occurring in the child's ways of thinking and feeling affect emotional perceptions in this period between "upper early childhood" and beginning levels of the preadolescent years.

EMOTIONAL DEVELOPMENT FROM SEVEN TO NINE YEARS

Because the child's school life occupies a large percentage of each day, the seven- to-nine-year-old child is experiencing many different and conflicting emotions relative to self-imposed reflections presumed to be (though they may not be) other people's reactions to the self. One of the times in life when the individual begins to view the self in the eyes of others who are significant in some way to his/her self-evaluations is directly in the classroom.

Every time a pupil says anything in the classroom the self is on display in terms of success, failure, or indifference (which turns out to be a form of nonsuccess). It is difficult in school life to do anything that is private or goes unconcealed for any length of time.

Emotions are developed in the context of social groups. In the family, children learn what that particular social group/system values, what it expects, and what it derides or rejects. Children in this age range have had some examples at home which typify values that may be in conflict with those of their peers. The child has numerous struggles with these discrepancies between home and school; these may ultimately result in the development of a conscience, morality, empathy with others, and in some cases, rejection of one form or another of a specific value orientation from home.

Identity-seeking in this age range may also involve a child in doing things that appear irrational, atypical, or unusual to parents and others who have known the child for many years. The child tries out, in a sense, various role characteristics that were not particularly relevant or noticed before in relation to a self-concept. Incongruencies between impressions one has of the self when certain behavior manifests itself and how others seem to perceive one's performance in that role characteristic become the final judgment. With this judgment of one's own degree of congruence with what one did and what was approved (in gesture, verbally, or in other socially approved form), come emotional levels of pleasure, shame, guilt, or of self-satisfaction and pride.

Some writers and researchers view emotions as part of one's genetic inheritance and in part as socially influenced. Others perceive them as more biological than social.[112] Sociologists typically reject the view that was popular along those lines in the nineteenth century, that (social) human behavior results from "biological determinism." This perspective indicated that all human behavior was the "result of genetically inherited *instincts* and *traits*. Traits are inherited through *genes*, the units of heredity, which also control the processes of development and growth."[113] Sociologists suggest that the complex interaction of people with one another and in various situations affects human behavior, as does the interaction "between the innate and the learned" characteristics in people. They state that people's behavior "is not rigidly programmed, but develops interactively with the environment."[114]

We learn from parents and other socializing agents what is significant for receiving approval, where the sanctions (positive and negative) are, and where one needs to be cautious and to avoid punishment. This learning process influences internal mechanisms (self-control) to guide our behavior in certain directions. Sociologists perceive the development of emotions to occur as part of a complex process of interaction between the individual who affects or has control of sanctions (parent, teacher, older sibling) and the child who is being controlled.

Emotional development is greatly affected by perceptions of ourselves, as Mead has suggested.[115] We view ourselves through our parents' eyes and decide that we are "good," "bad," "worthy," "lovable." "The self has a character which is different from that of the physiological organism proper. The self is something which has a development; it is not initially there, at birth, but arises in the process of social experience and activity, that is, develops in the given individual as a result of his relations to that process as a whole and to other individuals within that process."[116] The self is not separate from an emotional process and identification of emotions.

One must also be aware of the attitudes that others take toward a body build, physical appearance, and other characteristics (physically endowed) that people might find pleasing. In this sense, the genetically inherited traits of red, curly hair, for example, blue eyes, fair skin, or dark hair, dark eyes, and dark skin can affect interaction among people who find these features attractive in an individual. In themselves, however, as genetic traits "unfolding" they do not automatically engender social appreciation.

The acquisition of gender-related images for children comes from many sources in society, such as television, parents, peers, books, and hero/heroine perceptions of people in theater, sports, and other celebrated areas of life. These perceptions of what is feminine or masculine and desirable among one's own groups of male and female friends will affect emotional development in positive or negative directions.

General trends toward giving children more choices for their own behavior place the onus on also providing some implications (without a sense of threatening, but rather for purposes of providing information) for certain choices that may be made. These decision-making periods are often anxious ones for children. They want to be mature and independent. At times, however, they do not feel sure enough of themselves and want both or more choices. They do not want to rule out any one of the choices. This indecisiveness can create emotional upheaval for them and for parents who insist that the children have to follow through on a choice they have made.

Children seek maturity as a concept in relation to their own behavior. They want, simultaneously, the parental support that they may have had prior to this period of life. Conflicts arise within as the child tries to reconcile wanting something and not wanting it at the same time. Unreasonableness, irritation, and behaviors that on the surface seems totally unjustified arc, in part a manifestation of the anxieties that accompany growing up to one's ideal level of competence.

Children in this age range between seven and nine years old are neither as young, psychologically and emotionally, as the preschool child, nor are they early adolescents. They are in an in-between stage of leaving one complete range of childhood to *approaching* another significant time of life, that of adolescence. American society divides those life cycle periods in specific psychological ways. With an advanced technological society, too, and various changes in child-rearing perspectives, attitudes toward children in this age range are fluctuating. Even though the adolescent period seems protracted, in one way, in longer schooling processes prior to one's receiving a job and "being out on one's own" in some cases,[117] this period just prior to the adolescent period is not protracted. And it is often vague about expectations of children. It is similar to a bridge that one travels, either long or short, before reaching the base of a steep hill that will take time, energy, conflict, and physical growth to climb.

Encouraging children as well as adults to express their feelings is one among several recommendations made by psychologists, psychoanalysts, and other therapists interested in human behavior. The degree of expression, to the point of temper tantrum, varies among parents and teachers in terms of how much they are willing to allow. Each individual has a point at which affect, anger, and hostility can be controlled. With contemporary views that recommend urging the "hearing" of one's angry feelings, children are allowed the freedom to make them heard (without fear of reprisal) in relation to what the parents or teachers are comfortable in granting. If parents and teachers are in agreement with the principles underlying such expression, and which suggest that mental health can be achieved through venting one's feelings instead of withholding them, they will allow greater leeway, time, and energy for the implementing of values clarification, or feelings.

The next section will address problems of social development that involve moral issues, conscience development, contradictory and ambivalent love and hate, and other confusing issues that arise in the socialization process. Learning about role behavior, expectations of others and one's self, achieving self-satisfaction while pleasing others and adapting to one's own moral code, involve maturity, noting social cues in the environment, and generally finding one's place in one's world.

SOCIAL DEVELOPMENT FROM SEVEN TO NINE YEARS

Children in this age range are able to form relationships that can be sustained for a longer period of time than was possible earlier in their lives. They can argue with each other but return to relationships and continue to nurture them.

As children mature in responding to people in a variety of settings, they acquire a larger range of responses that become ready tools or techniques to be used at their disposal. Judgment of response continues to orient the way relationships will go. Adult assistance in explaining the behavior of people can help the child learn to perceive people's attitudes so to be less

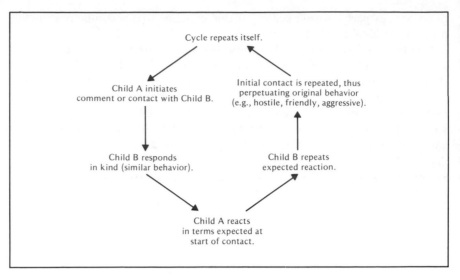

Cycle repeats itself.

Child A initiates
comment or contact with Child B.

Initial contact is repeated, thus
perpetuating original behavior
(e.g., hostile, friendly, aggressive).

Child B responds
in kind (similar behavior).

Child B repeats
expected reaction.

Child A reacts
in terms expected at
start of contact.

Concept Illustration 2–2

Circularity of Behavior and Responses (Emerging from Others) Recreating Themselves.

in need of evoking self-defensive reactions. If children perceive others as being unkind or vindictive, for the most part, they will be ever ready to identify many situations as calling for self-protective behavior in order to bolster a bruised ego.

The various ways of responding to people cover a wide range of behaviors, from laughing to playfully tusseling and becoming more serious with a response that reveals or describes one's feelings. Studies suggest that initial contact with an individual, e.g., aggressive, happy, sad, hostile, friendly, can sometimes create the tone for the action that follows.[118] Noting Concept Illustration 2–2, for example, one can see how the direction of feelings may go. One response evokes another from each person, in some cases setting up a chain reaction.

A child may come to school in a somewhat pleasant mood and be ready to interact easily and happily with others. An untoward event or a discordant response from another child can change that mood. The child can then begin responding to others in a sullen and hostile manner affecting others to respond in kind. The sensitive teacher may note what is happening and at least in her/his own behavior begin to ameliorate some of the intensity of responses which may be occurring. This does not suggest that the teacher should reprimand the children. It does mean that a change in mood can be influenced by the way the teacher's own disposition responds. The teacher who is aware of irritation in the children can, for a short period of time, at least, provide an activity that will alter and redirect the sentiments of the session.

Teachers may choose one of several directions in which to do this. They may read a calming poem (or story) to the children. They may lead them slowly into an activity that will help them vent their feelings, e.g., a game, song, or opportunity to express aesthetic impressions. What they do not do is hurry the children and thus cause more anxiety than has already been displayed in the classroom. Neither will they be too exacting and restrictive with specific and detailed assignments. Anxiousness, irritation, and fear in children are obvious in many ways. The teacher must learn to ease the children's feelings when possible.

There will also be times, as in testing, when anxiety has to be dealt with in order to proceed with work that must be done at that time. Sensitivity to the children's fears shows in the teacher's smile, emotional support, and responses to questions.

The classroom experiences not only provide more data for children's learning about interpersonal relationships, they also offer an arena for decision making about various personalities that one must encounter. This involves role-learning performance and its adaptability to one's socially perceived world (adaptability both in terms of external events and one's own judgment of them).

Role relationships and how one performs in them are complicated to study.[119] Our behavior is expressed in different ways and often smiles conceal stress rather than connote joy. In the attempt to understand how someone feels about something or another individual, judgments are often not accurate. Their accuracy is often not given the test in relation to its application in a given situation. Social learning varies, however, as researchers note.

Researchers who have been concerned with children's social development perceived the nature of children and their cognitive processes in various ways. Psychoanalytic theories of Freud seem to assume that children are, in part, aggressively seeking to satisfy certain sexual or other innate traits. Social learning theorists consider that children are affected by the environment, but that the effect occurs in different ways. Some children are considered to have stronger innate influences in this learning, according to some researchers, and other children have less. "Many social-learning theorists would find it difficult to agree with"[120] those researchers who consider that the child has little if any skill to use in adapting to the environment. The child in that view is seen as totally without energies or elements which would be ready to respond, and in that sense, the child is considered a passive entity.

Many social learning theorists, however, view children's activity as evidence of energies involved in interaction with others and in responding to them in assessing, judgmental, and perceptual ways. It is the reciprocity of behavior, one person judging the other, that affects in the individual a means of knowing one's world and the self in relation to it. Social interaction also affects the judgments building within the self and the quality of characteristics or energies one has that can be used in future processes of interaction.

The process of learning about others is simultaneously the process in which one learns about the self. The dynamics in a situation are both cause and effect, or antecedent and consequent, in the acquisition of judgment of one's self. These ebbs and flows, give and take, action and reaction, in interpersonal relationships are interpreted in various ways depending on the child's age, maturity, and ability to notice cues in other people's behavior. Sometimes these cues provide options for the child's tendencies to decide on one way of behavior or another. Learning of this kind occurs on the spot, often unanticipated by either of the people involved in the interaction process.

Social cognition is a form of learning that emerges from "the child's conception of others ('person perception'), the child's ability to take the perspective of another ('role taking'), the child's understanding of psychological causality ('intentionality'), and the child's moral judgment."[121] Researchers differ as to which of those aspects they study and to which they attribute most "cause" in the child's abilities of social cognition and subsequent (or inherent) behavior. Some see the children's social development, in part as a structure (role taking and social cognition); some see it as a means through which information is obtained selectively from one's environment; and some prefer the view that children's development in social relations is not a structural concept similar to stage development theories, but rather an increasing acquisition of knowledge (experiences) by means of social interaction, which translate themselves into guidelines for the self.

Children focus on the actions in a relationship. They learn to formulate principles (of meaning) which they apply to the ongoing activity in the relationship. In that sense, children do not know precisely what to expect when they enter into some activity with others, but they do expect to act on the cues they receive from others about certain options that one may take in one's own behavior. They are able to generate for themselves certain guidelines that they use to govern their own course of action and possibly to influence the other person's action as well. Youniss and Volpe indicate that their work with children's friendship patterns, although not offering a complete theory, does suggest that children's social development is both "self-generated and other-determined."[122] They suggest that "Social thought may be the result of a coconstruction,"[123] that occurs in the interactive process of individuals with each other. Together, children in their study were able to agree on which interactions seemed to signify a relationship of friendship among them.

Implications for a specific relation arise within the *dyad*, or basic unit of two people, interacting with each other. Those implications provide some knowledge for that relationship, but not necessarily all those that follow. The dynamics in one relationship are not necessarily effective in another, nor might they be the same every time in a relationship with someone known well. Ongoing relationships sometimes change the rules for the participants within systems of behavior on any given day or time. Predictability vacillates in the dyadic system, in relation to time, place, and moods of the individuals involved.

Children learn to understand that what they do can affect others. They also know that the other individual has some expectations of what can happen in a given relationship. The two are inferring from the behavior of each other what can happen, given certain actions that one may take. This kind of coconstruction of thinking, as indicated by Youniss and Volpe, is what constitutes social understandings (systems of interactive rules and procedures) that become "systems of relations."[124]

The means by which children's understandings of social events are tested need greater analytical distinction. Not all social situations involve an emphasis on certain perceptions. Turiel, for example, suggests that children conceptualize differently their attitudes toward behavior regarding how they should be governed by rules of a game, and the kind of behavior that should be prompted by moral predispositions. Social conventions are not always morally derived. Turiel indicates that to use game rules in order to test moral development seems inappropriate.[101] Responses to social conventions may differ from internalized constraints that are not of a moral nature.

The work of many researchers on the development of children's acquisition of social understanding suggests that many unresolved issues remain. Enlightenment in regard to clarification of issues, domains, and conceptualization of crucial questions has illuminated further what the next steps in research might be. This is a contribution to the way educators, parents, and others can understand children's behavior (as well as their own) in the classroom and outside.

Social development, understanding, cognition, whatever one may wish to call it, goes on throughout life. The complexities that arise in different situations, as well as changes that occur internally for people, contribute to a lack of predictability as to what will actually take place in the process of human interaction. The period between seven and nine years old is an introduction to complicated interpersonal interaction and relationships. As life does not become less complicated, but rather more so, in the relationships with others as one matures, the child in this period will have to build more layers of experience within the context of social events. This does not mean that life becomes simpler and that people's behavior becomes more clear. Researchers are discovering that conceptualization.

The complexity in interpersonal situations increases both with more knowledge and with less. How one chooses to mediate or modify what is learned in social relations, or with others, depends on, among other things, cognition, temperament, mood, self-concept, and typical ways of interpretation used by the individual. Seven- to nine-year-olds depend to a great extent on how their parents and teachers explain behavior to them. The terms they use, and the labels they give to describe characteristics in the behavior of others, and the value judgments ascribed to them influence the systems of judgment developing in the child.

Teachers, as well, who are present in children's groups almost every day, affect children's impressions and interpretations of moral, social, and other various interactional forms of behavior. Although their own early childhood behavior can come to the foreground to influence children they teach, they also need updated information to identify effectively with children.

SUMMARY

This chapter presented information on various categories of development of children, from birth to about nine years old. Children's development was perceived in terms of physical, motor, intellectual/academic, emotional, and social characteristics, and in that light each age range was discussed.

Even though it was recognized that much more research is required to answer some of the questions that emerged in carefully controlled and respected research, the data that were presented represented some of the most recent issues of value to parents and teachers.

Children's development is strongly influenced by adults who are responsible for their well-being. Many adults who are typically not aware of the information available for their use could benefit from knowledge that would facilitate answers to some questions on child-rearing processes.

Research data that indicated variations in the way babies and young children learn reflect relationships that need to be known among nutrition, genetic development, parental knowledge of the necessities for effective prenatal care, and general care resulting in healthy babies.

Orientations of psychologists, sociologists, social psychologists, developmental psychologists, and others approaching an area of study from their own disciplines provide very useful information that changes the emphasis on studies of socialization, cognition, social thought, and the like.

Brain development and the functions of the right and the left hemisphere in relation to certain skills in the human being have been the subject of interest to many researchers in the last twenty-five to thirty years. Sensitive instruments for the study of brain activity, as well as which skills are processed in each side of the brain and cortical areas, facilitate to some degree new data that are useful to educators. Even though the researchers themselves are cautious in the way they interpret the information, and warn that their findings are not totally conclusive, they nevertheless instigate critical postures toward some of the concepts that have been accepted in past years.

Human growth is affected from birth by the size of the body, certain genetic determinants that affect processes of the body, and also by the environment, nutritional advantages, and the particular people and care that they engender.

Comparisons to the work of Piaget in the intellectual categories, attainment of speech, language, and thought, as well as his work in moral development, are made to more contemporary researchers' studies. Freud's perspectives are commented on and applied in some cases to children's development, although they are not totally accepted in contemporary contexts. The work of both these men is greatly respected, even with some criticisms of certain conceptualizations or assumptions made by them.

The purposes and goals of this chapter were planned to provide information that could enlighten educators and parents and other adults interested in the well-being of children's development. No pat or easy answers were recommended. To do that would be oversimplifying what is involved in knowing and understanding children and ourselves in our own responses to them.

TOPICS FOR DISCUSSION

1. Describe some of the differences between what you thought infant development was like and what you found out it was by reading this chapter. Has this changed the way you will interact with infants?
2. To what do you attribute the changing nature of human interaction and attitudes toward young children and what they need in their development?
3. Observe children who are three or four years old. Note their patterns of initiating contacts with each other. What do they do? What do they say? Do you note that any of these contacts remind you of adult interchanges or not? Why?
4. Education in the United States has changed, or has it not? Comment on that question. State your comments with evidence, either personal, professional, or from readings. Does this for you represent a change for the better (for America's future) or worse? Does this represent a change for improvement of human life? Why or why not?
5. Visit a health clinic for children. Note what is being done for them. What is the highest incidence in cases among them? Why do they come to the clinic? What do children's health and vitality seem to need in terms of most support? Can mothers and teachers help in this process? What could be avoided by anticipating health problems among the young?
6. Are parents of today in better condition, psychologically or physically, to nurture babies or children than were parents in the past?
7. Do a brief case study on a child you observe at school. Note in three different visits, for one and one half hours each, exactly what the child did, with whom (s)he played or worked, spent time alone with, physical energy levels (e.g., high, medium, low, and how they were manifested). Characterize this child's orientation toward people (or life) at school. Why did you choose this child to observe? What was it about this child that attracted your attention or interest?

NOTES

1. William J. Meyer and Jerome B. Dusek, *Child Psychology* (Lexington, Mass.: Heath, 1979), p. 86.
2. William A. Kennedy, *Child Psychology*, 2nd ed. (Englewood Cliffs, N.J.: Prentice-Hall, 1975), pp. 47–54. See this section on intrauterine life of the unborn infant and an excellent set of figures on pp. 50–51 that demonstrate six stages in the emergence of the infant from the womb.
3. Fernand Lamaze, *Painless Childbirth: The Lamaze Method* (New York: Pocket Books, 1972). See also Frederick Leboyer, M.D., *Birth Without Violence* (Garden City, N.Y.: Alfred A. Knopf, Inc., 1975), and Frank Caplan, Editor, *The Parenting Advisor* (Garden City, N.Y.: Anchor Press/Doubleday, 1978), pp. 7–13. On page 8 of his book, Caplan makes the point that any method that helps a woman learn more about her body, preparation for what childbirth is, and how to share the experience with one's husband or relative or friend so that she has an effective experience in it, can be viewed as prepared childbirth, not necessarily as "natural childbirth."
4. Sueann Robinson Ambron, *Child Development* (San Francisco: Rinehart Press/Holt, 1975), pp. 67, 68. See also William A. Kennedy, *Child Psychology*, 2nd ed. (Englewood Cliffs, N.J.: Prentice-Hall, 1975), pp. 117, 119.
5. Kennedy, op. cit., p. 119.
6. Arthur T. Jersild, Charles W. Telford, and James M. Sawrey, *Child Psychology*, 7th ed. (Englewood Cliffs, N.J.: Prentice-Hall, 1975), p. 150. See also Paul Henry Mussen, John Janeway Conger, and Jerome Kagan, *Child Development and Personality* 4th ed. (New York: Harper, 1974), p. 132.
7. Jersild, Telford, and Sawry, op. cit., p. 150; and Mussen, Conger, and Kagan, op. cit., p. 132.
8. Ambron, op. cit., p. 74.
9. Meyer and Dusek, op. cit., p. 96.
10. Mussen, Conger, and Kagan, op. cit., p. 134.

11. Meyer and Dusek, op. cit., p. 97.
12. Caplan, op. cit., p. 136.
13. Ibid., p. 137.
14. Caplan, ibid., pp. 210–224. See also, T. Berry Brazelton, *Infants and Mothers* (New York: Delacorte, 1969), 296 pp.; Joseph Church, *Understanding Your Child from Birth to Three* (New York: Pocket Books, a Division of Simon & Schuster, 1976), 253 pp.; and Burton L. White, *The First Three Years of Life* (Englewood Cliffs, N.J.: Prentice-Hall, 1975), 285 pp.
15. Ambron, op. cit., pp. 104–150; Jean Piaget, *The Child's Conception of the World*, translated by Joan and Andrew Tomlinson (Paterson, N.J.: Littlefield, Adams, 1960), p. 28; Barry J. Wadsworth, *Piaget for the Classroom Teacher* (New York: Longman, 1978), pp. 13–15.
16. Henry W. Maier, *Three Theories of Child Development* (New York: Harper, 1965), p. 99.
17. Ibid., p. 96.
18. Ibid., p. 97.
19. Ibid., p. 101.
20. Lloyd deMause, Editor, *The History of Childhood* (New York: Psychohistory Press, 1974), pp. 1–3.
21. Ibid., p. 3.
22. Ibid.
23. Frank Reissman and S. M. Miller, "Social Change Versus the 'Psychiatric World View,'" pp. 64–75 in *Mental Health and Social Change*, edited by Milton F. Shore and Fortune V. Mannino (New York: American Orthopsychiatric Assoc., AMS Press, 1975), 330 pp.
24. deMause, op. cit., p. 3.
25. Meyer and Dusek, op. cit., p. 145.
26. Ibid., p. 160.
27. Ibid., p. 185. They write that "The process of fitting new experiences or objects into already existing structures is almost never completely faithful to the actual attributes of the objects." They indicate that accommodation and assimilation occur together, and that they cannot be separated, nor can one of them be considered as more important than the other; they are reciprocal to each other.
28. T. G. R. Bower, *Human Development* (San Francisco: Freeman, 1979), p. 296.
29. Ibid., p. 298.
30. Lee Salk, "Woe to the Parents Who Turn to the Experts," pp. 62–68 in *Speaking Out for America's Children*, edited by Milton J. E. Senn (New Haven and London: Yale U.P., 1977), p. 67.
31. Ambron, op. cit., p. 155.
32. Ibid.
33. Bower, op. cit., p. 304.
34. Ibid.
35. Ibid., p. 306.
36. Robert B. Cairns, *Social Development* (San Francisco: Freeman, 1979), p. 109.
37. Ibid.
38. Ibid., p. 79.
39. Ibid., p. 97.
40. Richard Flacks, "Growing Up Confused," pp. 21–32 in *Socialization and the Life Cycle*, edited by Peter I. Rose (New York: St. Martin's, 1979), p. 25. Flacks describes a source of strain that parents experience when wanting to grant their children autonomy or freedom of expression of certain perspectives, while their own commitment to "traditional virtues of cleanliness, obedience, and emotional control" interferes periodically with what they do allow, or tell their children. Sometimes they reprimand their children for a kind of behavior that they may not bother to notice at another time. This "absorption" of personality sometimes shapes an individual "who fears failure *and* success, experiences deep anxiety about his acceptance by others, finds it difficult to establish his own autonomy, and is, consequently, far more driven toward conformity and 'security' than toward independence and personal achievement."
41. Cairns, op. cit., pp. 3–12. The varied perspectives used by researchers of various disciplines are synthesized by Cairns to describe approaches to studying social development. Psychoanalytic views, behavioristic psychological findings, and developmental psycholog-

ical, as well as zoological, studies contribute to discussions on the historical understandings and insight on social development. The fallacies of "leapfrogging from studies of primates and rodents to the solution of human problems" are emphasized as are the necessities for studying "the biosocial organization of the individual, the structure of the group of which it is a part, and the nature of the interchanges in which the acts occur." (P. 9.)

42. *Items*, Vol. 33, Nos. 3/4, December 1979, Social Science Research Council, p. 62. Many writers indicate that the adult's personality is directly related to the treatment one receives from parents in the first few years of the child's life. "Recent research has cast doubt on this relationship, suggesting that there is no demonstrable correlation between the nature of these early experiences and an individual's behavior as a young adult." Although many developmental theorists have taken positions that present direct relationships between the earliest years of life and characteristics that show up or remain in an adult's personality, sociological orientations, as shown in Chapter 1 of this text provide reason for doubts given the considerations of changes in societal contexts throughout the years.

43. Kennedy, op. cit., p. 134. Since genetic research has provided insight on genetic conditions in human beings, more is known about relationships between hereditary characteristics and the environmental experiences of an individual. "Without an environment that stimulates, protects and nurtures his innate potential, it fails to thrive."

44. John W. McDavid and S. Gray Garwood, *Understanding Children* (Lexington, Mass.: Heath, 1978), p. 69.

45. Jersild, Telford, and Sawrey, op. cit., p. 153. The data from many studies indicate that "body size has both a genetic component and an environmental (principally a nutritional) component. What we see in nature represents the interaction of the two."

46. Ibid., p. 156. When a child is finally ready to walk, much of the groundwork has been laid in the months before, when the child's development in the "muscles of the upper trunk and arms" has occurred. Postural control in holding the head up, sitting, and the power to move the body forward affect the ability to walk when the child is ready to do so.

47. Meyer and Dusek, op. cit., p. 116.

48. Ibid., p. 117. To introduce training for any skill prior to the appearance of readiness signs in the child, "would be futile because the neuromuscular maturation would be insufficient to permit the child to profit from the learning experience."

49. Herbert Ginsburg and Sylvia Opper, *Piaget's Theory of Intellectual Development*, 2nd ed. (Englewood Cliffs, N.J.: Prentice-Hall, 1979), p. 19.

50. Ibid., pp. 19–20.

51. Ibid., p. 20.

52. Burton L. White, *The First Three Years of Life* (Englewood Cliffs, N.J.: Prentice-Hall, 1975), pp. 134–137.

53. Ginsburg and Opper, op. cit., p. 70.

54. Ibid.

55. Meyer and Dusek, op. cit., p. 104.

56. Ibid., p. 103.

57. Ibid., p. 108.

58. Ibid.

59. Betty Edwards, *Drawing on the Right Side of the Brain* (New York: St. Martin's, 1979), p. 27. For many years, the left hemisphere has been known as the dominant one, and the right hemisphere the subordinate one. Since language and other reasoning processes were considered to take place in the left hemisphere, it was considered major and superior in function to the right one.

60. Ibid., p. 30.

61. Ibid., p. 35.

62. Ibid., p. 36. She says, "It seems to regard the thing as-it-is, at the present moment of the present; seeing things for what they simply are . . . not good at analyzing and abstracting salient characteristics."

63. Eleanor E. Maccoby, "Moral Values and Behavior in Childhood," pp. 227–269, in *Socialization and Society*, edited by John A. Clausen (Boston: Little, Brown, 1968), 400 pp. Moral development involves learning how to conform with certain values of one's parents

as well as, in one sense, learning to accept them as one's own (or internalize them), p. 230. She states also that some conform willingly, having accepted those values as their own; some do not.

64. Alex Inkeles, "Society, Social Structure, and Child Socialization," pp. 73–129, in *Social-ization and Society*, edited by John A. Clausen (Boston: Little, Brown, 1968). Although an individual may feel that "society" makes certain requests or demands, it is often rather someone who has a strong interest to support or protect that is making the request, and not someone who is in fact performing a function as an agent of the larger social order or "society." P. 84.

65. Ellen Ward Cooney and Robert Selman, "Children's Use of Social Conceptions: Toward a Dynamic Model of Social Cognition," *New Directions for Child Development* Number 1 (1978), pp. 23–44. They use a stage analysis approach to study children's reflective reasoning as it affects social functioning. Five stages of children's conceptions of individ-uals, friendships, and peer-group relations were studied and applied to stages of social reasoning. These findings were examined in the light of an analysis of "spontaneous social comments and social interactions of individual children." Pp. 23–24.

66. John W. McDavid and S. Gray Garwood, op. cit., pp. 258–259.

67. Berkeley Rice," Brave New World of Intelligence Testing," *Psychology Today* (Septem-ber 1979), p. 37.

68. Ambron, op. cit., p. 212.

69. Ibid.

70. Ginsburg and Opper, op. cit., p. 81. See also Ambron, op. cit., p. 239. It is significant that children about three and a half have a vocabulary to describe their world in terms of about one thousand words, as noted by Howard Gardner in *Developmental Psychology*, (Boston: Little, Brown, 1978), p. 175.

71. Gardner, op. cit., pp. 238, 239. Bruner's work highlights the exploratory (scientific) ori-entation in children's play. Vygotsky focuses on the aspect of children's play that permits them to create new meanings other than those that have been governed by names of objects and affected by their uses. A stick can become something else in the child's play repertoire for the moment. This allows children to adopt "a hypothetical or pretend stance toward the present." P. 239.

72. Edythe Margolin, "Work and Play—Are They Really Opposites?" *Elementary School Journal* Vol. 67 (April 1967), pp. 343–353. A typology on the classification of work and play reveals that the two characteristics in an individual's learning can be diffuse. Both make serious contributions to an individual's development.

73. Gardner, op. cit., p. 184.

74. Ibid., p. 185. Vygotsky's work is compared to the work of Piaget and to the hypotheses in the Whorf–Sapir view, each of which shows a different path to the development of language, thought, and speech. Piaget presents views on the means through which action affects thought, and language reflects those levels; Whorf and Sapir's work indicates that language determines the way one thinks; and Vygotsky conceptualizes two separate streams, thought and speech, which become fused into one system of thought and lan-guage, and meanings.

75. Akhter Ahsen, "Eidetics: An Overview," *Journal of Mental Imagery* Vol. 1, No. 1 (Spring 1977), pp. 5–38.

76. Ibid., p. 11.

77. Barbara Biber, Edna Shapiro, and David Wickens in collaboration with Elizabeth Gilke-son, *Promoting Cognitive Growth* (Washington, D.C.: National Assoc. for the Education of Young Children, 1971), p. 63.

78. Cairns, op. cit., p. 354.

79. Alex Inkeles, "Personality and Social Structure," pp. 249–276, in *Sociology Today*, edited by Robert K. Merton, Leonard Broom, and Leonard S. Cottrell, Jr. (New York: Basic, 1960), p. 256. Inkeles says that to be aware of both the psychological and the sociological variables in the study of interaction does not reduce one or the other. "The result is a product of the interaction of the sociological and the psychological variables of situation and personality." P. 256.

80. Ibid., p. 271.

81. Ibid.

82. Ibid., p. 272.

83. Robert L. Munroe and Ruth H. Munroe, "Perspectives Suggested by Anthropological Data," pp. 253–317 in *Handbook of Cross-Cultural Psychology*, Vol. I, edited by Harry C. Triandis and William Wilson Lambert (Boston: Allyn, Inc., 1980), pp. 282, 283.

84. Ibid., p. 283.

85. Paul Mussen and Nancy Eisenberg-Berg, *Roots of Caring, Sharing, and Helping* (San Francisco: Freeman, 1977), p. 103.

86. Brian Sutton-Smith and Shirley Sutton-Smith, *How to Play With Your Children (And When Not to)* (New York: Hawthorn, 1974), p. 126.

87. Ibid.

88. Gardner, op. cit., pp. 267–292.

89. Ibid., p. 271. It is suggested that, ". . . abilities in the young brain are organized differently" from those of adults.

90. Some children when five years old understand and speak and use about two thousand words, involving sentences of at least four or five words. When about six years old, children have a vocabulary of approximately two thousand five hundred or more; at seven, many more words, more complicated sentences, involve about three thousand words or more. Some children may have about four thousand words in their usable vocabularies.

91. Munroe and Munroe, op. cit., p. 279. Affective behavior occurs in most societies. Those things that are valued, however, may differ among societies. These authors do indicate, however, that if a society turned out affectless people, it could hardly survive, because the cooperation and reciprocity needed for survival could not exist.

92. Jersild, Telford, and Sawrey, op. cit., p. 295.

93. Ibid.

94. Cairns, op. cit., p. 153.

95. Elizabeth M. R. Lomax, in collaboration with Jerome Kagan and Barbara G. Rosenkrantz, *Science and Patterns of Care* (San Francisco: Freeman, 1978), p. 54. At birth an individual is presumed to have fixed quantities of sexual energies that could regulate or "restrict" the "degree of satisfaction" gained from sexual energy or the *libido*. Freud changed the theory later to indicate that the *libido* was not only involved in a sex drive, but that it was an "energy reservoir for all of the life-preserving instincts. . . ." He perceived the libido as a source of mental energy, too.

96. Lomax, Kagan and Rozenkrantz, op. cit., p. 56.

97. Ibid., p. 66.

98. Catherine S. Chilman, *Adolescent Sexuality in a Changing American Society* (Bethesda, Md.: National Institute of Child Health and Human Development, 1978), 384 pp.

99. Discussion in earlier sections dealt with Piaget's work as well as the work of Vygotsky's, and that of others who were concerned about language development. Studies on the cross-modal functions in the brain also disclose relationships between motor development and intellectual skills.

100. Piaget, *Judgment and Reasoning in the Child*, translated by Marjorie Warden (Paterson, N.J., Littlefield, Adams, 1960), p. 143. Being able to reflect on one's reasoning occurs with abilities for introspection. Piaget indicates that "up to the age of seven, introspection seems to be completely absent. . . ."

101. Ibid., p. 143.

102. Ibid., p. 148.

103. Ibid., p. 206.

104. Ibid., p. 209.

105. Ibid.

106. Gardner, op. cit., p. 398.

107. Ibid.

108. Ibid.

109. Ibid., p. 400.

110. Ibid.

111. Ibid., p. 395.

112. Norman Goodman and Gary Marx, *Society Today*, 3rd ed. (New York: Random, 1978), p. 120. Sociobiologists perceive the biological bases in the individual, rather than social interactivity as the greater of emotions and/or social behavior.

113. Ibid. They also say that human behavior is learned through the socialization processes, rather than through the unfolding of predetermined traits.

114. Ibid.
115. George Herbert Mead, *Mind, Self, and Society* (Chicago: Un. of Chicago, 1967), p. 135.
116. Ibid.
117. This kind of job independence can vary among social classes and with the individual circumstances of the family or child.
118. Paul Mussen and Nancy Eisenberg-Berg, *Roots of Caring, Sharing, and Helping* (San Francisco: Freeman, 1977), p. 144. A study is reported on three groups of seven- and eight-year-old children who were given instructions that variously led them to think of sad and happy thoughts. The children who were happy and were subsequently asked to share money with other children showed greater generosity than did the others, who were sad. See also, p. 103, in which a discussion on the imitation of aggressive behavior seen on television indicates children's tendencies to follow in kind, to use those observations as models for their own responses.
119. Renato Tagiuri, "Person Perception," pp. 395–449 in *The Handbook of Social Psychology*, 2nd ed., Vol. Three (Reading, Mass.: Addison-Wesley, 1969), p. 432. "The subtlety and delicacy of the process of coming to know other persons has never been underestimated, but empirical, naturalistic, and theoretical evidence now available suggests that it is even more complex than one ever dreamt of."
120. David R. Shaffer, *Social and Personality Development* (Monterey, Calif.: Brooks/Cole, a Division of Wadsworth, Inc., 1979), p. 14.
121. William Damon, Editor, "Social Cognition," *New Directions for Child Development*, No. 1 (1978), p. vii.
122. James Youniss and Jacqueline Volpe, "A Relational Analysis of Children's Friendship," *New Directions for Child Development*, No. 1 (1978), p. 21.
123. Ibid.
124. Ibid.
125. Elliot Turiel, "Social Regulations and Domains of Social Concepts," *New Directions for Child Development*, No. 1 (1978), pp. 45–74.

SELECTED REFERENCES

AHSEN, AKHTER. "Eidetics: An Overview," *Journal of Mental Imagery* Vol. 1, No. 1 (Spring 1977), pp. 5–38.

AMBRON, SUEANN ROBINSON. *Child Development.* San Francisco: Rinehart Press/Holt, Rinehart and Winston, 1975. 508 pp.

BIBER, BARBARA, EDNA SHAPIRO, and DAVID WICKENS in collaboration with Elizabeth Gilkeson. *Promoting Cognitive Growth.* Washington, D.C.: National Association for the Education of Young Children, 1971. 65 pp.

BOWER, T. G. R. *Human Development.* San Francisco: W. H. Freeman and Company, Publishers, 1979. 473 pp.

BRAZELTON, T. BERRY. *Infants and Mothers.* New York: Delacorte Press, 1969. 296 pp.

CAIRNS, ROBERT B. *Social Development.* San Francisco: W. H. Freeman and Company, Publishers, 1979. 438 pp.

CAPLAN, FRANK, Editor. *The Parenting Advisor.* Garden City, N.Y.: Anchor Press/Doubleday, 1978. 569 pp.

CHILMAN, CATHERINE S. *Adolescent Sexuality in a Changing American Society.* Bethesda, Md.: U.S. Department of Health, Education, and Welfare, National Institute of Child Health and Human Development, Center for Population Research, DHEW Publication No. (NIH) 79-1426, Human Development, 1978. 384 pp.

CHURCH, JOSEPH. *Understanding Your Child from Birth to Three.* New York: Pocket Books, a Division of Simon & Schuster, Inc., 1976. 253 pp.

CLAUSEN, JOHN A., Editor. *Socialization and Society.* Boston: Little, Brown and Company, 1968. 400 pp.

COONEY, ELLEN WARD, and ROBERT SELMAN. "Children's Use of Social Conceptions: Toward a Dynamic Model of Social Cognition," *New Directions for Child Development* No. 1 (1978), pp. 23–43.

DAMON, WILLIAM, Editor. "Social Cognition," *New Directions for Child Development* No. 1 (1978) 144 pp.

deMAUSE, LLOYD, Editor. *The History of Childhood*. New York: The Psychohistory Press, 1974. 450 pp.

EDWARDS, BETTY. *Drawing on the Right Side of the Brain*. New York: St. Martin's Press, Inc., 1979. 207 pp.

FLACKS, RICHARD. "Growing Up Confused," pp. 21–32 in *Socialization and the Life Cycle*, edited by Peter I. Rose. New York: St. Martin's Press, Inc., 1979. 412 pp.

GARDNER, HOWARD. *Developmental Psychology*. Boston: Little, Brown and Company, 1978. 612 pp.

GINSBURG, HERBERT, and SYLVIA OPPER. *Piaget's Theory of Intellectual Development*, 2nd ed. Englewood Cliffs, N.J.: Prentice-Hall, Inc., 1979. 253 pp.

GOODMAN, NORMAN, and GARY MARX. *Society Today*. 3rd ed. New York: Random House, Inc., 1978. 592 pp.

INKELES, ALEX. "Personality and Social Structure," pp. 249–276 in *Sociology Today*, edited by Robert K. Merton, Leonard Broom, and Leonard S. Cottrell, Jr. New York: Basic Books, Inc., Publishers, 1960. 623 pp.

———. "Society, Social Structure, and Child Socialization," pp. 73–129 in *Socialization and Society*, edited by John A. Clausen. Boston: Little, Brown and Company, 1968.

JERSILD, ARTHUR T., CHARLES W. TELFORD, and JAMES M. SAWREY. *Child Psychology*, 7th ed. Englewood Cliffs, N.J.: Prentice-Hall, Inc., 1975. 588 pp.

KENNEDY, WILLIAM A. *Child Psychology*, 2nd ed. Englewood Cliffs, N.J.: Prentice-Hall, Inc., 1975. 553 pp.

LAMAZE, FERNAND. *Painless Childbirth: The Lamaze Method*. New York: Pocket Books, 1972. 191 pp.

LEBOYER, FREDERICK, M.D. *Birth Without Violence*. Garden City, N.Y.: Alfred A. Knopf, Inc., 1975. 114 pp.

LOMAX, ELIZABETH M. R., in collaboration with Jerome Kagan and Barbara Rosenkrantz. *Science and Patterns of Child Care*. San Francisco: W. H. Freeman and Company, Publishers, 1978. 247 pp.

MACCOBY, ELEANOR E. "Moral Values and Behavior in Childhood," pp. 227–269 in *Socialization and Society*, edited by John A. Clausen. Boston: Little, Brown and Company, 1968. 400 pp.

MAIER, HENRY W. *Three Theories of Child Development*. New York: Harper & Row, Publishers, Inc., 1965. 314 pp.

MARGOLIN, EDYTHE. "Work and Play—Are They Really Opposites?" *Elementary Journal*, Vol. 67 (April 1967), pp. 343–353.

McDAVID, JOHN W., and S. GRAY GARWOOD. *Understanding Children*. Lexington, Mass.: D. C. Heath & Company, 1978. 532 pp.

MEAD, GEORGE HERBERT. *Mind, Self, and Society*. Chicago: University of Chicago Press, 1967. 401 pp.

MEYER, WILLIAM J., and JEROME B. DUSEK. *Child Psychology*. Lexington, Mass.: D. C. Heath & Company, 1979. 658 pp.

MUNROE, ROBERT L., and RUTH H. MUNROE. "Perspectives Suggested by Anthropological Data," pp. 253–317 in *Handbook of Cross-Cultural Psychology* Vol. 1, edited by Harry C. Triandis and William Wilson Lambert. Boston: Allyn & Bacon, Inc., 1980. 392 pp.

MUSSEN, PAUL, and NANCY EISENBERG-BERG. *Roots of Caring, Sharing, and Helping*. San Francisco: W. H. Freeman and Company, Publishers, 1977. 212 pp.

———, JOHN JANEWAY CONGER, and JEROME KAGAN. *Child Development and Personality*, 4th ed. New York: Harper & Row, Publishers, 1974. 684 pp.

PIAGET, JEAN. *The Child's Conception of the World*, translated by Joan and Andrew Tomlinson. Paterson, N.J.: Littlefield, Adams and Company, 1960. 397 pp.

———, *Judgment and Reasoning in the Child*, translated by Marjorie Warden. Paterson, N.J.: Littlefield, Adams and Company, 1959. 260 pp.

REISSMAN, FRANK, and S. M. MILLER. "Social Change Versus the 'Psychiatric World View,'" pp. 64–75 in *Mental Health and Social Change*, edited by Milton F. Shore and Fortune V. Mannino. New York: American Orthopsychiatric Association, AMS Press, Inc., 1975. 330 pp.

RICE, BERKELEY. "Brave New World of Intelligence Testing," *Psychology Today,* September 1979, p. 37.

SALK, LEE. "Woe to the Parents Who Turn to the Experts," pp. 62–68 in *Speaking Out for America's Children,* edited by Milton J. E. Senn. New Haven and London: Yale University Press, 1977. 214 pp.

SHAFFER, DAVID R. *Social and Personality Development.* Monterey, Calif.: Brooks/Cole Publishing Company, a Division of Wadsworth Publishing Co., Inc., 1979. 624 pp.

Social Science Research Council. *Items.* Vol. 33, Nos. 3/4, December 1979, p. 62. 605 Third Avenue, New York, N.Y. 10016.

SUTTON-SMITH, BRIAN, and SHIRLEY SUTTON-SMITH. *How to Play with Your Children (And When Not To).* New York: Hawthorn Books, Inc., 1974. 274 pp.

TAGIURI, RENATO. "Person Perception," pp. 395–449 in *The Handbook of Social Psychology,* 2nd ed., Vol. Three. Reading, Mass.: Addison-Wesley Publishing Co., Inc., 1969. 978 pp.

TURIEL, ELLIOT. "Social Regulations and Domains of Social Concepts," *New Directions for Child Development* No. 1 (1978), pp. 45–74.

WADSWORTH, BARRY J. *Piaget for the Classroom Teacher.* New York and London: Longman, Inc., 1978. 303 pp.

WHITE, BURTON L. *The First Three Years of Life.* Englewood Cliffs, N.J.: Prentice-Hall, Inc., 1975. 285 pp.

YOUNISS, JAMES, and JACQUELINE VOLPE, "A Relational Analysis of Children's Friendship," *New Directions for Child Development* No. 1 (1978), pp. 1–22.

The Curriculum,
Its Programs and
Underlying Philosophics

Changes in Programs and Philosophies

Throughout the past fifty years, the curriculum of the schools has changed tremendously. As we leaf through guidelines, courses of studies, and programs for today's young children, it becomes obvious that they are far more complicated and articulated than they were in the 1920s. The trends in expectations for children and the manner in which children are expected to learn most effectively have changed the emphases in the lessons, books, and materials that are presented in today's classrooms.

A *curriculum* may be defined as a set of guidelines to be used by the teacher or others working with children at school; such guidelines include techniques, activities, materials, and books which are recommended for the teacher's use and which are expected to maximize the children's individual development. In this sense, both the planned and unplanned activities (those serendipitously arrived at) that are used for the instruction of children are included, as are tasks that the teacher introduces spontaneously when (s)he sees that the children would benefit from doing them.

Teachers who receive an unexpected visitor in the classroom who has to give the children information about inoculations that may take place soon will permit that presentation to be substituted for the activity scheduled for that time. What seems most useful for the children's growth, academically, psychologically, emotionally, socially, and intellectually at a given time will be offered in place of another, preorganized event. Children's anxieties need to be eased when they are to receive shots of any kind. Information that a nurse, doctor, or nurse's aide can give them serves an important purpose in their growth and understanding.

The curriculum consists not only of a planned, organized, sequential and specifically ongoing program, it also includes topics of an unusual nature that may be introduced because of a major event, or a school activity that may have to intervene. In general, however, the recommendations made for the structure of a curriculum are based on a rationale.

Philosophic Views, Goals, and School Policies

The curriculum includes a philosophy and goals that are made explicit in objectives, content, and implementation. The rationale underlying various programs is important in creating the curriculum. Decisions in regard to the rationale are much more complex and significant in their relationships to policies than they ever were. They are based on an educational philosophy, not only of a school system but of the tone of the times (or *zeitgeist*) and the social forces. Teachers may or may not agree with some of the concepts in a philosophy. Teachers are, however, the ones who implement the program, and therefore their manner of instruction may not always express an educational philosophy that is sought by the writers of the curriculum. This may be intentional or not. People do not agree on *how* certain subject matter areas should be taught. An educational philosophy or rationale, therefore, as it is placed on paper, may differ totally from the way someone interprets and implements that philosophy in the actual instructional process of the classrooms.

Typically, a group of people selected on the basis of choices made by school personnel in curriculum divisions will work on a new program for children in the elementary school. The group creating the program will represent teachers, principals, superintendents, subject matter specialists, and at times, consultants from universities. It is constituted of people from each of those instructional planning and teaching levels. Local groups usually have the privilege of making their own decisions, more so in some areas of the country than others.

Each state makes recommendations for certain subject matter areas of study. The local group may adopt those recommendations. When guidelines to the school system come in the form of legislative acts, the school must adopt those policies.

As the United States has a decentralized form of government, its educational system is similar to, or is a reflection of, the broader society. The federal government has guidelines, such as modes of action for desegregation, equal opportunity acts, and usage of monies that are accorded to various school districts. Local interpretations of specific ideas issued from the United States through governmental offices and agencies are distinct and bound to the specific group that understands its own needs. Particularly when governmental issues offer with them sums of money to subsidize various mandates (or recommendations for interpretation), local communities and governmental agencies or people try to adapt their activities as requested.

School policies have to reflect a realistic interpretation of specific groups' needs. Equal representation of all those who will be affected by such planning is necessary for at least part of an effective implementation of the policy. As well as equal representation of the people who will use the policy, up-to-date information is also needed if people are to work out school programs that will benefit many people.

Contemporary Trends in the Curriculum

The current trends toward problem solving, initiative, process emphasis in learning, creativity in thinking, originality, and the scientific objectivity of logic are all reflected in curriculum planning. Even though children need to learn what the correct answers are to problems that are given to them, educators are interested in how children arrive at their answers. Rote learning as a central mode of learning, is not valued as much as it once was. Rote learning (or memorization of words and dates without understanding their significance or meaning), is still a significant skill; it is not, however, the sole means of learning in school.

An emphasis on comprehension of what is learned has developed in the last twenty-five to thirty years.[1] Understanding one's society as well as knowing how to utilize knowledge is relevant to the preparation of youth for knowing how to live in, or change, its society. Taba suggests that one focus of teachers and those who create the curriculum for children should be to provide opportunities for learning that gear pupils toward a process of "becoming" and adapting to changes in social realities.

Following the line of thinking that emphasizes change and different interpretations of society, it is suggested that children be involved in learning that "include[s] processes of interpreting, questioning, and contemplating change."[2] It is further suggested that the content accepted as valid today (symbolically speaking), can become the "fiction" of tomorrow.[3] This thought too, underlines the importance of studying processes of becoming, of changing, of knowing how things work, and what affects change.

Contemporary thinking supports individualistic efforts in solving problems. Educational activities are less oriented toward valuing a single correct answer. Teachers are expected to ask when one child gives an answer, "Does anyone else have another answer to the problem?" Open-mindedness, flexibility, multi-perceptiveness, are qualities that are considered valuable in thinking.

People such as Taba recommend that educational processes in the classroom teach children how to think for themselves. They are to be developing ways of learning how to help themselves and to look within for their own resources for self-help. Her beliefs that children be taught to think, that it is not solely an inborn quality, carried weight along with several other educators who advocated the values of self-knowledge and self-help.

In a domestic society that offers many perspectives, individuals must ultimately decide for themselves what their best choices are. The bases for making effective decisions emerge from both personal and objectively oriented thought. Facts may not always persuade the individual. Regardless of what the individual uses for making the choice, however, the consequences of the decision rest with him/her. Emotions, temperament, mood, and other factors in a situation affect the individual's responses. Truth-seeking is not always a focus in deciding what course of action one may follow. The *locus* or place determining where and how the choice will be made, however, still remains within in the individual. To obey, to comply, or to deviate is a personal action. Educators can assist in these processes of thought to some extent. The curriculum can reflect the dynamics that may implement thinking. Techniques of thought that children learn about in the educational processes are expected to help them be effective in acquiring what they need for their growth.

Individuals and the way they think are also considered as part of significant ethnic and cultural groups throughout the country. "Cultural pluralism in the United States is now at a point where it may be used constructively to make a great improvement in intergroup relations in this country and at the same time to increase the economic and civic opportunity of the minority groups with lowest socioeconomic status."[4] Constructive understanding of groups for the concerns of each other is doing a great deal toward helping people know how to relate to each other and also to understand how people are similar to each other. The fact that through attempts of groups to understand each other, certain kinds of power become more open, accessible, and possible for equalitarian distribution, serves as a form of check-and-balance system against self-interests becoming too large in perspective.

Self-help, however, whether in the individual or the group, is learned, when possible, at school (in formalized processes) as well as in the home, through parental and sibling attitudes. The curriculum can be a strong force in facilitating the learning of self-help in socially accepted ways. There are many socially accepted ways in a democratic society. Many people are not aware of them. Too often, unfortunately, either because the teacher is not cognizant or the pupils do not experience diversionary perceptions (albeit of acceptable social forms), children as well as the teacher sense constraints more than they sense permission and encouragement to think about ideas differing from those of other people.

Principles of sociology and psychology, as advocated by sociologists learning theorists, and developmental psychologists, as well as those recommended by educators based on their research on ways that children learn, provide significant data that are useful for curriculum planners of today. Taba,[5] and Havighurst and Levine,[6] indicate guidelines that are pertinent to constructive planning for children in the classroom. Bruner,[7] as well, indicates the importance of providing challenges in activities that will facilitate problem solving, making order out of chaos, and learning how to meet unexpected (or contingency) actions arising in events. These reflect a changing society and an increasingly complicated technology.

As more researchers provide information on learning, language development, social cognition, and brain functioning processes (as indicated in the preceding chapter), it becomes clear that educators need to incorporate those findings into curriculum planning. If this is not done, children as well as educators of today lose out on an exciting means of experiencing learning as it can occur in the classroom. With an interesting curriculum that is realistically adapted to social directions (as indicated by sociologists and learning developmentalists), the classroom becomes more than just a fact-feeding place. It becomes a forum for challenge and a place that encourages constructive argumentative (and socially accepted) skills. Teachers and children can benefit from this perspective if it is presented effectively.

Considerations for Planning a Contemporary Curriculum for Young Children

1. Consider the meaning of the content for young children. Have they had any experience with the theme of content?
2. Examine the terms and concepts of the content. Will children be able to master them?
3. Are books that are available geared to children's experiences and using the new content appropriately?
4. How long can the children's interest be sustained by the curriculum theme under consideration?
5. Is there sufficient variety in aspects of the program to interest every child in it?
6. Can materials be adapted to individual differences in learning style, background, readiness, language levels, vocabulary of each pupil?

7. Can the teacher adapt his/her own style of teaching to the theme of the program?
8. Can this theme be supported by related ideas and concepts familiar to or introductory to continuing ones?
9. Can a variety of activities be built into the program so that children are introduced to different types of learning experiences at school?
10. Will the children be able to talk to their parents, siblings, relatives and others about what they are learning at school?
11. Can each child be provided with information that will enable him/her a position of leadership in the classroom?
12. Will each child be enriched because of any part of the curriculum? Will any of it be new to him/her? Will it be useful and contributive to the child's present or future?
13. If the curriculum broadens the child's horizons, that is, brings materials into the child's life that would not ordinarily be met in the child's "natural" surroundings, is the curriculum presented well, clearly enough to promote understanding?
14. Are unfamiliar ideas to the child introduced from a basis of familiar ones first?
15. Is the curriculum sufficiently open ended to permit children's contributions to it as it unfolds for them?
16. Are the tenets in the philosophy of the curriculum flexible enough to add new ones that are related or appropriate?
17. Do teachers have enough understanding of the curriculum goals and materials to be aware of its breadth and depth?
18. Are the children permitted to periodically deviate from or separate themselves from major objectives in the curriculum itself if they are pursuing learning and gaining from it?
19. Has the teacher planned an evaluative process in order to assess the children's understanding and functional usage of the curriculum activities and program?
20. Is the teacher sufficiently comfortable with the content of the curriculum to recognize when children do not understand part of it and are in need of assistance or clarifying activities/explanations?
21. Does the teacher know where to obtain assistance if the curriculum content is not clear to him/her? Does (s)he know where and how to obtain enriching materials for the curriculum?

Past, Present, and Future

In terms of what has been suggested by information on social changes, and the need to adapt to a transitional or "becoming" concept of learning at school, it is appropriate that teachers consider several approaches in implementing the curriculum. The work of researchers indicates what kind of world they anticipate for the future of today's young children.[8] Greater integration of the concept of cultural pluralism is expected throughout society. These perspectives will be reflected in the schools, communities, and individual groups of various ethnic values.

Any curriculum plan needs to obtain, besides its manner of presentation in the unfolding of its theme and content, various strategies that include challenges throughout, from start to finish. This does not mean that the challenges frustrate. It is necessary that they become pivotal to the child's skills and abilities. A discerning teacher is able to note when the activities are too easy or too difficult for any learner. Time is needed for the children to review, practice, and master various concepts prior to going on to the more difficult ones. But this happens at different times for different children. Their paces in learning differ.

A variety of strategies sustains a teacher's repertoire of teaching designs. Recommendations for strategies were made in Frazier's work relative to the need for helping children of all kinds in "adventuring, mastering, and associating."[9] He includes consideration of the extensive breadth of experiences that children can have and from which they can learn. They cannot help but learn because there is activity, consideration of prior experiences, and reaching out in each of the recommendations. The notion that there is something for every child at school must pertain. There is indeed enough variety in materials and activities available so that all children may find something they like to do at school and that represents constructive learning.

Historical Events Affecting the Present

The rights of today for various groups were fought for by courageous people of yesterday. Children can learn about these events at levels of understanding that are appropriate for them. This knowledge can help children understand some of the incidents that they hear about, and even help them create a channel for communication to adults about those events. It also provides them an opportunity to identify with their own groups, in which efforts to acquire equitability are still occurring. When children learn about the forthrightness of people who marshaled energies and thinking sufficiently to proclaim social needs, they are better able to know by what means some of these prizes were won. The privileges that they have now were not obtained automatically. Some one or some group had to fight for that right, privilege, or responsibility.

One does not have to go very far back in history—only the past ten years—to have evidence for the articulated needs of the oppressed. This evidence can help children be proud of a society based on speaking privileges that encourage concern for people who are not able to speak for themselves (for whatever reason). The system that supports concern for the interests of many, needs itself to be supported. Social consciousness is a prized quality in American society. It is the one quality that simultaneously enhances the individual and the society. It enhances the individual who has vision, sensitivity, and empathy to know that others are not as fortunate as (s)he may be. It enhances society because it strengthens awareness that individual nurturance of society makes society a better place for all people in it.[10]

The classroom is the ideal place to create a forum for the advance of privileges, responsibilities, and the protection of individuals and their society. In this sense, history is learned by the children. The history, however, comes alive for children who have lived through denial, inadequacy, and ineffectiveness in attempts to help themselves.

The ideal and the practical are mixed together as children discuss the past and present and how certain advances in science brought people what they have today. Minds, energies, persistence, and courage produce things that are used by many. Children need to hear about invention, trial-and-error efforts, and the grim determination that are often involved in the discovery of new ideas and technologies. They have to see themselves as part of that creative society. Teachers can inspire these views in them.

Children become able to understand how others were able to progress in a given field or discipline. Examples of the lives of others in the past who brought pleasure to people (even after their own inventive lives were over), can do much to revitalize children's goals and ambitions.

When children hear of the difficulties encountered and conquered by people in the past and that are often being encountered and conquered even today, they are better able to place in perspective what life is all about. They are better equipped (although not always, of course) to understand that persistence, good will, and belief in one's self and in others can be productive. The children in low-income groups and possibly in upper-income as well need to learn this. They often either take for granted that their lives will continue to be the way they are all the time and they can do nothing about it, or they think that their own efforts are not viable enough to create for them what they would like to have happen to them in the future.

Curriculum Activities on Past and Present and Future

In science: Inventors, writers, medical workers who brought valuable contributions to society.

In music: Composers, musicians, instrument makers who contributed to society.

In drama: Actors, actresses, stage writers who contributed to society.

In dance: Outstanding men and women in ballet, vaudeville, stage dancing who contributed to society.

In arts and crafts: Outstanding men and women who contributed to painting, drawing, crafts, design of society.

In fashion: Outstanding creators of fashion throughout the ages who contributed to society.

In television, radio, and journalistic forms: Outstanding people who contributed to the development of those communicative forms, past and present (behind the scenes or in public view).

Education is an excellent medium through which to revitalize children's hopes for the future and, through their own efforts, of obtaining what they

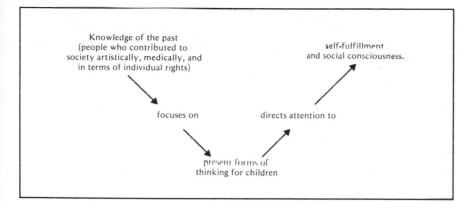

Knowledge of the past
(people who contributed to
society artistically, medically, and
in terms of individual rights)

self-fulfillment
and social consciousness.

focuses on   directs attention to

present forms of
thinking for children

Weaving Past into Present and Creating the Future for Children's Thinking.

Concept
Illustration
3–1

want. Teachers provide the materials and the working setting. The children can respond in kind. The teacher has to help them believe that they can do it. Note Concept Illustration 3–1. It demonstrates the principle of using accomplishments of people of the past to provide examples of models that may be worth emulating. Children need to feel that they have similarities in themselves that were present in those who accomplished unusual feats and discoveries in society.

Teachers who remember their own backgrounds at school often say that a teacher, or several of them, gave them in spirit and encouragement what they needed to feel as though they were "contributing" and significant individuals. Many lawyers and doctors have indicated this in one way or another.

Young children cannot understand the concept of time that reaches far back into history. They can, however, empathize with people, their families, and what the children did or felt. They do not understand the time sequence in biographies in the same way that they will when they are in the middle grades of the elementary school. The observation of holidays that celebrate the existence of people who are visible heroes or heroines of history, however, is within their understanding. The media, magazines, television, newspapers, and special programs bring to their attention as well as that of society's adults, what the feats or accomplishments of celebrated people were.

Young Children's Focus

The teacher has to become aware of the child's perspective in a variety of ways. The sense of history that many adults take for granted is not understood by children in the same way. Abstract concepts of time as an ambiguous something that occurred many years ago, is difficult for the conceptualization of young children. In fact, they consider that their teacher, about twenty-three years old, is old and lived in the "olden days."

The focus of the curriculum for young children must be on topics that accomplish at least two functions: First, the topic brings the children's attention to items, objects, events, people, and resources that have some familiarity to them; and second, it draws them from that point and introduces new concepts. It has been widely accepted that a curriculum must be relevant to the pupils who are exposed to it. One must also be aware that children must learn about people and events beyond their own experiences. Education's purposes for individuals is to broaden awareness and to extend knowledge of the pupils into spheres beyond their immediate contact. This should not be considered contradictory, that children need to be familiar with and also be introduced to things beyond their own environment.

In a given neighborhood, for example, a child may have a library, theaters, stores of various kinds, supermarkets, doctors' and dentists' offices, post offices, bus systems, lumber yards, and other forms of services and facilities. Children can be taught that these services involve money, either to support the facilities or to pay the people (i.e., doctors, nurses, theater operators) who manage those places. The money that people earn in their positions provide them with the means to pay for their food, houses, cars, and so on.

Children can learn about the profit-and-loss system up to a point. They learn that the supermarket clerk has a family that must be supported. Clerks have to pay someone else for things that they buy, too. Children can learn simple ideas about economic theory. They learn in the classroom what a penny, a nickel or dime can buy. These ideas are introduced in social studies units as well as in mathematical lessons. Whenever possible, however, the teacher must provide examples of subject matter principles that arise in "natural" situations of the classroom. When certain products are difficult to buy, or are out of season, children can be taught that scarce commodities become expensive. This is another principle of economics that will be introduced to children again on a more sophisticated level when they are older.

The curriculum in the primary grades is expected to include information that is accurate, simple enough for children in those age categories to understand, and that becomes a foundation for later, and similar, knowledge that will be presented to children in later grades. What children are learning in the earlier grades provides the basis for more complicated levels of skills, facts, and concepts that can be related to less complex and abstract perceptions. Children's learning proceeds with simple facts which themselves become part of the link in a learning chain of events.

The Child's Perspectives

Understanding how different children's experiences are from each other, the teacher knows that many points of view can develop when new information is presented to pupils. *Experiential differences* among people refer to the varied internal and external states that occur among individuals to influence the way they perceive the world. Even if the teacher shows everyone an experiment, an instructional lesson of some sort, or a picture of an object or individual, the children's responses will differ. They bring to the experience a variety of backgrounds and interpretations.

Family experiences, instructional experiences outside of school, extra-curricular activities that some children have, and illnesses affect in a number of ways the children's perceptions of school experiences. Even children in the same family have different psychological experiences from those of their sisters or brothers.

Part of the curriculum for young children includes activities and discussion on ways to solve problems, create new ideas, think independently, discover one's own resourcefulness and abilities, and know how to help others accomplish what they want. Prosocial behavior can be taught in school.[11] When children learn how to help others, their own self-perceptions are enhanced. To be valued by others contributes toward being valued by one's self.

Research on prosocial acts is difficult because of the complexities involved in measurement. It is indicated that a wide variety of behaviors may identify prosocial activity. Sharing what one has, helping someone in distress, risking one's safety for another individual's life, and being altruistic in some way, are forms of prosocial acts, as they are observed. Researchers, however, are trying to determine when an individual does these things without expecting some beneficial returns from doing them. The measurement of prosocial behavior is complicated because "the form and content of acts of caring, sharing, and helping are shaped by a host of antecedents (age, personality characteristics, motivations, capabilities, judgments, ideas, and the immediate contexts encountered . . .) and the intricate interactions among them."[12]

Teachers must help children as much as possible to bolster themselves against behavior in others that hurts their feelings as well as help them understand others and respond to kindness in others. Noting Concept Illustration 3–2 the teacher can see how essential it is to include in the goals of the curriculum a variety of ways to help children achieve solutions to problems that deal, not only with facts and issues, but also with interpersonal decisions and effectiveness in them.

These issues of interpersonal relationships and decisions that deal with courses of action in some activities with children are a form of a lifelong endeavor. If the teacher can help children develop rationales or mini-philosophies that can be used in self-guiding terms, this is a beginning in helping children acquire some "internal rules" that may serve them well. This does not mean that they will be bound by those ideas. It merely gives them some information that they may use if they wish.

One may be able to understand that in the teacher's efforts to help children become more dependable, and to know what their own abilities and skills are, the teacher's own self-concept builds. The efforts of the leader, almost like those of the coach of a team, can become translated into the performance of the players, whose work, in part, reflects the coaching skills. Watching the children one may obtain some ideas regarding the nature of the classroom most of the time.

Children's perceptions of the world need to be encouraged and modi-

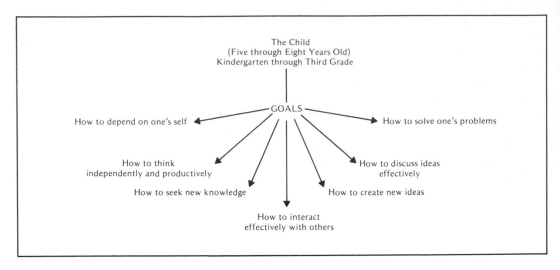

The Child
(Five through Eight Years Old)
Kindergarten through Third Grade

GOALS

How to depend on one's self

How to solve one's problems

How to think
independently and productively

How to discuss ideas
effectively

How to seek new knowledge

How to create new ideas

How to interact
effectively with others

Concept Illustration 3–2   Focusing on Young Children's Needs and Goals in Curriculum Development.

fied. Facts are presented in as clear a way as possible. Concern for children's feelings involves the ability of the teacher to imagine how it feels to be any child at any given moment. To help the children express what they think or feel, requires another set of skills and a complicated reservoir of information that needs updating as new research produces it.[13]

Meanings in children's development involve many experiences associated with concepts, either implied, inferred, or instructed. Symbolism builds on a variety of experiences with language and groups. Schools are excellent places to provide effective learning of subject matter as well as awaken children's perceptions which may be heightened in that context.

The mixed schools in urban areas represent various opportunities for children to learn about each other. As was indicated earlier, the cultural pluralism that prevails in the United States is becoming more evident in the curriculum and is reflective of different policy formulation for schools as well as the teacher's presentation of materials.

Young children do not have problems of adapting to one another's personality styles, typically, when efforts of the school and in the classroom, in particular, are made in that direction. Parents and families of various groups desire at times to be part of a larger culture, to be separate from it, and to be permitted to move in their own directions.[14] Cultural pluralism includes groups that wish to be separate from major events and activities that involve other than their own ethnic or cultural groups; it includes groups that wish to be assimilated into a "mainstream" of American life, as well as groups between those two concepts that wish to retain an identity until their own is strong enough to move into larger society.[15]

Children from families of various groups within a culture that is culturally pluralistic are going to have varied experiences, both at home because of their parents' points of view and at school because of their teachers' points of view. Teachers have to remain informed about various groups in order to understand some of the differences and similarities of hopes, goals, and expectations that pupils have for themselves.

Writers indicate that cultural pluralism can be used to the constructive advantage of a total culture. With federal assistance, and an "opportunity structure"[16] that mediates economic success for various lower-income groups, intergroup relations can progress to the point of involving broader segments of the population in civic opportunities. Communities are taking on greater and perhaps clearer identity than they have ever had in a constructive and socially acceptable perspective. Political strides toward community acceptance attest to this. Leaders of certain groups are sought and "courted" for the acquisition of voting blocs. Community identities have become clearer and stronger with well-articulated voices that advocate clearly defined goals and tasks.

Children are not directly involved in political themes through their own representation of themselves. They are, however, becoming more visible as people who have not been assisted in making decisions for their own best interests. The view is that they have been treated more as property of adults, rather than individuals who move in their own life space, and their decision-making powers have not been used by them, but rather have been taken from them.[17] With young children, this does not suggest the absence of guidance. It urges a different perspective in their regard, however. Vardin and Brody indicate that children have a right to fair treatment, which in itself involves a function of "particular political and social arrangements."[18]

The focus in the curriculum for young children has to be one that instructs them in the use of tools and techniques that are needed for self-expression. With such instruction, rather than having their best interests circumvented, by chance or design, children will have a better chance in knowing how to protect themselves from permitting a pre-emption of self-expression.

As teachers plan the curriculum for children, they must take both the sociological and the psychological perspectives in order to understand the orientation of the children in their classes. Noting Concept Illustration 3–3, one may obtain impressions as to how the conceptualization of children may be approached. They are pupils who come from varied experiential backgrounds, of varied belief systems, of varied financial support systems, and of varied idiosyncratic characteristics and attitudes.

The focus on the children from those perspectives provides greater assurance that the teacher will be aware of variety in the learning styles and preferences of the children. When children's orientations, interests, abilities, skills (as well as their embarrassing problems that make them feel ashamed or guilty are concerned), and other characteristics are known, the teacher can be more of a helpmate in the learning partnership than might otherwise be possible.

Concept Illustration 3–3 shows the significance of considering sociological perspectives as well as the psychological in the development of any curriculum for young children. Sociological perspectives refer to those that are oriented toward group, community, society, culture, nation, country, and world of which an individual is a part. They refer to the norms, rou-

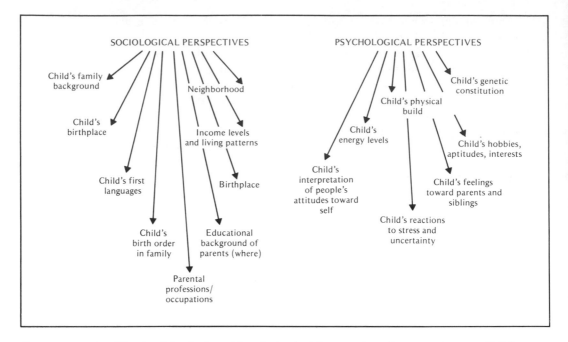

SOCIOLOGICAL PERSPECTIVES

Child's family background

Child's birthplace

Neighborhood

Child's first languages

Income levels and living patterns

Birthplace

Child's birth order in family

Educational background of parents (where)

Parental professions/ occupations

PSYCHOLOGICAL PERSPECTIVES

Child's genetic constitution

Child's physical build

Child's energy levels

Child's hobbies, aptitudes, interests

Child's interpretation of people's attitudes toward self

Child's feelings toward parents and siblings

Child's reactions to stress and uncertainty

**Concept
Illustration
3–3**

The Sociological and Psychological Perspectives Focus on Young Children.

tines, expectations, and reward and punishments systems that are important to any broad context in which an individual is reared.

Psychological perspectives concentrate more on each individual's impressions, style of thinking, learning, and responding to others and to situations. Psychological perspectives are less concerned with probing into group goals, society's perspectives, and group membership in ethnic or cultural groups than with probing into analytical relationships involving the individual's reactivity or response systems. Intra-individual differences are studied so that the individual's feelings and attitudinal changes can be measured and determined to an extent.

The psychologist sometimes perceives group goals or "society's" (or the collective) goals as interfering with the individual's "authentic" feelings and the desire to respond, subsequently resulting in suppression and the development of neuroses in varying degrees of conflict. When individuals are angry, irritated, or self-punishing because of their internal conflicts, to the point of being hampered in their abilities to function effectively, it is often erroneously perceived that external or group behavior stands in the way of self-expression.

The educator must include in a thinking design for the creation of a curriculum both perspectives, the sociological and the psychological, if a comprehensive view of the way a child is part of a family, group, area, or neighborhood is to be accomplished. Neither is complete without the other. The language to which a child has become accustomed, family patterns and expectations for the child's level of responses at any given age or time, affect the child's attitudes and orientation to people outside the home.

Children are often warned, advised, or admonished by parents on what is expected of their behavior at school. This can frighten children. When parents indicate that they expect a child to learn, to enjoy school, and not to fear the teacher, it is obvious in the way the child approaches the teacher and the classroom. These early experiences and expectations of school and the teacher are not defined in any way by school personnel that represents categories of children's messages from parents about the teacher. Often the teacher is not even aware of what the child has heard from the parent and whether the parent has transmitted to the child a fear of the teacher or of others at school.

Parents pass on to their children a heritage of their own memories of experiences at school. Some parents recoil in those images of what school was for them. They ask children to do what they themselves were not able to demonstrate as a pupil, in some cases. They are using, more often than not, their own parents' patterns and manner of admonishing or reprimanding children. Whether the intent at the time was or was not to protect the child from punishment at school, the child obtains from the situation with the parent a feeling that one had better be careful at school to "listen to the teacher," lest punishment result if the warning is not heeded. These are the children who either are afraid to smile or may go to the other extreme, often smiling stiffly and nervously to conceal the discomfort and fear that feel like a rock in their stomachs.

The focus on young children in the curriculum is different from the focus on older ones. There are many levels of understanding among young pupils who are in some cases receiving a "formal" education at minimal beginnings. They are learning how to be part of an organized group (i.e., how to or when one may get out of one's seat to obtain supplies, go to the bathroom, get permission to talk, among other things). The amount of formalization of rules, regulations, and expectations that face a child in the early years at school is great, considering previous experiences at home and neighborhood settings in many cases. The children have to learn simultaneously many new organizational techniques that are familiar to the teacher (who has done the directing often), but for the young pupil hearing them for the first time, the organizational framework is not as simple to understand. It requires time and experience for the child to feel comfortable in learning how to comply with the rules of the classroom. Each teacher, too, has different rules to govern the classroom, even though it is assumed that children are expected to create the rules for self-governance in their own classroom as educators view such policy.

Modes of the past are not always considered the best that should be used in current society. "Education must be more than management [of pupils]. The goal of education is the production of intelligent behavior—the production of autonomous, independent, self-directing, responsible, problem-solving forever-seeking persons."[19] To help children achieve self-respect, self-dignity, and self-worthiness results in admirable codes of teaching.

Helping children acquire self-respect is considered to be a better goal than the use of punishment in affecting certain responses to school work. Punishment is not considered an effective means of guiding the child's thinking toward more positive goals. It is suggested that too often punishment is used by people who do not want to take the time to use more positive or constructive modes of interacting with a child.[20] Helping children learn how to reason and how to perceive their own behavior in a light other than that which needs punishing will be treated in another section of the book, devoted to classroom behavior and subject matter instruction.[21]

Impressions that children have toward the teacher as an authority figure, as a helpmate, as confidante or strict disciplinarian stem from past admonitions from parents, siblings, and what children hear from their own peers or age mates. People's attitudes toward authority as a concept and/or toward authority as a person to be feared affect to a great extent how they conduct themselves in school or society. Those who have shared in creating rules of authority to be followed by others have a different attitude than those who are expected to follow certain rules blindly and obediently.

Thus children at school are obtaining some impressions as to what the concept of authority is, in their own terms as pupils. They are also discovering whether authority is on their "side" (functioning in their own behalf), and for the best interests of many, or whether it is something to foil, deride, and think of ways to undermine or deceive.

If parents have perceived the school as an institution which is superordinate in the sense of making rules for helpless but complying individuals in that context, children may also acquire a negative view of authority. Attitudes toward authority that prompt the child to fear rather than seek protection from supervising figures in school, will restrict rather than free the child in work at school. The child need not be intimidated, but rather can feel protected. Such a pupil who knows that if something in the classroom is not as it should be, will "risk" telling or asking the teacher about it without fear of reprisal. This does not always happen, but teachers need to help children acquire a sense of participation in the classroom in regard to the knowledge of an organizational system of some kind.

Authority as an aspect of education that is geared for children prior to school experiences is not often treated in the literature or research reports of children's perspectives in education. A readiness to respond to what is offered at school is a crucial pivot for children.

In the classroom that encourages freedom of searching, a shy child can be gently prodded to participate. Until the teacher discovers, however, that a child has been made distrustful of new learning contexts, the obstacle inhibiting the child's progress is not known. Parents who are knowledgeable of this blocking in the child's efforts to learn may be able to reassure the child that the teacher, while being an authority figure, is there to help not hinder or punish the child. Children typically think of punishment in the physical sense. Therefore, parents who admonish a child using that form of punishment as a threat are really standing in the way of a child's progress and growth at school and in several other social group areas.

In an effectively functioning curriculum the teacher helps the child become responsible for his/her own learning. Independent pursuits occur throughout the day in a variety of ways in activities geared to the children's successes and challenges. Authority as a concept is mainly involved in the children's awareness that they can receive help for their own learning efforts. As children learn that teachers can be asked to help in seeing that equality prevails among pupils, that children can have equal access to materials and equipment, and that kind treatment pervades classroom routines and behavior, children may be less reticent in actively seeking equitable practices in the classroom. Authority becomes turned inward, in a sense, prompting the child to become responsible for his/her own effectiveness and competence. The child learns that to protect one's self, one has to seek help at times from the teacher. To advance one's knowledge and growth, the teacher is there to help, as one form of authority in the school.

Reciprocity in teacher and pupil behavior is complicated. Both the teacher and the pupil have to cooperate in obtaining satisfying interaction. The teacher, however, sets the tone and atmosphere of the classroom and must be sensitive to children's unexpressed feelings that often hinder progress in learning. The next section involves various factions that influence a selection of activities for the curriculum.

Selectivity, Stability, and Sensitivity for the Curriculum

Even though the needs of young children are emphasized in the development of an effective curriculum, and it may be considered that they are too young to understand the dynamics of society in a limited sense, they must be aware of certain mechanisms that can affect them at school.

Every ten to fifteen years, changes in values occur. The complexities involve choices that individuals must ultimately make. These changes are reflected in society and in the schools, although not at the same pace. At times there is an obvious lag between what happens in places external to the school and what happens in the classroom itself. There are valid reasons for the discrepancy although the dilemmas are not easily solved without more information to illuminate the issues.[22]

Young children are growing up without models representing a former culture that may provide information for the changing perspectives of tomorrow.[23] It has been said that changes are occurring so rapidly that they surpass generational ability to present ideas to the young. For this reason, many educators suggest that children learn how to process information effectively, how to judge wisely, and how to select from among many issues or facts in order to arrive at sensible decisions for action.

A call for the scientific perspective in learning emphasizes that children learn how to make hypothetical statements, such as the "what if" (this happens), then what will the results be? The search is encouraged in the curriculum for questions that evoke new answers that have not yet been heard. Reserving judgment until more information is found and considering many perspectives are elements in scientific thinking. Children need to learn about scientific comprehensiveness in the consideration of ideas.

The teacher who implements a curriculum in which there are various facts, concepts, generalizations, and skills for discovering, measuring, and critically discussing findings is in a better position than teachers of former eras to provide children with broad ranges of approaches to the solution of problems. American society needs those perspectives. The children do, too, if they are to adapt to changes by using more effective tools and techniques to facilitate their thinking.

Educational systems, more often than not, have been approaching—as evidenced in the literature of the past fifteen years, at least—an emphasis on *how* one reaches solutions and on openness of thought (realizing that more than one answer to questions or problems can be correct). This far-reaching approach in education provides a deeper probing, broader searching, and more individualistic emphasis on critical thinking of a scientific nature than was true in the curriculum activities of former years.

Selectivity in arriving at answers requires the use of criteria. Choices that one makes, and the action that one follows after choices are made, require reasons and bases for identifying certain choices as the best ones. Schools have to provide the questions, the criteria, and the processes for arriving at choices. Table 3–1 suggests questions that can be asked of pupils in order to gear them toward seeking multisolutions before they decide on one or two. The purposes of these questions are to stimulate thinking that goes beyond a "yes" or "no" answer. They also create a mind-set that does not seek a rigidly prescribed single correct answer (even though there may be times when that is what the teacher will require).

It is true that the 1970s were a choice-offering decade to young people who realized that commitments might be delayed.[24] Changes in role interpretations of women in contemporary society, changes in the articulation opportunities of various groups in society, awareness of individualistic thinking made available through books, television, and newspapers, as well as movies and the theater (i.e., plays, musicals), have highlighted the numbers of choices open to young adults.

Mental health is affected by one's abilities to make choices that fulfill one's expectations as they are implemented. For this reason, although choices are open, they need also to be leading the individual to an effectively functioning life. Fluidity, remaining uncertain of how to make commitments or choices, and the disposability of objects in a rapidly and unreflective changing society lead toward confusion of identity.[25]

Growth of the self involves learning how to make choices. As was mentioned earlier in this chapter, in reference to Bruner's comments on how the school can prepare children for effectively functioning in their current and future society, children need to learn how to respond to contingencies.[26] Certain subject matter areas[27] lend themselves well to strategies recommended by Bruner and also by Kilpatrick.

With the expectation that technological development will continue to increase and that people will have to learn how to identify their own needs and answers to problems, and that brain functions and research will affect educational processes of the future, the curriculum becomes ever more

Table 3–1 Orientation of Teacher and Students in a Multifaceted Curriculum

Limiting Questions	Productive Multifaceted Questions
1. Is that true or not?	1. Can this be true? Why? In what instances would it not be true? How can we challenge it?
2. Do all writers feel this way? Yes or no?	2. Do writers have similar opinions? Can we know how they think? How? Why? In which instances would this answer be totally wrong?
3. What does the person who says he is "telling it like it is," mean?	3. "Telling like it is" means that _____ (pupil is asked to complete statement). Does one person have special authority to know what reality is? Why? Why not? Do you have knowledge of what reality is? What is the statement really saying?
4. Do most people agree on this? Yes? No?	4. Do almost all people think alike? Yes or no? Why so or why not? Are people the same or different? Why?
5. Do all Americans know what a democratic form of government is?	5. Are all Americans aware of what a democracy means for people, about people, and how it affects their lives? Why or why not? How does it affect them? Do they have to do anything to keep democratic processes working? Can little children help? How?
6. Should communities have health care? Yes? No?	6. What agencies help people in the community when they are sick? How did those agencies get there? Who helped? Where did people get the money for community services that help sick or poor people?
7. Is the English language the only language spoken in America? Yes? No?	7. How many languages do you think are spoken in America? What are some of them? Do you know people who speak more than the English language? Where do they live? Do your friends or relatives expect you to know their language even if it is not English? Is it important to know many languages? Does it help you and other people? Why or why not?

pertinent and significant in its content. It must be sensitive to the future.[28]

Identity, personal involvement, self-concept, critical thinking considerations, and a readiness to perceive ways to impose a problem structure and principles for solving them in a changing environment can provide children with a curriculum that can strengthen their skills as effectively functioning citizens in a society that may differ from the one many know today.

Educators have to consider the age and the maturity levels of young

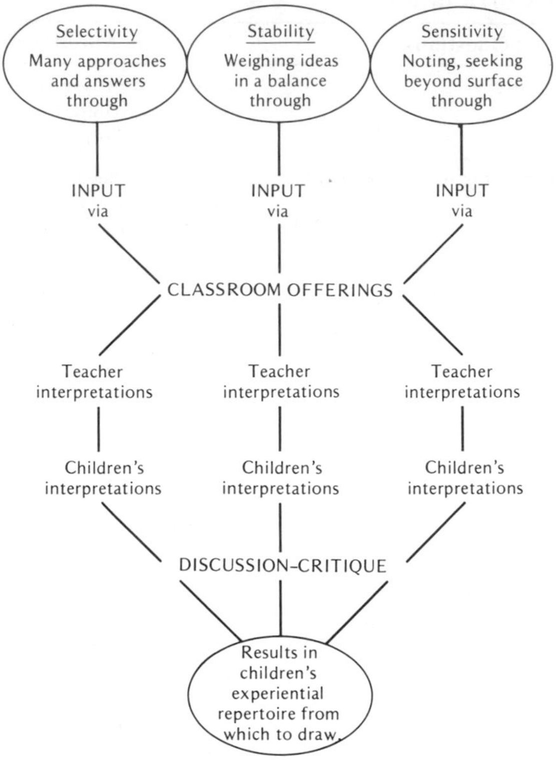
Selectivity
Many approaches and answers through
Stability
Weighing ideas in a balance through
Sensitivity
Noting, seeking beyond surface through
INPUT via
INPUT via
INPUT via
CLASSROOM OFFERINGS
Teacher interpretations
Teacher interpretations
Teacher interpretations
Children's interpretations
Children's interpretations
Children's interpretations
DISCUSSION-CRITIQUE
Results in children's experiential repertoire from which to draw.

Concept Illustration 3–4 Generating Selectivity, Stability, and Sensitivity in Young Children's Learning.

children for whom the curriculum is designed. When children are given activities that prove to be "over their heads" or beyond their readiness for comprehension, the fact should be recognized and those activities supplanted by easier ones that provide preparation for more difficult concepts. If some children, however, are ready to tackle more difficult problems and manifest this in their boredom with specific activities, they need to have experiences that advance their knowledge. Total readiness of a class is not to be expected.

Individually adapted curriculum experiences range from those having the simplest to those having the most difficult concepts and generalizations that need to be learned by children. Each subject matter area has its own technology and strategies recommended as ways to approach an understanding of it.[29]

Concept Illustration 3–4 indicates the many ways that the teacher and children together, give and take, probe and present, share and give critiques, on many ideas in relation to the subject matter presented in any curriculum. This is in keeping with the recommendation of those who are concerned that educators and other adults working in the interests of young children may perceive children's activities and experiences as occurring in a space identity of the children's. Even the subject matter as it is presented is not considered as a total block of information without the responses of children breathing life into its substance.

Children should be encouraged in the selectivity, stability, and sensitivity of an evolving curriculum, to be intuitive, to change the ideas that are presented, and to be aware that they are expected to bring different modes of thought to them. The curriculum in that sense can be perceived as an ongoing technological system that can be altered, that is balanced through the weighing of ideas and their viability, and that promotes an intuitive sensitivity which brings one beyond the data presented or leads one to extrapolate from them. Inferential thought is valuable; children are going to need it more than one might have believed decades ago. The evidence of impending and rapid changes in society warrant us in developing minds that can manipulate and reshape problem areas to make sense for the individuals who must live in different environments.

Society, Politics, and Law

"Natural" impulses of individuals in a population are mediated to some extent by collective rules or guidelines; these rules are created by a society, by its code of law, and by its political systems. It is assumed that people (at least in the American system of government) create their own laws to govern themselves.

Understanding that one grows in a democratic society, teachers and children in the schools assume that a relative degree of freedom of expression should be encouraged. But a question arises regarding freedoms and about our obligations to guarantee to the individual certain inalienable rights. Who permits the freedom? And who sees to it that someone else's freedom is not obstructed by another person's expression aimed at squelching it?

Teachers will be using these concepts in work with children. The crux of the problem lies in preparing material that is appropriate to the children's levels of understanding. This is done, to some extent, by having the children talk about a problem that is real to them after it has been posited by the teacher for demonstration by some pupils in the class.

All the abstract concepts of society as a collective representing a population of individuals in a given region, of politics, which may be perceived as a means through which people design ways of forming their governmental structures, and of law, which represents a codification system of a people and planned for protection of the majority and minority groups, are in their most formal aspects, very difficult for children to understand. They do not understand how these apply to their lives.

As children are reared in American society, they hear about the law in relation to being careful "not to break it." Traffic tickets are one example of children's understanding of what may happen if one violates the law in one's car or as a pedestrian.

In the course of development from infancy to childhood, and from adolescence to adulthood, people are going to learn which violations are more serious than others and how the law relates to them. They will also learn more about the specifics of any given law, if they are in a situation which forces a particular issue that has been translated into an offense of some kind.

The larger the population in any given area, and the more complex a society or culture may be in a variety of ways, the more it is likely that a complicated body of laws will exist to monitor the conduct of people in that area. Issues related to authority, coercion, protection of one's rights, equality, fair access to goods, services, and other elements in a society, and a number of other abstractions related to social justice and social consciousness—all of which are upheld by the people in a society—require time for children to understand. Abstract concepts are among the last that children learn as they develop. They learn about nouns, verbs, adverbs, and adjectives, which can be pointed to in some way and perceived in some objective (often tangible) fashion. Abstractions regarding justice, love of society or people on a broad basis, and other perceptions that are morally oriented beliefs or customs, involve time and associations that are appropriate to those behaviors and observations.

When children experienced with their parents some of the laws that regulated the purchase of gasoline for one's car on certain days, mandating the amounts that could be purchased and the like, they did receive some notions as to how the law can function. When the maximum numbers of miles per hour that could be traveled on an expressway was indicated as 55 instead of 60, a nationwide change was made in a relatively short time. Children can understand specifics in the way those affect them. What is more difficult for them to learn is the information that is indirectly related to the specifics, or not related at all at a given time in their lives.

Political decisions and speeches made in regard to them are not altogether alien to children's understanding; they have heard from parents and siblings about honesty or its opposite in political arenas. Voting time for the election of a president, or for local management, raises many political issues that children can hear people discuss. They obtain impressions of those often very unclear issues. In any case, however, they know that political systems exist and that they are related to "our president," and others in the White House.

Childhood, and Concepts of Society, Politics, and Law

Young children who are part of a specific governmental program planned to enhance their development, fortunately do not perceive themselves as unusual in that respect. They do become aware, however, through interaction with children in environments that differ from their own, that other kinds of neighborhoods exist, neighborhoods which may be better or worse than their own depending on how they compare them.

Children learn through the social studies[30] activities in kindergarten, and in first, second, and third grades what society represents, how the law is involved in governing or regulating society and the people in it, and why laws provide constraints on people's behavior in several ways. Teachers have to introduce social studies units, which themselves have many abstract concepts in them and from which children will acquire information (through direct experience in specifically related activities).

Children learn about society, politics, and law in an informal and a more formalized way at school through the curriculum that is created for them at their developmental age levels. It is true that those topics are sophisticated conceptualizations and not easy for young children to comprehend fully. When they have opportunities, however, to become involved in discussions on communities, how people pay taxes to provide money for the support of libraries, roads, safety agencies and the like, they are at least acquiring some elementary concepts upon which later more complex ideas can be built.

Even teachers have various views about society, politics, and law when they enter teaching. Unless one has been exposed in some way to a formal curriculum in any one of those areas, it is difficult to have an academically organized structure of political science, of sociology, or of law that is significant to use with children. Each teacher who does not have an emphasis of study in those areas has to acquire information that is accurate and then has to refine and adapt it to create activities for young children's programs.[31]

Each curriculum, and each activity in it, carries many assumptions regarding the content that is considered most important to children's development. One of the most important issues is that content be accurate in fact and in its manner of presentation. It is easy to understand, therefore, how difficult the social studies area of instruction may become. It deals with differences of opinion (which are valued) not only in popular understanding but in federal documents protecting the right of people to disagree.

Among other essential skills for children to obtain from a viable curriculum dealing with society, social issues, political conflict, and varieties of law that are focused on social justice, are techniques that can help them sustain a reasonable position or academic argument on a given issue. Children need help in learning how to defend an idea. They need to learn how to argue the merits of a given point, to allow others to present their ideas, and not to become hostile in the process.

The social studies offer the opportunity to hold many discussions led by the teacher's discerning guidelines that help the children conduct themselves in terms of formalized debating. These discussions can take place at the most elementary levels. The teacher helps children separate information and ideas from the people who are giving them. Adults find this difficult, admittedly. This does not mean that children should not be given the opportunity to differentiate between an argument on an academic issue and an interpersonal disagreement with one's friend or classmate.

Concept Illustration 3–5 indicates changing images that occur from childhood to adolescence and to adulthood in which challenges to earlier

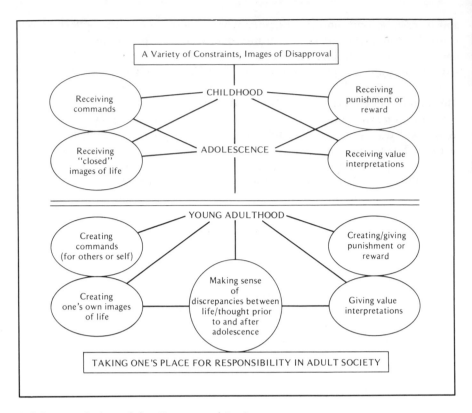

Concept Illustration 3–5

Adult Knowledge of the Concept of Society.

views may occur. Education is expected to affect changes in people. It is assumed that with new information an individual is willing to open for self-inspection formerly held perceptions of social constraints.

Teachers who interact with young children are themselves going through changes that involve recent challenges to their own views. They can keep an open mind when they work with children. They can help children through reasoning processes that pupils are just beginning to use in the primary grades.

Curriculum Reflections of Society, Politics and Law

As teachers' experiences in society reflect opportunities to view changing perspectives in an increasingly technological and multipluralistic society, they influence what and how children will be taught in the classroom. In this sense of change, and in a need to realign one's thinking with different political ideologies that arise with changes of people in offices at high federal levels, teachers are going to affect the curriculum, perhaps not directly, but indirectly.

Energy problems, ecology and imbalances, and varied impressions regarding the use of nuclear or solar energies introduce issues that warrant acquiring the best and the most information possible so that people are able to make intelligent decisions about their lives or about a voting process. Teachers who hope to obtain accurate data no doubt have to have a commitment that will urge them to spend the time to find what they need. Teachers are limited, to an extent, in shaping the curriculum that they use with children. Guidelines are usually given to them by a school system. In some cases, however, school administrators will allow some teachers a greater leeway in teaching what they select as appropriate ideas for the children.

Public schools that are part of a larger school system are at times held to certain county- or city-wide recommendations from a central office. This control varies with school systems in any state. Public laws hold public schools to certain legislative mandates to a greater degree than private schools are expected to offer a given curriculum format or content.

Issues that are sensitive to political crises, energy, or law are not easily approached in the curriculum. Much in that approach depends on individual teachers who have the courage to present in ways that are not blatantly offensive information that does not sound defensive, but rather constructive and academic. Opinions are held aside as much as possible.[32] The schools and teachers are subjects of study among social scientists, who analyze them as part of a bureaucratic structure of society. Some sociologists suggest that different organizational structures of schools could affect the learning of students in those schools. As perceived by some social scientists, too little change has occurred throughout the years in the curriculum and the way it is taught.

Quite as important as *what* is taught in the schools, is *how* it is taught, by whom, and in *what particular organization of the school*. Sociologists are concerned that not enough is known about relationships between the teacher and the teaching role, nor the structural properties of the school as an organization and the patterns of influence in the classroom.[33] Reasonable questions are asked regarding various differences that can be found among schools, the way children learn, and the way teachers use levels of coercion to conduct a classroom.

Among the more important questions that intrigue sociologists is one that asks what kind of social context in the classroom can produce better learning products in the students. This answer is anticipated in examining the ways that social organizations of schools (and differences among them) affect various kinds of student behavior in given organizational contexts.

An interesting translation of learning occurs between the sophisticated levels and abstractions that teachers conceptualize and the formulation they must make to transmit understandable knowledge to elementary school children. This, in itself, places the teacher in a posture of becoming another pupil. Although not evacuating the teaching role, the teacher psychologically has to adapt a conceptual framework that is more compatible with, or better related to, the child's level of development.

The personal changes in perceiving subject matter content and form that occur within the teacher's intellectual framework affect, to some extent, the way the children will receive it. Teachers conceptualize differently at thirty years of age what they learned at twenty years of age. Their own

Table 3–2 Components of a Curriculum on Concepts of Society, Politics, and Law

Changes Throughout a Lifetime of What Society Is, What Politics Are, and What Law Is		
(1) What society is from the perspective of a child	(1) What politics are from the perspective of a child	(1) What law is from the perspective of a child
(2) What society is from the perspective of an early adolescent (13–16 years old)	(2) What politics are from the perspective of an early adolescent (13–16 years old)	(2) What law is from the perspective of an early adolescent (13–16 years old)
(3) of a later adolescent (17–19 years old)	(3) of a later adolescent (17–19 years old)	(3) of a later adolescent (17–19 years old)
(4) What society is from the perspective of a young adult (teacher and others of similar age)	(4) What politics are from the perspective of a young adult (teacher and others of similar age)	(4) What law is from the perspective of a young adult (teacher and others of similar age)
Individual change in thought about global concepts that guide adult lives		

experiences in some personal and academic spheres bring changes to their perceptions of intellectual data. The children may benefit from these changes if the opportunities arise for appropriate instruction in those areas in which the teacher has gained greater sophistication of knowledge.

Noting Table 3–2 on components of a curriculum related to concepts of society, politics, and law, one may observe the changes that must occur throughout the lifetime of an individual who hears, listens, learns, and adapts to new information on any of those subjects. One must realize that as one matures from early childhood to adolescence to young adulthood, the degree of helplessness perceived from the perspective of an individual in society, part of politics and subject to codes of law, must to some extent become minimized. Greater knowledge and understanding of the dynamics of society help the individual to reason why certain elements work as they do. As persons who, in a sense, represent a highly technological society and who should be presenting information to children in the best way possible on how that society works, teachers must have the necessary information and updated concepts about it.

Children need help, as do teachers, in demystifying concepts that one grows up with from childhood. The prevailing views of society have to be related to the individual's psychological and educational framework of thought and conceptualization. Teachers have to help themselves and children translate everyday occurrences in terms of how they are part of a collective, a group of people or society. The "we" and the "they" are all a part of the same society, one that contributes to people's sense of pride and also to a sense of shame.[34]

Through a curriculum that attempts to represent society and the way children can be aware of their own relationships to it, teachers can identify major concepts as structural elements in children's conceptual frameworks. Politics as a sphere of argumentation seeking power to influence people regarding the direction that decision making may take, can be presented as part of a system. Mechanisms in any system are used to the advantage or disadvantage of groups or of people.[35]

The teacher will be pressed in a variety of situations to provide explanations for events in answer to children's questions about them. In some cases, children may be hearing conflicting views from friends, families, or nonfamiliar people. Some answers may relate to moral issues; some may affect ethnic or cultural perceptions of an event; and some may involve the teacher's own political impressions. In any event, the teachers have to perceive their own roles as individuals who have a professional obligation to perform as honestly as possible as that honesty relates to intellectual, academic subject matter. The teacher's directive has to come from giving the child information that can be used in his/her intellectual and academic fund of knowledge. Teachers have to be able, although it is very difficult, to learn how to separate or distinguish in their own minds between the deeply personal and the academic content of a slightly more objective type.

The manner in which information is given also affects children's impressions. When a teacher seems to overreact or appears angry or upset about a question or answer, a child may sense discomfort, or that something is being concealed. Very few studies have been conducted to find out what children say to their parents about school content or how the comments are related to the teacher's emotional levels when discussing any issue, moral or otherwise, thus insufficient evidence of any systematic nature is available.

As mentioned earlier in this section,[36] more information is needed to extrapolate the meaning and relationships between the organizational structure of the school and the manner in which children learn. Can the personal qualities of the individual in a teaching role be analyzed as distinguishable from the structural elements of the teaching role itself and how that role relates to the remainder of the school's total organization outside the teacher's classroom? These questions are not posed as challenges; they are information-seeking and analytical for the purposes of greater enlightenment on how schools work and how teachers function in them.

With greater forms and numbers of technological information systems, it seems more likely that finer analytical details can be extrapolated. Teachers should be able to benefit from these data and inferences. In the final analysis, it is hoped that children will be able effectively to learn more information and that which is essential to their well-being in a highly complicated society.

Children enjoy finding answers to a mystery as well as they enjoy games. Teachers often capitalize on this quality of search or discovery. Knowledge of techniques for teaching need to be supported by the data themselves that children will need in a rapidly changing world. It is possible to present information in a manner that is intriguing and in which children enjoy the search for meaning when they have a teacher who perceives the impetus for learning in a similar manner.

It is important that children understand their society and its dynamics (through the creation of mechanisms such as political systems and law), even when those systems represent complicated or sophisticated concepts. These concepts can be brought to the level of children's understanding when the teacher observes the children's thinking and behavior and influences impressions as to what they are able to comprehend. Several writers indicate the need for children to be able to articulate their views, difficulties, and anxieties but the children may need assistance in doing so. Child advocacy, family development, legal perspectives of children's rights in society, and ways to help people help themselves within a morally sound and legally sophisticated framework in society—all topics of interest to researchers and other writers—attest to children's needs to have the perspectives recommended in this chapter included in the teaching curriculum. Such perspectives would truly be triperspective in the capacity to consider several structural qualities to be implemented in behalf of teachers, parents, and children.

Writers who view children's needs and those of the family as being neglected in a large network (such as a complex, industrial society), suggest that an intermediate form of system be conceptualized to help ameliorate the problem.[37] They seek to identify "institutions that have been disregarded, sometimes even to the verge of destruction, but that still continue to be of primary importance in the life of ordinary American citizens."[38] The researchers term the institutions (of family, neighborhood, church, voluntary organizations) "mediating structures."[39]

Public policies are often made without the input of ordinary men and women to whom those policies mean and matter the most. It is suggested that a new paradigm for allowing the concerns of the people (poverty-stricken, low-income groups and the like, and voluntary associations) to be heard, be created in the form of mediating structures.[40] "Pluralism means the lively interaction among inherited particularities and, through election, the evolution of new particularities."[41] If the distinctive differences among individuals in the mediating structure are not sustained, through voices of people in the structure, then public policy is not serving the pluralistic society very well.

Public interest in the family is not intended to homogenize the individual differences existing in institutions such as the family. Those differences should be sustained. It is suggested that weak individuals, or uprooted people from vulnerable families, often unfortunately seek and submit uncritically to authoritarian concepts, views, or leaders and are "ideal recruits for authoritarian movements inimical to democratic society."[42] Such vulnerability needs to be protected. Individualism needs to be emphasized.

The educational system is one of the key factors in a family's recognition as a respectable component of society or the social structure. Berger and Neuhaus express concerns that the family in large systems has in large part been disfranchised.[43] One of their concerns is that the way of life of millions of American children and parents in lower-income segments of the population is often disparaged, and that such disparagement ultimately leads to an implicit self-contempt in the children for themselves. This disparagement may not be intentional (one would hope); however, it occurs, nevertheless, regardless of well-intended instruction. The researchers indicate that they do not suggest in this view, that "the lower-class child is being culturally raped when taught correct English."[44] They are referring to many other subtle ways that children in school sense criticism of a negative nature pertaining to their own families or parents.

From information currently offered by the research and writings of Keniston,[45] of Berger and Neuhaus,[46] of Berger and Callahan,[47] of Bruner,[48] of Vardin and Brody,[49] of Goodman and Marx,[50] and of others concerned about the social system and its functions, as well as for enlightenment of how the systems work, it is obvious that as educators we have much work to do in formulating a viable curriculum for children of today, children who will be the adults of a very closely approaching tomorrow. Among them there will need to be the informed and supportive leaders and informed participants of their own adult society. As their teachers and as adults concerned about the well-being of children and the world in which they need to function, now as well as in the future, we recognize that the task remains in our hands.

SUMMARY

This chapter was concerned with issues related to the development of a curriculum for children in the early grades of the elementary school. In that frame of reference, the issues, problems, and techniques that affect content in young children's programs at school are in part the substance of society, and of daily life in that societal context.

Writers indicate that in a rapidly increasing technological society, it is necessary that children and parents know how to define themselves in relation to their world. Children need a curriculum that is individualistic to help them identify who they are and what they are in what can become a very impersonalized world.

Teachers must be aware of their own obligations to grow and to realign their thinking in an adult world in a way that should be different from the conceptualizations they had of society, politics, and law when they were children.

Children in today's world are perceived differently as part of a large social system that attempts to be sensitive to the cultural pluralism perspectives, and that should sustain particular differences among people rather than homogenizing society. Children are considered as having their own spatial world made up of friends, school, and other nonschool or home environments, rather than being considered as properties of adults. It is suggested that children need to learn of choices, of effective means for articulating anxieties, and of ways of requesting help when needed. Rather than thinking of them as custodial objects in the space of an adult world, we should be teaching them more about the socially learned or acceptable "scientific" ideas that are open to them.

Teachers, like their pupils, need the updated knowledge that is becoming more accessible each day, particularly in the social sciences, in genetics, physiology, in brain functioning, and in political interpretations of a culturally pluralistic society. The depth and breadth of knowledge and facts that researchers disclose should provide the best curriculum facts, concepts, skills, techniques, and generalizations in the subject matter areas taught in the elementary schools.

Schools have taken for granted that certain subject matter areas belong in the curriculum, as may be observed in course guidelines. More current information that closes the gap between new knowledge and past instructional guidelines has to be recognized by curriculum writers.

Too often, people confuse the sophisticated knowledge and conceptualizations of higher educational research with ideas that are susceptible only to adult minds. More attention must be paid to the manner in which young children learn about societal concepts so that such instruction can be understood at early childhood levels. Higher educational information from the social sciences can be translated effectively through social studies units transmitted to young children. With the support of valid data to be used in the development of a curriculum for young children, teachers who understand children and who understand, as well, the concepts of social sciences and other subject matter areas, will be able to meet the challenges that face teachers and children in the 1980s.

TOPICS FOR DISCUSSION

1. Collect three courses of study (dated between 1960 and 1980) from school systems or curriculum libraries. Note differences between past and present guidelines for early childhood education. How has the focus of subject matter instruction and curriculum development changed in the last twenty years? Do you think the changes represent an improvement in educational practices for the benefit of children? Why? Why not?

2. Select five children from your neighborhood or from classrooms. They should be in the five- to eight-year-old age range. Ask them six questions that will give you impressions of what their awareness is of politics, law, society, or social problems. Note age differences and ask questions that are appropriate to their age levels. Gear the questions down to specifics that veer closer to the children's direct experiences so that they may understand your questions.

3. Plan a mini-unit that could be taught to six-year-old children (first grade) in which they could learn about community problems and the way people in the community could go about solving them. Problems could be focused on obtaining a library, a hospital, a health clinic for children, or a recreational center for families.

4. Ask four teachers of children four through eight years old where or from whom and how they developed their views/concepts of authority in the forms of people, institutions, objects, or symbols.

5. Find three objects or photographs that represent for you impressions of society, politics, or law when you were in your childhood years. Discuss each of them and why you remember them as evidence of your ideas at the time. Have some of these impressions carried over to the present for you? Why? Or why not?

6. Observe six-year-old children in three different classrooms. Note their ideas on society, politics, and law. What did the teachers do or say to help them articulate their concepts? How would you have elaborated on the teacher's work? Do you think that children generally have wholesome ideas that can be productive in their later years where concepts of society, politics, and law are concerned?

7. How do parades and major celebrated public events affect children's perceptions of a visible or real society of people? Give specific examples.

8. Cut out photographs or illustrations from magazines or newspapers that can be used as a collage that represents clothing, fads, recreational forms, dance, music, and art of various historical periods in our history. Arrange them in layers that vertically or horizontally show how you perceive the chronological events from past to present of different historical perspectives of American society. This could be done with children in the classroom. You choose the major objectives that would pictorially show how social changes influence the way people dress, decorate themselves and their society's environment, and participate in fads, novelties, and entertainment.

9. Interview four principals of elementary schools on the changes they have seen in educational practices and curriculum orientations of the past twenty years (in their own lives or in educational books and journals).

10. Discuss the concept of "mediating structure" recommended by Berger and Neuhaus, and by Berger and Callahan.

NOTES

1. Hilda Taba, *Curriculum Development* (New York: 1962), p. 67.
2. Ibid.
3. Ibid., p. 175.
4. Robert J. Havighurst and Daniel U. Levine, *Society and Education,* 5th ed., (Boston: Allyn, 1979), p. 477.
5. Taba, op. cit., p. 174. She recommends active approaches to the curriculum in which one may take a posture toward learning that is critical, unaccepting, and challenging.
6. Havighurst and Levine, op. cit., p. 545. At least three areas of change in the social structure affect teaching and the way the classroom will function: one area relates to the emphasis on education as a lifelong process; a second involves the need to help children become action-type learners; the third involves intergroup understanding.
7. Jerome Bruner, *The Relevance of Education* (New York: Norton, 1973), p. 104.
8. Havighurst and Levine, op. cit., p. 5. As we move from an era (1900 to 1970) of a youth-oriented society, one of very unequal income distribution, and of dwindling energy resources or reserves, it is expected that more of the population will be involved in service-oriented jobs or professions, will be oriented toward the values of a thirty-five- to sixty-year-old group, and the "lowest fifth of the population will secure a higher proportion of the total income of the society."
9. Alexander Frazier, *Adventuring, Mastering, Associating: New Strategies for Teaching Children* (Washington, D.C.: Assoc. for Supervision and Curriculum Development, 1976).
10. Havighurst and Levine, op. cit., p. 545.
11. Paul Mussen and Nancy Eisonberg-Berg, *Roots of Caring, Sharing, and Helping* (San Francisco: Freeman, 1977), p. 3. The definition of prosocial behavior, as the researchers use it in their study, includes "actions that are intended to aid or benefit another person or group of people without the actor's anticipation of external rewards."
12. Ibid., p. 13.
13. See information on social cognition in Chapter 2 of this text.
14. Havighurst and Levine, op. cit., p. 459. Groups such as the Amish, Hutterites, and Seventh Day Adventists often prefer that they be permitted to pursue their own patterns of life, finding them superior to the "mainstream" in society.
15. Ibid., p. 459.
16. Ibid., p. 477.
17. Patricia A. Vardin and Ilene N. Brody, Editors, *Children's Rights: Contemporary Perspectives* (New York: Teachers College, 1979), p. 11.
18. Vardin and Brody, ibid., p. 12. See also Jack C. Westman, *Child Advocacy* (New York: Free Press, 1979) p. xv. The study conducted by the Carnegie Council on Children, chaired by Kenneth Keniston, discloses analytical data and interpretations that point out the need to view children's development in the parent-child, government-family relation-

ships in a manner different from that of the past. *All Our Children,* by Keniston and The Carnegie Council on Children, focuses on government, families, and the well-being of children in the process of learning to articulate effective planning. The report is published by Harcourt, New York, 1977. Families are seen as needing assistance in some cases, but without having their prerogative for choices taken from them. This view is also supported by Peter L. Berger and Richard John Neuhaus, in their book, *To Empower People,* published by the American Enterprise Institute for Public Policy Research, in Washington, D.C., 1977.

19. Arthur W. Combs, *Myths in Education* (Boston: Allyn, 1979), p. 135.
20. Ibid., p. 132.
21. Comments on modes of classroom interaction will be made later in this text in sections dealing with subject matter instruction. Discipline, classroom management of routines, materials, traffic flow in the classroom, and the teacher's manner of giving directions, distributing materials for instruction, and general philosophic attitudes toward children's learning and self-help are relevant to discussions on sanctions for children in the classroom and modes of achieving favorable self-concepts.
22. Taba, op. cit., p. 54. The rapidity of technological change in a culture is absorbed through the environment and various artifacts; the social institutions, however, in regard to values, attitudes, and behavioral changes, lag behind the advances. Conflicts that occur among institutions and individuals because of these inconsistencies between an advanced technology and human behavioral values are common in Western industrial societies.
23. Ibid., p. 55.
24. William Kilpatrick, *Identity and Intimacy* (New York: Delacorte, 1975), p. 43.
25. Ibid., p. 9. He suggests that a future shock mentality and attitudes toward mobility and restlessness generate in people an accelerated need for novelty (in people and things). He suggests that identity confusion among people is in part a result of their unwillingness to arrive at choices and to make commitments which follow with an ability to sustain those commitments and choices.
26. Bruner, op. cit., p. 104. He further suggests that children be helped in finding problems which are much like puzzles that can be put together, that is, children should find the appropriate puzzle form to impose on the manner of approaching "a trouble" of some sort.
27. This topic will be discussed in the next part of the book, which presents subject matter areas that children experience at school.
28. John U. Michaelis, Ruth H. Grossman, and Lloyd F. Scott, *New Designs for Elementary Curriculum and Instruction,* 2nd ed., (New York: McGraw-Hill, 1975), p. 450. They indicate, too, that with an increasing population and automation, people will need to attain self-identification countering an impersonal world. They recommend that "ethnic heritage studies, bilingual-bicultural education, and career education" can be used in the curriculum to help children achieve positive self-concepts and individuality. P. 450.
29. Ibid., p. 333. They suggest that a broad range of strategies of teaching are involved in the instruction of social studies. Problem solving, inquiry approaches, decision making, and development of major ideas are among the strategy type models that can be used with children to stimulate a variety of modes in thinking.
30. Social studies involve several social science disciplines, from which concepts and generalizations are drawn and used as the substance for activities offered to children in the early grades. These will be discussed in a later chapter.
31. Bruner, op. cit., p. 100. Pedagogical practices involve certain assumptions. Bruner indicates that pedagogical theory is different from (and not as neutral as) scientific theory. He sees it more as a political theory, because it makes certain assumptions about a consensus in society. In any case, he suggests that "The psychologist or educator who formulates pedagogical theory without regard to the political, economic, and social setting of the educational process courts triviality and merits being ignored in the community and in the classroom."
32. Phillip C. Schlechty, *Teaching and Social Behavior* (Boston: Allyn, 1976), p. viii. Schlechty suggests that in times of tension, faculty do not take on the characteristics of intellectual communities, but rather of hostile camps of people.
33. Ibid., p. 5.
34. Lou Benson, *Images, Heroes, and Self-Perceptions* (Englewood Cliffs, N.J.: Prentice-Hall,

1974), p. 106. Humankind has from its earliest evidence of existence viewed the world in terms of good or bad, evil or virtuous. Evil is attributed to other people, according to Benson, rather than to one's self. It is because of the fear of being considered evil that one sees it in other people. He suggests that it is important to understand that human nature includes many kinds of qualities, from those that make one proud to those that do not.

35. Norman Goodman and Gary T. Marx, *Society Today*, 3rd ed. (New York: Random, 1978), p. 414. "Almost any social relationship may be characterized by competition for control of resources and of others' behavior. This struggle as it takes place on the level of the social system—private corporations, public bureaucracies, and especially, government— is known as politics."

36. The work of Schlechty poses many questions in regard to this topic.

37. Brigitte Berger and Sidney Callahan, Editors, *Child Care and Mediating Structures* (Washington, D.C.: American Enterprise Institute for Public Policy Research, 1979), p. 1.

38. Ibid., p. xii.

39. Ibid.

40. Peter L. Berger and Richard John Neuhaus, *To Empower People* (Washington, D.C.: American Enterprise Institute for Public Policy Research, 1979), p. 28. Mediating structures are defined as *those institutions standing between the individual in his private life and the large institutions of public life.*" The authors are concerned that mediating structures such as family, neighborhood, church, and voluntary associations, will not be heard in public policy formulations unless a new paradigm for their voices is created.

41. Berger and Neuhaus, op. cit., p. 44.

42. Ibid., p. 20.

43. Ibid., p. 21.

44. Ibid.

45. Kenneth Keniston, *All Our Children* (New York: Harcourt).

46. Berger and Neuhaus, op. cit.

47. Berger and Callahan. op. cit.

48. Bruner, op. cit.

49. Patricia A. Vardin and Ilene N. Brody, Editors, *Children's Rights* (New York: Teachers College, 1979), 182 pp.

50. Goodman and Marx, op. cit., 592 pp.

SELECTED REFERENCES

BENSON, LOU. *Images, Heroes, and Self-Perceptions*. Englewood Cliffs, N.J.: Prentice-Hall, Inc., 1974. 434 pp.

BERGER, BRIGITTE, and SIDNEY CALLAHAN. *Child Care and Mediating Structures*. Washington, D.C.: American Enterprise Institute for Public Policy Research, 1979. 84 pp.

BERGER, PETER L., and RICHARD JOHN NEUHAUS. *To Empower People*. Washington, D.C.: American Enterprise Institute for Public Policy Research, 1977. 45 pp.

BRUNER, JEROME. *The Relevance of Education*. New York: W. W. Norton & Company, Inc., 1973. 175 pp.

COMBS, ARTHUR W.. *Myths in Education*. Boston: Allyn & Bacon, Inc., 1979. 240 pp.

FRAZIER, ALEXANDER. *Adventuring, Mastering, Associating: New Strategies for Teaching Children*. Washington, D.C.: Association for Supervision and Curriculum Development, 1976. 138 pp.

GOODMAN, NORMAN, and GARY T. MARX. *Society Today*, 3rd ed. New York: Random House, Inc., 1978. 592 pp.

HAVIGHURST, ROBERT J., and DANIEL U. LEVINE. *Society and Education*, 5th ed. Boston: Allyn & Bacon, Inc., 1979. 617 pp.

KENISTON, KENNETH. *All Our Children*. The Carnegie Council on Children. New York: Harcourt Brace Jovanovich, Inc., 1977. 255 pp.

KILPATRICK, WILLIAM. *Identity and Intimacy*. New York: Delacorte Press, 1975. 262 pp.

MICHAELIS, JOHN U., RUTH H. GROSSMAN, and LLOYD F. SCOTT. *New Designs for Elemen-*

tary Curriculum and Instruction, 2nd ed. New York: McGraw-Hill Book Company, 1975. 482 pp.

MUSSEN, PAUL, and NANCY EISENBERG-BERG. *Roots of Caring, Sharing, and Helping.* San Francisco: W. H. Freeman and Company, Publishers, 1977. 212 pp.

SCHLECHTY, PHILLIP C. *Teaching And Social Behavior.* Boston: Allyn & Bacon, Inc., 1976. 333 pp.

TABA, HILDA. *Curriculum Development.* New York: Harcourt Brace Jovanovich, Inc., 1962. 529 pp.

VARDIN, PATRICIA A., and ILENE N. BRODY, Editors. *Children's Rights.* New York: Teachers College Press, 1979. 182 pp.

WESTMAN, JACK C. *Child Advocacy.* New York: Free Press, a Division of Macmillan Publishing Co., Inc., 1979. 431 pp.

Priorities in Communication: Helping Children Express Themselves

Prerogatives for Language Expression

Many people tend to take for granted the skills developed for the expression of one's thoughts and ideas through language. Teachers, parents, and care-givers are responsible for teaching children a complicated structure of thoughts, ideas, words, grammatical structure, and the meanings that are associated with all of those concepts. Adults who are concerned for the well-being of young children can rapidly become aware of children's attempts to express themselves.

Functional language that has to be used to ask for items in a store, to give information about where one lives, a telephone number, a street address, and a myriad of essential facts that help people in emergency situations, is among the first that children will learn. Teachers and parents are aware that this form of language is a lifeline. Children need to be able to understand significant messages and they need to be able to give them well. Adults who are typically accustomed to habits of language forget how new language is to children.

Aesthetic, expressive, and creative language as it bursts forth from children requires less monitoring by adults for correct grammar, sentence construction, and appropriate vocabulary meaning than does academic work. Adults should have a sensitive ear for children's expressions. Communication (or assistance in it) does not work unless an appreciative listener is involved to let the child know how (s)he is progressing.

From Infancy to School Years

Babies with normal hearing can sense immediately the sounds around them. Parents can, if they wish, easily observe their infants and the responses they make in gurgles, sighs, odd noises from the respiratory system, nose, and other parts of the body. Effective hearing shapes the child's abilities in terms of the receptor's skills in adapting to the sounds and noises of the environment. As meanings develop in association with those sounds or noises, the child learns how language functions to mediate one's behavior with others.

From birth, the child is able to note sounds, as demonstrated in research.[1] What those sounds mean, however, will develop from the infant's experiences with care-givers and others in the environment. Care-givers are able to detect the meaning of the child's sounds.[2] In that sense, the infant is affecting the behavior and activity of the care-giver, as well as the other way around.

Language development, expression of the self, hearing sounds or voices, unpleasant or pleasant noises—are all part of the child's incoming indicators of an environment that will yield millions of items of information. From among the variety, depth, and breadth of those sounds, the baby will select things that will have meaning relative to its own organism and mental development.[3]

The infant's entire body is in motion, receiving sensory images and sounds from the surroundings. Within a few days, however, the infant is able to show responses by a movement of the head, mouth, eyes, in the direction of sounds, movement, and smells as well. This combination of reactions facilitates beginning skills in language and in personal expression. Fortunately each human being who has healthy responses is equipped for self-protection and growth. The infant grows; the environment and the people in it vary in terms of how the baby will be cared for in nourishing growth.

The complexities involved in the human being's need to be the initiator in self-growth belie the writing that attempts to simplify explanations of the process. Adults must know how to help expression of language in the infant's repertoire of experiences. Opportunities arise in the usual course of the day when parents are feeding, bathing, playing with or dressing the baby. Many years ago, the process of learning language was not emphasized as one that had an important place in the home. The almost natural effects of it practiced by many babies in the crib, when crawling, bathing, or eating made it appear as something no one was doing anything to foster. Yet, without being aware, many parents were automatically or intuitively doing what they enjoyed in their interaction with infants. Talking, cooing, and singing softly to them attracted attention from the baby. Eyes were fixated on the parent's (or parents') face(s). Babies were observing mouths, eyes, chins, cheeks of the parent. Responses to sounds were being made.

While children are active in the process of their own language development, parents, teachers and other care-givers must be equally active. Since the 1950s, American educators have been increasingly concerned about the child's learning to read effectively. As it became known in the United States that too large a proportion of people were not able to read at even minimal levels, educational leaders began to accept the burden of responsibility for this lack.

Researchers studied reasons for the low levels of reading scores among Americans. A seriousness of purpose took hold. Educators have for many years remained concerned about identifying better ways than those of the 1950s for increasing the students' reading skills. Materials, motivation, psychological characteristics of learners at school, teaching styles, and other aspects of the reading process and teaching have been examined.

Diagnoses of reading problems are also a significant part of young children's instruction.[4] Although children's development is also perceived as a trial-and-error process, there are recognizable differences within and among children that signal early problems. Teachers have to know how to respond to and identify problems and to implement the solutions for them when necessary.

Before children are able to respond effectively to reading instruction, they have to have had many successful experiences in language usage. This does not mean that children who have had difficulty cannot be taught to read. It means that typically in the public school setting, with large classes, some children who have problems in language development may need added and more concentrated help in learning to read.

Language development is part of the reading process which begins at home when children start to symbolize sounds as a part of their vocabulary and speech. Although several researchers are defining the way thought, speech, and other aspects of language development occur many answers are still left unchallenged, and new problems are emerging in regard to the language development of young children.[5]

The following sections on the ways that children learn how to express themselves at home and at school will proceed from the point of view of needing to hear (listen), speak (produce sounds), read, and write—aspects of human development. As listening to someone speak is among the first elements in knowing what is significant to any human group, children's awareness of words, sounds, sentences, meaning, and its relationship to objects and obtaining what one needs/wants will be discussed first. Following that will be oral development, expressing, pronouncing, saying, announcing, speaking, and demonstrating one's ideas in the use of speech. A third and fourth section will concentrate on discussion and some activities related to the instruction of reading, a complicated process at best, and on the equally complex act of writing, of putting down on paper, in societally acceptable symbols and words, the ideas or needs that facilitate the human being's functioning in his/her own social group as well as those of other people.

Children Listen

As parents talk to their children, language is heard and repeated by the new family member. A great proportion of language spoken in the home is spoken automatically, that is, it is hardly considered instructional for the child. But many parents discover after their children begin to attend school that their own roles in their children's language learning were far more crucial than they themselves had considered them to be.[6]

Language instruction at school differs from language usage at home in that the school program has a regularly sequenced and organized plan for the children's instruction. Children are placed into a context of organized expectations; the organization is related to the subject matter, rather than to meaning as it is in a child's day when language functions in the way it usually does at home. Parents' use of language when they want to give a message, directions, or explanation emerges as a "more natural" function of language than school instruction. The organization of language instruction, in its more formalized sense, the language occurring within subject matter periods, is based on sequential development of children's abilities.

Children are hearing, in normal processes of learning; however they do not hear the same things that adults hear. The work that researchers have done, raising questions about the points at which children begin to hear phonemes as separated or distinct from each other, is a case in point.[7] Adults hear the letters of a word, and may even visualize it as well. Children hear a total expression of a word, and until they become accustomed (as can happen beyond infancy and toddlerhood) to recognizing the letters that are part of a word, they cannot know which letters or sounds are symbolized in the total word. Thus as children are learning language usage and words as they are composed of letters and sounds, they do not hear what the adult hears (or visualizes) in the process of language development.

Parents can point out the letters to children as perceived on packages, signs, and various other places that objects are seen with large letters on them. This type of pointing out to children is done in the normal process of activities that go on in the usual routines of home life. It is not done as a formalized lesson in the way it occurs at school. Parents who are aware, however, of the process of language development, can in many ways facilitate gains that can be made at school in the formalized setting of the classroom. Formalized in this sense refers to organization of routines, preplanning by the teacher, readiness of materials at hand that will be needed by the teacher and the children, with attention given to the quality and quantity of work to be done at a given time in the school program.

Critical Listening

Children need to be taught how to hear certain sounds in words. They first hear words and may echo the words in the best way possible. They imitate what they hear. This skill is enhanced when children are able to watch the speaker and are intent on repeating correctly what the speaker says. It presents a foundation for many other forms of productivity as well.

Adults are among the best sources for children to learn about names and language structures.[8] Imitation of adults and their speech patterns provide an external speech model for children, which is ultimately used for thought processes and the inner speech that children use when they are thinking. The inner speech, however, is perceived as having to occur before thought processes can evolve.

Inner speech, as Vygotsky uses it, is speech that one uses for one's self.[9] Sometimes, even the vocalization is absent. External speech that the child hears is an objectification of thought turned into words; the inner speech functions as speech being turned into thought, thus one process is the reverse of the other.[10]

Children who listen to language attentively are often very competent in repeating accurately what they hear. As a consequence, they speak with assurance, a quality that attracts the ears of other listeners, and is helpful in the child's cognitive development.

Voice inflections and intonations of speech patterns are present as early as the first year of life. A child hears the fluctuations of tone in the parents' or siblings' voices and is able to match a string of babbling sounds to those convincing levels. A pseudo speech, one that sounds as though it is a clear message (in babble form), represents strong beginnings of language development and should be encouraged. Although the speech is an imitation, or pseudo in that sense, it is real for the child, thus it represents an authentic speech pattern in its earliest phases.

Parents can at various periods in their young children's time at home name and call attention to the following:

- sounds of the doorbell
- a child's tricycle bell
- the telephone
- the automobile engine
- the squeak of wheels or a door hinge
- the venetian blinds or window shades being pulled up or down
- patter of rain
- sound of the clock (ticking or chiming)
- sound of water running from tap in kitchen or bathtub
- sound of mixmaster or kitchen beater mixing batter
- crunch of leaves under one's feet
- skates or skateboards
- bouncing ball
- click of light switch
- tearing paper
- opening and closing an umbrella
- musical bells (high and low)
- kitchen utensils

Attentive or critical listening at home provides a substantial foundation for a child who will be expected to be aware of what is said at school. By being given a start in becoming accustomed to listening to adults and others at home, and being expected to respond as a respected individual, the child is learning to adapt to relevant school patterns of behavior. Although teachers may be aware of this progression of the child's language development, parents may not be (at least in the same way that teachers are taught at the university).

Parents need to know, early in the child's language development, that critical listening in the home context can be applied mainly to physical sounds of words and general meanings, when it is appropriate to explain to the child. Nursery rhymes, singing games, poetry, and stories provide rhythmical qualities of words, all of which are helpful to children in establishing a critical listening orientation toward speech and language. Children enjoy hearing "Whoosh!" for the description of the wind. They enjoy, too, hearing someone say, "Kerplunk!" for the dropping sound of a heavy object. Teachers need to explain to parents how simple everyday speech and functions can help children develop foundations for language upon which later work can be built in school. Although this information is elementary to the teacher, it is not to some parents, who would like to know more about the way that language develops in human beings.

The next section emphasizes speaking, self-expression in creative ways, routine questions and answers, and other aspects of an environment that involve children in conversation or in both routine and nonroutine activities.

Speaking

Infants are ready to respond to the environment, as studies show, in a variety of ways. Experiments conducted to determine infants' preferences for sounds and music indicated that they sought speech sounds more than music.[11] This was demonstrated by the frequency with which the infants' sucking on nipples turned switches on and off for recordings of music or speech.

An infant, hearing the voice of mother who feeds, protects, and bathes him/her, is soothed. Infants turn their heads toward the mother's voice. They have discrimination skills from the moment of birth. The approval or facilitation of those skills depends on the people in their environment. The human equipment for speech, language, and other aspects of communication is ready in normal children for use from the moment of birth.[12] When the infant's interaction pattern with its care-giver is interrupted, for any reason, the infant becomes upset. Studies indicate that the baby's babbling, cooing, and body movements provide an interchange between the mother and infant, and these sounds and movements become a conversational mode and a communication system between the mother and child.[13]

Routines that the mother followed in feeding, bathing, and putting the child to bed were sensed by the child.[14] When someone different from the usual care-giver (or the mother in this case) took care of the infant, the difference was sensed by the baby. For this reason, researchers state that an interaction pattern has been established by about two months old between mother and child. This is a significant communication system of one, the infant, waiting for the other, the mother, to do something, to speak or act in behalf of the infant. The infant responds.

Speech develops, in one sense, with the beginning of sounds or phonemes, the simplest unit of sound. Parents hearing the infant's sounds, begin to identify them with words that have meaning in a given culture, or even in a given household. Babbling that is enjoyed by infants conveys a mood or tone to the mother, who recreates some of the babbling sounds to represent words for the baby.

Sounds that linguists recognize as phonemes (/p/, /t/, /b/,) are examples of sound elements in language patterns that are intended to become associated with meaning. There are approximately forty-six of these sound qualities or phonemes in the English language. They are not always the same as the twenty-six letters (or graphemes) of the English alphabet. The letters of the alphabet are used in spelling and to assist at times in pronunciation. (As any reader knows, many letters are silent and not to be pronounced, as for example, in the word, *known*, the *k* is not pronounced as it usually is when its sound is "acknowledged.")

Children do not, however, need to understand the academic aspect of the language in order to speak effectively. In any culture, an infant's sounds can be recognized as part of words that are significant to that cultural framework or its lexicon. The babbling stage is the same across cultures; the words that the care-givers or parents recognize in the babbling sounds or phonemes are usually part of a baby's communication system by the end of the first year. The parents use the words in association with the infant's sounds and the repetition of the words used, as they are connected to given acts, food, or objects, constitutes the interaction system in which infants learn to speak.

Children put words together between one and a half and two and a half years. These sentence-like speech structures emerge from the child's system of rules and the manner in which (s)he has interpreted the speech system. Some writers call sentence attempts in babies' early stages of development, a telegraphic-type language. It is obvious that words of action or intent are missing from what the child actually expresses. "Up," means, "Pick me up." The bare minimum of words and meaning is stated although typically the child understands more than what has been said. The adult who knows the child is able to comprehend the meaning intended by the minimum of words expressed.

An infant's first useful words recognized by parents may be, "Ma-ma," "Da-da," or "muk," for milk. When an infant uses a word, such as "muk," it may also be considered a holophrase. A single word that represents more than a single word for naming an object, but rather is intended as a request by the child, may represent a sentence or a phrase, thus it is called *holophrase*.

By the time a child is about a year and one half, it can speak some fifty words. During that time, the label (nouns) for objects, persons, places, and events (Christmas, Easter, Hanukkah, Passover) are given. The child learns to apply those labels, discovering through adult responses his/her attempts are correct. The child repeats the correctly received responses. Upon those reciprocal processes of spoken and socially approved words by parents, the infant acquires the acceptable vocabulary for functioning effectively, within the parent-child context at least.

Syntax, or the way in which children put words together, stress on syllables, intonation, and voice patterns continue with all speech production. Children hear them daily. What they adapt to their own styles of speech is a result of a complicated system of internal almost automatic decisions. Although speech patterns are not formed without thought, they are both conscious and involuntary at times. Exact imitation of speech does not occur. The child hears sounds in certain ways; the child has his/her own physiological attributes and characteristics, which are applied to speech and language production.

It is incredible, however, to realize that from birth to about two years old a child has typically learned a large proportion of knowledge about meaning, production of speech, and various aspects of language development that formulate the beginnings of a complicated system of communication and human interaction. For the infant who has an impairment of some type, particularly one in hearing or vision, language development becomes for the most part a different process than the normal infant's. The language process is different in that different parts of the brain have to become involved in a sensory receiving and translating function of language, meaning, and speech production.

Forms of speech are one of the most significant aspects affecting the personality, cognitive, emotional, and social development of the individual.

Not only the speech production, itself, but how the individual conceptualizes what is said or seen in the environment, affect the intellectual development of the person and, in turn, the way others will perceive the individual's characteristics.

Physical characteristics of the child influence impressions that others have of him/her, speech and language also contribute to impressions made on others. As the child learns to respond to certain cues and expressions in the faces of others (regarding impressions about one's self), the child also thinks of words that describe those impressions (which may be enhancing or not where the child's self-concept is concerned). The words and language used to describe one's environment greatly affect how the individual perceives it, whether it is negative or positive in relation to the child's point of view regarding one's self.

Speech, intonation, voice inflections, the use of a range of voice levels and dynamics are learned from others in the first two years of life and retained or not in later years. When children have access to hearing or seeing role models who are aware of voice control or speech intricacies and usage variations (e.g., in professions involving formal communications or acting), their refinement of language usage and production may be enhanced.

Differences among the views of Piaget, of Vygotsky, of Whorf-Sapir, and of Bruner, as well as Mead's views on social learning, demonstrate the significance of learning and its relationship to the development of thought and language—and also how those skills affect self-impressions.[15] Thought and language develop in different ways; some theorists conceptualize thought as occurring before language; some view it as occurring simultaneously; some view language as a function that develops parallel to thought. In any case, however, language has a crucial role in relating to and defining one's world of other people, things, and events.

Speech and Communication from Two to Five Years

Psychological willingness to identify with (or be like) someone who is significant in some way for the child, affects the language forms that the child will use. Words that the child uses are often based on the child's interpretation of the world, that is, on both the child's interpretation and that of the person preferred by that child.

Certain people become the focus for the child's mode of speech production, and consequently one of its more important motivators. Communication beyond the babbling stage provides a forceful reason for wanting to talk. Social interaction is a powerful medium not only in the development of an individual's temperament and responsiveness to others but in the way that individual thinks about him/herself.

Recent studies on language development of infants in the first two years of life suggest that cognitive and attachment theories used in analyzing children's development of language and speech be examined closely.[16] The studies disclose that the amount of interaction, and the quality of interaction, of the child with the mother may influence the infant's competence in communication and cognition.[17] The studies prior to the one referred to here had been, because of Piaget's findings and researchers' statements regarding attachment theories, tending toward minimizing the role of the mother in cognition and language development. The researchers who investigated the quality, frequency, and degree of stimulus provided by the care-giver or the mother of the baby advise that verification of data should be made across a variety of situations in which the baby is involved with materials and different forms of environmental experiences.

It seems that theoretical data change every ten to fifteen years in specific content. Statements that are made from data, and which appear plausible and valid at first thought, are sometimes contradicted in later studies when some one or some group tries to verify the findings. The researchers indicate that earlier work on the investigation of mothers' and children's interaction consisted of limited samplings of a temporal and descriptive nature, which analyzed behavioral patterns of interaction, rather than influences of interaction quality on later language of the individual.[18] They further suggest that although it may make sense to postulate that the rules acquired by an infant in the preverbal interaction process with a parent may provide some facilitation for language development, data for testing the hypothesis on that assumption have not been collected.[19] Thus one often makes assumptions based on commonly viewed perceptions rather than on data-based investigations. It requires some scientific human skills or sophistication in such areas at times to discern differences between statements that do not reflect research-tested findings and those that do.

Teachers who work with children, therefore, must be sensitive to the words they use in statements made to mothers and other care-givers regarding the responses of children. Too often, when an observation is made by a teacher, telling a parent about a "deficiency" the teacher considers the child to have, the parent attributes greater accuracy and validity than should possibly be accorded to the statement. The parent may become overanxious about diagnoses of a child's abilities or personality characteristics. Teachers who sometimes have less knowledge about psychological data, may overgeneralize and make comments about a child, compared to an experienced psychoanalyst, who would not.

Generally speaking, one can appreciate and have respect for those who have worked within the scientific constraints of investigating anything as complicated as influences on language development of young children. Positive as well as negative findings in such research are contributions to contemporary knowledge on speech and interaction patterns between the child and parent. Piaget's findings suggest that the infant explores for its own organism's benefit and that language, from interaction upon objects, develops in the process of formulating a cognitive structure. This is perceived also in the light of findings from studies that suggest stronger relationships between maternal behaviors and cognitive measures than between maternal behaviors and language skills.

Interdisciplinary studies involving developmental psychologists, social learning theorists, and psychologists interested in brain and social functional interaction will discover new theoretical connections. A continual puzzle must be taken apart and placed back together in unusual ways in order to find out the components of language development, facility, cognition, and how they interweave in the fabric of cognitive and speech development.

Social or human interaction, wherever and whenever it occurs, affects an individual's speech, except in cases of individuals who are ill, incapacitated, or under unusual stress, among other things. Children in the age range of two to five years old are typically acquiring more words in their vocabularies, speaking to more people and spending time with children at school.

The number of words in children's vocabularies varies greatly depending on the people with whom the children interact most often, their playmates, and the general patterns of language interaction that occur in their homes. By the age of two, some children know or have heard and understood at least about 300 words. Each year, given normal circumstances, they acquire several hundred more. By the age of three, a child may have about a 700-word vocabulary; by four, between 900 and 1,200 words. By the time a child is in kindergarten, (s)he may be able to use and understand about 1,500 to 2,000 words.

Differences among children vary in terms of when or how they use their vocabularies. Adults provide explanations and words for them that other children cannot supply. Experiences with many meanings as they are applied to specific words are necessary in order for the child to assimilate the fact that a single word can have several meanings in different contexts. Interaction with adults when the child is acquiring language is significant. The model for correct pronunciation of a word assists in the child's development of his/her own vocabulary.

Speech and communication in children between the ages of two and five develops at a rapid rate, for the most part. Particularly when they are with each other at school or in the neighborhood, they are engaged in talking at play, at directing one another, and at following or creating ideas for more involved interaction among or between them. The nature of the experience can inhibit or facilitate a higher proportion of speech production. When children are pretending (or role-playing) they are performing family functions involving conversations between a mother and father, or among siblings, they often use more language that they have heard from those sources.

Speech, play behavior, and communication in this age range have been of interest to several researchers. Piaget's work on the preoperational stage of thought, as he defined it, demonstrated in his view the way children acquired the use of symbolism, or symbolic representation of things and experiences that are not immediately present in one's environment at a specific time. Children in this age range are able to extend their thoughts and language to ideas beyond those that are present in the environment. They are able to play, imitate others (through memory of their impressions of others), and generally refer to objects that are not at hand. This is a form of abstraction in its beginnings of language development and referents.

Play has been recognized by many writers in the field of early childhood education, of psychology, of psycholinguistics, among others, as a significant stage of children's development. Cognitive, intellectual, emotional, social, and speech development are considered to be pivotal in the child's developing skills in the experiences of play, both alone and in the company of other children. Play is no longer regarded, for the most part, as a totally passive or nonlearning experience.[20]

From several points of view of writers of various disciplines, the play behavior of young children assists in the opportunity for practice periods in the use of speech. When this speech is used with other children, who may or may not be concerned with accuracy as it may be compared to events or objects in the environment, children can acquire greater levels of speech usage. Having an audience of another child or adult provides greater impetus, for the most part, to convey a message, whether that message is "just to talk," or to give an item of information that may be functional to another individual.

Evaluation of children's speech in terms of correct pronunciation, word usage, or syntactical modes used in conversation or in play situations with other children is not the predominant function of or by the children. Even though the children may correct each other on ideas that they may want to accept or to build into a "scenario" at play, they seem, however, to be less preoccupied with precise speech. As long as it flows and moves the play along, the children seem, for the most part, to accept it without criticism. This does not mean that criticism of speech is totally absent. It is not, however, of major interest to the children when they are deeply absorbed in the play fluidity and social interaction of the situation.

The cultural references to activity conceptualized as play differ from society to society. Fun, recreation, and relaxation are, in part, concepts that denote for many a minimization of the energies required when one is at work, or on the job from which one earns a living. From the viewpoints of some other people, employed or paid in the capacity of doing something they enjoy, the job and "fun," may be almost synonymous.

The experimentation, manipulation, and discovery-seeking behavior that occurs at play, or when an individual is not rushing into identifying immediate answers to a given problem, often resembles the searching of the scientist who is expected to solve problems of an unusual or continually vexing nature (e.g., disease control, socially widespread problems). An attitude of deeper analysis or probing occurs when it is expected that an easy answer may not be the correct one or the best solution. Children's play behavior with the involvement of speech, communication, and the presentation of new ideas that arise from symbolic thought encourages imagery that is useful. Some writers suggest that perhaps the play behavior of young children may "go underground . . ." until about seven through twelve years old and resurface through involvement in adventurous games or exploratory activities.[21] Daydreaming in the adolescent years is perceived to be an example of such gamelike or pretending behavior. Through this, an individual may also learn how to empathize with others, acquire better understanding of role behavior, and enlarge abilities related to imagery formulation, among other skills.

Play behavior at school may be enhanced in the interaction with other children; this does not mean that children do not learn about imagination and symbolic representation from adults as well. Bruner, Vygotsky, and some early childhood educators consider it important that children have contact with adults as part of a necessary development of language, thought, and play behavior.[22] Reciprocity in language is as important as one person listening in a one-way sense to another. Speech, action, reaction, and another action or stream of words setting into motion that circularity and continuing process of speech production and creation of higher levels of imagery and thought, are significant in children's development.

The means through which speech and communication occur for children in the age range of two to five years old varies to a great extent at times. The background at home through which children learn their earliest forms of speech production, and the schools that children attend in various parts of the country, are examples of those differences. Teachers of children in kindergarten as well as those in the prekindergarten schools have mixed philosophies among them. Some want to be formalized in their approaches to language instruction; some do not. Play experiences may be minimized in deference to time for more formalized programs of instruction. This is not to say that there is not a place for several modes of teaching, either in the classroom or outside of it.

Experiences in playful manipulation of objects and ideas should be a lifetime adventure. If people do not continue to search in a nonrigid manner for new conceptualization of currently accepted views, progress may be minimized. Enlightenment for currently unsolved problems occurs in many instances through the playful, experimentation of perceiving an idea in a way that is different, or even appears to be absurd, compared to current standards or norms of some kind.

Attitudes toward play and work emerge from the cultural proscriptions about those categories of activity in any given culture.[23] Some see work as totally separated from play behavior. Play is not perceived as having a serious quality to it. It is rather viewed as something one does after one's work is finished.

In the context of American education of young children, however, play has been redeemed as more than just an opportunity to release fatigue. Many educators and psychologists, as a matter of fact, consider that play is a way to re-energize one's muscles. In that attempt of refortifying one's energies, one is able to withstand the rigors of dealing with difficulties or complexities that one meets in one's intellectual pursuits.

Recreation has been discussed as a means of balancing one's achievement energies and activities. Playful engagement, as a human enterprise or function, has a significant contribution to psychological as well as intellectual and physical spheres of thought. Thus play has been taken from the categories of passivity, nonutilitarianism, and nonsignificant aspects of human activity, into the categories of the energetic useful (cognitively and creatively), and is recognized as having greater significance in the total context of human words.

Teachers who work with young children may have mixed feelings about the specific play activities that are either part, or not, of the total curriculum offered to children at school. Their own feelings about what children ought to be doing, and the particular context in which they should be doing it (as a "work" activity or not), affects the amount, intensity, or format that the children will experience at school. The skillful teacher is able to sense when the children are learning, regardless of whether there is formalized program planning or not.

Children need to be permitted many opportunities for speech. They hear rhythmic qualities in stories that are read to them by the teacher. They also learn from poetry and jingle-type forms of limericks. Language, a play on words, sounds, meanings, and social or functional interchange, provides an excellent medium for the reservoir that children need for themselves as they develop their own inner speech, as referred to by Vygotsky. The external speech of others in the environment becomes the inner speech and the child's own internal mechanism that assists in the development of language as well as thought.

The age range between two and five in children's language development, in thought, content, conceptualization, symbolic imagery, language fluidity with ideational rhythms, is intensive and extensive. The richness of experiences and the quality of interaction with others who are able to respond to the child and contribute toward the child's feelings that what is said is important, does an immeasurable service to the child's linguistic and cognitive development.

Parents are often in need of more information regarding their own importance in the ways that they can help their children in the development of language. They also need to have some information about the fact that when children appear to be acting in a manner that is "stubborn," it is often merely a result of the way the child sees the world and the language that is used to describe it. The nature of thought, as Piaget suggests for the young child's modes of communication, is that it is difficult to become engaged in a reasoning process, or to reverse back in one's thinking and reflect on what one had said prior to arriving at an answer.

By the time children are about five years old, they have acquired most of the basic structural forms of their language.[24] Some children attend a prekindergarten or nursery school prior to four, and they hear formally structured thought in stories and directions of the teacher given to the children. They learn how to lengthen a sentence and to apply transformational rules of grammar through listening to various speech forms of the teacher that occur in daily routines. Parents, too, can be helpful in the same way at home by listening to the child's speech and extending what the child has said.

To the child who may have said that a pencil was lost, a parent may say, "Would you like me to help you find your pencil, which may be in the box in your bedroom?" Transformations from the child's statement, as well as questions generated from it, focus on certain word changes to pronouns or verb forms. The child can understand them because the original statement was the child's. These extended sentences in themselves do not create children's understanding of transformations in speech, but they do provide opportunities for children to hear them in the context of familiar speech forms.

With a greater number of studies on language development, grammatical knowledge, syntax, vocabulary, and meaning in speech development, plus their relationships to the development of thought and abstractions of conceptualization of complex ideas, more data will enlighten scholars as well as parents who are interested in young children's development. Because speech and language are significant in a culture that is oriented toward scientific precision and intricacy of thought leading to abstractions, it is important that teachers and parents help children in the best way possible to maximize their development in communication. Functional and social aspects of communication are central to the well-being of a child's growth and his/her ability to function effectively with others.

Children who learn two languages at home or learn one that has dialectical properties that differ from what is referred to as Standard English (SE), present to some teachers a problem of discerning differences that may be developmental or dialectical. The misunderstanding of language differences as they relate to Standard English often interferes with equalitarian attitudes.[25] Each language has a structure of its own and should not be considered inferior as a communication system that is effective or functional for people. Languages or dialects that differ from Standard English forms are not to be considered deficient or underdeveloped.

Linguists consider dialects to be the combination of language variations that are used as a communication form. Standard English is perceived as one among several dialects in the United States. In the context of dialectical variation, a language with its own systematic and structured code can not be considered as superior or inferior to other language forms. Appropriateness in language usage relative to an individual's preference for usage, may vary among the judgments of individuals. Social devaluation of a language form leads to misjudgment of an individual's personality and intellectual capacities.[26]

Some children who learn two languages at home in their early childhood years and are bilingual before they enter school, are able to function effectively in both (e.g., Spanish and English).[27] They know how to interchange words and syntax in both languages. Children who have heard mainly one language at home and have to learn English as a second language have some problems at the start, but later seem to circumvent them. It is important for second-language learners to understand word usage in a semantic sense before they acquire an understanding of syntactic rules.[28] This is true of any language learner.

When children experience at school enough role models who use the language desired for new learning, they are able more easily to acquire the language than they may be if drill methods are used. It is suggested that if teachers are to be ready to help children having problems learning English as a second language,[29] they must have sufficient facility to expand on children's language; often a native speaker of the language to be learned is able to accomplish this, recognizing quickly what the children's problems might be.

Contemporary issues on whether children should learn to read first in their own native language, before they learn how to read in a second language, are unresolved. Some parents want their children to learn to read in non-English first. Studies do not show any advantages one way or the other to the learning in one language or the other.[30] It is also suggested that if children do start with the second language, they can acquire easily a bilingualism that is prized by many people. Facilities in reading two languages, equally understood as well, can be very useful to the individual's functioning effectively in his/her society or in interpersonal relationships.

Some schools provide opportunities and time periods in the school day for children to experience two languages, one English and one non-English. This depends on the neighborhood of the school, supporting funds to provide for teachers who may instruct adequately in two languages, and factors related to psychological attitudes among families in a given area.

Differences between the appropriate time to teach English or non-English to preschool or school-aged children may be observed, although there is not adequate research on the topic.[31] When the first language is the stronger, however, in the child's development, it is suggested that the child become literate in it. Activities that can help all children advance in language development are essential in any case, whatever the age or language preference of children. Teachers who are able to up-date their information on bilingualism and are able to exercise astute powers of observation can do a great deal to help children.

Children in kindergarten can be given excellent opportunities for hearing stories, poetry, songs, and conversation from the teacher who is aware that the children may identify with their teacher and use him/her as a model for speech patterns that they can emulate. The use of music or musical instruments provides opportunities for pupils to hear differences among sounds, recognize high and low tones, and the loud and soft ones as well.

Auditory discrimination and visual observation skills help children note the differences among letters, sounds, and symbols and their relationships to word structures and meanings in conversation. Voice inflections, intonations, pitch, speed, and ranges of speaking as they differ among individuals, are valuable observations for children to acquire. They need an adult's assistance in these perspectives. Although children are able to build on a structure that has begun at home, they need to hear further abstractions descriptive of language as it is used by many people.

As children move into the first grade, where more formalized routines have to be involved in the total program of the day, they need support, information, and caring supervisional qualities. It is assumed that they want to learn, regardless of whether they appear to meet the challenge presented to them on some days. The teacher who is able to understand what motivates children in the various behavioral forms that they show is able to see below the surface levels and to identify with children who want to be competent.

The next section presents information on the communication process as it is manifested and developed in children from six to nine years old. This age range represents the educational grade range of first through fourth grades, going beyond information typically presented in early childhood texts. In this view, developmental differences can be adequately considered, children at eight years old, for example, can have skills of a nine-year-old in the fourth grade.

Speech and Communication from Six to Nine Years

The skills that children bring to the first grade in which formalized reading, writing, and mathematical processes begin, varies among and within pupils to a great extent. Compared, however, to the kindergarten in which many different activities were presented, and at varying structural levels, the seriousness of tasks in the primary grades involves increasingly more difficult problems and coordination of skills.

Even though children may be six years old, chronologically, when they are in first-grade groups, teachers note that there can be about a two or three year maturity difference among pupils in their emotional, social, or academic elements of behavior. Skillful teachers, typically, have prepared several levels of subject matter in any one area so that when the children are learning about reading or new ideas in language arts, lessons that move from simple to complex are available. Individual differences among children are noted by the discerning teacher, who adapts the appropriate matching lesson to the children's abilities. In this way the children have an opportunity to succeed in their work. The teacher does not plan something for them that is beyond their understanding.

Teachers need to learn how to judge the appropriateness of a concept to the children's abilities to comprehend it. New ideas are introduced, reviewed, and then followed by further opportunities to review what has been learned. In the process of review, as well, teachers have to have many different activities ready, ones in which the same concepts are embedded and that can be offered in a different way to the pupils.

During the primary grades, children are acquiring in their language a larger vocabulary, longer sentence construction and usage, and a greater mastery of some of the earlier understandings of syntax and grammatical structures that approach those of the adult stages of development. By the time children have reached kindergarten, they appear to be able to use various syntactic structures; however, their language usage demonstrates that they are still learning to master grammatical constructions that will, in time, become more like those used by adults.[32]

Some of the discrepancies between language usage and the child's understanding of what is being said become obvious in various ways when a child is tested on a knowledge of grammatical rules. What children say may be accepted by adults as correct expressions, grammatically; however when the children are questioned about specific structures, they do not understand them.[33] In this they may be compared to adults, who have a vocabulary of understanding that is more extensive than their vocabulary of common usage. Children can often understand certain language forms or words, but may not understand the intent of a message when words, even those that are familiar to them, are arranged in a different syntactical structure.[34] An example of this was shown when some children at five or six years old misunderstood the intent of a message in a sentence that indicated one child told (or promised) another that a task would be done by the person who promised the action. "Rosalie promised Jody that she would clean the table." A five- or six-year-old child may understand this message to be that *Jody* was told to clean the table. The significant observation here is that children, even though understanding what the word *promise* means, may still not understand it when it arises in a grammatical structure that differs from the one they may have used or heard most of the time.[35]

Even though teachers may develop greater sensitivity to and awareness of what children are able to do, say, or understand, they must, simultaneously, encourage rather than inhibit children when they express themselves. To correct their grammar or language (especially in mid-statement, rather than to continue talking, using correct form), is to stultify what they want to say. With greater depth of information on how children learn, should come the concomitant awareness that children need an understanding adult to hear them express themselves at school or in the home.

Children's attempts at language should be taken seriously as representing sincere efforts to communicate effectively. Studies reporting a lack of understanding in children's perspectives of language and syntactical variations should be used by teachers to help themselves help young children in the acquisition of greater competence, while also not lowering one's subtle expectations of what children are able to do. There is a fine line between not pressuring children, and interfering with what they are trying to say, and also allowing them to speak in a natural spontaneous manner, and being unaware of their trial-and-error attempts at effective language forms. The teacher can be aware of the child's mistakes in using various forms, but also know that frequent exposure to desired speech models can greatly facilitate children's language learning.[36]

Writers indicate that children can learn to use a variety of language styles, regardless of the one they may have learned before they came to school. One study reports changes in young children's abilities to describe objects (that were not visible to the listener). Training sessions of only about fifteen minutes for each child were given once a week, for four weeks in all. The experimenters themselves were suprised at how quickly the children adapted to an adult style of speech to describe objects, where they were (under the box, etc.) and in what kind of box they were. They used compound sentences and descriptions of greater length and complexity as they noted pictures of more complicated content.[37]

Flexibility of speech styles is important to note in the light of research that describes children's skills at a given age and also suggests that what children have heard at home may interfere with some learning at school. Limitations of abilities in speech among young children seem to be, according to writers and researchers, more related to the models available to children than to some unique qualities that can be anchored to styles that children acquire early in life. Children's speech can change when they hear others use a variety of speech styles that appear relevant to the experiences and understanding of children.

Grammatical construction of language is also part of the total speech pattern that children emulate as they observe adults or others with whom they want to identify or to whom they are attracted in some way. A child in reciprocal conversation with a teacher who is listening to the child explain what s(he) has seen just completed is hearing what the teacher says in response. The style of language and the grammatical structure are parts of the total message, and children are able to hear it. Writers indicate that when children are given the opportunity to talk about what is of relevance to them, they are far more likely to use greater detail, longer sentences, and complex linguistic forms[38] than they ordinarily might use.

Often, teachers are asked to listen to children more often than to talk to them. It is assumed that children will want to express themselves more often if they have a "willing ear" that is ready to listen attentively and with unhurried interest to what is being said. Program goals of kits that are readily available for purchase vary in terms of whether the teachers do more of the talking than do the children. The teachers are expected to listen to children in order to hear aspects of conceptual understanding, word usage, syntactical awareness, and other speech elements. It is assumed that when children are heard by an astute teacher, more help can be given the children. The teacher who knows each child's strengths and weaknesses in language facility is considered to be in a far better position to give the child intelligently guided help.

For the most part, programs reflect specific areas of guidance for children at different developmental levels in speech abilities. The teacher judges which aspects of the program should be used for which children. In a general sense, however, most of the writers that criticize kits, or their usage, for children's language development, emphasize that the teacher be considerate of children, be sincerely interested in what each child has to say, and be conscious of the fact that children use the teacher as a model for their own language expression.

Children imitate to an extent what is heard in their environment. Linguists indicate that children cannot imitate what is not already a part of their own speech structure. They may bring a message to someone and attempt to deliver it in verbatim terms, but they can only do so to a point. They shift part of the message to fit their own language structure.[39]

Teachers have to use programs that are comfortable for them. Just as children will speak or not, as they desire, so it is with teachers. If programs are not familiar to them, if they have not had some opportunity to study them, and know how to use them with their own specific group or with individual children, those programs will have little use for them. Many teachers make their own activities to encourage the children to practice certain word forms. With activity books that are available for teachers to use with pupils, teachers are often able to design or to adapt their own ideas.

Even though grammatical construction and word forms are often studied in research reports, almost every book on language development of children that relates to teaching, includes significant statements that point to the teacher's attitudes during interaction with children, and to the teacher's awareness of children as people as much as the teacher needs to be aware of his/her self.[40]

An emphasis on the child as an individual with his/her own style of speech (and speech rules that are internally formed within the child's own schema or framework of thought) provides for teachers a basis for designing their own activities that are appropriate to the specific pupils in the room. It is significant that books on children's linguistic development reflect various points, depending on the author's feelings about what is important for children to know as they develop educationally and psychologically at school. Some authors emphasize the number or frequencies and percentages of children who are able to produce evidence of knowing one language form or another. Some, while including that information, also make a plea for perceiving the pupil as a human being who is trying to learn and who needs emotional and courteous support from a teacher committed in behalf of the child's well-being. It is as if the counting and the percentages are less important in some cases to consider during the early years of language development than is the creating of a receptive environment that encourages language expression (correct or not as a grammarian might view it).

Opportunities for speech and communication have to be created at school and at home. Note Table 4–1 in which suggestions are made in which children may be encouraged to talk, describe an activity they enjoyed (or did not like). Questions need to be asked to encourage language. Some writers indicate that teachers should ask open-ended questions more than the yes or no type.[41] Psychologists, too, recommend for purposes of allowing the child to practice speech and thought patterns that children be asked open-ended questions that evoke lengthy answers, thoughtful, individual words that express the child's own feelings.

Parents sometimes want information on how they can help their children at home. Teachers take for granted the knowledge they have acquired in their own preteaching courses at universities or courses given as part of in-service programs. Parents of young children can benefit from the recommendations of the teacher. When parents know what to do and realize how much their help can facilitate some of the work attempted by the children at school, the results of such cooperation from parents can be noticed in the children's work in the classroom.

Table 4–1 indicates the number, quality, and frequency of activity types that can normally arise at school and home to enhance a child's speech and communication development. In the typical day for children, their academic and interpersonal skills associated with language expression can grow with almost minimal attempts of adults around and ready to initiate reciprocal interaction among or with children.

The table gives examples of things that can be done. Those ideas are enlarged upon as follows:

1. General talk for children at all age levels recommended here includes discussion about parties, friendships, planning for vacation trips, trips to the museum, libraries, lists of food needed for meals to be cooked,

Table 4–1 Activities that Occur at School and Home to Encourage Speech and Communication for Children*

	General Talk, Planning Trips	Critical Analyses	Social Issues	Music	Cooking	Poetry	Science	Mathematics
At School								
Six (First grade)								
Seven (Second grade)								
Eight (Third grade)								
Nine (Fourth grade)								
At Home								
Six (Neighborhood/peers; family/parents, siblings)								
Seven (Neighborhood/peers; family/parents, siblings)								
Eight (Neighborhood/peers; family/parents, siblings)								
Nine (Neighborhood/peers; family/parents, siblings)								

*Parents and teachers may want to check out in the following manner their application of the above: S = Seldom; M = Moderately; O = Often.

ingredients to be included, clothing to be purchased, activities for the day and for future days or special events. (If possible, argumentative topics should be avoided at meal time.)

2. Critical analyses arise and can be encouraged when individual members and visitors discuss ideas that are significant for their own lives or changes that may be occurring in their own family, or societal events, policies, etc. Television news media and documentaries provide the *nuclei*, or seeds, for discussion, at whatever level, formal or informal. Advertising media and the various pitches made among them can be discussed in a constructively critical manner.

3. Social issues are critically relevant in people's lives; parents can focus, for their children, attention on social issues involving people other than themselves, and conditions of people in other countries and opportunities or the lack of them to obtain adequate and nourishing food. Political views geared to children's levels of comprehension can be discussed.

4. Music is an excellent means for encouraging vocal expression; rhythm facilitates difficult sounds, changing them into less self-conscious sounds and expression; music in itself is a kinesthetically arousing form of encouraging vocal expression and dynamics of tone levels.
5. Cooking offers many opportunities for discussion. We must plan the ingredients that have to be included in anything even as simple as jello. Recipes or directions for salad, puddings, cakes, icings, cookies, and soups involve planning, cooking, order of mixing ingredients, setting temperatures for cooking, and serving the food. Making sandwiches requires planning for the ingredients and the order of each step in the sequence. Making any kind of food, dessert or casserole, involves accounting for each ingredient that goes into it and how and when it is to be included.
6. Poetry lends itself well to reading aloud; the sounds and musical rhythm provide another element to speech that is essentially human. Poetry is written at all levels of appreciation; the adult selects what is judged to be appropriate for children. Children usually like to create their own poetry, rhyming words, nonsense syllables, and jingles or limericks (after they have heard some).
7. Science relates to the wind, various weather elements, the air, space, water, cars, tricycles, household appliances, pulleys, wagons, liquids changing from one form to another, such as water to ice. Very few processes and energy, or forms of matter changing from one condition to another do not relate to scientific principles as humankind is generally aware of them.
8. Mathematics involves counting, systematizing, classifying, spatial relationships, and size relationships—all of which come up frequently in the interaction that adults and/or siblings have with young children. A myriad of opportunities arise to involve children in counting food, packages, bottles, drinks, judging, relating, comparing and arranging sizes of objects, toys, blocks, shelves, books, and numerous other objects that are found in many households.

Children can be given many opportunities for communicating ideas and feelings in the classroom. They often enjoy games that feature sounds of the environment. Teachers need to have a file of such ideas handy on the desk, as well as a picture inventory that demonstrates effectively objects, animals, and natural foliage of the environment.

The teacher asks one child to imitate a sound of the environment outdoors while the children try to guess what it is. These imitations often become the words that are used in a story, song, or poetic attempt. To make sounds or objects (clocks, typewriter, barking dogs, rain, thunder, etc.,) "come alive," helps children adapt to the creative ideas they will develop when they need to write, either individually or as part of a classroom project.

Effectively delivered speech among people is enjoyable. It is worth helping children become competent in both the presentation of an idea and the recognition of the validity of one. Part of the teacher's work in assisting children to acquire speech that is enjoyed by others involves helping children develop a habit of listening that becomes sharper and more astute as they mature. In a sense, the teacher helps the children learn to appreciate well-articulated language written or expressed aloud.

The imagination of the teacher becomes a "teaching tool" that constantly replenishes itself with ideas that encourage and sharpen the sensory images of children. For this reason, the never-ending need to update and try new activities or gamelike tasks, teachers must provide focus for the children's hearing, practicing, and discriminating among many sounds of the environment as well as the sounds of letters in words. Props that are used in the classroom add new ways to attract the pupils' attention. For them, it is as though a unique lesson is introduced. The objects used for a lesson may be unusual, but the principle of attuning ears to higher levels of sensitivity in recognizing various sounds is not new.

Children's breathiness in speech may be caused by tension, inadequate air in the diaphragm, or an illness, such as a cold. When children have been very active in games, running or rushing around, they may not have sufficient air in the diaphragm to speak clearly. Then, too, the manner of speaking often reflects the psychological feelings one has about the message or intent. Uncertainty, fear of what might occur after one speaks, or anxiety about a given subject affect the quality of sound in the production of speech. Secret messages used in activities encourage sensitivity to speech sounds as well as the ability to discover something that is not obvious to everyone. Using various tubes and unusual forms through which children may speak or create messages to one another introduces another way to capture children's attention to a unique "language creator."[42]

Children's abilities to speak are closely related to their physical attributes as well as their thought processes. The teeth, oral cavity, throat, nasal passages, and respiratory system affect the sounds that will be produced. Health and energy levels influence speech, too. Forceful sounds, words, and ideas convey the message in that vein. When an individual is ill, the energy that is involved with abilities to bring air to the wind passages, which in part deliver speech, may be at a low ebb. The speech sounds are thin, not very vibrant, and consequently reveal the physical weakness of the individual. These low-energy sounds may also come from an individual who is depressed or otherwise psychologically limited in fully expressing him/herself.

Handicaps related to sight, hearing, or other functionally and physically limiting parts in the sensory receiving-or-sending system of the individual, can affect the sounds that an individual hears or produces. These limitations can offset an individual's abilities to receive proper cues of knowledge from the environment. People may have a high level of intelligence and not be able to communicate clearly. The perplexities that are unraveled by people working with children and adults in special education reflect that physical disabilities do not coincide with thinking disabilities. When children who are handicapped are given a task that involves language-free responses, they often demonstrate effective learning of concepts.[43]

As language production is so closely a part of the child's personal identity, it is important that the teacher respect what the child says as a significant effort to convey an idea or message.[44] Because there will be wide variations among children in their attempts to communicate, teachers must be aware that their quickness to match the children's speech with their own correct speech forms can discourage children's attempts as well as deflate the children's self-impressions.

When the teacher notes that children need to acquire greater competence or ease in producing certain speech sounds, s(he) may introduce games with objects: blowing feathers into the air or naming objects that have within the name those letters that the children need practice in saying. Such a procedure minimizes focusing attention on the inability of any child to produce a given sound. The teacher's concentration on often using words that involve certain sounds that the children need to master in speech can help immeasurably to provide, in subtle ways, the needed practice or repetition without embarrassing the pupils.

Children sometimes substitute sounds such as *th* in words needing an *s* sound. Lisping often occurs when children have lost their temporary teeth (front central incisors); at times, however, children whose parents lisp may continue to use speech substitutions even when all permanent front teeth are in place.

The early childhood years are complex in the rate and quality of learning that continues in children. The developmental aspect of learning, therefore, has been recognized fortunately as a condition in which children are learning to acquire every day, greater facility in a given skill or ability. They may not be working on a specific ability in the same way that an adult says, "Today, I am going to work on my backhand stroke"; they are, however, constantly listening and sensing the activities in their environment.

The realization that children are working through various stages of development, and that few stages are considered as totally past or fully mastered in an individual's progress, indicates that educators and other professionals are aware that a constant process must continue toward increased mastery of any given skill. The timing of help that is given, or that intervention of instruction occurs, depends on several qualities in a situation and in the specific child who may need assistance of some kind.

Problems that children may manifest in speech can be in part developmental and in part a typical mode of early childhood levels of growth. The significance of these differences between normal pupils and those needing professional attention lies in the degree and extensiveness of interference with intelligible communication.[45] Unusual intonation of speech, inability to use appropriate words to express an idea, unusual articulation or timing qualities in self-expression manifest variations from the normal production of speech. Teachers who work with young children should try not to confuse the normal attempts in early years of language development with problems that need to be recognized and assisted by professionals who work with children's problems in speech.

Hearing may be impaired, for example, when a child has a cold or a disease that occurs in early childhood education. Mucous in the head passages obstructs sound and clear reception of external speech. An easy way to check whether children do have a hearing loss is to recommend an examination. Various ways to detect chronic hearing loss are suggested, such as observing whether the child holds his/her head to one side and leans the ear toward a direction, or asks the speaker to repeat often what has been said, is often ill, fails to pronounce words properly, or does not seem to become involved in playing with other children.[46]

Frustration levels can result from occasional inadequate hearing for otherwise normal children who do not suffer from impairment of hearing. Psychosocial anxieties, however, escalate for children who are expected to hear effectively, yet do not.[47] Adults expect appropriate responses and are irritated when children do not cooperate, yet often the children do not hear well enough to know what adults want of them. One of the most unfair problems in schools is to expect something from children when they cannot physically respond in adequate terms because of an impairment of which an adult is not aware.

Temper tantrums, expression in physical terms instead of verbal modes, and impulsivity, among other response mechanisms, become the major means through which some deaf children react to the environment.[48] Although such children should not be isolated from others who do not have hearing problems, adults should be aware of the problem so that their expectations are more reasonable.

As children mature and progress through the grades from first through the fourth in elementary school, they experience many activities geared toward communication. When they are learning to read, they have to verbalize, pronounce sounds correctly, decode the letters with appropriately matching sounds and meanings. Speech and communication, therefore, are major themes throughout the curriculum.

Whenever possible, the teacher should offer expressive activities for children through choral readings (entire class reciting a poem in unison or in parts); individual readings, or poetry presented to groups or the total class; puppet monologues or small group presentations with stick, bag, or pâpier maché puppets; descriptive stories with illustrations that children may respond to and indicate what they see or like; and dramatic representations of situations or events that children can recall and present to the class.

Sharing, speaking, reciting, dramatically presenting any idea that emanates from the children's minds emphasizes the pleasure (if the teacher orients it in that direction) of communicating to others who become the receptive audience. As has been indicated in many of the examples mentioned earlier, the model of the teacher who is perceptive, looks at children when they speak, and shows that the children's words are important, is a crucial part of any language program for pupils at school. The attentive attitude of the teacher can be reflected in the children. When they are an attentive audience for their classmates, they are also hearing more effectively than they might be when they listen only half-heartedly. The teacher must plan to avoid as many distractions as possible during the time that children are trying to convey ideas through language expression. This in itself indicates to children that communication among individuals is worthwhile.

Speech, language development, and the variety of communication modes among families are an indication of human interaction types that many people take for granted. The spontaneous communication interaction of small units of people, who interact frequently with one another, is typically accepted as a normal development. While this is true, the communication process as it develops at school is far more planned in the way it is permitted to function. It is spontaneous only to a point. The children are not permitted to talk at any time they choose. For this reason, the unnaturalness of a speech environment must be tempered periodically in order to encourage "freedom" of speech or naturalness of expression.

Through listening to stories in the earlier grades at school (kindergarten and first grades in particular) children acquire a sensitivity to rhythmic language as well as hearing significant ideas conveyed in books. Vocabularies can be extended through children's learning about new concepts, too. The internalized timing mechanism, however, that lets pupils know when they should speak and when not to, is acquired through time and experiences.

As children progress through the grades, they learn from each teacher how much conversation will be tolerated within or outside of normal curriculum activities. Pupils begin to sense the idea of when to be silent and not to submit to the temptation of saying what they think at any time they wish. This adaption to the teacher's expectations for expression (and when to withhold them) is one of the most important skills a child has to learn as part of a pupil's role. In this context of the classroom and with each teacher, a timing gauge has to be internalized; this is something that is not explicitly taught but which children must learn, nevertheless, if they are to function effectively with any given teacher.

The design of reading programs at school, as well as the activities planned for children's participation in the language arts, can contribute toward freedom of expression if the teacher considers it important to children's "natural" development at school. Reading and language arts throughout the school day incorporate opportunities for a large variety of speech and communication techniques. The next section emphasizes these aspects in the pupil's school day.

Reading Skills: Preparation and Enjoyment

The act of reading includes participation in various activities other than sitting down in a formalized session of reading instruction as teachers and pupils know it. Children are involved in reading when they are shown words or symbols that represent an idea, object, event, or person. They are surrounded by symbols every day, for the most part.

Young children are aware that the scribbles (as the message may appear to them and to which they see others respond) have a meaning. They sense, too, that the codes are important (e.g., letters and words representing ideas or action). As they mature, too, they learn that reading is a valuable skill. It affects the personality to a great extent.

The sophistication that comes with having competence in reading, as young children may perceive it in its affective sense, is worthy of acquiring.

They see their older siblings reading, their parents and others who seem to do it in relation to work, paying bills, receiving relevant information on directions that need to be followed, and commenting on something that they may be reading at the moment, all of which influence the children's impressions of the importance of reading in daily living.

Young children hear as they ride along with their parents or others in a car, someone indicating what various signs say or direct people to do. Advertising and store posters that provide information about merchandise, prices, and the like, indicate to children that people have to learn to read to translate the symbols and concepts displayed in various places. These observations that children make, plus the parents' comments on the relevance of reading skills to how one may function, affect their desires to learn how to read.

In a society where the abstract is valued in the conceptualization of ideas from representative symbols (over and above asking someone to perform a given task), young children learn that certain characteristics in regard to that form of competence in people stand in high esteem.[49] They sense the importance of stating an idea well so that it focuses and receives appropriate attention from someone. This awareness of valuing articulation skills in an individual is perceived by children long before they are able to verbalize an understanding of the means for acquiring such skills. Further, to be able to show someone that the skills needed for reading are mastered symbolizes gradual attainment of a favorable self-concept for the child, at least in regard to some level of competence in one's total personality construct.

Functional reading skills, or those that children see parents and older siblings use in order to facilitate completion of tasks or involvement in daily activities (e.g., shopping, following traffic rules, signs, or signals) differ from reading that brings pleasure to the individual who has sought out a certain magazine, journal, newspaper, or book to read. The degree to which children see this use of written materials varies among families. Although it is true that electronic media have made inroads into and may have reduced the frequency levels of an individual's use of written materials directly at hand in the environment, the television set, nevertheless, discloses written or symbolic cues as well as pictorially presented ideas. These need to be translated in some way for the individual's own mental or intellectual framework of thought.[50]

Parents who consider competence in reading to be significant for their children's development will pursue the means to help their children accomplish goals in literacy. They do it in many ways by the attitudes they reveal in acquiring books, purchasing them, using a library, and involving children in reading or discussion of something that has been read.

Some homes with an inadequate financial base or means of subsistence cannot or do not contain as many reading materials as the owners might desire. But libraries and various programs designed for young children are accessible, and children can acquire an early appreciation for the libraries' ongoing checking out and returning system and can learn to use it at optimal levels.

Preparing children for the enjoyment, awareness, and beginning receptiveness of skills in reading can begin in their infant years. It can be accomplished, not in a rigid or formalized manner, but in the same way that toys are playfully and experimentally used. Just as children do not need to have toys forced upon them, neither should books be used in this manner. A certain tentativeness exists with many activities or objects that are introduced to children in their early years. Many different experiences are needed before children acquire meaning and facility in usage of language.[51] What needs to be ensured is that they have the experiences and the opportunity to know about the varieties of things, people, and events that are in the environment and can be enjoyed.

The next sections will indicate how very young children begin to become aware of reading as an act of obtaining information from written symbols, sounds, words, and ideas. Even while they are not expected, at first levels, to understand that the words expressed by an adult who is looking at any written print are part of a direct relationship between the reader and the content read, children can, nevertheless, sense that a variety of information exists in different forms. Children from one year old to their toddler years can have many print-related experiences, whether in books, pictures of objects and words, or simply watching parents reading a magazine.

Reading Orientation in Infancy and to Two Years

In the last fifteen years, more books for young children have been published than ever before in United States history. Books are made out of strong cloth instead of paper so that infants will not be able to tear them. Beginning books, which show objects and one word naming the objects, provide a start in the child's library. Books that have objects covered by a fabric which can be touched by the child give a tactile, sensory, stimulation as well as a visual one.

Even before children begin to handle books on their own, parents who have held the child while showing a book have been sensitizing the child to the reading act, that of obtaining something from viewing a book. Psychological satisfaction, stimulation, talking, smiling, explaining, or conversing while looking directly into the child's eyes represents a significant human contact, which is very crucial in learning how to relate to others. (This can be done without a book, too, of course; the book provides a focus for both individuals for the moment.)

Reading with one's parent or older sibling can become a very special time for a child. A pleasant interchange of eye contacts that the child experiences in the reader's eyes responding to the child's responses, is building a basis for the acquisition of knowledge about one's environment. Sharing one's time, words, and responsiveness to ideas with another is one of the basic elements of a relationship with someone. One does not have to be able to verbalize feelings about a relationship in order to have one or to sense it as an infant does. Gestures, contact, and tone communicate feelings.

Infancy to sixteen months is an extraordinary period of growth. The child learns each day about people and what is expected from them depending on the age, relationship, and personality predispositions of those involved.

Talking, seeing people, using certain objects in the home, walking to various places in the neighborhood with one's parents, seeing many objects in the street (cars, street-cleaning vehicles, motorcycles) or in the sky (airplanes, helicopters) introduce the child to things that will be seen in books. Books reflect life. Life reflects books. Children's books which illustrate these objects with appropriate words are significant beginnings for a very young child

Children recognize boxes or containers of their own food. They become stimulated by the sight of them, especially when they are hungry. Letters or pictures on those containers represent beginning translation of symbols to letters and words as well as the sounds of words. Print and object become associated. Sounds and letters become connected in their use with children.

Focusing on objects and affiliating them with words for and functions of those items can provide information that will be applied later to similar objects that are seen by the child in books. This is a form of readiness for reading that is also practiced at school. Observation and discrimination among objects, sounds, shapes, and other aspects of differences among things help the child in recognizing uniqueness among letters and words, both in form and in sound.

As writers discuss a readiness for reading and the best time to involve children in beginning processes, they indicate that the opportunities for practice may in fact be the reading process itself.[52] As reading readiness activities at school involve storytelling, critical listening, concentrating on objects or symbols, repeating the words or sounds and story ideas, establishing eye contact between reader and listener, as well as other qualities of sound production to be noted by the teacher (instructing the child), any such activities that occur prior to school are reading instructional activities even if they are not occurring in a formalized context of the schoolroom.

The parent is considered to be the child's first teacher because many things that happen in the home are in themselves an act of instruction, perhaps not intended as such, but they teach the child something that will most likely be encountered again later and will be recalled as well for further application to a given item of knowledge. Whether these results eventually are construed as positive or negative in relation to a child's development is a separate issue. In a number of cases, however, parents are typically teaching their young children more that can be used later, at school, than they may realize.

Thus, the act of reading, usually involving itself with books or magazines, whether the parent's or the child's, is obvious; reading, however, is also occurring when the parent calls the child's attention to this box, that ball, the red bicycle, the yellow top, the pink blanket, and whatever item in the environment is being used or pointed out to the child. As the differences among sounds, objects, shapes, and textures, among other things, become pivotal in sensitizing children to the reading process, the home, in which a myriad of items are seen and sounds are heard, provides a profitable laboratory for the educational context of learning.

Many parents are unaware that children, between infancy and two years old, are learning how to discriminate among sounds, things, shapes of letters in illustrated books and in magazine graphics or illustrations, as well as in songs and language used by people in the child's environment. The normal activities of the home can, if guided in terms of recognition and affiliation with words heard and seen in signs, boxes, cans, or magazines and books, become part of the child's early reading orientation.

Special programs have been offered through experiments to determine whether or not children who do not normally have an environment in which an adult encourages communication can learn effective forms of cognitive growth and intellectual functioning.[53] Young children between the ages of eight and twenty-four months were given help by tutors who came to the homes of the subjects for a period of one year (an hour a day, five days each week). Children imitated the sounds of the tutor, played with and responded to games initiated by the tutor, learned to repeat names of objects, looked attentively at books and generally became responsive to the activity offered to them.

Between eighteen and twenty-four months, the child was shown illustrated books in which one subject was illustrated on a page. Naming and labeling or saying something about the object was the purpose of the task given to the child. Alphabet books and simple single-object books made of durable cardboard or cloth were helpful in presenting ideas in colorful and sturdy form.

Simple stories can be told about single objects, animals, or people. Children learn how language and books yield information. As an adult discovers what a child's preferences are, repetition of certain activities follows, and may also be enlarged upon in various ways. The adult has to know at what point the child is tiring in any activity and to terminate it.

Print awareness, symbolic relationships to ideas, language, or speech, as well as recognition of sounds and their association with objects or people, are significant characteristics of reading with books in hand. These elements occur, however, long before a child is able to understand what school is. Writers offer several explanations for the way that children can acquire reading skills yet not be aware that they are, in fact, reading.[54] It is also suggested that schools take advantage of the amount of information children have on reading before they are introduced to formalized instruction at school.[55]

The next section on reading development deals with developmental ages of children between three and five years old. Many children in this age range attend nursery or prekindergarten (at about three and four). Most children at five years old are in kindergarten or with children of similar age in a formalized instructional setting. Public and private schools organize grade levels in various ways, depending on the number of pupils and teachers and the physical space available to the schooling environment.

Reading Orientation from Three to Five Years

Children's vocabularies increase greatly in the years between three and five. Not only are children with others their own age, they are also with different adults and a greater number of different people representing backgrounds that vary from their own. This widening circle of new relationships, in itself, contributes a great deal toward new knowledge about the way things are in the child's world.

Consider the three-year-old child who discovers, seeks, pokes about in everything. The child does not know what to expect to find, for the most part. The motive for moving around the house stems from a never-ending quest for finding out about what is available for the child. Adults do not have to motivate the child, it is true. The interest in the child's desire to taste, to touch, and to know about the nooks and crannies of a house pressures the active search to pursue constantly for the surprises in the environment.

Typically, any nursery school to which a child of three or four may go provides storybooks, large objects on which to play (e.g., large blocks indoors, tricycles, slides, and swings outdoors), large pictures, and magnifying glasses with which to study scientifically the bugs, butterflies, flowers, leaves, and other creations of nature. The alphabet is usually shown in some form. It may be in trainlike strips across the top of the blackboard or bulletin board. Children become accustomed to seeing large (capital) letters as well as small (lower-case). They know that those letters represent something that is significant (or ought to be) for children.

Children know that there are songs and poems that represent the memorization of the alphabet. They realize that the letters together symbolize something else. That is, different from an "ABC" song, when individual letters are placed along side each other in special relationships (e.g., boy, dog, cat) those letters become ideas that are messages to people. They are not sure, until they recognize parts of a word, how those letters affect the spelling of a word. They have a hazy notion of the letters as having some importance to adults. They cooperate and try to remember as they are requested to respond about a word.

At three, children see illustrations in storybooks. They recognize the association between pictures and the words in the text of the book as this is pointed out to them by the teacher. They focus on the picture as the adult reads to them. The adult may show the child the significance of certain letters. Usually the letters of a child's name are the first that become important. Parents may help the children write their names by showing them in capital (or upper-case) letters each letter in a name. Later, when the child goes to school, the child learns the manuscript forms. Typically this is not too difficult for the child to manage, although in some cases, it may, for various neurological or psychological reasons, be difficult.

Reading for the three-year-old consists mainly in hearing stories read, in picking up one's own books of nursery rhymes, poetry, or simple stories on going to the store, hospital, or dentist's office. The children see large letters in the newspapers. When they go for a ride in the car, they typically note the signs, not only for traffic signals, but also those on benches representing advertisers' slogans or logos. Gradually these objects and symbols become meaningful.[56] Children are able to understand more of what they see in print than educators or parents are aware. Studies need to be conducted to ascertain certain limitations and strengths that children in this age range have even before they reach school instructional levels.

Until formalized instruction occurs, teachers of children in the three-year-old age range, must provide pupils with stacks of books on various topics such as scientific phenomena (e.g., clouds, thunder, sun, moon, space), and stories that intrigue children who enjoy hearing about animals, families, pets, magic, shapes, colors, cars, people from all backgrounds and countries.[57] Many "beginning" series exist, presenting scientific concepts to children in an attractive and simplified manner. A teacher or parent has only to go to the library or to the educational supplies stores that have exciting books and pamphlets of many levels of complexity or simplicity.

Scientific ideas must be presented accurately, even though they are simplified for early readers. They are presented in a way that explains why or how certain phenomena occur in nature. They are less complicated and abstract than in reading material geared for older children.

Books that provide adults with ideas to be used with children, and that children may like to look at as well, are to be found in bookstores and in catalogues.[58] Parents and teachers may acquire more ideas than they are able to exhaust in presentations to their children. As children differ in terms of readiness for certain ideas or complexities at various psychological levels of understanding, a choice of activities should be available from which to determine appropriateness for certain children.

Because contemporary writers are aware of the psychological orientations that people have in relation to solving interpersonal or emotional problems, many books are available that discuss visits to the dentist's or doctor's office so that children's fears and anxieties may be minimized. Friendships, rejections, loyalty, and the like are discussed in stories that are presented simply enough to permit a child to understand the major theme. Bibliotherapy refers to books that can be used to help an individual reason, be assuaged by, or find solace in some way through reading or hearing the story about another individual who experienced similar pain or psychologically disturbing effects and solved his/her problems in some way, even though it may have been only a temporary solution. Empathy or identification with the major characters of a story help the reader or listener "work out" a problem. A sense of isolation is ameliorated to some extent, as well as being substituted by new alternatives for action.

No one knows the specific point at which a child of three moves to the capacity of a four-year-old relative to any intellectual activity. The developmental process of growth in any cognitive or emotional area is not obvious at all times. For this reason, we must be aware at all times that the child's abilities are not as clearly marked as a date on the calendar that denotes chronological age. The calendar is an invention of humankind. It keeps a record of dates and years. It does not, however, indicate as clearly a sharp line or level of any achievement in the individual. Often, although people may be aware of this on an intellectual level, they forget that children have their own rates and depths of knowledge acquisition and expect too much of children or hurry them into performing up to levels beyond their abilities. This can have negative effects.

Human accomplishment in reading and other linguistic areas occurs mainly, we are told, in the left hemisphere of the brain. Even though it may be located or identified in that manner, the human being does not function in limited parts. The body as a total entity is affected by anything that touches even a tiny area of it.

Amazing combinations of thought and feelings are occurring in the child of three, four, or five years old. These children are learning, through seeing objects close at hand (touching them), what those objects do, what they are called, how they work, and how the printed word labeling each of those objects may look. Differences in coding and functioning of the right hemisphere of the brain, which processes spatial impressions of the individual, compared to those in the left hemisphere, which processes logical and sequential language, emphasize skills development in certain areas at one time, but not at another.[59] It is recommended that children be given material that involves spatial development and nonverbal imagery in skills development as well as linear reading skills. Word recognition can be approached in the perception of the total configuration of the word (right-hemispheric activity) as well as the perception of its individual letters (left-hemispheric activity).[60]

Various forms of language recognition may occur in the right hemisphere of the brain when those impressions involve total spatial patterns; coding of a symbol or pattern may be processed when that pattern represents another idea. It is the linear processing of reading or logical order of an idea in writing that is assumed to be performed better by the left hemisphere. The critical aspect of judgment and analysis of what the individual does is described by reasoning and thinking that occur in the left hemisphere of the brain. This aspect of learning has been considered the major area for educators. Researchers of cognition and sequentially developing knowledge consider that with the information that has been disclosed by research on the activities of the right hemisphere of the brain, educators should be including in the curriculum for children a more comprehensive plan for developing the right hemisphere as well as the left.[61]

Interestingly enough, young children show the ability to judge many differences among objects and seem free from constraints that are placed upon them later in school to perceive the world in a given way. Creativity is more fluid and expressive prior to children's learning to read and being held to the linear perspective of a given learning context.

Most of the teacher-or-parent activity with young children should engage children in conversation and discussion about objects and things of a reading nature in the environment. Rather than being concerned about which part of the brain does which coding or functioning for the human being, it is safe to include rather than exclude a variety of tasks (appropriate to the child's abilities). One of the exciting aspects of a child's early education is that no one is certain about the child's performance levels or skills related to many tasks that are part of later disciplines or subjects taught at school. It is known that children are able to do well in a wide variety of tasks; it is also known that intimidation, or premature correction of what they do, can inhibit them psychologically and physically in implementing a task.

Each child's individuality in skills, as well as attempts to master a task, must be respected by the teacher. Regardless of the size of a pupil, as is evident in the small three- or four-year-old child, teachers must perceive that child as a total, intricate system bursting with potential that can be channeled well in the child's behalf. The teacher is there at school to help the child, not by engraving the child's inadequacies in his/her self-concept, but rather by bringing out the child's growing powers to read, to see, to express, to sing, and to communicate with friends (teachers as well as pupils). Teachers need to check their own behavior often to determine whether they are allowing themselves to take undue advantage of the child's vulnerability and helplessness as a young pupil unfamiliar with his/her own rights; the child needs someone to help build his/her own self-respect. The teacher should be doing this if the child is to become confident in his/her skills, and in what s(he) says or does as a respected human being.

It is helpful for the child, as well as the teacher, to look at books that emphasize emotional, social, and interpersonal aspects of development.[62] A series of books, referred to as *Ready-Set-Grow*, discusses children's responsibilities, handling one's emotions effectively, expressing one's self well, feeling satisfied with one's abilities rather than overly critical, all from the point of view of a child and not in the lecturing, moralizing tone often used by an adult to a child.[63]

As teachers and parents interact with children, it is easy to forget the children's perspectives toward the world and toward their own self-expectations, as they think others would approve or not. Children are constantly trying to adapt to adult expectations (as well as those of other children) and to measure up to those standards or criteria. Books that help children, while interacting with adults, understand the degree to which dissonant behavior is normal or natural among people, do a service to children. Adults take for granted much of what has been learned throughout the years and assume that children, even at three or four or five, know similar reconciliatory means for assuaging one's own damaged self-concept.[64]

The ideas presented to children at their levels of comprehension reflect contemporary psychology on the same themes of adequate knowledge of self and an acceptance of human frailties as a comprehensive part of the human being and of humankind.[65] Good and evil reside in the same dimension. As one seeks to pursue one's goals in desirable, socially acceptable terms, what also exists in the mind is the opposite of those goals. Thus one is aware of bipolar of good and evil while struggling to remain within one sphere or the other. Because the abstractions that adults reason with, and perhaps rationalize in order to acquire a semblance of self-knowledge and surcease from anxiety, are typically complex, it is worthwhile that books for children can adapt such abstractions to comprehension at earlier levels of children's experiences with life.

Hard-cover, spirally-bound books for young children are available describing children's activities at understandable levels.[66] Charmingly presented books on topics or objects that are present in most children's surroundings (or in television pictures) are available in supermarkets as well as in the library.[67]

Books for use at bedtime are plentiful. Among the list are two that are easily enjoyed by young children.[68] Some children enjoy the same books to the point of wearing them out. If they desire newer ones or different ideational themes, a trip to the library is a worthwhile investment. Besides being an excellent outing to an interesting place, a walk or ride to the library as well as checking out books to take home for a couple of weeks or so, is similar to acquiring something new in one's psychological repertoire. It removes one from the mundane and routine habits of daily tasks. As children browse among the choices available to them in the library, they are also becoming familiar with other categories of reading and subject matter that can be of interest to them in the future.

Many opportunities arise in the school day of children in the three- to five-year-old age range, to experience pleasurable and informative stories on the varieties of people in society. Differences among families, in size, composition, origin, beliefs, attitudes, and appearance provide excellent story ideas and are informative. Children will receive instruction related to this area, when they learn about social studies in part of the school day. Social science generalizations from about seven social science disciplines [69] are used to create subject matter study forms for children in elementary school. Differences and similarities among families and people from various ethnic and racial origins will be part of a study period. Stories about such differences, however, are helpful in paving the foundation for understanding presentations of sociological and anthropological differences in later grades at school. [70]

The kindergarten includes a great number of activities that affect in one way or another children's abilities in reading. The classrooms, indoors and out, has a reading readiness orientation. Whether the content is oriented

This kindergarten boy matches the correct symbol with the correct word on the weather chart in a science and language arts lesson. (Photo by Gerald J. Margolin.)

It is important that children help each other during a reading lesson. Charts are used to a great extent in early reading activities. They facilitate for the children materials that the teacher makes for a particular lesson in the knowledge that the children can be successful in reading. The teacher knows what the children are ready for and will find pleasure in reading. (Photo by Gerald J. Margolin.)

toward a social studies understanding or whether it is diverse in subject matter, nevertheless, the room is geared for many levels of skills that exist among the children for whom the room has been prepared.

The five senses and also a knowledge of kinesthetics on how the body moves or feels to the individual, and sensitivities toward feelings of balance, provide receptors to the child's repertoire of reading awareness. Children's activities that involve touching, tasting, smelling, seeing, and hearing, and tasks that contribute toward a feeling of balance and appropriate state of readiness, are foundational to complex levels of understanding words and concepts.

Teachers have to call children's attention to shape, size, smell, textures,

Listening centers offer a chance to hear clearly articulated stories while typical noise levels of the classroom are kept from disturbing one's concentration. These listening headsets permit individualistic activities to occur even while the teacher and children are doing other things in the classroom. (Photo by Gerald J. Margolin.)

and auditory differences among things in the environment. Children may hear or see many phenomena and objects in the classroom. They will not form concepts about them, however, unless their teacher gives names to those events and objects. The associational effects of ideas and words, plus facts and conceptualization, become one of the most useful contributions to a child's framework of intellectual constructs that a teacher can provide.

Writers have drawn together some ideas that can be used directly with children.[71] Some have recommended themes and activities that teachers themselves might bring into the classroom. Most books on curriculum for young children include many ideas that the teacher or parent may adapt to the specific pupils who will be using the projects.

Charts are used by the teacher to write stories that have been dictated by the children. The children then use those charts as offering reading content that is already familiar to them. Note the action between the two children shown using the chart together in the photo on page 188.

Listening centers, such as that shown in that photo, provide opportunities for children to listen through individual headsets so that distracting sounds of the environment are prevented from interfering with stories they are hearing. Noises, voices, and children's activities are typically a part of the kindergarten classroom. As listening is not an easy skill to acquire relative to new words and stories, children need to concentrate totally on what they are hearing.

Children read charts that have their names on them showing that they have a responsibility for doing something in the classroom. They may be expected to distribute crayons or paper to a small group of children. They may be monitors for seeing that all the blocks are put away after they have been used, or all the activities at a mathematics table are cleared when time to stop has been signaled.

As children read notes showing their names associated with responsibilities of some sort, as they read the calendar with days of the week, figures for each day, names for each month, and holidays that are celebrated or observed, they learn how words are significant in telling people what to do. When new ideas or words are introduced, children need a few examples of appropriate usage in the context that renders meaning to the words and concepts.

Teachers have to be aware that children do not yet know enough about spelling, and associating the correct letter with the sound that is part of a word. Because of this weakness in recognizing letters through sight and sound, children have to hear clearly what the teacher says. They cannot yet visualize the letter that is being pronounced by the teacher. This realization will come for many children, after many experiences in seeing, hearing, saying, and sounding out some of the words they hear.

Teachers may have to exaggerate sounds or words in order to help the children hear clearly the letters that may otherwise be swallowed in pronunciation and lost to the children's hearing and discrimination of sound. This kind of consciousness that a kindergarten teacher must have for the inability of young children to visualize the letters that represent certain sounds in words is helpful in sustaining articulation that children must hear if they are to learn. Exaggerated expression of sound or words may sound peculiar to adults who are not accustomed to kindergarten activities and the nature of children who are trying to learn how to become more mature. In order to retain interest in a variety of language expressions, teachers often create stories that may have repetitive sounds that will provide practice in hearing and saying the sounds that give children difficulty. Jingles, poetry, and four-line songs introduce easy forms for the practice of words and letters in certain words. Games can also involve the pupils in practice that can be valuable for them in the long run.[72]

As is true of individuals at any age when involved in learning a new fact, concept, or subject matter area, listening critically is essential, or at least concentrating on a given item of information. With children in the three- to five-year-old age range, listening, noticing differences among things and events as well as people, become central to the first step in internalizing knowledge. Reading is a complex act. It is psychological as well as physical (involving learning with the five senses as receptors that feed information to the brain). Three- to five-year-old children are taught to perceive that certain elements of things or words are more important than others. Their learning experiences prior to the first grade in school are less formalized, but are complex and broad-reaching, nevertheless.

The next section indicates how experiences of children between the ages of six to nine build on what they already know. This period of children's education is typically the beginning of frequently formalized and organized activities (sequentially organized at times) carried out in both large and small groups. Teachers differ in the manner of teaching, of organizing into large or small groups, and in how didactic or fluidly instructive they may be. The next section includes discussions of these issues of teaching strategies, organization, and environmental arrangement of classroom instruction for six-to nine-year-old children at school.

Reading Skills and Performance from Six to Nine Years

The first grade for many children at the age of six represents very serious efforts in beginning reading. Even though the kindergarten in some cases may have introduced routines for children and may have had many readiness for reading tasks as part of the daily schedule, the first grade nevertheless is different in several ways.

When one considers the increased number of tasks, and the increasingly difficult activities that are introduced to children in the first grade, as well as the knowledge needed to perform effectively in several subject matter areas, it is not surprising that some children become overwhelmed in the first few weeks of school. The first grade has to be organized skillfully if the children are to move from one activity to another with ease. The teacher's awareness of children's needs, anxieties, and abilities can often alleviate traffic patterns and routines to some extent during the first few weeks. Many teachers do not introduce complicated tasks or routines for performance in those learning tasks too early in the first grade. Simpler tasks are presented first so that pupils are able to sense accomplishment. Review of learning that may have occurred in the kindergarten (e.g., recognition of simple words, labels, shapes, colors, among other aspects of learning) provides opportunities for the teacher to know what the children can do. It is important that the children have a sense of satisfaction or success at least in the first two weeks.

All through school experiences, teachers have to be conscious of the fact that learning proceeds through the completion of some tasks in which pupils gain self-confidence. Gradually as new information is presented, the children add on to what they already know. They need the teacher's approval as much as they need an inner sense of satisfaction. If they do not feel that they are making headway and that their efforts are productive, they may stop trying. This contingency has to be avoided. The teacher can skillfully observe when it may be occurring, or showing tendencies to occur.

There may be about twenty-five or thirty pupils in the classroom. The teacher must, nevertheless, know each of them well. Even though each pupil cannot be known in terms of how work is done at all levels, all of them need to be known within a few weeks. Seeing children for several hours a day, watching them work and watching the way they respond to their classmates, permits a teacher to know a great deal about them. The way in which each child is given help relative to what the teacher has observed about the child's skills and abilities becomes crucial to that child's success. A teacher must know how to plan effectively to provide the appropriate task that is commensurate with pupil abilities to meet success in the task. When the teacher knows how to adapt activities to children's abilities so that successful efforts result, children can learn rapidly at times. The teacher, however, should know children well after planning such adaptive activities.

READING GROUPS AND LEARNING STRATEGIES

Before children are placed in groups that represent a similar level in ability for the pupils in them, many activities have taken place in the classroom. These experiences provide for the teacher's judgment a means through which some placement of children can be made and one in which pupils will be able to learn effectively. Children typically do not find it easy to concentrate when the total class is being taught together; they seem to lose focus because of distractions of other pupils.[73]

Grouping in its best usage, permits the teacher to observe the children's progress as well as to concentrate on a few at a time. Individual skills can be noted much more effectively in small groups than in the total setting of an entire class. Many activities are conducted in small groups when the teacher has to notice, follow carefully what the children are doing, and has to record the children's progress. When songs are sung or taught, when poetry is presented as a choral reading or recitation, or when directions need to be followed to participate in a game, the total class may work together.

Too many things are taken for granted about children's comprehension skills.[74] Studies have indicated that young children between five and a half and six and a half have found it very difficult to distinguish long words, phrases, sounds, and syllables. They do not know where the separation between words lies. They hear sounds and often cannot associate sounds as parts of words.

It requires time for children to realize too, that spaces between words represent a way of marking off the words as individual representations. For this reason it is recommended that the teacher become very familiar with what the children are able to do and not to assume that they understand the terminology used in reading instructions.[75] One study revealed that advanced work of children in the first grade that required recognition of the tall letter (such as an "l,") in the middle of a long word, was difficult.[76] These examples verify the necessity for teachers to check themselves when they ask children to do something by way of recognizing words, sounds, letters, and the like. It is one thing to challenge pupils, quite another to do it with the realization that it may be too difficult and may confuse them.

It is noteworthy that even while developing strategies in the classroom for organizing and grouping children for reading instruction, a teacher must be aware that learning to read is not only an exercise in putting words, sounds, symbols and ideas together in a way that makes sense for the child. The children who seem to be successful in reading are those that have a reservoir of syntactical knowledge, who are able to note clues in relation to other words in context of the material being read, and who are aware that the words convey meanings similar to those that one hears in spoken words.[77]

It is recommended that the teacher present many opportunities for children to practice the recognition of words, word order, inflections, and cues in their relationship to the context in which they are seen. Even though the teacher meets with the pupils in groups in order to have reading instruction for them, there is still a great deal that must be done before the children use the primers. Matching symbols and sounds, seeing the words on cards or other shapes,[78] noting contextual clues, seeing words associated with objects, and many other activities provide children with the opportunities to make sense out of seeing and hearing the sounds, meanings, and sentences that compose their language.

The teacher can recognize the abilities of children who are ready to read from preprimers and those who need more practice reviewing words and simple sentences or phrases that are affiliated with pictures of ideas, things, or people. With that recognition of differences in the pupils' skills, must come an understanding of and empathy with the children's perceptions as they see other classmates reading from books that they themselves are not yet able to use. Teachers must be aware of and understand the psychological effects that competition and the abilities to read have on children. Children's feelings will be hurt when they are not able to be in a group that they see is advancing beyond their own. Encouragement and support are needed by pupils.

Many activities and games are available, commercially or in booklet form, to show the ideas that teachers may need to make suitable tasks for each child at any level of readiness. This supply of materials for children to use at any level of complexity makes school life easier and more pleasant for all concerned. The children are able to participate at all times because some place in the classroom there is something that they are able to complete successfully. Here, again, the skills, imagination, and empathy of the teacher come into focus.

There are no concrete guidelines for creating groups for beginning instruction in reading or any other grouping of children in classrooms. The decisions as to which children will be placed where, when, and how, depend greatly on the circumstances in each case. Teachers may also want to change the pupil periodically from one group to another as soon as the child demonstrates a need or level of skill to change either to a more advanced or less accelerated group.

Some of the signals that a teacher must note are those that show a child's displeasure or unwillingness to read, comments about being in a group that the child finds disparaging in some way, or tendencies to criticize often, complaining about almost everything at school. The teacher must be attuned to various changes in the pupils' behavior so that adaptations can be made in the activities given to them for participation. Levels of readiness make a vast difference for each child between enjoying what (s)he is able to master and wanting to avoid any attempts to take part in learning.

The reading process as planned by the teacher includes the need to have children develop their vocabularies, note the structure and analysis of words and word parts, comprehend syntactical structure or general awareness of how to put a sentence together so that it makes sense, understand cognitive aspects of subject matter content, know how to adapt new meanings to one's vocabulary of word recognition and usage and to acquire a reservoir of words for easy recall. These opportunities can occur throughout the school day, during planned lesson periods as well as those that arise spontaneously. With the teacher's awareness that the children need practice in language and reading skills, a continual effort toward that end can be made for the children's benefit. It requires acute observation on the teacher's part, in listening and seeing what each child is saying and doing when (s)he speaks or reads.

Some teachers may use three reading groups in a class of about twenty-five or thirty. Some may divide the children into about five groups if the teacher can manage the preparation of materials for them and if there seems to be a pattern of similarity among the children in five different groups. To consider the criteria for grouping, test scores may be used, children's facility with language and words affect their reading skills, psychological and emotional maturity are considered, as well as cognitive developmental levels and general intellectual capacities.

Children are given opportunities to read aloud as well as silently. When the children are beginning reading, oral presentation or recitation is essential because the teacher has to know how the children are pronouncing their words. As pupils advance, however, they are given some opportunities for reading silently, followed by answering questions about the meaning of what they have read. Teachers may often ask the children who are sitting in a five-member group to listen while one of the other children reads, and to follow the words on the page, and in that sense they are reading silently.

Because reading has been recognized since at least the 1950s as an extremely important skill for an individual, it has become one of the most concentrated areas of study in the schools. Books have been written to amplify for the teacher the different ways of teaching, whether to use phonic approaches, word-analysis approaches, or contextual cues for word recognition and comprehension. There are also many gamelike readiness activities for formalized reading. Whatever manner is chosen by the teacher relates to the teacher's own predispositions leading toward a comfort in style, attitude, and general organizational modes that facilitate activity in the classroom. The teacher's personality, as well, influences how the children will learn. Technical material, varieties of activities, and books in themselves do not determine whether a reading program will be effective or not. The teacher's manner of using materials, the feeling of concern for the children's learning how to read and to enjoy reading affect the success or lack of it in a classroom.

Teachers need more confidence in their own choice of reading interaction with pupils. They need to persist in efforts to show children that their well-being is important to the teacher. The speed in learning to read is less important than are the goals of mastery, persistence and the enjoyment of the search and progress toward those ends.

FIRST GRADE

For children in the first grade, teachers may use a basal reader approach in reading instruction along with many activities in which the basic skills are needed for language and reading development. The basal readers approach typically includes workbooks that can be used for readiness activities, a few preprimers, a primer and a beginning reader's book.[79] Most public schools systems (and private ones as well) use this approach.

The basal readers are controlled for the level of vocabulary, syntactical usage, comprehension, and story content. The preprimers may have, for example, about 40 to 110 words in a cumulative vocabulary, whereas the primer has from 120 to about 310, and the first reader's books may have as many as from 230 to about 475.[80] Thus, the series of books range from below 100 to almost 500 words. This range represents a judgment made on the way children learn and how much they are able to assimilate with comprehension in a span of guided reading materials.

When these basal readers are used, specific instructions for their use are given so that the teacher sees explicitly described sequences of development that can be followed. The teachers are expected to depend mainly on and follow the directed planning of the books and guidelines. Some teachers enjoy doing this; others do not. Some teachers prefer their own creative planning and activities with children and do not like the limiting specificity of certain instructional guide books. In any case, ever since competence in reading has become a nationwide concern for the public and children at school, many teachers and schools are expected to use the basal reader approach considering that approach to be failsafe.

The basal readers provide instructional activities and even the exact statements that teachers can make to children when any lesson is introduced. There are also suggestions in some cases for ideas that the teacher may follow in a creatively adapted manner. Individualized instruction is much more a part of the reading program than it was many years ago. This means that writers of most basal reading programs are aware of individual differences among children who are part of a large classroom. Thus instructions for individual differences can be included for the teacher's judgmental use with certain children.

Like any material given to the teacher to use in a structured and sequential sense, the readers and workbooks may prevent creative ideas on the teacher's part. Discretionary use of anything in the classroom depends on the wisdom and judgment of the teacher, who enjoys a variety of forms in the classroom. Some teachers may use the workbooks in a supplementary fashion and obtain ideas from them, but not turn the children loose to use them in a haphazard or nonsupervised manner. When children use workbooks that are not overseen by the teacher, they may be making the same mistakes over and over again without the teacher's knowledge. The teacher can help the children only when errors are known.

Some school systems, in an attempt to diagnose each child's level of development and to effectively help every pupil improve at his/her own pace, use what is conceputalized as a systems (or systematic) approach in the instruction of reading. With these plans for recording children's progress, come intricate charts that reflect children's levels of mastery in the recognition of words, beginning and ending parts of words, vocabulary knowledge, and a number of other aspects of effective reading skills.

One need only look at the textbooks and packaged plans that various schools use for reading instruction, not only in the first three grades but in later or intermediate grades as well. The principal of the school is often given the opportunity to choose which of the readers published by many companies will be selected for purchase and presented to the teachers to use in the classroom. Often the principal will ask the teachers which textbooks they would prefer (along with guiding plans for the teachers using the books with children).

Some school systems make the selection in the administrative offices asking the advice of consultants or specialists in the fields. The manner of selection of purchase and eventual choices made depends on the individual school system and whether it is centrally oriented in its decision-making processes or more oriented toward the instructional or teaching staff's participation. Often the state department in which a school system is located may recommend, but not mandate, the purchase of a particular series of reading texts. These rulings vary among states and local school systems. Teachers may note this and find out how the system works in their own schools. Sometimes principals of schools appreciate a teacher's interest in this regard; sometimes they do not. Again it depends on the individual situation and how the teacher's interest is expressed.

Some teachers realize that even though the readers occupy most of the reading period, they nevertheless have to have many individual activities prepared for independent work of children who finish their work faster than others. While the teacher may spend about twenty minutes with a group in which directed reading is occurring, the children in the other two, three, or four groups may be working at an activity (e.g., matching words to pictures, matching letters to word components). When the teacher works with a group that needs more help, more than twenty minutes may be spent. This suggests that the rest of the class, while not working directly with the teacher, must be involved in activities that can carry them through without the teacher's detailed supervision.

If the teacher knows that time must be cut shorter on a given day for any group, activities that serve to review what the children have learned can be used rather than the basal readers. Children enjoy change just as do teachers. Discipline becomes less of a problem when the teacher has a large variety of tasks and activities congruent with many children's abilities and interests.

Effective placement and identification of activities affect the children's usage of tasks when the teacher is not able to provide individual supervision. Teachers who acquire, through purchase or creating them, activities maintained in boxes that are labeled for easy recognition by the pupils find that their classrooms run smoothly. When children are able to take something from the shelves, go to a table and work quietly with a purposeful activity, they are often happy with school and do not need to distract others in order to stimulate themselves. This independence in occupying one's time wisely can carry over into efficiency of time outside the school as well.

Teachers of pupils in kindergarten and primary grades must realize how varied in pace and form the developmental levels of children are as they try to adapt to many different school skills. This suggests that change may occur rapidly in some children at times; in other children it may not. If children's concerns are at the heart of the teacher's orientation in teaching, attention will be given to these subtle differences among pupils.

Teachers simply have to be observant of each child. They have to notice when some pupils are ready to move to another reading group. Most books dealing with children's instructional needs advise that groups have limitations as well as advantages. Groups facilitate the teacher's lesson planning so that it is focused on several children's skills at similar levels. They also allow children who are ready to read at more advanced levels to work together. For children to wait too long for someone to read is frustrating. By the same token, teachers must be careful not to treat "slow" readers differently than the "fast" ones. Children sense these attitudes on the part of the teacher and take on toward themselves those same orientations. If they think that the teacher is irritated or "disgusted" with them, they themselves accept those attitudes as real, and unfortunately shift them into part of their own self-concepts.

Gradually, through the first grade, pupils realize what the seriousness of school is all about and they know more or less what will be expected of them in the second grade. Typically, they have learned a great deal in the first grade, even though all the skills presented to them may have not been fully mastered. The second grade is an extension of activities and subject matter areas that were introduced in the first grade. New forms of writing may be introduced and more complex aspects of science and mathematics.

SECOND GRADE

The second grade for reading instruction of pupils at school involves increased complexities in vocabulary development, comprehension skills, and word-attack competencies, and broader varieties of reading opportunities in books, stories, basal readers, chart stories, and a number of experiences that involve language exchange among the pupils and teachers. Reading becomes a more integrated part of everything that children do. Following directions and comprehension skills are involved in almost everything the children do, from following instructions for a simple game to a complicated test-taking situation.

The children are not only in reading groups in many schoolroom routines, they are also keeping their own records of completed activities. They are learning how to organize materials and to be accountable for work expected from them at various times in the school term. Classification systems for their own progress become apparent to them. Their own notebooks, folders, card files, and other forms of keeping track of their own work sensitize them to organizational schemes that are similar to a reading systems approach.

At seven years old, children are often comfortable with school. They are no longer novices and know how to conduct themselves in classrooms, for the most part. So much of what pupils learn at school is not written in explicit form. They are learning about informal relationships among people. They are learning how people respond to each other when certain products are seen (e.g., a picture painted or drawn by a child). They are learning how to get in the good graces of the teacher or other children. They need friends.

Accountability for one's progress becomes more apparent and more necessary in the second grade. Children's awareness among themselves of which child is advancing and which one is not is no secret. Reading, mathematics, and other subjects become serious endeavors. All children, one would guess, want to succeed and to be admired by their peers. The second grade, although more familiar to children as far as its routine aspects of school are concerned, is for some children tedious in its difficulties and in its advanced expectations upon them. Some teachers indicate that the children seem tired and frustrated. This is sometimes noted too at sophomore levels, both in high school and in the second year at college or the university, when students show signs of periodic boredom and frustration and restlessness. Such times present the greater challenge for teachers who wish to motivate students to enjoy what they experience in instructional modes.

Basal readers in the second grade have a cumulative vocabulary of 950 words to 1,700.[81] Teachers are cognizant of the need to build on those readers with poetry, stories, and chart stories composed by the children. Vocabulary should constantly be gaining, through ideas presented in class and library books, and providing children with an appreciation for the variety of words that can be used to express exactly what an individual wishes. Fun with words and one's language becomes an active teaser in children's appetites for learning.

Children are also having a wider range of experiences than they did in the first grade. Their comprehension levels are typically advancing. Teachers must be aware of the appreciation levels that pupils have for certain books. In a typical second grade, children's reading skills may differ by a range of three grade levels, from grade one to grade four. If a child is bored by a basal reader, the teacher may have to adapt to the use of other books or activities. Some school systems have gifted programs so that children who are advanced in reading, mathematics, science, or other areas, may attend at least for part of the school day, one of those advanced programs.

Some of the basic approaches in helping children to recognize words and sounds (or decoding symbols to words) are still used in the second grade. Because not all children are mastering words and comprehension at even minimal levels, the skills must be practiced. The children who are increasing their achievement in comprehension and word-recognition skills also need practice for greater facility in using new levels of concepts and vocabularies.

Some programs geared toward enhancing phonics skills are recommended for children's use in the kindergarten and primary grades.[82] These activities offer opportunities to recognize sound and letter and word combinations. Vowels and consonant sounds may be emphasized along with rules for guidelines in pronunciation. Some of these programs are the

Phonovisual Method, Phonetic Keys to Reading, the Carden Method, or Words in Color. Depending on the ability levels of the children, the teacher may choose a simple or more advanced component of these programs.

The wisdom of the teacher must be relied upon to make the choices for the best gains of the students. The choices made for grouping the children and subsequently deciding which groups will receive which materials do not represent an easy decision. It seems that with materials available in the numbers and programs produced today, a multifaceted approach may be used. Some teachers may use along with basal readers, an individualized reading program in which simple books created by others than writers of educational activity books may be introduced (having only limited numbers of words and sentences). General language experience approaches involving the children's dictated stories of their own ideas can be used; the ideas they present are written on charts (by the teacher). The children know the content since they saw the teacher write what was dictated. This is done more at the first-grade level than at the second, but it may in certain classrooms prove to be very effective in correlating the components of reading, writing, seeing, and saying.

Word-attack skills must continue in the second grade because new words are encountered, many of which may be unfamiliar to the children. Even though language skills proceed from one's own natural background or context of spoken words, school language in the process of learning about new concepts (such as mathematics, science, social studies, and health, among other subject matter areas) presents totally unfamiliar words and concepts.

Skills needed for recognizing words involve the recognition of sounds (phonics), noting configuration (shape or outline of words), recognizing structural units within a word (structural analysis), recognizing relationships between a sound or phoneme and the printed grapheme or letter, as well as being aware of vowel combinations or consonant blends in words and such beginnings and endings of words. Children are able to recognize words through an awareness of meaning when they see them in a given context. Often even if they do not know the letters in the words, the sounds, or how to pronounce them, the context of a word as it fits into appropriate meaning of a sentence, helps them in knowing what the word is. Teachers can help children use a variety of approaches in learning to read.

With more research conducted on methods of reading and more knowledge revealed on how the reading process occurs, teachers can avail themselves of new ideas and practices. What they must remember, however, is that their own views and intuitive approaches to children's learning are often very reliable modes for helping children. To the teachers who know their pupils well, the processes of teaching seem to come to mind almost without thought. A delicate balance between acquiring the most recent information and using one's own best educated judgment can be maintained. Even with the frequency of listening to the children read, the teacher's attention and pleasure in hearing the children's appropriate levels of pitch, variation of tone, and expression as they are related to ideas become significant to the children's willingness to read.[83]

Teachers working with children in the second grade enjoy the abilities of the pupils because they are slightly advanced over the novitiate status of the children in the first grade. Grouping may be done in terms of the skills range of the total class. Developmental levels increase, sometimes rapidly, sometimes slowly. The more that the teacher has available for reading, not only in books themselves, but in charts, poetry, drama, writing letters and presenting them, choral reading, jokes, riddles, and many other forms of communication activities, the better for the students.

Technical aspects of how to recognize words, how to say them, how to use them appropriately in a sentence or story or how to recall meanings of them in proper contexts can be practiced. What matters a great deal is the general atmosphere of the classroom, which engenders language expression and enjoyment of it.

The student's experiences in the third grade may be similar to those in the second. This depends on the teacher and the organization of experiences in school. When a child is eight years old and is interested in reading books of various types and is looking for topics in the library that bring him/her to wider ranges of reading, success in reading may be developing.

THIRD GRADE

Children in the third grade are beginning to use the library with greater ease than they might have earlier in their reading development. Some children show an advanced knowledge of library use and reading skills when their parents have introduced them through their own interests and trips to the library.

Functional skills in reading are emphasized in the third grade because it is assumed that the child has gained some reading skills in basal readers and is able to move from the structurally programmed books into more generally oriented materials. Comprehension skills become more relevant as the reading matter itself becomes more complicated.

One writer suggests that six skills may be used in helping pupils learn how to understand what they read.[84] First, children need to understand the basic meaning of a passage; second, they should be able to detect an organization in the passage; third, they should be able to analyze the material; fourth, they should synthesize it; fifth, they should evaluate it; and sixth, they should be able to respond creatively to questions asked about it.

Even though word-attack skills and expression of words are noted, as well as the children's general abilities in articulating ideas of readings given orally or read silently, teachers are ever concerned that children understand what they read. Technical skills for aproaching new passages that are unfamiliar to children are stressed in the third grade. Questions are asked by the teacher so that word meanings can be recalled, inferences can be drawn from what was read, the child can become aware of critical clues regarding the explicitness or implicitness of an idea and can be helped to recognize the writer's mood, tone, or attitude about an idea.

Basal readers in the third grade reflect a cumulative vocabulary range of about 1,900 to 3,300 words.[85] This alone gives some impression as to the increase of words when one compares the second-grade readers with the third. Differences in skills among the children increase to a greater extent in this grade level. There can be a range of skills that represent six grade levels among pupils in the third grade.[86] Some pupils are capable of reading at the first- or second- or third-grade level; while others may be able to read at the fourth-, fifth- or sixth-grade level. One among the children may be at the fourth-grade level in reading skills, a few may be at the fifth-grade level, several at second, and slightly more at third; one child may be at the sixth-grade level. This suggests that teachers will have difficulty grouping the children in clusters for reading instruction. Individualized reading instruction and multifaceted levels of reading must be considered at this point. Materials to guide children at different levels can be obtained through various programs. The teacher, however, must make the choices and adapt them to individual pupils in a given classroom.

Teachers have to select their own plan for record keeping on each child's progress. When specific programs are purchased, however, they often include a means for checking children's mastery of reading skills (e.g., word attack, phonics, recognition of certain word endings, beginnings, consonant blends, and the like). Systems approaches to reading include record keeping of very specific mastery components in the children's reading development. Curriculum laboratories in universities or colleges as well as in large school systems (or small ones too) have a variety of programs that the teacher may check for comparison.

At times, school systems select their own means of assessment and recording of children's progress in reading. The evaluation forms may be simple at general levels of usage in the classroom. They can also be complex, represented on large sheets shown on a classroom wall, indicating exact items of mastery acquired by each pupil.

Testing in reading is strongly related to a means of diagnosis and prescription for next steps or sequences in children's learning. These recommendations for strengthening the skills of pupils may be made at varying levels, from remedial approaches to more typical or normal developmental levels. Typical measurements made to ascertain a prognosis for growth in reading are related to the "rate [of reading], comprehension, vocabulary, and word analysis."[87]

It is recommended that children can be taught that it is sometimes better to read rapidly when scanning for specific facts without actually reading all the details, looking for topical headings or major sentences.[88] To read rapidly for no specific purpose seems unjustified by some writers.

Remedial work in vocabulary knowledge and recognition includes the use of dictionaries, calling children's attention to words and their meanings, and provision of practice in noting relationships between words as well as emphasizing synonyms and antonyms.[89] Word lists in themselves are not recommended as a way of improving children's facility in comprehension and recognition of specific words. Usage in context and experiences with specific purposes planned by the teacher seem to ensure greater development of vocabulary skills. Prediction and measurement of which words are needed most by individuals remain uncertain in research conducted so far.[90]

Concerns for the semimechanical means of having children answer questions on the reading that they do in the primary grades are expressed by Spache, who indicates that an underlying assumption, the value of repetition, is questionable.[91] He says that the practice seems to reflect a view that children will be able to increase their comprehension and growth in reading skills if they answer questions on main ideas or details and conclusions of stories or assigned reading.[92] Again, rather than a generalized approach, it is recommended that different questions be asked in relation to specific content in order to help children learn how to read critically, searching for certain facts, identifying omissions of ideas or words needed to convey better meaning, sensing distortion of ideas, or usage of biasing terms.[93] Teachers need to know how to ask such questions at varying levels of difficulty for the pupils in any classroom group.

Word-attack skills as they are typically taught in the classroom are questioned by researchers.[94] Relationships between the students' knowledge of rules learned in isolated word practice on sounds and construction of words and their recognition of words in reading processes themselves do not hold. Learning to read words during the act of reading books or stories, rather than emphasizing word learning through synthetic skills involving sound and word construction drill in isolation, appears essential for improved reading ability. Varieties of word-attack skills are needed for children who are having difficulty in reading. These approaches, however, should be presented to children when they are reading and can note the words as part of a broader context of ideas and meanings.

Teachers may wish to try a simple sentence test for children in the primary grades to find out what the pupils' feelings are about reading. The responses provide information on the child's attitudes toward and satisfactions in reading.[95] The test is conducted individually with each child, who listens to the teacher ask for the word that needs to be filled in after the child hears the sentence, such as, "I cannot read when _____." Older children can read the test and complete it by writing the words in themselves. It can give the teacher impressions about books that the child likes, the child's preferences for certain reading groups, or even whether the child likes to read aloud to the class.

If teachers would like to know about several ways to analyze children's reading, many test forms are available. The test constructions guide teachers in what to look for in the pupils' oral reading.[96] Accuracy, comprehension, and the rate of a child's reading are measured in the Gilmore Oral Reading Test, Gray Oral Reading Tests, Individual Reading Placement Inventory, San Diego Quick Assessment Tests, Standard Reading Inventory, Classroom Reading Inventory, and Diagnostic Reading Scales. For each of these tests, comments are made about content validity, construct validity, reliability, and concurrent validity, as well as a general description of the tests themselves.[97] Most of these tests are conducted in an individual, rather than group, manner. They also test, for the most part, the pupil's skills in word recognition, oral reading, comprehension in both silent and oral reading, and the speed of reading. They are age-graded, of course.

The disabled reader is viewed as an individual who needs more help than the individual classroom teacher can provide. Being below the average reader in one of the primary grades at more than two years qualifies an individual for special diagnoses of specific difficulties in reading. For the secondary levels, three years below the average grade placement for a pupil where reading skills are concerned should alert teachers to the pupil's need for remedial help.[98]

It is interesting to note that classroom teachers who have materials appropriate to flexible modes of instruction in reading are typically able to help children make up a deficit of six months in their reading abilities.[99] Even in the third grade, competent teachers can bring children who have had a three- to seven-month lag in adapting to grade-level performance in reading up to grade level by knowing how to help the children.

After the primary grades, however, in the intermediate grades of the fourth and fifth, many children (60 per cent of them) are outside their grade placement. This means, then, that less than half of the children would be within the expected year of grade placement.[100] For this reason, a one-year lag in children's reading skills below grade placement is not considered a reasonable time period or identifier of children's needs for remedial services. Fortunately, many of the children in this one-year deficit seem to overcome it through the competent attention of their teacher.

This indicates, again, how important it is that the primary grades teacher have a variety of materials and techniques that can be used to back up some of the impressions the teacher has about certain children needing help in given areas of reading. The deficiencies can be alleviated to some extent when a teacher is able to identify some of the problems of the pupils.

Parents need to know how to support the child's efforts in learning how to read. When a parent begins chastizing a child for being lazy, uninterested and the like, it is not helpful, but rather engenders negative overtones to the reading process. Being available to hear a child read, a parent can be supportive in receptive attitudes; this transmits significant information and reassurance to a child.[101]

The end of the primary grades at elementary school represents the winding down of an early childhood range of behavior, personality, and school role. It represents an entrance into the close-to-puberty period when children are in a physically developing stage toward maturity. Nine years old and in the fourth grade marks the beginning of early stages of youth. Some children are mature at this age particularly when they have friends who are older than they and who are close to their early teen years. With each age range, parents as well as teachers have to be aware of the children's advancing and widening circles of friends, concepts, interpersonal understandings, and intellectual capacities that can manifest themselves. Thus while adults who interact with children may know them to some extent in terms of what can be expected, adults also need to be aware that the differences among children will become greater and more intricate. If children are to be given an equitable consideration in adults' interactions with them, teachers and parents will have to be ever aware of unexpected behavior, both pleasantly surprising or disconcerting at times.

FOURTH GRADE

In the fourth grade, children can have reading skills that facilitate unusual types of learning. At the same time that teachers are aware of pupils who comprehend and read well in a variety of subject matter areas, there will be several children who appear to be younger and less mature in reading comprehension patterns.

Basal readers in the fourth grade typically have a cumulative vocabulary of about 2,800 to 3,500 words.[102] Although the words themselves may indicate an advance in quantity, teachers are often advised to note whether the content of the readers is of interest to children nine years of age. It is incumbent upon the teacher to acquire reading materials that reflect current perceptions of children in that age range. Societal contexts vary from group to group as well as from decade to decade. If the text appears outmoded to the children, they will not respect or dignify its use.

Children are also at times able to pronounce a word in the context of reading even if they do not know or understand the word. Teachers have to check comprehension often by asking for answers to questions in which the children's answers would reflect comprehension. Basal readers build into the lessons for children the gradual acquisition of words that many children should be able to comprehend. What the teacher has to do, however, is to constantly seek assurance of comprehension as well as noting correct pronunciation of words.

Dramatic presentations in puppet shows or plays, a television mock-up station, and other forms of communicating media provide excellent opportunities to have children (in a relatively unself-conscious manner) use colorful and informative language and reading materials. These props or purposeful activities give pupils the experiences needed in using words that are a more natural process for them. The teacher can recognize many qualities among the children's presentations that reveal what they know or do not know. These spontaneously presented activities separate children from the structured basal readers and permit the use of a variety of words that are more within their own sphere of knowledge.

The teacher's imagination is always challenged. Even though materials and books may be available for children in the age-graded group for which the teacher is responsible, each classroom group is different when the teacher observes closely the inter- and intra-variations among pupils. Fourth grade children show increasingly greater differences in maturity levels of reading and in sophistication in personality and interpersonal relationships. Such differences present yet another consideration in selecting reading matter of relevant content within the children's readability levels.

Teachers are given graded levels of materials, but if they do not have them, and they desire other materials that may be of greater interest to students, readability determinations may be made by following a formula recommended by some educators.[103] By identifying three passages of one hundred words each (from a book or journal that appelas to the teacher who has decided to use it with the pupils), the teacher counts and plots on a graph the average number of syllables and the average number of sentences in the reading material selected.[104] This may give the teacher greater confidence that the pupils would be successful when presented with different articles hand-picked by the teacher. It is recommended, too, that even though a given selection for children may appear too high for their success in reading, it may nevertheless be offered if the children are interested in it. High interest can encourage "reaching" to understand by reading at levels beyond one's ease.

As children in the fourth grade will be expected to read in various content areas such as social studies, mathematics, science, ecology, and other topical issues related to technical terms and concepts, it is necessary that they be introduced to various terms as well as a critical way of reading. They will need help in learning what the technical terms mean, how to conceptualize the terms in relation to other content encountered in reading, and how to recall the correct term when it appropriately applies.[105]

Newspaper articles have topics and content that afford excellent opportunities for an argumentative focus. Children need to read for truth, accuracy, and journalistic influences as well as the *who, what, why, when*, and *how* questions that emphasize significant facts about the material. Journalists have to support their data but they also feel the need to influence readers and use emotionalism to do so in some cases. Scientific topics in documents or books, even while representing subjectivism, must submit proof of facts by providing documentation for readers to use for verification. The scientific viewpoint, different from a journalistic one, must be dispassionate and not one-sided in reporting what is found in a particular research report. A report on scientific research includes the negative as well as positive points. Whether further comments are made to present the implications of the results of any research depends on the writer and the purposes of the total article.

Classroom discussion of articles read by the pupils can help greatly in teaching interpretation. An excellent lesson is learned when children hear the diversity of perspectives that exist in groups. They also need to learn how group opinion can be swayed when one or more individuals present forceful argumentation for one point or another. Children must learn how to protect themselves from being influenced easily by colorful language or anger transmitted in messages from individuals either in class or in the written materials presented to people.

Social studies content introduces to pupils the importance of knowing one's facts so that the individual is not unduly influenced by a convincing speaker who may not have all the facts needed to make intelligent decisions. Intelligent reading becomes essential at each grade level that pupils approach in the elementary school and in later contexts of schooling.

Films, filmstrips, resource speakers, and field trips are used not only in the language arts aspect of elementary school programs; they can also be used in any of the content or subject matter areas that can help pupils acquire greater comprehension and specific facts in technical knowledge about scientific or social studies backgrounds. Intellectual capacities for scientific data can build on interest, regardless of how unsophisticated the reader's skills may be at any given point. When information is important to a reader, it is attained.

Children in the fourth grade enjoy literature in many different forms.

Family interrelationships, parental patterns of interaction with youngsters, and interpersonal relationships with friends at school, home, or other places that a child goes with him/her family are all represented in literary materials. Bibliotherapy, which refers to the use of books to enable children to vicariously experience problematical situations of characters, provides opportunities for discussion in the classroom. Children are able to hear or read about the ways in which individuals in a story solve their own problems that are often painful prior to the final action, or decision made, by major characters.

Sources are recommended for obtaining books that are appropriate for children who are grappling with various problems.[106] Books about death of a loved one, about reassurance against fears of abandonment, separation feelings, and several other anxieties experienced by children can be used effectively with pupils. Discussion may follow in some cases. Hospitalization, changes in life style, and the need to develop courage in facing difficult problems of a personal nature are often discussed in class and alleviate, at least for some children, some of the uncertainties they may have had. At times, reading and discussion of this kind can introduce anxiety for children who have not thought about such problems. In any case, the teacher has to observe the children in order to know how to present literature in the bibliotherapeutic vein.

Generally it is recommended that various types of literature be offered to children in grades beyond the primary levels in which interests and capacities for understanding are developing. Comprehension is always sought by having children identify the main ideas in a selection, select significant details, indicate the organization and sequence of ideas, draw inferences, anticipate meanings from the general flow of ideas, summarize the material, detect differences between opinion and fact, note relationships between the graphic materials (e.g., maps, charts) and the written explanations that relate to them, and attain visual images that can be described in relation to the article or book that has been read.[107]

Children should also be encouraged to write their own stories and to read them to the class. Illustrations can be included with such detail or general representation as the pupil wishes. As the pupils read critically and learn how to comprehend literature, they are adapting styles that may be incorporated into their own choices of developing booklets or orally presented work.

Children in the fourth grade can be given activities that the teacher can make; some can be made with the children's assistance. The activities provide enjoyable exercises that strengthen skills in comprehension.[108] Most of all, the teacher's attitude toward reading experiences for children determines the extent to which the pupils will respond to instructional efforts. Every child may not succeed, but many will, or at least will want to get involved when the teacher demonstrates attitudes of faith in the children's efforts.

Studies indicate that when children apply their own ideas to words used in definitions or story material, they are able to retain them more effectively than when learning them by memorization alone.[109] Wittrock reported the results of three ways used in order to test superiority of method of children's instruction of vocabulary words. One way was to have the children write the definition of a word after reading it, another way was to read the word and trace a picture of it as given, the third way was to read the definition and draw one's own image of the definition. The researchers indicate that when children generate their own image in relation to a verbal definition, they are creating their own idiosyncratic relationship to the idea.[110] They also suggest that when children are expected to generate ideas or to imagine their own distinctive definitions of words (upon meeting new ideas), they will retain them more effectively than they do when only reading about the new words. Wittrock recommends that learning at school be conceptualized as a "generative cognitive process," using both the verbal process of reasoning and spatially or imaginatively oriented processes.[111]

Although learning to read is important for the acquisition of knowledge, opportunities to use one's thinking processes to elaborate relationships between new stimuli and knowledge gained in past experiences are relevant for broader educational gains. Comprehension skills can utilize the individual's capacities to bring past experience to new information encountered by the student in reading processes. Some researchers are urging that instructional techniques use more than verbal means to involve children's responses in reading.

Wittrock proposes at least three implications for teaching all of which are based on his research (as well as the research of others) related to hemispheric activity of the left and right sides of the brain.[112] The first implication for teaching children is that better methods utilize the multiple processing that goes on in either side of the brain rather than teaching toward mainly the left hemispheric activity, which emphasizes logical, linear learning forms. Second, the complicated processes of reading involve not only the recognition of shapes and sounds, but also the conversion of meaning into speech and intonation patterns of pitch, emphasis, and selection of syllables for word patterns, and that complicated set of functions involves both the left and the right hemispheres of the brain.

Pictures seem to help children learn vocabulary more effectively than only a visual presentation of the word itself. Imagery instructions related to vocabulary learning seem to improve learning. In this sense, the children are bringing to the instructional situation their own processes of learning and meaning, rather than reproducing what they are expected to learn in the exactness of someone else's presentation.

The third implication that Wittrock describes for teaching lies in the relationship between inductive and deductive methods of teaching and the manner in which the brain halves interact with each other.[113] He indicates that inductive learning, which involves the ability to synthesize parts into wholes, can be more effective for students who are "right-hemisphere-dominant." For students who are left-hemisphere-dominant, learning processes that involve deductive learning, that of proceeding from the rules to examples demonstrating the use of rules, was the more effective means of instruction in a curriculum on language learning.[114]

Even though pictures are processed in the brain in an imaginal and spatial form, the learner might be encouraged to describe the pictures in sentences. Wittrock indicates that this manner of instruction may be considered not only a pictorial mode of learning but also a verbal-semantic one.[115] Imagery and semantic-verbal processes interacting with each other can produce beneficial effects for the learner.

As research discloses more data on effective ways of learning, as well as the identification of internal functioning during processes of learning, educators can adapt instruction in the classroom to that knowledge. The same comments made by researchers on the activity of the brain when reading was the focus of concern can be made about writing. The coordination of skills related to decoding letters and sound relationships, understanding semantic and syntactical arrangements in written materials, and creating one's own ideas in the form of written expression involves challenging thought processes. Learning to write stories, reports, summaries, or other forms of descriptions is one of the last instructional activities that children receive in an organized curriculum. Writing instruction begins, however, in subtle ways when young children ask others to tell them what something written on paper means or says. Children often show how they will write a letter or note long before it is expected of them at school. Their scribbles are a delight to see. Their translations of their own writing are even more impressive.

Writing—A Personal and Functional Mode of Expression

Common sense tells us that the strongest drive to learn something is implemented and propelled by a purpose. When children want to write a message or to show that they are somewhat like their older brothers or sisters, they are ready to do something about it. They are ready to watch someone who is writing and to try to imitate the letter formulations.

Even though formalized patterns of writing are not introduced to the child below two years of age in American society, the child is very much aware of writing. In a literate society writing is necessary and the lives of citizens are geared toward knowing how to respond to many things in writing. It becomes the trademark of sophistication for individuals, as well as creating a foundation for the history of human groups.

For young children, prior to school attendance, writing typically has minimal impact or meaning unless the teacher places an emphasis on writing in various ways that are commensurate with what children are able to understand or to use. Being able to do it, however, as they imitate the scribbling appearance of their parents' writing, can be important to them. It becomes a symbol of maturity to some extent.

Children's writing stems in part from their opportunities to hear and enjoy language. Adults who encourage children to create or even to respond to forms in functional modes of writing are doing a service for children. A fill-in form that requires a name or address and telephone number or a birth date can be implemented in the best way possible by a young child. Writing includes to a great extent, the signatures of a child on a card, a thank-you note, and any other brief messages, such as "I love you."

Some educators and researchers consider that writing should be taught before children learn to read. It is considered to be a personalized form of communication and allows a child to bring his/her own experiences to the written symbol.[116]

If children want to put letters together to form what they think are words, it is recommended that they be encouraged to do so, regardless of spelling considerations. Plastic letters, placed together to form words or a child's name, are useful in a child's early experiences in expressing something in "writing." This kind of writing emanates from the child's perspectives rather than someone else's standards and is in this sense a motivating and valuable place to start.[117]

Music, songs, singing games, riddles, and other rhythmic aspects of communication among individuals provide excellent opportunities for children to appreciate sounds and messages conveyed through language and music. Parents can introduce these early in a child's experiences at home. Musical sounds and their rhythmic qualities attune the child's ear to dynamics of rhythm and tone ranges in speaking and to rhythm of words in writing.

Imagery, spatial relationships and sequences, ideas evoked through song or poetry, and games stimulate language expression and the enjoyment of it for children. It does not take much on the part of many adults who are with children to tell a short story, ask a riddle, sing a simple song or describe a picture in a few seconds. Doing so can trigger many ideas for language expression and writing for children. Even though adults find it difficult to take seriously the efforts toward writing that children may make, it is actually those early efforts that lead to improved skills by the time children reach school. Parents must learn to see how their spontaneous and informal efforts affect developmental levels of competency.

Writing in the First Two Years[118]

When given a crayon or pencil, many children will happily scribble on a large pad. As long as they are given a large enough sheet of paper to scrawl on with abandon, not worrying about their scribbling extending beyond the sheet of paper to the carpet or wall space underneath it, they do well in their attempts to use the paper. They usually show it proudly to an adult and expect to have it admired. All they need is a smile if the adult does not have time to comment or to look closely at it.

Parents can give children crayons and used sheets of wrapping paper or large paper bags that have been torn open and spread out. Parents can also place simple words or pictures on the paper and the child may want to adapt them in some way. Here a caution needs to be made.

The parent playfully shows the child various examples of writing. One would not seriously expect a child to start "writing" in the first two years of life. What can result, however, from this interaction between parent and child is an appreciation of writing materials such as pencils, crayons, and chalk that can be used to mark up a large sheet of paper or wrapping that is no longer needed. Some parents have permitted their children to create "designs" on paper which later become the outer wrapping of a small gift. Some children have had the joy of writing all over a piece of muslin which later became a skirt for themselves or an adult who enjoyed children's creative efforts.

Experimentation, discovery, manipulation, and curiosity motivate the child in this age range to try expressional statements with any writing utensil. Finger painting offers the opportunity to move colorful, easily managed nontoxic paint around on a smooth-surfaced paper. Often the shelf paper that has a shiny surface, spread out on a table (which has been protected by newspapers) becomes the artist's medium for self-expression. Children like to write letters of the alphabet or their names or pictures at their level of ability.

Children in their first two years of life are manipulating many objects and materials. Their curiosity leads them to touching and testing surfaces for the variety of tactile sensations it gives them. Many parents have discovered, much to their dismay, that the child who sat quietly in the crib, waiting for the parent to remove the diaper, had already involved his or her sensory equipment to feel and spread the contents of the diaper. Knowledge gained from reaching out (or into) the environment provides the child with more ideas, experienced firsthand from which to draw statements of expression when the child describes or recalls an incident.

Children enjoy the sensation of soft surfaces, such as that found in the use of clay. They like to carve something out on the surface of the clay. They also like to do this in sand wet enough to have a consistency that will not be powdery but can hold a firm stroke or impression made by one's hands.

For Parents:

Crayons and pencils should not be given to a young child unless paper is provided at the same time. The child will understand that the two are to be used together. The suggestion to draw something the child likes will also convey the idea that the writing instrument can become an artistic form for developing pictures either for the child's or the adult's pleasure.

Materials That Can Be Used for Writing

Shelf paper

Butcher paper

Large newsprint pads

Old oilcloth

Wrapping paper

Old, washed sheets

Old, washed pillow slips

Wrong side of old greeting cards

Billboard sheets from advertising agencies

Computer sheets (used)

Thick, nonsharp writing utensils can be offered to a child who is being supervised by a parent. Moving with a sharp instrument in one's hand is very dangerous, and children should not be allowed to do it. Children like to put things in their mouths, too, and this must be prevented by adults who are responsible for children. When someone is not available to watch the child using a drawing or writing utensil, these writing or drawing activities should not be offered.

Young children see older siblings writing letters, painting signs or posters for school assignments and voluntary organizations (e.g., scouts, small neighborhood or school clubs). They like to imitate their brothers or sisters and may be encouraged to do so at the children's levels of skills. The child's self-concept can be enhanced when an older sibling allows the younger one to accompany work production at the sibling's side.

Very often when children draw or write something, they describe their work as a design or may use a few words to label what has been done. Children's early attempts are not going to be recognizable to older siblings or parents as representative of reality. Parents and others need to become accustomed to the fact that young children's work is expressive of an idea or feeling, not in a way that can be explained when the child is more mature, but the product can honestly represent a child's efforts as an aspect of communication. Teachers need to help parents become aware of the importance of respecting children's attempts to learn.

Parents may plan to:

Include the child's notes within other letters written by the parent.

Request that the child write a grocery list with the parent

Create the child's own imprint notes, such as an insignia made by the child

Recommend a thank-you note to a sibling after having done something thoughtful for the child or parent

Have the child create a cover for several styles of notes

Write a note to a new neighbor welcoming him/her to the neighborhood

Write a note to a friend asking him/her to visit

Invite a relative to a social gathering

Write a get-well note with an accompanying illustration

As parents write thank-you notes or send birthday cards, they can tell their children what they are doing. Valentine's day, Thanksgiving, Easter, Christmas, and other occasions during the year present opportunities for parents to do thoughtful things for people. Sending a card, signing one's name with an added personal note, and allowing a toddler to make his/her "mark," can begin the experiences of writing upon which later ones will be built. Attitudes are conveyed and impressed upon a child who sees that writing to someone extends warmth and pleasant social relationships. This occurs even without a young child's being able to verbalize intellectually how social interaction takes place.

The major effects of having a child draw or write something that is sent to another individual are that communication modes manifest themselves for the child. It is a beginning for the child in seeing how effective social interaction is in the form of a functional or expressional note of consideration for someone. Nothing is perfect in form. The child's encouragement is the major focus at this time.

Attitudes toward writing continue as the child develops and realizes the depth of skills that can be acquired toward that end. *Depth,* as the term is perceived from the adult point of view is different from the term as intellectualized by a child. Understanding in regard to depth or refinement or advanced skill develops only with experience and involvement with any given skill. Between three and five years old, communication and aptitudes in that context become more varied, extensive, and focused in terms of interest in special topics. In terms of Piaget's classification system of children's intellectual or language development, children are (between two and four years old) acquiring the ability to see in their mind's eye, representations of things that are not present in the environment. In fact, the child thinks to a lesser extent, in terms of words, but rather in terms of images.[119] This tendency can be an advantage when the child draws or writes "messages" to others.

The creativity reflected in the speech of children two years old also indicates that the child senses fewer constraints to abide by given rules in language usage than will be noted in later years. The children's references to reality applied to their own internal firsthand feelings (rather than the adults') about the environment or an event permit them to talk in terms of the spontaneous representations of images that they experience when they use language.

Writing from Three to Five Years

Children in the age range of three to five see writing of various kinds in personalized forms of letters or notes as well as newspapers, booklets, and business correspondence that parents have in the home. They see it when a parent or sibling writes a letter or checks in sending out payments for bills. The frequency of seeing adults writing letters or reading them has an effect on children when the adults comment on those letters. Children acquire knowledge about writing when specific items are pointed out to them.[120]

In this sense of explanation and descriptions of letters to and from home, parents can be very instructive and instrumental in advancing a child's knowledge about and appreciation of writing. Illustrations with writing beside or underneath them also indicate to a child how the message relates to the "spatial image."

Although some parents may think that writing involves formalized methods of teaching if the child is to learn it, such parents can be given assistance by a teacher who tells them writing starts long before a child comes to school and sits with other children who are simultaneously learning how to formulate letters that represent words. A child does not have to know the alphabet, as many parents surmise, prior to learning to write his/her name or other words that are of interest to that child at any given time. The organizational syndrome often seems to overcome parents who are accustomed to thinking that nothing happens without formalized and sequential instruction. Consequently it is assumed that to show the child how to write a card, letter, or word without the curriculum organizational knowledge to precede it, is out of order or inappropriate. This is an unfortunate assumption. Children can learn "out-of-order" knowledge if one conceptualizes experiences that take place in the home as being out of order or prior to formalized learning at school.

One of the first items of information that children like to write is their own names. Teachers may write the child's names on products (illustrations or collage, or clay modeling forms) that each pupil does. Some children become so intrigued with the letters of their own names that they write them all over a large sheet of paper without any relationship of space considered for one letter being next to the other. The letters of the child's name become the illustration on a large sheet of newsprint.

When the teacher is not rushed in having to move from one child to another quickly in order to meet a time schedule, (s)he may show the child how to form each letter of his/her name. In that sense, the child is receiving explicit instruction in writing. Typically, however, the teacher tries informally or not, to help each child learn how to write his/her own name each time a child's product is being identified. Queries such as, "What letter comes first?" precede at times the teacher's beginning to write. When the child responds, the teacher shows the child how to write the symbol representing the first letter of the name. There is an awareness on the part of the teacher that each time something is shown to the child, the child is learning. Whether the instruction occurs in an informal or formal and organized sense is beside the issue. The teacher takes advantage of having the child's attention on a given problem or item of learning and realizes that this is one of many accumulated experiences that contribute to a child's mastery of concepts.

Teachers print the children's names on cards that label lockers or places that each of the pupils use to hang coats or sweaters while they are at school. For young children of three or four, the teacher will also place a symbol (e.g., picture of a toy, train, doll's head) so that the pupils may easily recognize their own locker or place in the coat room.

At three and four, children gain in abilities to write figures representing numbers as they do in writing letter/symbol forms. Writing a 1 with one lollipop beside it, helps children learn to recognize a one to one correspondence between an item and a figure. Parents can teach children many skills at home without being aware of the concept that is being taught and the formalized or technical name applied to the concept as educators refer to it.

Children are encouraged to notice the shapes of objects that represent the shapes of letters. An o can represent a mouth wide open singing. "Ohh-h, say can you see?" A k can remind them of a person with one arm and one leg forward like a tin soldier seen from the side view. An s can remind them of a garden snake, or a garden hose before it is filled with water that straightens it out. A t can remind them of a table, a j of an umbrella, an r of a person hunched over. They can make up their own analogies. Children like to imagine that inanimate objects come alive in the form of an animal or person. In this manner, they will remember the shapes of letters. How they reproduce them when they begin writing is another matter. It is still difficult for them to control their writing when they begin to become familiar with many different letters. Practice in writing is needed to ensure greater ease in handling the pencil or crayon and in acquiring greater control over the mind-eye coordination required in the mastery of writing symbols in the order and spatial representation desired.

Various games and activities can be offered the children to allow them opportunities to practice the formulation of letters (on paper or in the air). Parents can do these activities with children at home.

Sky Writing

Children like to trace letters in the air like airplanes whose smoke fades in the distance. They follow a leader who stands in front of the class, back turned toward the class to avoid the confusion of right to left.

Guess What Letter It Is

One child faces the class and places his/her fingers in a position to represent a letter. The class mimics it back by hand and then asks if that is the letter the child had in mind. The leader chooses another child to create the letter that will be copied and guessed by the class.

What Kind of Note Do I Send?

A child asks the class what kind of note to send if I want to invite someone to my party. (An invitation, should be guessed by the children.) Another child is chosen. What kind of note do I send to tell someone I like what she gave me? (A thank-you note or I-like-it note can be the answer.)

Some commercial kits present sequenced practice for children by pictures with sandpaper letters next to them representing a sound and letter that marks the beginning of the word descriptive of the object in the pictures. The tactile sensation in tracing the letter helps the child remember it. If the children are introduced to letters made of circles, the sequence of letters they learn will consist of whole and partial circles. Thus, they learn an *o*, then an *a*, which is a manuscript form[121] rather than a printed *a*. An *e* consists of an incomplete circle. It is usually easy for children to learn the *i* and *l* as letters having only straight lines in them. An *h*, and *n*, present similar characteristics.

Readiness for writing is similar to readiness for reading in the sense that adults must sense children's awareness of letters and the sounds representing certain symbols. The children's attention span in watching someone write also gives the adult an idea as to the degree of their interest in the written forms.

Adults also need to remember that it is not perfection that is sought in early attempts; rather it is the effort to do it that is emphasized. If a child tries to write, this is significant. Encouragement is needed so that the child will become involved repeatedly and willingly. The practice in writing is the necessary continuing thread throughout a child's efforts.

One writer indicates that the teacher can notice the degrees of readiness that exist among the kindergarten pupils by attending to at least the way children are able to differentiate their right from left hands, the way they are able to practice a left-to-right hand eye-sweep direction in following a series of pictures, their awareness of sizes and shapes and spatial relationships among things and letters, their awareness of the fact that handwriting identifies something in the environment or an idea of some kind, as well as being able to participate well in activities that involve the skills related to a knowledge of direction, shapes, sizes in sorting objects, and the like.[122]

Directional placement of hands or objects needs to be called to the children's attention. They will not be aware of the significance of writing from left to right unless it is pointed out to them. Singing games are often used to help children practice differentiation in the use of either hand. This again is an area in which parents can be helpful. They can ask their children to carry objects with their right hands, with their left at times. When children put their shoes on, they need to know which one corresponds with the right or left foot. Teachers can make parents aware that this skill in differentiating direction, knowing the right from the left and also when one moves from the right to left, helps children in preparing to write and to read. The parents may be more willing to support the teacher's requests for practice at home when they are aware of its benefits to skills development.

Helping children to observe in a concentrated fashion what they see around them, or helping them practice recall of certain ideas and things they contacted, can support a habit of being more acute in watching and remembering. Powers of observation need to increase as children learn how to write and read.

Some teachers begin with simple sentences for children four years old by showing them how writing looks after a child dictates or tells the teacher what to write. The assumption in this experience is that the child seeing the teacher write what has been said, will realize that speaking can be symbolized in writing. The child recognizes some of the words after the teacher has pointed them out. Since the child told the teacher what to "say" or write, it is evident that the child knows the words to some extent. Familiarity with the content of writing presupposes recognition of the words in a message.

The form used for four-year-old children is referred to as manuscript writing. It is composed of straight lines and circles for the most part. It is assumed to be easiest for children to do themselves, because the letters do not have to be connected to each other (as is done in cursive writing), less skill and motor control are involved in forming the manuscript letters than is needed for cursive writing, the manuscript letters are assumed to be more transferable in reading to the letters in print seen by the child in books, manuscript writing is assumed to be more legible than cursive, progress seems to be greater or faster in the attempts to write manuscript rather than cursive forms, manuscript writing seems to help children's achievement in spelling and reading, and it seems also to be contributing to more numerous and better written products by young children.[123]

Some teachers also provide wide-lined paper for children to draw boxes, a cart, a door, and various objects that will become part of letters. They can begin to draw circles and straight lines, vertically and horizontally, that provide practice needed for creating shapes of letters. This can be done in unhurried practice periods until the children become accustomed to sensing a fit between spaces and shapes.

The simpler the sequences given to children in the early stages of writing practice, the better they are for the children's gradual increases in learning. The teacher must remain with the same style in the early grades since the children will be practicing the manuscript form in its lower- and upper-case style. (See Concept Illustration 4–3)

Prekindergarten activities involve children in a variety of ways in writing skills of a simple nature. Whenever possible in its appropriateness to the children's experiences, the teacher subtly introduces purposes and presentations of writing that can be done either in small groups or with the total classroom group.

Young children need to learn that the lower case letters (as in their own name, following the first capital letter) are different in form from the first or capital letter. Mark learns that the first letter of his name when it is written, is *M*. The rest of the letters are written in lower case, i.e., "ark." Miriam learns that the first letter of her name is capital "M," the rest are in lower case form, i.e., "iriam." (See Concept Illustration 4–3) Teachers can show parents these differences. Many parents teach the children to write their names in all upper-case, or capital, letters. Teachers can show children that they have another way that their names can be written, rather than to criticize the way they have learned from their parents.

In the kindergarten children will be learning some words that evolve from an experience that the teacher plans for them. Even though words will be introduced in the first grade that will be used in children's pre-primers, they are typically introduced in kindergarten unless the school or the teacher has acquired an organized sequential program.

The kindergarten program may include writing of children's names, labels, or colors and shapes. The children's production in writing, however, is not of as great concern as it will be in later grades. The kindergarten is an excellent place to introduce many ideas, skills, and experiences to children. It permits children to become familiar with many units of work that include social studies, science, ecology, mathematics, language arts, health education, nutrition, rhythms, music, and art. The children's performance in that work, however, represents responses to introductory levels, not refined techniques that may be expected of pupils in later grades. For this reason, criticism, reprimands or demands for perfection when children forget what the teacher told them, are minimized. Rather, encouragement to try and not to worry about mistakes is the main theme. This applies to efforts in writing as well as other subject matter areas that are in focus.

Children in kindergarten may be ready for work that is introduced in the first grade; some, however, may not. As the children in kindergarten may be about four years and nine months to a year beyond that, they represent varying stages of readiness for writing. By the time many pupils are placed in the first grade (between five years and nine months to over six years old)

Sometimes space is permitted for an illustration and a few words or a title under the drawing or painting.

Concept Illustration 4–1

they are interested in writing and may have had some successful early experiences. The first grade becomes an organized learning laboratory, which can in the beginning week or so be conducted in terms of reviewing what children may already know; after that the teacher places the children in learning groups for reading and other subject matter areas, and the record keeping for pupil progress becomes concentrated.

Writing from Six to Nine Years

FIRST GRADE

Some educators recommend that children in the first grade be given some time to practice what they already know in handwriting readiness activities before they are taught new letters. Pupils can also be given opportunities to make large illustrations of squares, circles, lines in different directions, and half circles and to adapt character-like features or objects from those shapes. This prepares them for shaping letters in a more concentrated manner than was expected of them earlier.

Some teachers provide a large and durable cardboard background that the children can use to support a sheet of newsprint. (See Concept Illustration 4–2) The children practice their handwriting and shape representation on those sheets. Some newsprint sheets, about half the size of those used on easels for painting, also include at the bottom of the sheet a few lines that can accommodate writing if the teacher wants to place the child's comments about his/her illustrations below the work. (See Concept Illustration 4–1)

It is recommended that children be given the opportunity to create sto-

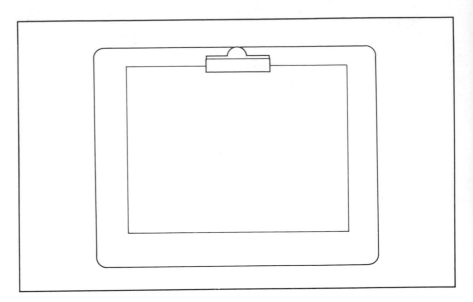

Concept Illustration 4–2

A clipboard to which a sheet is attached for drawing or writing what the child wants to express.

ries as the teacher writes their words on the chalkboard or on a large sheet of tagboard (heavy chart paper). Sometimes teachers write the story for the children first on the chalkboard and later take more time to write the manuscript letters on a chart that will be used often in the following weeks. Some objectives that are suggested for the pupils' attainment in the first

Manuscript Alphabet (Upper and Lower Case)

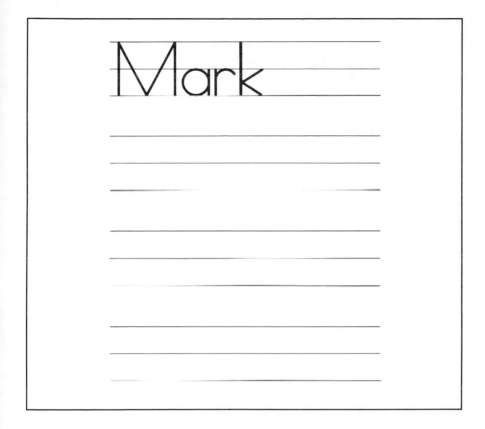

grade are that they be able to write with the teacher's help a two-sentence idea that has been created by the class, that they be able to create a two-line idea of their own that they can write, that they know how to begin and end the necessary strokes to create letters and words, that they understand how spacing is significant to a word, that they know all the letters of the alphabet, that they know how to plan for a two-finger margin at the paper's left side and a one-finger space between letters,[124] and appropriate spacing between words as the teacher decides is attainable, and that children should be able to write correctly their own names.

Concept Illustrations 4–3 and 4–4 show the differences among spatial distributions of lines drawn for the accommodation of children's writing. As the children gain greater control over their own letter formations they are able to contain them in smaller spaces. In the first grade, children receive both the lined and unlined paper as the teacher considers appropriate to the maturity levels of the children. The purpose of lined paper is to aid the pupils, not to frustrate them. Thus, unlined paper is often used to allow greater freedom and fewer constraints for the children.

Some instruction is given to children observing the teacher at the chalkboard. A few children at a time can attempt writing at the board. Many teachers in kindergarten have encouraged children to do this without supervision, just to experiment with "writing." They copy the letters that are

```
┌──────────────────────────────────────────────┐
│                                              │
│     Mark                                     │
│  ─────────────────────────────────────       │
│                                              │
│  ─────────────────────────────────────       │
│  ─────────────────────────────────────       │
│  ─────────────────────────────────────       │
│                                              │
│  ─────────────────────────────────────       │
│  ─────────────────────────────────────       │
│  ─────────────────────────────────────       │
│                                              │
│  ─────────────────────────────────────       │
│  ─────────────────────────────────────       │
│  ─────────────────────────────────────       │
│                                              │
└──────────────────────────────────────────────┘
```

Concept Illustration 4–4

provided in games or the large heavy rubber letters of the alphabet one often observes in classrooms.

Ideas for writing centers in the classroom can be obtained by consulting various booklets providing quick tips for teachers.[125] Because practice and continued involvement in a variety of skills related to observation of shape, awareness of sequence, increased powers of noting differences, and coordinating ideas with words, are aspects of writing techniques, they need to be offered in a broad variety of tasks. Children need to have different experiences that direct their attention to concepts about writing, techniques, and motivating devices to draw them into participating, fully absorbed, at various levels and times in the classroom.

The teacher can place on the bulletin board ideas such as the following:

Do you like to receive notes or letters?
Which notes did you like best?
On which occasions do you remember feeling happy about something someone wrote to you?
Would you like to tell someone about your pet?
Would you like to invite someone to a party?
Would you like to help someone who feels sad about something?
Why do you think that people like to write letters to each other?
Can you think of someone that would enjoy receiving a letter from you?

Children can be encouraged to write neatly so that what they write is legible. This should not be overemphasized to the point of distracting them from efforts to write. It can be mentioned periodically. It suggests that clear writing is easier to understand and less likely to misinform someone about the message conveyed.

This paper does not have many spots on it made by an eraser. We can understand what it says. It is pleasant to read a message that is not clouded by spots.

Teachers can save boxes in which letters cut of felt or strong cardboard can be kept. Children enjoy moving letters around making words out of them. Flannel boards, too, provide manipulative experiences for children. The appearance of a word, a letter from a child's name, or one's parent's name can be exciting to discover (much like anagrams or other word games that involve letters that form words after the letters are unscrambled).

Activities that can be stored in small boxes or small fabric bags, with a drawstring to close the top, can keep tiny parts in the appropriate place. Children will return boxes in the proper place. When teachers acquire many activities needed to involve children in practicing what they are attempting to master, organization of those materials is necessary. It not only ensures a more effective use of them (in the parts remaining together), but it also permits a longer lifetime for them. Some teachers like to put some of the activities away and bring out new ones so that children will not tire of them. In that way of rotating tasks that are presented to children, the teacher can avoid boredom that might otherwise result when the same activities were offered to the children too often. Organization is significantly related to the teacher's ability to sustain records in knowing which materials are used more often and more effectively than others.

Some teachers use old workbooks in which sequenced story ideas are clearly shown in pictures. Cutting these small pictures out, laminating them if desired, or placing adhesive tape backs to the pictures, allows a child to place the pictures in order as the ideas are depicted. Sequential development of an idea is an important characteristic in writing, as well as being aware that one's writing of a story must move in a left to right direction. When children can manipulate things that represent themes, words, or ideas they are gaining facility in techniques that lead to writing skills.

Children's work should be displayed captioned with "Good Ideas," or "Our Best Work," or "Our Class Writes Well." Each child's best work can be placed on construction paper backing or among several others in a paper-framed form on the display board.

Teachers should save a file of ideas that they notice when they visit the classrooms of other teachers, when they read various journals published for teachers, or when they encounter ideas in various books on the curriculum variations for children. The newspapers often have sections that suggest games that can be created for children using the newspaper as a focus. Parents can use the same games at home; they often will do so when the teacher indicates how much it can help the letter and symbol recognition of children.

Some teachers also like to help the child acquire boxes of word cards. The teacher asks children to tell the class what words they want to write or ideas they want to talk about. The same principle of identifying key words that are significant for the children is used as the teacher goes to each child while others are busy writing letters and symbols or simple words that they already know. Children enjoy having their individual file boxes of words that are important to them. The children themselves know what they would like to write about; in that sense, the school does not impose unknown words (not that to do so at times is unjustifiable) but rather the child's knowledge initiates requests for further association with words and new constructs of knowledge. Children are better able to retain what comes from their own experiences and attaches itself to related concepts in the external world.

The first grade is a bridge in a sense, between earlier exposure to a variety of activities and ideas that make up the experiential background of pupils and later knowledge that builds on what happens in this introductory period of school life. The maturity of the child contributes to the manner in which a child perceives the world. What is pivotal to the child's acquisition of depth in learning and intellectual development generally, is the quality of naming and explaining that goes on in the environment relating experiences with concepts of various disciplines.

By the time children are ready to enter the second grade, they are aware of what is expected of them. For some it is pleasant, for others it is symbolic of chores. At least with some successful experiences, children can look forward to a new start, being with different classmates at times, and gaining new knowledge. Parental support makes a difference, too, in children's anticipation of school experiences.

SECOND GRADE

Although it must be remembered again that children who are about six years, nine months, and who may be seven years old, enter the second grade at school, they represent various backgrounds and skills which they bring with them to the experiences of that classroom. The teacher arranges for different types of activities that will at least recognize the children's successes. That means that a range of ideas have to be presented to them. Writing skills are evident among the pupils. What they have actually produced in the year preceding the second, has to be discovered by both the teacher and the pupils, themselves.

The teacher will plan both formal and informal types of experiences for the practice periods in handwriting manuscript forms.

Concentration on form and shape of letters occupies the children most of the time in handwriting periods. They are still working on the mastery of manuscript lower and upper case letters and the appropriate time to use them.

Children are also involved in the purposes for writing. They are encouraged at all times both by observing the teacher writing on the board and by noting carefully the situations in which writing is appropriate.

Children will gradually become interested in various styles of writing. They will notice the differences among their classmates and the teacher. They will compare these styles to their own.

Boxes with the letters to be practiced will be placed around the room.

Pupils can use the letters as models for their own work. The teacher places certain letters out on days that they should be practiced. The boxes

Children send their warm wishes to other children in the hospital.

can be of various colors. Consonants can be of one color; vowels of another. The teacher may vary the experience in terms of the needs of the children. When the children are finished with their papers, they place them inside the boxes, which have a slot on top.

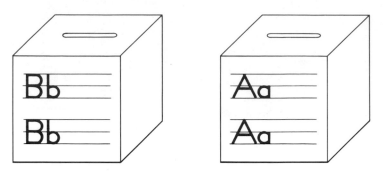

The children know where to obtain the lined paper for their practice in manuscript writing. In some cases, the teacher gives them an allotment to keep in their own desks and notebooks to use when they are finished with other activities.

Often the teacher builds an area that the children may want to use in the back or side of the classroom. It is separated from other areas by a three-sided screen. The screen can have papers completed by the children tacked on it displaying careful work. Each child should have the pleasure of seeing a paper of his or hers on that screen.

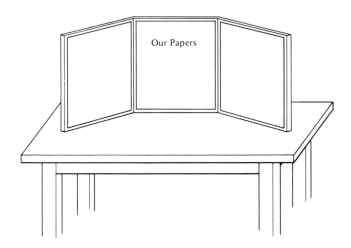

The Writing Corner

Themes on writing motivate children's desires to write.

My Pet
My Favorite Friend
My Favorite Food
Things I Like Best to Do
Things I Like Least to Do

My Favorite Colors
My Best Work
Places I Like to Go
My Favorite Relative
I Like Myself Best When I . . .
I Like Myself Least When I . . .
My Spare Time
My Hobbies
People
Downtown
Airplanes
Cars
Buses
Trains
Telephones
Walking
Jogging
Hopping
Swimming
Horses
Cows
Country Roads

Children in the second grade are still working on the refinement skills needed for more precise form of letter shapes, sizes, and knowing when to use capital letters. They learn increasingly about simple punctuation marks, the apostrophe, the exclamation point, the quotation marks as well as the period, comma, and question mark. They have been seeing these punctuation forms in their reading, but it is another issue to remember to include them in one's writing.

The teacher has to use those punctuation marks whenever possible and explain briefly to children why those symbols are used in writing. They have to be associated to speech as well. As soon as children see these expressive components of writing used frequently, they can become accustomed to the necessity for them. Some children, however, have difficulty as do adults in knowing when to use (or not to) certain punctuation marks.

When certain skills need to be emphasized or reviewed, the teacher has to plan several lessons to focus on repeated problems that are evident in the children's work. Activities, too, are planned as enrichment or as opportunities to review and refine skills that continue to present problems to pupils. This is one of the reasons that teachers must have a cupboard full of various activities geared toward children's practice on almost every skill imaginable. In this way the teacher is able to do what is called individualized instruction, at least in being aware that children have different problems at different times during their attempts to master ideas presented at school. Individualized teaching involves also the teacher's one-to-one work with the pupil, knowing exactly how the child responds to an idea and where the child is in the process of learning. Strengths and weaknesses of each pupil have to be known if the teacher is to help each child. Record keeping of children's progress is a companion feature to a teacher's working face to face with one child.

Even when children are working in small groups, teachers are able to create charts that show what children have done. Some teachers have a chart posted at each learning center, which has a concentrated focus on a few tasks that children attempt and may even complete when they participate in that center. Cutting out letters from magazines and newspapers and pasting them in design format or to form one's name involves classification of letters, coordination of hand and eye, skills involving the creation of order from several materials, and imaginative efforts, among other things. The teacher can have a chart above the learning center and may have the picture representing the activity or a word describing any of the skills involved in completing the task. A check mark after a child's name indicates whether the task was attempted, unfinished, or completed. These various record-keeping devices help the teacher and the child know how the child is faring.

Some teachers have created paper that gives children ideas and space allocation for words that have letters extending above and below the middle of a space. The teachers supply paper that has at the beginning of each line a simple house. The child notes parallels to letters such as g, which extend below the floor of the house, h extends to the roof of the house.

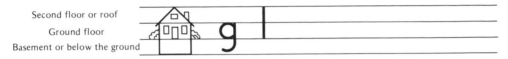

Second floor or roof
Ground floor
Basement or below the ground

The house design is placed at the beginning of every group of four lines as a guide.

This awareness of space above and below the middle space for letters in a word helps children acquire better spacing for word units.

The ingenuity of the teacher and skills in implementing designs for children's practice in handwriting often make the difference between progress or deficit lag for pupils. The teacher who has a sensitive awareness of what can be done by children (e.g., so that they are challenged sufficiently but not frustrated) is an excellent source of support. Novelty introduced into daily lessons gives the teacher new energy at times as it does the children.

Children can be shown forms for the correct spacing and indenting of letter writing. Bulletin boards, chalkboards, and other presentation backgrounds can be used to show pupils how a short letter is written with the upper right-hand corner used as a place to write the date, then the salutation, the major body of the letter, and the closing information and signature of the writer.

These forms have to be shown, not only on the board, but also in the various learning centers or small group activities planned by the teacher. Repetition of learning skills is necessary if the children are to gain from the teacher's efforts. Sometimes, the teacher will write at the left-hand side of the paper what the children need to fill in for the major portion of the paper. The word *Date* placed before a line ————————, that permits space for the pupil to fill in, helps the child remember that the space needs to be allocated for the date in most messages or letters written by the child.

Subtle reminders for what children need to remember in writing can be placed around the room, above the chalkboard, and in unique cardboard three-way fold and stagelike backgrounds that set the activity apart from the rest of the classroom. Children can work independently to increase mastery of writing skills without disturbing classmates or needing close supervision by the teacher. The teacher can, by a quick glance around the room, see how everyone is working. The interest of pupils in the activities can occupy children so that they want to accomplish their tasks rather than allow anyone to distract them from work.

By the end of the second grade the children typically have been involved in writing forms, filling in their names or dates in various activities given to them by the teacher, writing short notes either with the entire class or by themselves, identifying the key words in written materials, learning about the precision needed in saying or writing what one means, and a variety of other elements related to writing. They are still perfecting their handwriting and remembering the proper form of each letter or symbol that they write. At least they are trying to do so even though they may not always succeed. It takes many experiences and practice to bring them to the point of sufficient motor control and perceptual coordination to perform well in their writing activities.

Some teachers may begin teaching the cursive writing to children at the end of the second grade. Children view the cursive writing as "grown-up"

Cursive writing

because it is more like the script seen in letter writing, and is less like the manuscript print. Some teachers like to wait until children have fully mastered the manuscript writing before they introduce cursive. The transition is often made by showing how the manuscript letters can be joined. Many teachers in the third grade begin cursive instruction whether manuscript has been mastered or not.

THIRD GRADE

By the time children are close to eight years old and in the third grade, they have had writing experiences at varying levels of success. Some pupils are eight and older, but their chronological maturity does not ensure motor coordination and perceptual developmental levels that support the skills needed for writing. Typically, the teacher expects to help the children refine writing techniques whether the manuscript writing is still used or the cursive writing is introduced. Teachers have to observe children's work to the degree of knowing how each of them writes. Otherwise the children cannot be helped effectively.

Maturation levels are considered before a teacher begins instruction in cursive writing. Some educators consider that waiting until children are ready to learn a new technique is better than introducing it prematurely and thereby introducing failure or frustration to pupils. The teacher has to be discriminating in knowing how and when to teach new techniques. For the children who need more help, individualized instruction can be provided. The attitude of the teacher giving this help reflects whether the teacher thinks the child is slow, or just going through a normal process of learning. Children need the teacher's support and patience and can sense irritation or annoyance when the teacher feels it toward their work.

The content of written materials serves to motivate children to observe the manner in which writing must occur. With purposes in mind, children are more interested in knowing how to write and give better attention to the techniques that they need to know to carry out a project of their own desire. In that sense, teachers need to be aware of the range of activities that can interest pupils in the third grade. They have acquired some levels of maturity. There will be problems in writing, however, that individuals find difficult even in adult stages of performance.

Punctuation seems to present difficulties to adults. Some writers think that either it has not been taught well in schools, or there are simply some mechanical aspects to punctuation that are difficult to master.[126] The relationships between meaning and punctuation contribute toward difficulty in learning, when one is younger in elementary school, what correct punctuation may be. Quotation marks around a conversational statement, or a period at the end of a complete sentence may not be as difficult as knowing where to place a comma. In any case, punctuation has to be emphasized in terms of major principles. When children have to learn so many things such as spacing of words and letters or symbols, what to say and how to say it, new forms of cursive letters and symbols, as well as adapting to various new items of information, they have a great deal to master. Gradually, as they move through various activities focusing on similar needs for punctuation marks, they may acquire the habit for punctuating correctly.

Children can learn to edit their own work by hearing the teacher ask them to look for any places in their work that need a period, a comma, a question mark, or an exclamation point. They can also be helped in looking for those punctuation marks in books they read. Consciousness levels, in a sense, are being raised to becoming more aware of the need for (and the absence of) punctuation marks in the necessary place.

Some teachers have had children stand in front of the class, as part of sentences or other dramatic presentations, and have deliberately emphasized the position of quotation marks, exclamation point, or other needed punctuation form. Anything that brings the children's attention to usage of a writing symbol can be optimally shown in an activity or dramatized (puppet-show) form so that pleasure and instruction are correlated.

Activities that present pictures and words asking what is happening in the picture can be included in learning centers or small groups of task-focused participation. Separate punctuation marks written in bold form, pasted on strong cardboard, should be placed in the correct position for usage. This should be checked by the teacher when the child is finished with the activity. Some activities are color-coded and self-correcting. When the children place one part with another, they can see that the same color matches and is the correct answer.

Capitalization has to be emphasized whenever possible. The teacher points this out to children whenever a proper name label is needed. The name of a city, town, or person can be shown often to emphasize the appearance of a capital letter at the beginning of written forms of a name. Children also need to recognize the need for a capital letter to be shown at the beginning of a sentence, writing the name of the month with a date, and several other forms that require capitalization either because of where the word appears in a sentence or because of the special attributes of a name or word.

Apostrophe symbols present different problems in that children need to know when they are used to show possession, when they are used as a contraction of two words, or when they have to be used followed by an *s*. Every opportunity that the teacher has to bring these forms into contextual usage will provide the children with another chance to learn and understand the mechanics involved in various punctuation problems.

Children like to play the role of newspaper journalists who tell others how to create stories and how to write in correct form. They may often be given the opportunity to edit a group of papers while the other children who are reporters respond as they think their role counterparts would be expected to respond.

Humor has to be injected often into the teaching and learning situations at school. Children need release from their serious efforts to measure up to the teacher's, their own, or their parents' expectations. Their writing can include jokes or riddles that introduce a playful and experimental aspect to their school activities.

Humor sometimes permits a creative effort of form to be used. A child may want to write something in the shape of a square or triangle. To deviate from standard forms can be noted as representing something that is unusual or funny. Creativity is appreciated for its own sake. When the teacher begins instruction of cursive writing, however, deviation from correct form does not accomplish the children's goals related to humor. All efforts toward correctness of form should be taken seriously as a sincere effort on the part of each child.

A significant change in writing manuscript to cursive is one related to how the pupil places the paper. Manuscript writing itself does not slant as does cursive. Note below the difference between the manuscript, "a," and the cursive "*a*." The major stems of the letters change.

The child's paper has to be placed not in a perpendicular fashion, but slanted toward the right for the right-handed child. The teacher demonstrates, however, the way that manuscript letters are joined and then shows differences among the cursive letters. Words will be used to show how letters look when they are joined to each other in a meaningful context.

Children who are left-handed are permitted to slant their papers in the direction that is easier for them. They are encouraged to be comfortable in their writing. Their concentration needs to be focused on the formation of letter shapes. As pupils become more competent in their writing of letter formation, they can then concentrate on better form, better slant, and uniformity of space usage for words and between words.

Children should have their own folders for examples and products of their writing, dated according to completion. They should be encouraged to design their own folders or writing portfolios. They may want to paste various pictures on the cover in collage style or they may want to draw their own illustrations along with their own names. Uniqueness, recognition, and appreciation should symbolize classroom work, both from the teacher's perspective and the children's for each other.

Topical headings for the children's work either on the cover or within the folder may follow suggestions made by the teacher such as the themes below:

	WRITING AND THINKING	
Ideas	I Like Stories	Ideas
	I Enjoy Hiking	
Create	I Went Fishing	Create
	I Like to Cook Outdoors	
Write	Find the Word I Left Out	Write
	A Funny Riddle	
Do Your Own	A Scary Moment	Do Your Own
	A Loud Noise	
	The Day My Friend Moved	

Introduction to standard forms in writing cursive letters can be followed up with activities in which those skills are practiced. Holding the children to perfection levels can be inhibiting, therefore the manner in which the teacher encourages children should be one of emphasizing the children's efforts, "You really tried on that one! You are making much better loops (or up strokes, or consistent slants, or whatever) in your letters." The comments must be stated in positive rather than negative terms. "I can see that you have really been trying! Your work shows it!"

Children's gains are developmental; one skill builds on the other. Children do not achieve higher levels of competence simultaneously. This is why they need to know that they are proceeding in the correct direction. (Everyone learning a skill needs this reassurance in order to know how to practice.)

A B C D E F G H I J K L M
N O P Q R S T U V W X Y Z

a b c d e f g h i j k l m n
o p q r s t u v w x y z

1 2 3 4 5 6 7 8 9 0

When children manifest fatigue, teachers can alternate activities and introduce a game that will actively involve them on their feet, moving around to music or their own rhythmic beat. The teacher must be ready with ideas as well as trying to motivate children to be creative and suggest their ideas. Fatigue should not be confused as a lack of cooperation on the children's part, nor as evidence of delaying tactics or laziness. The teacher must honestly review his or her own techniques to determine whether children are expected to do too much too fast and to reach idealized levels of performance before they are able.

Parents also need to be aware of trends in children's learning. They need to know that even though their children are being taught differently from the way they were when they attended elementary schools, the manner of instruction is typically based on reasons that emerge from current research. Not that everything in the classroom is based on sound research, but parents need to support the children's efforts in doing what they are expected to do in school regardless of the familiarity of those techniques to the parents' knowledge. The updating of research findings as it reaches the teacher is not always translated to technical skills used directly with children in the classroom. In any case, when new information does come out in journals or periodicals, teachers can share it with parents at such levels that parents want to pursue technical information.

Educators like any other professionals who continue studying to update their knowledge know that change is sometimes in order. They are aware that modification and refinement of classroom instruction are needed. Although the last word is not apparent anywhere, the parents need to know that educational techniques are being studied, are being brought to teachers' attention when possible, and are revised as needed when it is feasible to do so. Differences among school systems and teachers are obvious in the awareness of recent knowledge about classroom instruction. In-service classes are given by school systems in hopes of keeping their teachers informed. Educators are individuals with their own preferences for teaching styles. Parents can be encouraged to recognize that their children are going to have different experiences with teachers whose style may or may not be congruent with their children's learning aptitudes or predispositions in the process of classroom instruction.

As writing is based not only on intellectual development but also on motor coordination and perceptual levels of pupils, it can be affected by the parents' expectations and attitudes of satisfaction with the children's work. Self-concepts are fragile. They can easily be hurt. Just because writing is a school subject, it cannot be considered as totally separate from the child's personality development. Parents need this information from the teacher. It can be presented in an empathic manner and with the teacher showing that understanding of the parents' disappointment or levels of expectation may be out of synchronization with reality.

Children's skills in the third grade are becoming more differentiated in terms of intra- and inter-individual differences. Their experiences contribute to the meaning they bring to their ideas and writing.[127] When their knowledge is sustained by sophisticated experiences outside of school, they are able to perform differently than other children who have not experienced similar problems or issues in their lives.

Racial misunderstanding as experienced by some youth is deeper for those youngsters who have not yet read about it or lived near someone who has. Reality is introduced differently for children. At times they can approach their formal experiences at school with greater perceptiveness than their teachers may have despite the teachers' formalized knowledge of similar topics. This is not to say that the teacher's instruction in language skills related to children's expression of feelings about their own contacts with reality is invalid or not useful for the children. It emphasizes the powerful impact of firsthand experiences on children's perceptions of the world, whether that world is noted at school or outside of it.

Children's cognitive styles contribute to the way they will adapt to writing skills. Differences in the way they perceive problems and respond to ways of solving them reflect their tendencies to be reflective (e.g., to take more time to think of possible alternatives) before they speak or act, to be impulsive (e.g., to speak immediately upon thinking of at least a small part of the solution), and the degree to which they are more dependent on the context (e.g., field-dependent, or dependent upon what is seen in the background) or can ignore the background to some extent (e.g., be field-independent) and make adjustments in thinking in terms of individual thought).[128]

Writing quickly or perceiving differences accurately are not always a symbol of high intelligence. The more researchers study differences among individuals, the more they discover learning styles that do not necessarily coincide with common assumptions made by educators.

Children in the later childhood years (beyond eight) have strong drives toward competence in some areas more than others. Their cognitive development does not always match the formalized levels of school expectations. When they develop through personal experiences information about death, social relations, or the arts they bring that knowledge in passionate terms to their work in school tasks. Their comments on a particular experience can be precocious and highly perceptive.[129] Although the children may not have a range of knowledge in discussing the broad issues of the problem area that has affected some of them, they can, however, reflect an awareness of distinctive issues as shown in their personal writing or creative stories.

Most books on early childhood do not include a discussion of children's development the year after the third grade or the intellectual progress of nine-year-old children, but the next section in this book includes the work of children in the fourth grade as symbolic of difficult transitions from early childhood to an initiation of middle or later childhood years. These issues are sometimes overlooked in terms of the developmental effects of early childhood on a preadolescent period and how early cognitive and affective patterns emerge in the differentiating effects of personality development and learning or performance at school.

FOURTH GRADE

Teachers may see before them in the pupil who is in the fourth grade an individual who seems mature, yet is childlike in stature and personality. The same child who may be viewed as being nine, going on forty (rather than ten), has to receive permission from parents to go to an event that is presented mainly for adolescents and young adults. The incongruent lags or discontinuities between sophisticated thought and actual performance in school tasks are evident in the fourth grade. Although the differences may have been evident in earlier grades, they are obvious in the readiness (or lack of it) of children in the fourth grade to proceed as many teachers might expect.

Motor coordination in writing skills may not be as much of a problem among nine-year-old children as the content of writing may be. Children may have had sufficient experience in writing various forms at school, as well as at home, although they manifest distinctive differences in the way they function when doing them. Some may find writing an unpleasant chore. Some pupils may enjoy certain aspects of it. They may enjoy creative writing more than having to follow an outline for a book report. They may become irritated with reminders of technical omissions in their writing. They may also have developed strong ego-related feelings to their products. Teachers' knowledge of those feelings can affect the manner used in approaching the pupils. Children should always be respected as individuals with feelings, but pupils in this age range have become more self-conscious of their characteristics and their own behavior with people. Although their words may sound at times as though they are sure of themselves, they need support from their teachers and parents.

Talking, reading, describing people and events, and debating issues provide opportunities for children to write. Through discussions, children hear the rhythmic quality of language that often becomes part of their writing. Teachers can recommend ideas for writing such as those below.

Some teachers encourage pupils to start a daily log. Only one sentence a day, if desired, can begin a child's experiences in recording impressions of events. Although this may be considered a diary type of activity, it need not be personalized to the extent that some diaries are. It can be viewed more as a record-keeping function. Children in this age range would probably want to write more than one sentence describing an experience or event. Beginning with brief comments, however, children realize that sometimes they will want to say less, sometimes more. They may also illustrate ideas in their record books.

```
┌─────────────────────────────────────────────────────┐
│              An Expressional Challenge                │
│                                                       │
│  Things I Like Best About Myself                      │
│  Things I Like to Do All the Time                     │
│  Things I Wish My_____Wouldn't Bug Me About     │
│  How to Find Happiness                                │
│  The Best Show I've Seen                              │
│  My Favorite Friend                                   │
│  A New Hobby                                          │
│  Outer Space                                          │
│  Finding Myself                                       │
│  In My Private TIme, I Like _____                │
│  Would You Like to Know How I _____ ?            │
│  My Ideal                                            │
└─────────────────────────────────────────────────────┘
```

Folders are needed for individual work. Pupils may decorate the covers in as elaborate a manner as they wish. This can be done during an art period. Individual preferences of the pupils are obvious in the topics they choose to write about most often. Their folders, as well, symbolize productivity in various themes. The teacher should show an appreciation of various interests. Whenever possible, pupils should present their work to the class. They may either report on something related to their folder materials or on a hobby about which they have written. Often, after pupils have written something, they are better prepared to talk about it.

It is recommended that pupils be aware of the importance of

Originality in writing.
Clarity of expression.
Appropriate choices of words.
Using correct form.
The tone of language used.
Imagery in descriptive writing.

Instruction on outlining is helpful for pupils in knowing how to guide themselves in writing a report or organizing one. A title is written first, then the major topics are indicated. Under each major topic a child may write one or two subtopics. The concluding or summarizing statements close the report. The numbering of these topics can be developed as the teacher gives examples by using a composition or story that most of the children know. Often a book or story, in the way it is presented, lends itself well to the articulation of an outline form. Teachers need to look for those examples that can be clearly demonstrated to children. Sometimes tapes or films can be obtained from educational commercial sources, describing the design of outlines.

Children, nine years old, are still having some misunderstanding about syntactical arrangements.[130] They confuse subjects of a sentence with the action of a sentence in some cases. They interpret, for example, the sentence, "John asked Bill what to do," to mean John told Bill what to do.[131] Although many writers assume that children by the age of five have mastered their native language structure, Chomsky does not agree. Many children are still acquiring syntactical knowledge through five to ten years old.

Teachers should have sentences written and cut up into separate words. Children can place the sentences on the ledge of the chalkboard by placing individual words in an order that makes sense to some extent. Changing these sentences around so that variations of meaning can become evident to children can provide opportunities to learn that words acquire different meanings depending on where they are in a sentence.[132]

Poetry and creative stories exercise children's imagination and the use of words to create colorful ideas and images. When the teacher encourages uniqueness in children's writing, they will understand that they should not copy other people's ideas. The teacher has to tell the children that each person is different and has unusual ways of describing something that has happened to him or her. Children can be taught to appreciate differences in people's work.

A collection of poetry books in the room and various selections and types of poetry posted on the bulletin board can help children appreciate many topics treated in poetry. The environment in the classroom encourages or inhibits children's appreciation of and familiarity with poetic forms. Examples of the poetry of famous writers, of children's anthologies, and classics of years past can be tacked to a corkboard. Changing those displays often can attract children's attention to different topics. Pictures or photographs that capture the mood of a poem are expressive and exemplary of work that children may use as a model.

The children can be given the opportunity to read their favorite poems. This alone shows that the teacher values poetry. Sometimes teachers read verbal imagery forms to children before they write their own. Discussions that set mood and tempo create an atmosphere of acceptance if the teacher concentrates on developing a slower cadence in some cases for talking and writing. When the children are not rushed, they are often able to become reflective. Some teachers use music that is soothing and restful if a mood for "dream-making" is desired.

Skills involving proper spelling can even be introduced in poetic form. Rhyming of words shows children how they are similar in some parts. The words children use for their own stories are kept in their own dictionary boxes. Different words outside their own initiated usage can be shown to them in a sentence and copied for their dictionary. Meaning, concentration, observation of letters, symbols, and sounds can be emphasized as children see new words that they are asked to know how to spell.

Each teacher has a preferred method for teaching children how to spell. Often various styles may be adapted to a given classroom of children. Most techniques involving spelling include visual and auditory discrimination as well as kinesthetic imagery. Some researchers indicate that 75 minutes per week devoted to spelling is the maximum time that ought to spent.[133] If teachers encourage in children some of the positive attitudes toward recalling the correct spelling of a word, the formalized time spent per week for spelling practice or testing can be 60 minutes. Attitudes toward correct spelling that can focus children's attention on individual letters, as well as reminders that the children edit their own work, can contribute greatly toward positive orientations. The desire to spell correctly brings skills to the fore, at least as much as the child can do at any given level of development. This does not mean that a child does not need technical assistance in learning to spell. It does mean that the pupil's willingness to meet the challenge and enjoy the effort toward that end can facilitate success.

Children's dialectical differences can often make spelling difficult for them to learn. Standard forms of the spelling of a language or dialect different from the one they are accustomed to using present a challenge to the way they hear sounds and relate them to letter symbols. Here, again, teachers must understand at the start that the theme of communication should not be discouraged. It is essential to human relationships.

If children need individual help, the teacher can arrange for it in various ways. Sometimes it can be provided by opportunities to focus on certain words that help the child recognize sound and letter correspondence (e.g., *d* in find). The writing and language of children are as much a part of their personality as any other acts and must be respected. Following that guideline, the teacher should consider that school instruction is simply another facet of the child's instructional and intellectual world. The child's background has not been a void. It has content and validity. Some writers chastise educators for the way children of different dialectical usage are treated so that they themselves begin to devalue their own background. Teachers must be careful not to contribute toward children's lowered self-concepts in that manner.

Children's learning at school is abstract to a great extent in that pupils solve problems that are often not a part of their own experiences in life outside of school.[134] Cross-cultural studies on differences of educational contexts in which children learn, indicate that nonschool children in cultures other than American ones, learn about problem solving directly in an environment that will involve the activity itself, once learned. Children in American society sit in a classroom that poses problems unfamiliar to them and that involve elements or characteristics the pupils do not know from experience. Children are expected to write and read about situations that are not present in the immediate environment, as well as knowing how to measure and define common attributes in concepts.[135]

If the children at school are often outside of their own immediate contexts of understanding, and their learning in order to be effective must bring their own experiences to the language they use, it is essential that their efforts to write, speak, or spell not be derogated. To do so is to undermine the children's ready foundations for learning whatever the school can build on to the children's developing responses.

Because pupils must learn to express academic ideas that have little relationship to their own experiences, it becomes more essential that they invest meaning in the words they are learning to use. In unschooled societies, where people can show what they mean in the context of certain problems immediately at hand, symbols not directly related to the situation are less important than are words in American societal usage.[136] When discussion of a problem is separate from its own context of need, symbolic forms become more important in terms of representing the ideas (not present in the environment).[137]

Comments made about the "efficiency" of learning directly in the context of use of such experiences are also supplemented by observations that recognize what schools are able to do in building technological knowledge that can be useful to children in nonschool societies (if their countries are to become more industrialized). Decisions regarding the feasibility or wisdom of becoming industrialized, however, are another matter, not discussed in relation to choices or techniques of schooling for children in some other cultures.

Some developmental psychologists envision the schools as being responsible for the pupil's developmental level in a cognitive sense and as required to provide the best cognitive realization for a pupil at a given stage of his or her own abilities or capacities to learn. This suggests that all children will not be taught in the same manner.[138] It is also expected that fulfillment of each pupil's intellectual and emotional potential be guided by the school.[139]

Children's writing falls within the context of the recommendations made by developmental psychologists as well as researchers in reading education. The emphasis is made upon children being given the opportunity to use what they know from their own background and experiences as content for speaking, writing, and reading. Enlargement on those experiences comes with school activities enjoyed with other children and with new contacts, which are themselves becoming a natural part of the children's environmental contexts. New experiences enmesh themselves with the old in a gradual process of learning.

Experiences at school can be considered as add-on knowledge to the children's own backgrounds. The children's past experiences in their own familiar surroundings are the initiating focus for them (and can be the starting point for the teacher's instructional activities for them). Their personal backgrounds, however, should not represent the total of their education. Meaning has begun for them in their own lives at home or in the neighborhood (and through television, in part, if they have a set). It can be enlarged upon at school, which is a place that provides opportunities to associate ideas with one's personal framework of thought. It is the skillful teacher who knows how to link the child's meaning systems with school terminology in a way that engenders pride in the child for reaching out beyond his/her easy grasp.

Through the process of writing and the teacher's patience with pupils as they stretch their skills, children can be inspired by a world that is yet unknown to them personally. It can become their own environment through reading and writing about it.

Collections of the children's work should be displayed around their classroom, reflecting the nature of interests that exist among people in the class. An emphasis on reaching out toward new ideas can be made by the teacher who supports pupils in an atmosphere that persuades experimentation and a playful attitude toward learning. One of the reasons children fear trying something new is that they have been conditioned to think in a success-failure syndrome. Their teacher, however, can help them perceive attempts to learn about something unfamiliar to them as part of finding out about themselves (new attitudes, for example) and relating that to a world of which they can be a part if they wish. Not to try may sometimes mean that they are closing themselves off from something they may like very much and may bring them a great deal of satisfaction in the future.

Growth in writing and conceptualizing abstractions about things, events, people, and places occurs in relation to associated experiences. Fear of growth in and of itself can block one's hopes and goals toward knowing more, seeing more, and coming in contact with more people of one's choice than might be possible when one remains in one's most comfortable or most familiar surroundings. Although children may be fearful of low evaluations (by others, themselves, or their teacher) on their writing or conceptualization attempts, they must be urged to continue at their own levels and in self-competing or self-challenging modes.

The classroom can be filled with materials, kits (either commercial or made by the teacher), cassettes, listening head-sets, varieties of curriculum offerings, paper and various media for writing, magazines for cutting out pictures and ideas, paints for illustrating poetry, stories, scientific or mechanical devices, and a host of other things to stimulate the lives and work or activities of nine-year-old children. As indicated earlier in this chapter, nine-year-old children are sophisticated in their thinking related to some ideas, often close to adult stages of perceptiveness. Schools and classrooms must capitalize on that.

SUMMARY

This chapter dealt with a crucial subject matter area in young children's lives. Communication forms and self-expression influence an individual's personality development and mental health. Interpersonal relationships are affected by communication skills.

Most books on early childhood education deal with early years through age eight. Although this is typically the age range of early childhood education, another year, the ninth, has been included in this chapter to provide some highlights and insight on the preadolescent perspectives that are beginning to emerge in children's development. A child in the fourth grade has just begun an advanced or intermediate part of childhood at school and home. The differences among children in the fourth grade become more distinct as they reach out to various aspects of the environment. Sophistication among some pupils is obvious. The teacher and parent have to be aware of the variety of influences and potential skills that are developing in this period of childhood.

The chapter emphasized ways of encouraging children to express themselves and enjoy learning about the uniqueness of their own forms and talents in expression as well as learning about communication techniques that are used by others. Learning how to listen critically, to speak, to understand, to read, and to write at various age levels provides significant patterns of communication at school and home.

Effective communication can make the difference between being somewhat happy and effectively functional in one's world or feeling alone and alienated from others. The increasing number of topics and interpersonal interests that show up in reading, writing, and other forms of communication suggest that the range of interests of individuals can be satisfied. The child has only to look for reading materials that bring meaning and pleasure for him/her.

From the time a baby arrives, the communication that occurs between the infant and parents affects various interaction patterns. Speech, the child's hearing and brain coordination processes, efforts at the production of speech, listening skills, ability to read later in the fourth year of life—all are affected by physical abilities, psychological capacities, and interpretations of what the child hears, sees, and senses from those in the environment. As language expression is a form of behavior, adults have to be aware that their attitudes toward the child's language can influence the child's self-concept and mental health.

Parents can help children attain competency in communication skills by supporting the children's efforts at fluency, problem solving in language, and generally assisting the children in new attempts at mastery of language expression, be it reading, writing, or speaking or listening critically to what someone else says. Informal instruction at home precedes significant learning that occurs in the formal, organized, and sequential arrangements of the classroom.

Audio-visual materials, cassettes, listening centers, a variety of books, pamphlets, pictures, dictionaries, and technical materials for communication activities may overflow in the cabinets and shelves of a classroom. The teacher seems to have the strongest impact on children's learning gain, however, in knowing how to use those materials effectively with the pupils and to provide a classroom atmosphere that welcomes learning activity.

TOPICS FOR DISCUSSION

1. Tape or record three different samples of about 15 minutes of speech heard in three children: (1) a two-year-old; (2) a three-year-old; and (3) a four-year-old. Compare differences among them in terms of fluency, pronunciation, breathiness, facial expression, if possible, and some contextual elements describing the circumstances of speech.
2. After doing a case study on an infant's development in the first year of life, relative to physical, social, emotional, and cognitive characteristics, discuss with others or on paper what you think are crucial periods in a child's development. Why do you think so? How can parents help at these times?
3. Why is it necessary for teachers to understand children's development in the first few years of life? How does this knowledge affect attitudes toward and perceptions of young pupils?
4. Create a plan for a classroom of children in the first grade. Design a schedule for them that you think would enhance their language development.
5. Design a program that would help parents become involved in a language program focusing on hearing, speaking, and readiness activities typically carried on in the kindergarten.
6. List the books you would have in your classroom in order to accommodate the skills of children in the first, second, and third grades. How would you arrange an attractive library corner for them?
7. Create and describe the use of five games that would give the pupils an opportunity to match and coordinate letters and symbols. Choose the grade level that is of interest to you.
8. You are giving advice to a first-year teacher who will be teaching kindergarten for the first time. What will you recommend for organizing an effective and comprehensive lan-

guage development program? What audio-visual aids will you recommend? What supplies will you need to have or order? What books will you advise to have on hand for free-time browsing, but also for the teacher's use with the children?

9. Design a schedule for six weeks that can be submitted to a principal who asked a teacher of the first grade to submit such a schedule prior to instruction. It should include the subject matter that will be taught each day and the time allotted for periods each day. Unique events should be included as planned for special days. Are field trips part of your program? Should they be? Are resource speakers part of your program? Are they appropriate? Can they contribute to the pupils' general knowledge? How?

10. Identify areas of content that are integrated effectively with children's having opportunities for language experiences. What will these areas contribute to children's development in critical listening, recognizing letter shapes, sensing rhythm in words or phrases?

11. Design six bulletin boards that can be used in a classroom for children in the second grade who need practice in symbol, sound, letter-shape associations, writing announcements of importance, thank-you notes, invitations to a party, business letters requesting something, and letters of appreciation to a resource person who visited the class.

12. Create forms that require fill-in responses for children in the third grade. Discuss your purposes for each form and the benefits you hope that the children will derive from giving the needed responses on those forms.

NOTES

1. T. G. R. Bower, *Human Development* (San Francisco: Freeman, 1979), p. 50. The ability to localize sounds in terms of their direction or source is present at birth in varying degrees.

2. M. M. Lewis, *Language Thought and Personality in Infancy and Childhood* (New York: Basic, 1963), pp. 13–22. The child's cries seem to start with discomfort; these are early efforts in speech development. Comfort cries are also an aspect of learning to express one's self; those sounds are like vowel sounds, a, o, or u. Babbling occurs about several weeks after the child's birth and sounds as though the child is playing with sounds.

3. Margaret Bullowa, Lawrence Gaylord Jones, and Thomas G. Bever, "The Development from Vocal to Verbal Behavior in Children," pp. 101–114 in *Monographs of the Society for Research in Child Development* Serial No. 92, 1964, Vol. 29, No. 1, *The Acquisition of Language,* edited by Ursula Bellugi and Roger Brown, 191 pp.

4. Dolores Durkin, *Teaching Them to Read,* 3rd ed. (Boston: Allyn, 1978), pp. 461–493. See also George D. Spache, *Investigating the Issues of Reading Disabilities* (Boston: Allyn, 1976).

5. Lev Semenovich Vygotsky, *Thought and Language* translated by Eugenia Hanfmann and Gertrude Vakar (Cambridge, Mass.: M.I.T., 1979).

6. Grace A. Ransom, *Preparing to Teach Reading* (Boston: Little, Brown, 1978), p. 6. Sensations remembered in association with the use of words are retained in normal perceptual development. She suggests that the sensations obtained from body balance, organic sensations of hunger or thirst, and kinesthesia ("being aware of what your body is doing") as well as the senses involving hearing, seeing, touching, tasting and smelling all affect perceptual development.

7. Bullowa, Jones, and Bever, op. cit., p. 112.

8. Susanna Pflaum-Connor, *The Development of Language and Reading in Young Children,* 2nd ed. (Columbus, Ohio: Merrill, 1978), p. 8. The dialogue that occurs between adults and children provides significant cognitive development for children. Adults provide the model that children use for the organization of their own thought and speech, as Vygotsky indicates.

9. Vygotsky, op. cit., p. 131.

10. Ibid.

11. Peter A. de Villiers and Jill G. de Villiers, *Early Language* (Cambridge, Mass.: Harvard U.P., 1979), p. 16.

12. Bower, op. cit., p. 320.

13. Ibid., p. 321.

14. Ibid.

15. These differences were discussed in Chapter 2 of this text.

16. Inge Bretherton, Elizabeth Bates, Laura Benigni, Luigia Camaioni, and Virginia Volterra, "Relationships Between Cognition, Communication, and Quality of Attachment," pp. 223–269 in *The Emergence of Symbols. Cognition and Communication in Infancy,* edited by Elizabeth Bates and others (New York: Academic, 1979).

17. Ibid., p. 268.

18. Ibid., p. 266.

19. Ibid.

20. Edythe Margolin, "Work and Play—Are They Really Opposites?" *Elementary School Journal,* Vol. 67 (April 1967), pp. 343–353. This article was among earlier works dealing with the attempt to codify (through a typology of play and work) the similarities between scientific characteristics of discovery, manipulation, suspended judgment on evaluative processes, absorption of interest to the exclusion of concern about time consumed, and other significant aspects of learning and intellectual development involved in play.

21. Jerome L. Singer, "Imagination and Make-Believe Play in Early Childhood Education. Some Educational Implications," *Journal of Mental Imagery* Vol. 1, No. 1 (Spring 1977), pp 127–144.

22. Note comments in Chapter 2 of this text in which the words of Vygotsky are discussed. See also the introduction of Jerome Bruner, pp. v–x in L. S. Vygotsky's *Thought and Language,* edited and translated by Eugenia Hanfmann and Gertrude Vakar (Cambridge, Mass.: M.I.T., 1979).

23. Edythe Margolin, "Parental Attitudes Toward Work and Play in Four Countries of Western Europe," U.C.L.A. Grant in 1968. Unpublished Report. This was a pilot study to provide a basis for further research in play behavior.

24. There are wide variations in this among children from various backgrounds, and experiential differences in language usage.

25. Courtney B. Cazden, "Suggestions from Studies of Early Language Acquisition," pp. 3–8 in *Language in Early Childhood Education,* edited by Courtney B. Cazden (Washington, D.C.: National Association for the Education of Young Children, 1972). See also Courtney B. Cazden, Joan C. Baratz, William Labov, and Francis H. Palmer, "Language Development in Day-Care Programs," pp. 83–99 in *Language in Early Childhood Education,* edited by Courtney B. Cazden (Washington, D.C.: National Assoc. for the Education of Young Children, 1972).

26. Cazden, Baratz, Labov, and Palmer, op. cit., p. 90.

27. Pflaum-Connor, op. cit., p. 58.

28. Ibid, p. 60.

29. Ibid.

30. Ibid., p. 64.

31. Ibid., p. 66.

32. Carol Chomsky, *The Acquisition of Syntax in Children from 5 to 10* (Cambridge, Mass.: M.I.T., 1979). The rate of acquiring syntactical structure decreases after the age of five, but the quality increases in terms of mastery that becomes more similar to adult forms of language (p. 2 of Chomsky's work). Although it has been a popular assumption that children have mastered, by the age of six, most of the structures of their own native language, Chomsky suggests that children are actively involved until ages nine or ten in the process of acquiring effective usage and understanding of syntax (p. 121 in Chomsky's work).

33. Ibid., pp. 2–5.

34. Ibid., p. 4.

35. Ibid.

36. Ilse Mattick, "The Teacher's Role in Helping Young Children Develop Language Competence," pp. 107–116 in *Language in Early Childhood Education,* edited by Courtney B. Cazden (Washington, D.C.: National Assoc. for the Education of Young Children, 1972). See also Jean Berko Gleason, "An Experimental Approach to Improving Children's Communicative Ability," pp. 101–106, in *Language in Early Childhood Education,* edited by Courtney B. Cazden (Washington, D.C.: National Assoc. for the Education of Young Children, 1972).

37. Berko Gleason, op. cit., p. 104.

38. Mattick, op. cit., p. 110.
39. Daniel I. Slobin and Charles A. Welsh, "Elicited Imitation as a Research Tool in Developmental Psycholinguistics," pp. 170–185 in *Language Training in Early Childhood Education,* edited by Celia Stendler Lavatelli (ERIC Clearinghouse on Early Childhood Education: U. of Illinois, 1971). Since children have to acquire deeper than surface structure of sentences and transformational rules, they do not learn language by imitation, but rather, they filter through their own language system, what they hear and ultimately express.
40. Mimi Brodsky Chenfeld, *Teaching Language Arts Creatively* (New York: Harcourt, 1978), pp. 3–34. See Chapter One on the unique individualization of self-expression, creativity, self-knowledge. Chapter 2, pp. 35–65, provides many ideas that are useful for teaching.
41. Mattick, op. cit., p. 111.
42. *Messages* Penguin Books: Australia Ltd., 1978, 31 pp. This illustrated booklet demonstrates various ways to produce objects and ideas for conveying messages.
43. Philip L. Safford, *Teaching Young Children with Special Needs* (Saint Louis, Mo.: Mosby, 1978), p. 48.
44. Ibid., p. 49. The teacher must learn to adapt to the various dialects and speech forms of children so that the children's linguistic abilities in their own native language forms are appreciated. If children sense an attitude of "condescension and noblesse oblige" in the teacher's receptiveness of speech, they are not encouraged to pursue further efforts in development in that context.
45. Bernard G. Suran and Joseph V. Rizzo, *Special Children: An Integrative Approach* (Glenview, Ill.: Scott, Foresman, 1979), p. 129.
46. Ibid., p. 116.
47. Ibid., p. 122.
48. Ibid., p. 123.
49. Jerome Bruner, *The Relevance of Education* (New York: Norton, 1973), pp. 50–51. The skills that are acquired to use language as an intellectual tool not only involve years of experience toward that end, but also permit cultural orientations toward high levels of technology.
50. The content of what is seen is not discussed here; what is of concern is that children learn to become adept at translating symbols, sounds, word usage, and concepts as seen in any context that introduces reading. What children ought to read, to see, or to hear is a separate issue. The subject relates greatly to parental desires, school contexts, and general societal values as well.
51. Vygotsky, op. cit., p. 83. Complex psychological processes are involved in the child's learning to understand concepts, from the first moment that a word is introduced, throughout the variation of experiences and reconceptualization of word meanings as a child matures. Word meanings evolve within the child as different opportunities arise for the use of any given word.
52. Pflaum-Connor, op. cit., p. 132.
53. Genevieve Painter, "A Tutorial Program for Disadvantaged Infants," pp. 79–100 in *Language Training in Early Childhood Education,* edited by Celia Standler Lavatelli (ERIC Clearinghouse on Early Childhood Education: U. of Illinois, 1971).
54. Mary Anne Hall, Jerilyn K. Ribovich, and Christopher J. Ramig, *Reading and the Elementary School Child.* (New York: Van Nostrand, 1979). The authors indicate that some people view reading as beginning for children at birth, when they are exposed to the environment of sounds, people, things, and events. p. 55.
55. Ibid., p. 56.
56. Ibid. Children in this age range were able to recognize Ivory soap, McDonald hamburger, Coca-Cola labels when they were asked to "read" the label. They were also able to recognize the word within the context of manuscript print. When they were asked if they knew how to read, they said, "No."
57. There are books that provide adults with techniques and knowledge about the way to transmit ideas to young children as well as books that can be used directly with children who concentrate on the book and illustrations themselves.
58. Ann Cole, Carolyn Haas, Elizabeth Heller, and Betty Weinberger, *Children Are Children Are Children* (Boston: Little, Brown, 1978). This book describes activities, educational

practices, foods, sports, and holiday observances, among other things of children in various countries, such as Japan, Nigeria, Soviet Union, Iran, France, and Brazil.

Excellent catalogues are available from various companies, bookstores, department stores, children's book and record shops in most cities. Libraries have information about those catalogues if parents or teachers are not able to secure them directly from the vendor's sources.

59. Ransom, op. cit., p. 11.
60. Ibid.
61. Ibid.
62. Gunilla Wolde, *Betsy and Peter Are Different* (New York: Random, 1979) and Gunilla Wolde, *Betsy's Baby Brother* (New York: Random, 1975) are books, well-illustrated and appealing in form and content, which present in charming ways the individual's attempts to reconcile differences among feelings and people.
63. Joy Wilt, *Mine And Yours* (Waco, Tex.: Educational Products Division, 1978). This book helps children understand that it is all right to disagree with someone and that the other person, as well, needs to have the "space" or freedom to disagree without punishment. It also indicates how people sometimes take advantage of each other, without intending to do so. See also Joy Wilt, *Saying What You Mean* (Waco, Tex.: Educational Products Division, 1978) Psychological communication in words, gestures, and feelings is emphasized in this pleasingly illustrated book. Again, adults can learn from the clear messages throughout the book, which emphasize adult and child interaction as well as child-to-child interaction.
64. Joy Wilt, *You're All Right* (Waco, Tex.: Educational Products Division, 1978). People make mistakes; make wrong choices in buying something, in choosing friends, and in many other human acts. This fact does not condemn an individual personality as an unworthwhile entity. To be human is to make mistakes. The child's way of dealing with mistakes affects the self-concept and can, with adequate and appropriate help, permit him/her to surmount feelings of self-contempt.
65. Lou Benson, *Images, Heroes, and Self-Perceptions* (Englewood Cliffs, N.J.: Prentice-Hall, 1974), pp. 102 and 365.
66. John E. Johnson, *My School Book* (New York: Random, 1979), describes the child's school day in words and illustrations that are very appealing. Color, format, durability, content, and tone of words used are attractive and uplifting in spirit for children.
67. *Eggs* in Wonder Starters series. (New York: Grosset, 1971). Hen's eggs which are eaten at home as well as other eggs that are the origin of young animals, are described and shown in clear, illustrated form.
68. *Sleep* in Wonder Starters series. (New York: Grosset, 1971). See also Mabel Watts, *The Bedtime Book* (Racine, Wis. A Whitman Book, Western, 1963), 28 pp. This book describes the ways that many animals and birds sleep, all in their own places or environment, suggesting that each creature has a place for sleeping just as the child has his or her own bed.
69. The social studies as children know them in later grades at school include generalizations and concepts from the social sciences of anthropology, economics, geography, history, political science, sociology, and social psychology. Some writers also use philosophy or psychology as areas from which to draw generalizations of knowledge.
70. Cole, Haas, Heller, and Weinberger, op. cit., pp. v–viii provide insight on how the authors compiled their book on children from various lands and cultural origins.
71. Joy Wilt and Terre Watson, *Listen!* (Waco, Tex.: Creative Resources, 1977). These authors have also published books on visual experiences, on tasting and smelling, on touching, and on rhythm and movement, all of which are very useful for children at home and in the classroom. All were done by the same publisher in Waco, Tex.
72. Ransom, op. cit., p. 255. Games can be adapted to the levels of children's skills. Two children can be partners, helping each other in a variety of ways to sort sounds and objects, to place them in trainlike order on a ledge, using sound and word dominoes on a desk.
73. Dolores Durkin, *Teaching Them to Read*, 3rd ed. (Boston: Allyn, 1978), p. 194. Durkin indicates that even if it were appropriate to bring a total class of young children together, who were similar in skills and the like, it is still wiser to teach them in small groups and

of course, individually, when possible. To instruct a total class at one time is not to ensure learning of each child.

74. Ibid.
75. Pflaum-Connor, op. cit., p. 118.
76. Ibid., p. 119.
77. Ibid., p. 124.
78. Durkin, op. cit., p. 229. Games can be used by making a large figure pasted on to cardboard, and on which a mouth with an opening has been created. Words in the form of a banana or other shapes, can be placed as children say them, into the mouth of the cardboard figure. A paper bag or small box can be placed behind or stapled to the back side of the mouth-opening and can catch the words as they are placed through the silt.
79. Robert M. Wilson and Maryanne Hall, *Reading and the Elementary School Child* (New York: Van Nostrand, 1972), p. 56.
80. Ibid., p. 57.
81. Ibid.
82. Ibid., pp. 74–76.
83. Ransom, op. cit., p. 371. Oral reading is important in the second grade. Children can at this level know how to use proper tone, rhythm, emphasis, and appropriate phrasing. Many opportunities to read aloud or to express ideas provide essential elements of an effective reading program.
84. Ibid., p. 330.
85. Wilson and Hall, op. cit., p. 57.
86. Ibid., p. 278.
87. George D. Spache, *Investigating the Issues of Reading Disabilities* (Boston: Allyn, 1976), p. 442.
88. Spache, op. cit., p. 443.
89. Ibid.
90. Ibid.
91. Ibid., p. 444.
92. Ibid.
93. Ibid.
94. Ibid., p. 445.
95. George D. Spache, *Diagnosing and Correcting Reading Disabilities* (Boston: Allyn, 1976), p. 387.
96. Ibid., pp. 163–191.
97. Ibid.
98. Ibid., p. 5.
99. Ibid.
100. Ibid.
101. There are several other ways that a parent may help in the child's reading efforts at school and at home. These will be discussed later. The topic is also included in several books that indicate how parents and teachers work together for children's gains at school and at home.
102. Wilson and Hall, op. cit., p. 57.
103. Durkin, op. cit., p. 118. The Fry Readability Scale is one among several assessing approximate appropriateness for the reading of pupils in given grade levels.
104. Ibid. Most reading formulas attempt to measure difficulties in vocabulary, structure of sentences, and content in relation to a given category of individuals. See also Durkin's pages 50 and 51 of the same work. Fry's readability scale offers a relatively easy way to assess difficulties and appropriateness of reading materials for a set of pupils and although it is approximate in its measurement, it is preferred by many teachers because it is less complicated than other computational formulas.
105. Ransom, op. cit., p. 407. It is suggested that in the fourth grade the teacher divide the children's reading time into blocks for reading literature, free choices, and for study and comprehension skills directly related to given technical areas. In later grades, it is recommended that teachers in the content areas themselves teach the children reading skills related to vocabulary recognition, meaning, and rate of reading orally and silently. Social studies, mathematics, science, for example, have many terms that represent com-

plicated concepts. When children meet them for the first time, it is difficult unless the teacher helps the pupils in comprehending and visualizing the words or terms.

106. Joan Fassler, *Helping Children Cope* (New York: Free Press, a Division of Macmillan, 1978), 162 pp.
107. Harry A. Greene and Walter T. Petty, *Developing Language Skills in the Elementary Schools*, 4th ed. (Boston: Allyn, 1971), p. 490.
108. Evelyn B. Spache, *Reading Activities for Child Involvement*, 2nd ed. (Boston: Allyn, 1976), pp. 194–223. There are also ideas for games that can be played (in teams) by the children in which both knowledge and physical activity are involved. Newspaper ads are used, too, in an instructive and enjoyable manner.
109. M. C. Wittrock, "The Generative Processes of Memory," pp. 153–184 in *The Human Brain*, edited by M. C. Wittrock and others (Englewood Cliffs, N.J.: Prentice-Hall, 1977), p. 171.
110. Ibid., p. 172.
111. Ibid., p. 176.
112. Ibid., pp. 177–180.
113. Ibid., pp. 179–180.
114. Ibid., p. 180.
115. Ibid.
116. Carol Chomsky, "Write Now, Read Later," pp. 119–126 in *Language in Early Childhood Education*, edited by Courtney B. Cazden (Washington, D.C.: National Assoc. for the Education of Young Children, 1972).
117. Ibid., p. 120.
118. In the first year, children may see written forms and receive impressions but not create them themselves. Sometimes children make attempts to hold instruments in their fists, but it is not until about two that children are more interested in using crayons to draw or write. Some children may do so before they are two.
119. Herbert Ginsburg and Sylvia Opper, *Piaget's Theory of Intellectual Development*, 2nd ed. Englewood Cliffs, N.J.: Prentice-Hall, Inc., 1979, p. 82. The child's use of language does not suggest that verbal symbols are used in the major part of his/her thinking. Since the child perceives the world in terms of his/her own internalized system of meanings, the child's and the adult's meaning of a word often are not the same. Language has to become much more central to the child's habitual form of communication before verbal meanings more closely approximate an adult's reference point.
120. When adults give simple reasons for communication, received or sent out from home, they are helping children understand the relevance or importance of written modes of communication. Specificity or exactness is not the major function of parent explanations when children are very young.
121. See Concept Illustration 4–3 to note a manuscript form of the letter *a*.
122. Walter T. Petty, Dorothy C. Petty, and Marjorie F. Becking, *Experiences in Language* (Boston: Allyn, 1973), p. 211.
123. Greene and Petty, op. cit., pp. 141–142.
124. Petty, Petty, and Becking, op. cit., p. 215.
125. Sandra Nina Kaplan, Jo Ann Butom Kaplan, Sheila Kunishima Madsen, and Bette Taylor Gould, *A Young Child Experiences* (Pacific Palisades, Calif.: Goodyear, 1975). A section on writing centers and tasks appears specifically on pp. 123–129 in which simple activities are sketched for easy adaptation. See also, Doreen J. Croft and Robert D. Hess, *An Activities Handbook for Teachers of Young Children*, 3rd ed. (Boston: Houghton, 1980), pp. 131–136.
126. Greene and Petty, op. cit., p. 257.
127. Howard Gardner, *Developmental Psychology* (Boston: Little, Brown, 1978), pp. 433–438. The examples are given of children who experience poverty and know more than others who do not, what some of the principles in social problems are. Also, children who are involved in music or art can proceed to adult levels of perceptions and this knowledge is reflected in what they say or do, as well as in the choices they make and the reasons they give for those decisions.
128. Ibid., pp. 446–454.
129. Ibid., pp. 433–438.

130. Chomsky, op. cit.
131. Ibid., pp. 17 and 120.
132. Chomsky's examples might be adapted from her study.
133. Greene and Petty, op. cit., p. 400.
134. Gardner, op. cit., p. 424.
135. Ibid.
136. Ibid. Note the reference to Olson's work (1976).
137. Ibid. See the comments derived from Scribner and Cole's study (1973).
138. Ibid., p. 426.
139. Ibid., p. 427.

SELECTED REFERENCES

BENSON, LOU. *Images, Heroes, and Self-Perceptions.* Englewood Cliffs, N.J.: Prentice-Hall, Inc., 1974. 434 pp.

BOWER, T. G. R. *Human Development.* San Francisco: W. H. Freeman and Company, 1979. 473 pp.

BRETHERTON, INGE, ELIZABETH BATES, LAURA BENIGNI, LUIGIA CAMAIONI, and VIRGINIA VOLTERRA. "Relationships Between Cognition, Communication, and Quality of Attachment," pp. 223–269 in *The Emergence of Symbols. Cognition and Communication in Infancy,* edited by Elizabeth Bates and others. New York: Academic Press, Inc., 1979. 387 pp.

BRUNER, JEROME. *The Relevance of Education.* New York: W. W. Norton & Company, Inc., 1973. 175 pp.

BULLOWA, LAWRENCE, GAYLORD JONES, and THOMAS G. BEVER. "The Development from Vocal to Verbal Behavior in Children," pp. 101–114 in *Monographs of the Society for Research in Child Development.* Serial No. 92, 1964. Vol. 29, No. 1, in *The Acquisition of Language,* edited by Ursula Bellugi and Roger Brown, 191 pp.

CAZDEN, COURTNEY B. "Suggestions from Studies of Early Language Acquisition," pp. 3–8 in *Language in Early Childhood Education,* edited by Courtney B. Cazden. Washington, D.C.: National Association for the Education of Young Children, 1972. 134 pp.

———, JOAN C. BARATZ, WILLIAM LABOV, and FRANCIS H. PALMER. "Language Development in Day-Care Programs," pp. 83–99 in *Language in Early Childhood Education,* edited by Courtney B. Cazden. Washington, D.C.: National Association for the Education of Young Children, 1972. 134 pp.

CHENFIELD, MIMI BRODSKY. *Teaching Language Arts Creatively.* New York: Harcourt Brace Jovanovich, Inc., 1978. 359 pp.

CHOMSKY, CAROL. *The Acquisition of Syntax in Children from 5 to 10.* Cambridge, Mass.: The M.I.T. Press, 1979. 126 pp.

———. "Write Now, Read Later," pp. 119–126 in *Language in Early Childhood Education,* edited by Courtney B. Cazden. Washington, D.C.: National Association for the Education of Young Children, 1972. 134 pp.

COLE, ANN, CAROLYN HAAS, ELIZABETH HELLER, and BETTY WEINBERGER. *Children Are Children Are Children.* Boston: Little, Brown and Company, 1978. 212 pp.

CROFT, DOREEN J., and ROBERT D. HESS. *An Activities Handbook for Teachers of Young Children,* 3rd ed. Boston: Houghton Mifflin Company, 1980. 257 pp.

DE VILLIERS, PETER A., and JILL G. DE VILLIERS. *Early Language.* Cambridge, Mass.: Harvard University Press, 1979. p. 16.

DURKIN, DOLORES. *Teaching Them to Read,* 3rd ed. Boston: Allyn & Bacon, Inc., 1978. 549 pp.

FASSLER, JOAN. *Helping Children Cope.* New York: The Free Press, a Division of Macmillan Publishing Co., Inc., 1978. 162 pp.

GARDNER, HOWARD. *Developmental Psychology.* Boston: Little, Brown and Company, 1978. pp. 371–472.

GINSBURG, HERBERT, and SYLVIA OPPER. *Piaget's Theory of Intellectual Development,* 2nd ed. Englewood Cliffs, N.J. Prentice-Hall, Inc., 1979. 253 pp.

GLEASON, JEAN BERKO. "An Experimental Approach to Improving Children's Communicative

Ability," pp. 101–106 in *Language in Early Childhood Education*, edited by Courtney B. Cazden. Washington, D.C.: National Association for the Education of Young Children, 1972. 134 pp.

GREENE, HARRY A., and WALTER T. PETTY. *Developing Language Skills in the Elementary School*, 4th ed. Boston: Allyn & Bacon, Inc., 1971. 571 pp.

HALL, MARY ANNE, JERILYN K. RIBOVICH, and CHRISTOPHER J. RAMIG. *Reading and the Elementary School*. New York: D. Van Nostrand Company, 1979. 374 pp.

JOHNSON, JOHN E. *My School Book*. New York: Random House, Inc., 1979. 20 pp.

KAPLAN, SANDRA NINA, JO ANN BUTOM KAPLAN, SHEILA KUNISHIMA MADSEN, and BETTE TAYLOR GOULD. *A Young Child Experiences*. Pacific Palisades, Calif.: Goodyear Publishing Company, Inc., 1975. 231 pp.

LAPP, DIANE, and JAMES FLOOD. *Language/Reading Instruction for the Young Child*. New York: Macmillan Publishing Co., Inc., 1981. 535 pp.

LEWIS, M. M. *Language Thought and Personality in Infancy and Childhood*. New York: Basic Books, Inc., Publishers, 1963. Pp. 13–22.

MARGOLIN, EDYTHE. "Parental Attitudes Toward Work and Play in Four Countries of Western Europe." U.C.L.A. Grant in 1968. Unpublished Report. 32 pp.

———. "Work and Play—Are They Really Opposites?" *Elementary School Journal*, Vol. 67 (April 1967), pp. 343–353.

MATTICK, ILSE. "The Teacher's Role in Helping Young Children Develop Language Competence," pp. 107–116 in *Language in Early Childhood Education*, edited by Courtney B. Cazden. Washington, D.C.: National Association for the Education of Young Children, 1972. 134 pp.

MCPHEE, GRIBBLE. *Messages*. Penguin Books: Australia Ltd., 1978. 31 pp.

PAINTER, GENEVIEVE. "A Tutorial Program for Disadvantaged Infants," pp. 79–100 in *Language Training in Early Childhood Education*, edited by Celia Stendler Lavatelli. ERIC Clearinghouse on Early Childhood Education: University of Illinois Press, 1971. 185 pp.

PETTY, WALTER T., DOROTHY C. PETTY, and MARJORIE F. BECKING. *Experiences in Language*. Boston: Allyn & Bacon, Inc., 1973. 529 pp.

PFLAUM-CONNOR, SUSANNA. *The Development of Language and Reading in Young Children*, 2nd ed. Columbus, Ohio: Charles E. Merrill Publishing Company, 1978. 230 pp.

RANSOM, GRACE A. *Preparing to Teach Reading*. Boston: Little, Brown and Company, 1978. 556 pp.

SAFFORD, PHILIP L. *Teaching Young Children with Special Needs*. Saint Louis, Mo.: The C. V. Mosby Company, 1978. 376 pp.

SINGER, JEROME L. "Imagination and Make-Believe Play in Early Childhood Education: Some Educational Implications," *Journal of Mental Imagery* Vol. 1, No. 1 (Spring 1977), pp. 127–144.

SLOBIN, DANIEL I., and CHARLES A. WELSH. "Elicited Imitation as a Research Tool in Developmental Psycholinguistics," pp. 170–185 in *Language Training in Early Childhood Education*, edited by Celia Stendler Lavatelli. ERIC Clearinghouse on Early Childhood Education: University of Illinois Press, 1971. 185 pp.

SPACHE, EVELYN B. *Reading Activities for Child Involvement*, 2nd ed. Boston: Allyn & Bacon, Inc., 1976. 243 pp.

SPACHE, GEORGE D. *Diagnosing and Correcting Reading Disabilities*. Boston: Allyn & Bacon, Inc., 1976. 397 pp.

———. *Investigating the Issues of Reading Disabilities*. Boston: Allyn & Bacon, Inc., 1976. 482 pp.

SURAN, BERNARD G., and JOSEPH V. RIZZO. *Special Children: An Integrative Approach*. Glenview, Ill.: Scott, Foresman and Company, 1979. 532 pp.

VYGOTSKY, LEV. *Thought and Language*, translated by Eugenia Hanfmann and Gertrude Vakar, Cambridge, Mass.: The M.I.T. Press, 1979. 168 pp.

WATTS, MABEL. *The Bedtime Book*. Racine, Wis.: A Whitman Book, Western Publishing Company, Inc., 1963. 28 pp.

WILSON, ROBERT M., and MARYANNE HALL. *Reading and the Elementary School Child*. New York: D. Van Nostrand Company, 1972. 355 pp.

WILT, JOY. *Mine and Yours*. Waco, Tex.: Educational Products Division, 1978. 128 pp.

———. *Saying What You Mean*. Waco, Tex.: Educational Products Division, 1978. 128 pp.

———. *You're All Right*. Waco, Tex.: Educational Products Division, 1978. 128 pp.

————, and TERRE WATSON. *Listen!* Waco, Tex.: Creative Resources, 1977. 159 pp.

WITTROCK, M. C. "The Generative Processes of Memory," pp. 153–184 in *The Human Brain*, edited by M. C. Wittrock and others. Englewood Cliffs, N.J.: Prentice-Hall, Inc., 1977. 214 pp.

WOLDE, GUNILLA. *Betsy's Baby Brother*. New York: Random House, Inc., 1975. 22 pp.

————. *Betsy and Peter Are Different*. New York: Random House, Inc., 1979. 22 pp.

Wonder Starter Series. *Eggs*. New York: Grosset, 1971. 24 pp.

Wonder Starter Series. *Sleep*. New York: Grosset, 1971. 24 pp.

Mathematics:
Who Needs It and Why?

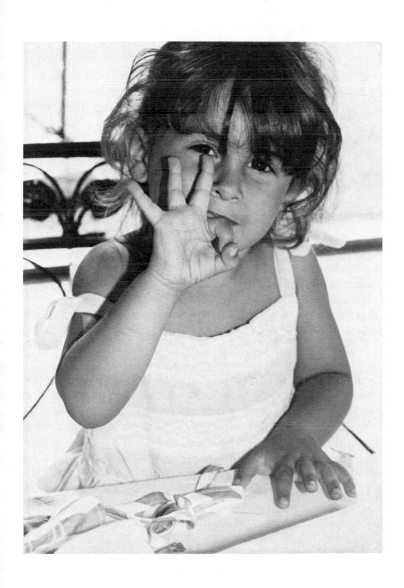

Functional Mathematics

It would be difficult to imagine how people would function without knowing how to count, add up a grocery list of prices, buy food, or measure anything, without having a knowledge of mathematics to some extent at least. Contemporary society, with its increasingly sophisticated computer systems, quality-counting points urging objectivity or competition, and a myriad of counting mechanisms, challenges one to be without some measure of knowledge about mathematical systems or functional usage.

In early years at school, pupils are not often aware that what they are learning will have significance for their lives outside of school. It is mainly in retrospect that school children begin to sense that their current knowledge was at first initiated in earlier grade levels. The skills of the teachers, therefore, rest heavily on their being able to motivate pupils so that mathematical operations do, in fact, become central to many things that they do and consider significant.

Children enjoy participating in activities that they can do well. Teachers can offer simple tasks in mathematics so that pupils enjoy doing them, and in that reflection of pleasure they should be able to continue sustaining positive attitudes toward achieving success in more difficult tasks. Children do not need to know, in their early contacts with mathematical functions, how the current mathematical ideas were derived or comprehended as a total logical framework in itself. They need to get a grasp of it in terms of their own direct experiences as those activities relate to computing, counting, measuring, estimating, and the like. They need to become familiar with a rudimentary vocabulary that links itself into a numerical, geometrical, or algebraic conceptual system. This is done when children experience simple tasks that have been within their own background in daily living.

Before children attend school and hear about formalized systems of mathematics or shapes and sizes, among other concepts, they have experienced being at the market with their parents, buying things, and hearing people count up a total that has to be paid to the person at the cash register. Their impressions are not clear, as they will be later on, when they have had more experiences counting, adding, subtracting, and the like. The first words, ideas, human exchange, and receiving something when money is exchanged present glimmers of factual, partially systematic data. It is upon these early experiences that school instruction bases itself and gradually takes the child to higher levels of learning.[1]

Writers indicate that mathematicians do not always agree on what mathematics is. What is recommended as an emphasis in the contemporary curriculum is this: the structure of mathematics as a subject matter area, its laws and principles, its logical relationships, correct terminology related to operations of a mathematical nature, and students' awareness of its usefulness in understanding space, size, capacity, density, and other formula computations that can be used to quantify aspects of the world.[2] It is also recommended that the content selected for instruction should be identified in terms of, first, a theory related to society and what its needs seem to be, second, a subject matter theory, related to the organization and logical process of the subject matter itself, and third, a psychological theory, related to the needs of the individual learner.[3]

Another source recommends that children be assisted toward mathematical understandings by learning how to solve problems, become successful with activities of a mathematical nature, understand the utility of mathematics, and have fun with it.[4] Attitudinal aspects of pupils in a mathematics program at school are emphasized as highly significant to their success and progress in learning.[5] One study is reported in which children were praised, shown approval through facial expressions of the teacher and touched, symbolizing approval by the teacher. The children's performance in tasks increased when they had such approval and decreased when they did not.[6]

Favorable Directions for Mathematical Efforts

Many young children below the age of three show considerable interest in toys and components of toys that are placed together (after having been taken apart). Fractional pieces are, in part, capable of being described as an element of the mathematical system. When parents use the terminology of the principles of fractions, children are beginning to acquire knowledge that will be used again when they go to school.

It is suggested that when a child recognizes that a piece of toast that (s)he has broken off from the total slice of toast is a part of the whole slice, the child has begun to understand the concept of fractions.[7] The word *fraction* applies to a part, or piece, from a larger whole. Children will need many opportunities to take things apart and put them together again. When they do this, words or phrases such as *pieces, sections, parts, all of it, the whole thing, a complete whole* may be used. Even using the word *fraction* to denote a part of something can accustom children to the conceptual reference to the mathematical term.

For children under three, parents, or other adults and siblings with them, can count toes, hands, toys, food, and other objects in the environment. Rote counting of objects, people, or household utensils begins a familiarity with the one-to-one correspondence of things to a number. Many children enjoy counting from one to ten because they hear their older siblings do it.

Parents can be very helpful in remembering to use mathematical terms or numerals, or shapes of objects, which cannot only be realistic for a child's experience in accomplishing something, but can also serve to practice terms and associate them with activities that have a social utility. Noting Table 5–1, parents can recognize how much their own contributions to children's spontaneous activity at home can facilitate learning that will become the basis for later work at school.

Children at the age of three are able to create circles, intersect lines,

Table 5–1 Mathematical Concepts* for Children Under Three

	Count Objects	Count Toys	Count People	Count Hours	Count Days	Count Months	See Shapes	See Sizes	Hold Weights	Draw Figures	Counting-Type Songs
First year	At kitchen table	At play In bath	Guests	Meal-time			Ball	Big toy	Ball		One Little Piggy
Second year	At kitchen table	At play	Guests Family	Meal-time	To birth-day	To birth-day	Ball Balloon		Ball	1, 2	Ten Little Blackbirds
Third year	At kitchen table	At play	Friends Family	Meal-time	To birth-day	To birth-day	Circle Square	Big Little	Ball	1, 2, 3	Ten Little Blackbirds

*Parents can introduce any concept of large, small, tall, short, round, square, bigger, smaller, fat, thin, full, empty, and other words that represent symbols of number, size, shape, position. Any time they do this they are giving children words that symbolize concepts of mathematics.

and draw various shapes. Their visual imagery products can be related to names of mathematical shapes that they have produced.

Children are handling many sorts of toys, teething objects, rattles, blocks that fit into one another, animal shapes, eating utensils. They have to accommodate their manner of handling them as they note variation of such objects. Some objects are large and they hold only a part of one. Some that are small can be contained to a greater extent by holding the objects with both hands. Parents can call the child's attention to something that is *too big*, or *too small*, or *too heavy*, or *too light*. These are concepts related to capacity, weight, volume, size, and perhaps shapes of an unusual nature. A ball is shown as a *round* ball. The parents can think of these terms whenever possible to help the child associate mathematical concepts.

Once the parent, while taking the child for a walk, points out ideas of a mathematical nature, the child may adopt the habit of noticing shapes (circles, triangles, squares, rectangles); sizes (big, little, huge, gigantic, tiny, very small); position (up, down, between, low, high, level or even with something else, uppermost, layered); and number (first, second, third, one, two, ten, one hundred, a thousand).

The words denote concepts. The formalized aspects of the concepts become a new association when they are linked into structural components of a mathematical system. See Concept Illustration 5–1.

Animals are an attraction for young children. Whenever they see a very small puppy, a kitten, a tiny monkey, they often are willing to approach it, with an adult overseeing the action. The number of legs, the tail, the eyes, the nimble movement, provide another opportunity for a child to concentrate on shape, size, and number of characteristics of the animal. Activities at school for kindergarten children often show several sets of eyes from various animals or birds.[8] Children learn about sets of two and their significance in experiences as well as sets of two being part of a mathematical system and structural way of referring to a concept.

Cooking has many opportunities for counting, measuring, filling liquids in cups, spoons, mixing bowls. The measuring process shows children how important it is to know correct amounts for ingredients. They will under-

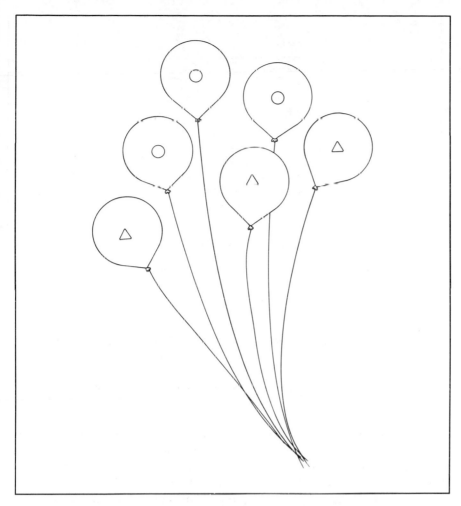

Six Balloons: Three Have Circles, Three Have Triangles. Parents can use construction paper in different colors to paste over the above. Talk to the child about the number by counting; describe shapes in the balloons. Later children will learn about "sets" at school. Equivalent and nonequivalent sets are taught in kindergarten and first grade.

stand how much better food tastes when the amounts of flour, salt, sugar, and milk are correctly included as a recipe indicated. The time that something has to be thawed, or baked in an oven, or cooked on the stove becomes significant in relation to the proper result of food. Parents can show the child how the temperature is set with, of course, the comment that only mother or another adult turns on the stove. It can be dangerous.

Timing for cooking, baking, or allowing something to cool in the refrigerator becomes an understanding that the child assumes is essential in all households. Common knowledge accepted by adults is new to young children. They observe events around them. They need, however, explanations and comments from adults who realize how necessary it is for children

```
        Count the trees we see.                         _____
        Count the colors we see.                        _____
        Count the cars we see.                          _____
        Count the people we see.                        _____
        Count the flowers we see.                       _____
        Count the birds we see.                         _____
        Count the dogs we see.                          _____
        Count the tricycles we see.                     _____
        Count the airplanes we see.                     _____
        Count the strollers we see.                     _____
        Count the construction machines we see.        _____
        Count the street-cleaning machines we see.    _____
        Count the policemen we see.                     _____
        Count the kittens we see.                       _____
        Count the smells we like.                       _____
        Count the apartment houses we see.             _____
```

Concept Illustration 5–2

On Our Walk.

to hear. All these associations of time with temperature, the clock, the effects of proper attention to accuracy in measurement, are the foundational contributions for the child's mathematical beginnings.

Parents of young children do not themselves use workbooks. Ideas of what is useful in the development of learning come from an underlying awareness of relationships between the humanly conceived structure of disciplines (or subject matter areas) and what is seen in everyday life. Going to the store, to the cleaners, to the park, to the library, are routine activities. They are the stuff of life. Upon them are built order or at least the minimized chaos that scientists have attempted to develop. The process of counting, relating, and assessing represents an accumulation of knowledge.[9] See Concept Illustration 5–2. A simple orientation toward one's environment in a semistructured sense begins a sensitivity for conceptualizing order among objects, sounds, and people even when one is outdoors in less boundary-enclosed areas than are found in the home.

Technologies are based on objectivity, precision, and an appreciation of timing. Logic, appropriate sequencing, and proportionate applications of ideas to functions and processing create the inventions that contemporary society takes for granted. Space missiles, airplanes, medical and surgical techniques related to building, and changing body parts were accomplished through scientific precision.

Noting Concept Illustration 5–3, the associations between logic and order of a mathematical system and the terms or processes relevant to understanding those associations are indicated. The child sees, hears, and performs the connection between the surrounding phenomena and his/her own views or experiences, related to meanings of a system devised by mathematical writers. Repetitious experiences and variety of them begin to bring together some meaning about an everyday world and a system of abstractions that become real. The more the child experiences a labeled

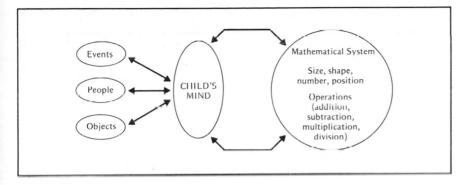

Linking Reality to the Discipline of Mathematics.

reality, the more the ideas (or concepts) become automatic and internalized. Formal introduction to those concepts at school simply represent what the child already knows in part.

Children in American schools must understand two systems of measurement; one is the English system, and the other is the metric. Most countries use the metric system, and the United States is tending in that direction.[10] Actually the metric system has been legal in the United States since 1866, but only recently has it begun to be used in daily purchases at the market or gasoline station. In medical practice, however, and generally in chemistry, metric measurement has long been the rule, decades before there was popular evidence of such usage.

Although contemporary changes in measurement from a foot to a set of meter units, changes from the gallon measurement to liters or litres, and from temperature in Fahrenheit units to centigrade and Celsius can be confusing to people learning them after living with the former measurement units, the metric system is not as confusing for today's children. The units that were learned earlier by adults now have to be accommodated to a different system, thereby presenting a challenge to parents.

Children may not find as difficult the system they are learning in contemporary society because it is the primary one they are learning. They do not have an interfering set of terms, that is, they have not been given labels that adults thought were the only reality of their own time. Adults find the new terms conflicting with an older reality. The children do not. See Concept Illustration 5–4.

Advantages Parents Give Children
Provide children with a flexibility.
Expose them to ideas and many labels.
Show them measured items.
Demonstrate ways of adding things.
Demonstrate ways of taking things apart.
Use terms that emphasize a function.
Be open to change.
Understand differences and similarities.

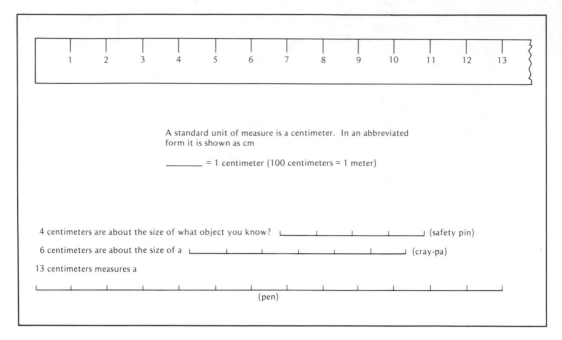

A standard unit of measure is a centimeter. In an abbreviated form it is shown as cm

_____ = 1 centimeter (100 centimeters = 1 meter)

4 centimeters are about the size of what object you know? └_____┘ (safety pin)

6 centimeters are about the size of a └_____┘ (cray-pa)

13 centimeters measures a

└_____┘

(pen)

Concept Illustration 5–4

What Is a Centimeter?

Show differences in stacks of objects.
Show equal sets of objects.
Find simple and clearly illustrated books on objects.
Develop an appreciation of details in objects.
Build an awareness of gradation in size.
Help develop pleasure in concentration.
Help develop achievement after persistence.
Share joys of accomplishment of child.

Mathematical Concepts from Three to Five Years

From three to five, children are seeing relationships (through experiences they have in counting, measuring, weighing, and balancing) between specific numbers and how those abstract concepts relate to things that they touch and rearrange. Although they may not understand specifically how those functions relate to a larger mathematical system of constructs, they have had some familiarity with the functions and have been introduced to words or symbols needed for conceptualizing some meaning that may be attributed to measurement.

Formalized programs now available for young children suggest that more children than in several years past will receive simple concepts of mathe-

I Sing and I Count.

matical instruction in preschool environments. Teachers of kindergartens usually build such instruction into their daily programs. Many children already know nursery rhymes, fingerplay songs, or poems that deal with number concepts. Games introduce ideas of large, small, smaller, teeny-tiny. Directions for certain activities, "Put your right hand in the air; Put your left hand in the air," lead to specifics—all of which inform the child about defined labels and actions of a classifiable nature.

Some three-year-old children who have been exposed to number concepts and games are familiar, at least to the extent of rote knowledge, with counting-type songs. Memorization of songs that contain number concepts, as well as addition and subtraction, are often obvious among children in the three-to-five age range. (Ten little babies sitting on a fence, One went away and then there were nine," etc., give children vague ideas of numbers and their properties.) The teacher should not think, however, that all children understand the functional operation of those numbers.

Rote Counting

Whenever possible, the teacher counts with the children the number of pupils in the room. Counting opportunities occur every day. It is up to the teacher or parent at home to capture those moments. Note Concept Illustration 5–5.

Memorizing numbers is one step in the understanding process of order and one-to-one relationships of object to number. Children, however, do not understand the groupness of a number over one. They need to see grouped articles and the associated figure many different times and places before the concept takes on a wholeness in perception.

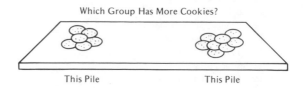

Which Group Has More Cookies?

This Pile   This Pile

Hearing children say a series of numbers from one to ten or even twenty when they reach kindergarten does not ensure that they have a knowledge of those numbers' properties. For example, if a child who counted quickly up to twenty were given a group of objects to count, and asked to point to each one that was being counted, it would not necessarily follow that this task would be done correctly. In like manner, when children are asked to specify between two groups of objects which one had more, they find it difficult unless the teacher helps them count each of the groups.

Counting is not easy for all children. They may remember the words for numbers, up to a certain point;[11] the meaning of the numbers, however, or the reasons for the number names being said in a certain order does not seem to make sense. Rote counting, however, provides a beginning for recognizing the number names and how they can be used to apply to an activity or song.

Many children upon entering kindergarten are able to count to ten or higher, and may also be able to count by ten's (ten, twenty, thirty, forty, etc.).[12] Many can recognize what the numerals from one to ten look like and may also be able to write many of them. The variation of children's abilities have to be assessed by the teacher so that the children are given the help they need.

Cardinal and Ordinal Numbers

Children can learn, as they are assigned different numbers, how a given order provides access to an activity at a given time. They learn, too, that numbers are assigned to an object in order to identify it and distinguish it from others.

Cardinal number provides an identity that does not necessarily relate to the time that the number was given. It does not necessarily define position or place in the numbering system. It tells how many of something are contained in a pile or set of materials.

Ordinal number describes a relative position of an object or person among others. Something can be third, fourth, fifth, and so on in a group of about fifteen. The highest number relative to an opportunity to do something may be one in that case or it can start with the last person counted. Serial order is suggested in ordinal-position counting.

Children often start a game by counting themselves from one to five saying, "Now I'll go first, you go second," and so on. Others waiting for

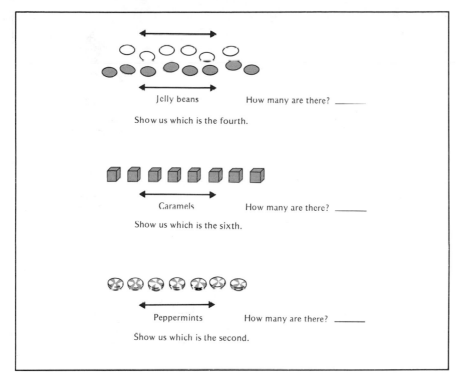

Jelly beans   How many are there? _____

Show us which is the fourth.

Caramels   How many are there? _____

Show us which is the sixth.

Peppermints   How many are there? _____

Show us which is the second.

How Many and Which Ones? Show Us.

their turn to participate understand that their numbers identify when they go into the game.

Note Concept Illustration 5–6 and adapt from the suggestions there. Teachers need to keep many different and safe objects available for repeated tasks involving counting, also those that encourage noting relationships among objects. The mathematical system increases its complexities based on these more elementary functions that kindergarten children are learning to perform.

Teachers should save buttons, wooden doweling, empty spools of thread, and small empty boxes that can be used for counting and classifying. By retaining in different boxes of various shapes, colors, and sizes, a number of buttons, discs, old crayons, and tiny cards with pictures of objects on them, the teacher can have ready for pupils at all times exercises in counting cardinal and ordinal numbers. Classification of objects, which is done often in the classroom, requires many repeated activities involving the children's ability to note differences and similarities as well as number.

Storing tiny boxes with singularly classified items in them can save the teacher time and energy when the children need functional tasks to practice. Their manipulation of buttons of various sizes and shapes, their placement of various colored toy boats, cars, wooden dowling of various lengths, all provide purpose in learning concepts related to mathematical elementary principles. Children need many of these experiences handling, arrang-

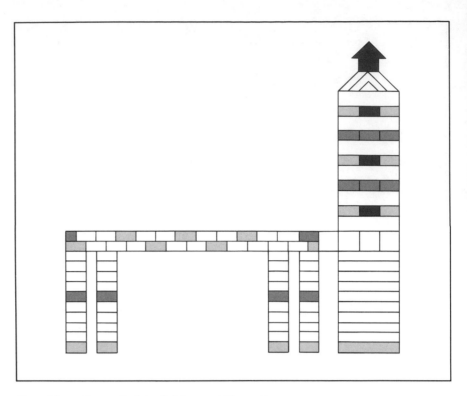

**Concept
Illustration
5–7**

How Many Boxes Build a Bridge and Tower?

ing, and counting objects before they will be able to comprehend the symbols they will meet later in mathematical logic and sequences.

Parents can organize these boxes at home. After birthday parties there are many wrappings, boxes of various sizes and shapes, and ribbons of various widths and lengths. These can be mounted on durable backing. Ribbons can be pasted down to show various lengths and widths. Boxes can be piled on top of each other. They can also be pasted to each other to resemble a progression from base level largest up to smallest at the top. Children learn from this counting and measuring in relation to specific numbers.

Children are not forced into adapting ideas to symbols. They gradually work into an understanding of them. The teacher or parent is careful not to crowd too many concepts at the same time. This only serves to confuse. Simplicity, clarity, and organization help the child want to learn and master ideas. The child is not aware of how much needs to be "covered" in a concept. It is endless in reality. While the teacher may have some goals planned for the child, it is best to let the child's comprehension become one of the factors that influence the breadth and length of conceptual elements that should be tackled.

As parents and teachers try to help children in learning names, symbols, functions, and operations of various numbers of objects, they remember the importance of attitudes, orientation, and positive perceptions that are needed in approaching subject matter. If the children feel overwhelmed

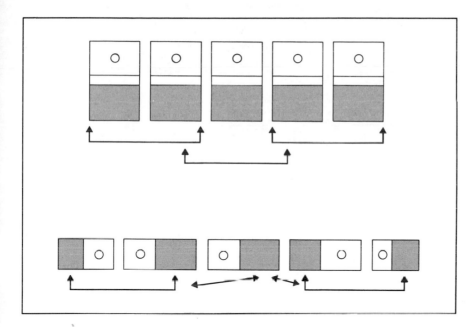

Find the Gray Blocks and Count Them.

by too much data or materials, they will withdraw. They will dislike the subject. It takes longer to bring them back to an involvement in it when they have been antagonized by it than it does to go slowly in the first place.

Parents can draw numbers for children without creating an atmosphere of instruction. Playful, experimental, relaxed attitudes in the demonstration of figures, 1, 2, 3, 4, 5, 6, 7, 8, 9 permit children to see them. Typically it is best to show those figures with a cluster of objects that represent them. In that way, children begin to associate cardinal and ordinal number with the symbols that represent their concepts.

Shapes, Sizes, Positions, and Relationships

Children between the ages of three and five have often been shown or have been given balloons, balls, and toys of a variety of shapes. They have learned, in some cases through experiences, what the attributes or properties of those shapes are. They can recognize that a ball is round and that some objects because of a roundness are able to roll away from them.

Some five-year-old children are able to draw a square, a circle, and a triangle. This form of visual discrimination provides a beginning of the kind of perceptual awareness they need for an understanding of geometrical properties.[13] It is suggested that because certain shapes in the child's environment occur with high frequency (such as cereal boxes, windows, and doors), the reasons for articles being in those shapes should be recognized by children.[14] This provides an opportunity for the child to perceive rela-

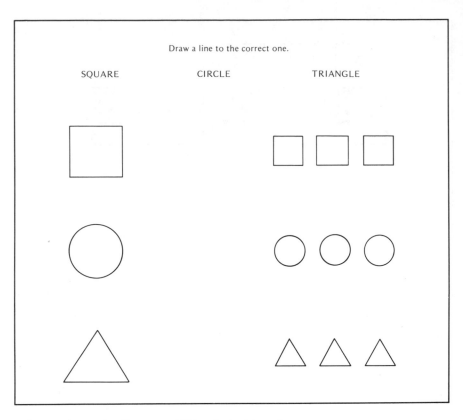

What Is the Right Shape and What Is Its Name?

tionships between objects and the functions they serve. It also leads to assumptions about predictability of when certain shapes will be preferred over others, depending on the functions planned for them.

Sizes of objects make minimal sense unless they are shown next to each other in comparison. Many experiences are needed for pupils to recognize differences and similarties in sizes. Changing and rearranging objects of various colors and of interest to children have to be done often if children are to acquire concepts of size differences.[15]

If the teacher cannot have available boxes of various sizes and shapes for the children's use in comparing the sizes, pictures of objects of similar dimension may be cut out of magazines and laminated for durability or thickness for handling. The teacher will have to use judgment in being sure that the pictures do not throw the child's judgment off through errors of perspective. Only one object should be taken from a picture. Relationships in perspective can be deceiving. A tall building, for example, can appear large in the foreground whereas an airplane which is actually larger, can seem smaller when it is shown in the distance or high above the building.

The teacher can use objects that are part of the classroom to compare a small crayon with a larger one, a small chair with a larger one, and a shorter child next to a taller one (being careful not to embarrass either of the children while making the comparison). A large sheet of paper can be compared with a smaller one as well as yardstick compared to a 12-inch (or 6-inch) ruler.

Positions that identify places in space, in design, in a room, give children relevant information that will serve them well in many different subject matter areas. The recognition of up, down, beside, on top of, between, in front, in back, and underneath are concepts and references that are difficult for them to learn. Words that identify position in space are abstractions. They are more difficult to learn because the referent is typically dependent on several other objects. The concept is only real when it relates to another item or person.

> Where is the chair? Is it on top of the Table? Is it beside the table?
> Where does a person wear a hat? On what part of the head?
> Where is the icing on a cake?
> Where does a person find a drawer?
> Where does a person put a toothbrush?

Encouraging the child to use the words that denote position in relation to another object can be very helpful. This concept will be relevant to geometric principles, to mathematic placement of figures, to reading, because of discrimination sensitivity needed in the recognition of various letter shapes.

Relationships of objects to each other in space and in terms of psychological concepts related to function are necessary for young children to learn. And objects surround them in their daily life at home, in the neighborhood, and at school.

Placing something at the right side, instead of the left, gives the child an appreciation for the direction that must be followed in reading, writing, and in arithmetic. Opening a book from the left-hand cover and reading to the back is reading to the right. Relationships of one place to another, that is placing a fork to the left of the plate on the table, familiarize the child to some of the customs of a culture. Placing the napkin in the lap, placing the glass of water in a certain place on the table near one's plate, give the child some impressions of norms and expectations. When they are aware of these customs, they will be more comfortable when they are with others who expect the same things to occur.

The relationship of a fork to a knife, the pencil to paper, the soap to water reflect knowledge of objects that are used together. Meanings are built up on relationships between things and people, places, and positions when they are used to meet one's goals.

Even positions in walking, standing, and riding a tricycle demonstrate effective utility of things that provide solutions for people. Children can understand why heavier items have to be placed at the bottom of a stack. They can learn to judge the benefits of thin materials needing to be placed between those of heavier qualities if one is to be protected from the other.

Children enjoy using blocks to build structures and bridges. Their attention can be called to the different shapes and sizes of the blocks. They begin to recognize the common circles or round shapes as well as the square and triangle.

My feet go_____ the table when I sit down.

My carpet is_____the floor.

My eyes are near the_____of my head.

My hands are at the_____of my arms.

My house is at the_____of the street.

Icing is_____the layers of a cake.

My soles are at the_____of my feet.

I wear my hat on_____of my head.

I like to stand_____to my brother.

I like to sit_____when I am tired.

I have to stand_____when I pledge allegiance to the flag.

I like to swim_____the water.

I put peanut butter on_____of my bread.

I put cheese in_____two pieces of bread.

I do not like dirt_____my fingernails.

Concept Illustration 5–10

Where Do They Belong Most of the Time?

Handling objects of various shapes that are also of various textures give them more experiences in building concepts. They realize the lightness and fragility of a balloon compared to hardwood blocks, for example. They learn to handle them differently. Holding them in a controlled manner, anticipating what happens if they let go of either one, gives them an awareness of the nature of materials.

Soft toys permit tossing around without serious damage resulting in rough interaction. Certain lighter weight, less durable toys can weaken and ultimately fall apart.

Relationships to type of use, nature of fabrics, and characteristics of the way something is put together all combine to affect the manner of usage. Thus relationships not only to position, size, shape and texture affect pleasure, but also an endurance quality over time.

Children's realization of relationships begins to build a form of logic, thinking ahead, anticipating cause and effect. Mathematical concepts require anticipation of possible outcomes. The greater number of experiences of this kind that children have, accompanied by explanations of events by interested adults, the better will foundational skills be developed.

One of the more difficult concepts for children to learn is that of relationships between size, such as small, smaller, smallest. They have difficulty recognizing gradations among several objects that are each increasingly larger than the other. Given five items in a row and mixed regarding different sizes, children do not place them easily from smaller to larger as they should be appropriately represented in size.[16]

Nesting blocks or a set of dolls within dolls provide effective opportunities for children to place items from smaller to largest in their relationships to each other. And parents and teachers can save boxes that can be placed one within another. Children may use these to place before them in a row

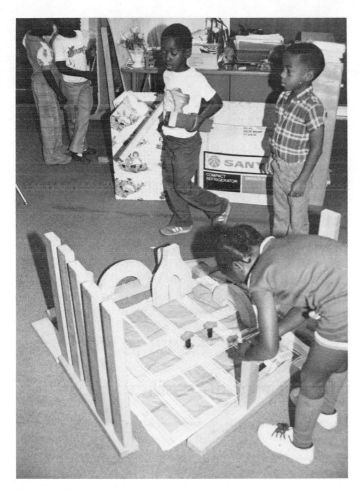

Kindergarten children find that building structures with blocks is not easy, but it provides many opportunities for judging relationships, planning, and ultimately finding satisfaction in one's work. (Photo by Gerald J. Margolin.)

from smaller to larger or place them within each other. This helps to develop anticipation of size increase or decrease.

Judgment of spatial relationships is very difficult. To judge what fits into a space requires many experiences with objects. In a society that emphasizes abstraction to a great extent, children are not having enough experiences with tangible materials. These experiences are needed, particularly at the early levels of relating ideas with things and with names.

Puzzle assembly accustoms the child to judging spatial relationships. One can learn from simple three-piece puzzles how to fit a piece into the place that completes the picture. Young children can start with simple, inlaid puzzles and become more proficient to the point of using five or six pieces that are cut in ways that do not give easy clues. Puzzles are typically part of any nursery school classroom. They provide hand-eye coordination. Spatial discrimination requires experiences with space judgment and objects in their appropriate places. Often an adult can assist the child by saying "Where do you think this piece belongs?" If the child still needs help, the adult may say, "Shall we try it over here in this space?" "Do you think it might fit if we put it here?"

Sometimes the adult presents the child with a picture that has something missing from it. A house without a door, for example, can be shown to the child. The child may point to the place that has a missing object or may try to draw it in. This demonstrates awareness of relationships.

A bus without its wheels can be drawn on a sheet of paper. The child can be asked what is missing from that bus. When the child shows that the wheels are needed, the questions, "Where should the wheels be placed on that bus?" This helps one become used to noticing where the proper placement of items should be. It attunes pupils to refine skills of observation. It teaches them to seek completeness. It also heightens their awareness of the presence of oversights or errors.

A child can be asked to draw a large circle at the top of a sheet of paper and then to draw a large circle at the bottom of the paper. Next, a square can be drawn between them. Then a larger square can be drawn outside the square that has just been drawn. Again, an emphasis on relationships and space and size gives the child another set of opportunities to try out the needed powers of sensitivity to those concepts.

Days, Months, and Time

Even though children may hear daily comments about the day or time, they are not aware of the system in its abstract sense as an invention of humankind or a record-keeper and measurement of time. It is difficult for them to interpret the symbolization of the clock, except in relation to what it looks like when they are permitted to do something that has meaning for them.

There are several references available to identify the reasons for the child's difficulty in successfully knowing how to read the clock or even to understand the duration of time.[17] Duration of time as it passes is a psychological phenomenon. The mood and temperament of the individual affect how the length of time will be perceived. Piaget's work and the writings of many who have interpreted his perspectives of the way individuals acquire mental development and thought provide stimulating rationales for the difficulties children face at school (or home) when they are expected to understand adult thought and explanations of things in the environment.

The difference between the knowledge children are able to extract and abstract from their environment when the concepts relate to a logico-mathematical experience and that which they gain from a physical experience, as Piaget views it, is that the logico-mathematical experience involves the way one reflects on one's own action, rather than generalizing from touching the objects themselves. When a child examines an object, feels it, turns it around, looking at from several angles, and notices its properties, the child is able eventually to make judgments about its texture, size, pliability, its durability (hard objects as different from soft or fluid ones), among

	Tuesday	Thursday
What day is it between the two?		

	Sun. Mon. Tues. Wed. Thurs. Fri. Sat.
What day is the beginning of the (school) week?	

Fill in the number on the correct day:

JULY						
Sunday	Monday	Tuesday	Wednesday	Thursday	Friday	Saturday
		1	2	3	4	5
6						

Our Calendar.

Concept
Illustration
5–11

other attributes. Where the ability to make judgments in a logico-mathematical experience is concerned, the child must be aware of internal thought processes in reference to the objects viewed.

When the teacher or adult realizes the extent to which humankind's terms for abstract ideas face the child in a myriad of experiences daily, it is not difficult to empathize with a child's problems in learning. Repetition of experiences is vital. For this reason, it is essential that parents, in the spontaneity of home experiences, use the opportunity to let the child touch, reason, manipulate objects in various positions and talk about them when possible. With two types of experiences, the physical and the logico-mathematical one, children are sensing the physical properties of objects and they are also acquiring meaning from the environment in terms of the names, functions, and thought processes that are required to understand those objects.

Children gradually will learn what the clock represents, why it is used, and how it affects the activities of people in the environment, at home or at school. Several recommendations are made by curriculum writers who have been interested in ways to use Piaget's findings to create programs for young children.[18]

Children want several reminders to help them become familiar with reading and interpreting the calendar. Large calendars with clearly marked numbers and names of days help them easily to recognize the significant information. See Concept Illustration 5–11 for suggestions.

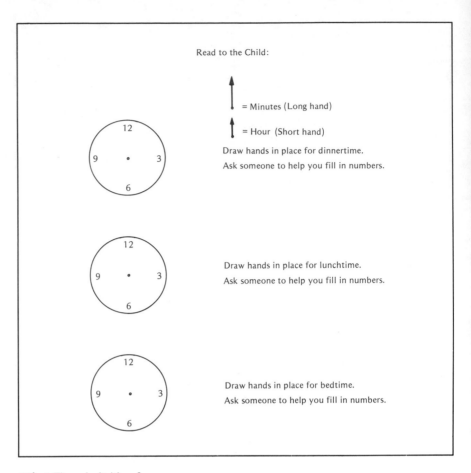

Read to the Child:

↑ = Minutes (Long hand)

↑ = Hour (Short hand)

Draw hands in place for dinnertime.
Ask someone to help you fill in numbers.

Draw hands in place for lunchtime.
Ask someone to help you fill in numbers.

Draw hands in place for bedtime.
Ask someone to help you fill in numbers.

**Concept
Illustration
5–12**

What Time Is It Now?

When children are given the opportunity to create a calendar and to handle a card with each date on it, they derive greater meaning from the concept. Some teachers have a child place the correct date on a calendar each morning before the program of the day begins. Since time is an abstraction, the children need to experience handling of the "pieces" of time, so to speak. Anything that is created to provide touching, placing correctly, changing when needed, parts of the abstraction, the child acquires a stronger relationship between idea and reality.

Telling time is another spatial and temporal concept that challenges young children's abilities. They need repeated experiences with the concept.[19] Many children are able to understand that 8:00 A.M. is a time for breakfast. Twelve o'clock or noon is the time for lunch for some people. When the parent tells the child, showing where the arrows are on the clock, that it is time for lunch, nap, dinner—whatever routine or function may be appropriate to that hour—the child begins to recognize the correct time.

Note Concept Illustration 5–12, which gives an opportunity to fill in the appropriate answers to the clock's indicators of time. The parent or teacher may create this on a larger poster size. The child can try out different time positions. If the chart is covered with laminated processing, figures can be erased and the chart can be used repeatedly. The poster is more durable than paper and can withstand less than gentle treatment.

Children enjoy a challenge within reason (their own reasoning capacities). No one enjoys being frustrated by constant difficult presentations. Most children are curious enough in their search for solutions to problems and to find out how things work, to persist, despite difficulty, in their efforts with materials. They must, however, be given a reasonable chance to succeed. Learning to tell time orally, and to rationally understand the concept underlying the system are accomplished by having many opportunities to identify such concepts and their relationships to the way the real world functions. The variety of activities that will be available depends mainly on the adults who are responsible for children's learning.

When the family plans to go on a trip of some kind, there are many opportunities for children to be involved in planning. Various clock hours as well as the calendar of days (or months) can be shown prior to the date and time of departure. It may be annoying for parents to hear children ask often whether the day or time is getting nearer for the family's vacation point of departure from home. But children need those opportunities to help them understand the system of time.

Children can hear the planning that is involved in allowing adequate time needed for traveling to the airport, bus terminal, train depot, or whatever form of travel terminal is expected. Some educators recommend that children be a greater part than they usually are in the early planning of a family vacation. Children are learning how to solve problems of time, decisions that must be made in their contingencies upon time allotments, and several other issues that arise when people have to coordinate travel of any kind.

For children between three and five, abstraction of a high level should not be expected. They need things that allow them to turn, to wind, to move from place to place. They need to experiment with objects that are like ordinary household items. They need things that are durable and safe. Plastic clocks that can be wound, that tick, that have handles to help children turn to the hour and minutes as they investigate the correct time, can facilitate experiences.

Sixty minutes and twelve hours involve counting systems different from those that children learned earlier in their counting experiences. Thirty days in a month or thirty-one also introduce a new counting unit of time. Children are trying to balance this information out with each new record-keeping device they see.

Whenever possible, if the adult keeps the processes simple and uncomplicated, not going from one to the other idea, expecting it to make sense to the child, the child will gradually learn the various counting units. If the parent concentrates on one kind of measure of time and discusses it simply, this is adequate. It has to be remembered, however, that differences among a 12-hour day, a 60-second minute, a 60-minute hour and the 30/31-day month (except February with 28, but 29 in leap year) as units of measuring time in different forms, present inordinate stresses on the intellect.

Adults have accepted this without question after acquiring the habit. Children are accepting it, too. But they should not be considered inept because they do not acquire the habit quickly and easily.

When an adult tells a child that something will be done *later*, the child is learning a concept of time. The clock can also be used in this regard.[20]

Two o'clock is _____ than four o'clock.
Five o'clock is _____ than six o'clock.
One o'clock is earlier than _____ o'clock.
Seven o'clock is _____ than three o'clock.
One o'clock comes sooner after the noon hour than does _____ o'clock.
Dinner at _____ o'clock is _____ than lunch at _____ o'clock.

Sooner, later, before, after, at the same time are concepts that give the child impressions about time or temporal relationships. These concepts will be touched on again when the child goes to school. Time is important in any schedule.

Daybreak, sunset, A.M., P.M. develop meaning as they are used appropriately in relation to something real that is happening to a child. Sunrise, the direction from which it occurs, gives the child an appreciation of another abstract use of direction in space. (Many adults still find it difficult to locate themselves in relation to the north, south, east, and west direction. Even with specific intent to remember, directional skills frustrate adults.) Conscious and deliberate attempts to associate time concepts and directions with certain definitive terms will help a child, however, so that by the time (s)he attends school, the words are not strange but represent meaning and purpose for the child.

Children can make clocks easily with paper plates. They write their own numbers on the plate, with some help. A brad in the middle of the plate piercing two hands for the clock provide a manipulative object that can be used to "create" time as the child wants it. The clock can be decorated by drawing or pasting little flowers around it. A child may want to place a design on it. In the back, the child can write his/her name in manuscript letters.

Alarm clocks that can be automated or set to ring at a time set by the child show how time reminds people to segment their day at significant times. Children learn that setting an alarm can be helpful in being sure that one wakes up in time for school, for dressing, for allowing enough time to be picked up by someone who is taking a passenger to another destination. Bus schedules need to be consulted when a ride is needed. The alarm clock helps people in keeping their schedules.

Children know that their favorite television programs are shown at a time familiar to many. They can check in a newspaper or television schedule. Children learn to expect schedules in various places. They begin to realize that information can be secured in many places. They do, however, need to acquire techniques to translate those items of information.

Parents can also show a child, by indicating the direction of a clock (from the top of the circle to the right toward the left and back up again), how we think *clockwise*. When we say something goes *counterclockwise*, we point left from the top, down, around to the right, and up to the top again. These terms are remembered as simple words, not concepts in depth. Deeper awareness occurs with time and experiences related to hearing the words used in appropriate contexts.

Mathematical Functions and Operations

"I have two cookies. Now I am taking one away and putting it here on the table. How many do I have left?" This operation of subtraction is seen by most children very often. The operation of addition, "Here is one cookie. Now, I'll give you another. How many cookies do you have?" happens frequently for many children.[21]

Addition, subtraction, division, and multiplication are practiced by children all the time. They are not aware of it. The terms are abstractions, devised by humankind to simplify and order a complicated world. The desire for accuracy, objectivity, equality, is assisted by systematic operations, as children will learn at school.

It is easy to show children when several are together how they can share among themselves six toys, or six pieces of candy, crayons, or whatever they are using. Boxes, sheets of paper, ribbons, pencils are shared, divided. Children experience subtraction and addition in their play activities.

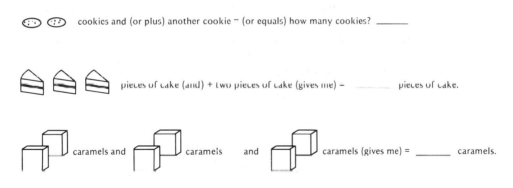

cookies and (or plus) another cookie − (or equals) how many cookies? _____

pieces of cake (and) + two pieces of cake (gives me) − _____ pieces of cake.

caramels and   caramels   and   caramels (gives me) = _____ caramels.

They measure the length and size of pieces of candy if they are cut before eating. Fudge, squares of penuche, brownies, chocolate chip cookies, are carefully observed in terms of size when they are divided among friends.

When a pie is cut into four pieces, how much is in each of the four pieces if they are divided evenly? If a pie is cut into six pieces, how many sixths of a pie do we have? Fractions that result from cutting a whole object into pieces of that whole object are part of a division process that will become basic to children later in school. The process, however, is very real when it involves the division of something a child likes to eat.

Some of that candy, *part* of that candy, a *piece* of one of those candies all represent fraction terms that will be used in formalized and symbolic operations later in school.

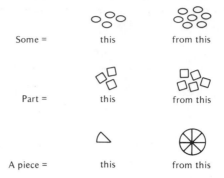

Some =   this   from this

Part =   this   from this

A piece =   this   from this

Children can have experiences with equality of sets. They will be shown two empty cans. One marble will be added to each proportionately to the other. The teacher will draw on the board what is happening in reality.

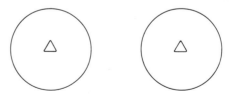

The teacher has shown them at other times before an experience with the drawing, how equal sets of objects are part of daily living. A knife, fork, and spoon for each person can be considered, when placed side by side, as being an equal set of items.

Simple one-to-one relationships can be demonstrated within a circle that represents enclosure of a set.

Are these equal or unequal sets?

Gradually, they become more difficult with more items in the set. The major idea of comparison in mathematics and the quality of one side (of an equation) with another resides in this simple example. Is it the same on both sides? Are these equal or unequal? How can we make them equal?

Children can use paper sacks they can see through and place marbles or candies in each of them. They can see how an equal number of marbles or candies look when held side by side.

The purpose of having them handle objects and place them in containers is to have them make the transition from the real bag to paper and pencil representation of that experience. Mathematical symbols are created to

The teacher is helping kindergarten children learn to use the materials planned to provide an understanding of sets, a mathematical concept. Children place the figure 3 under a set of three flannel rabbits around which yarn has been placed to represent the concept of a set. These items can be placed on a flannel board, an easy manipulative device for instruction. (Photo by Gerald J. Margolin.)

represent real experiences. Computing with larger figures later in school is based on an understanding of what those figures represent.

Are these bags (or sets) of marbles equal?
Why?
How can we make them equal sets?

A word of caution here to teachers and parents: When children are very young, that is, under five years old, they should not be expected to perform in workbooks by themselves (if at all). Workbooks may be used as ideas for parents/teachers but should only be used *together with* the child. Too many adults are frustrating children by expecting them to perform fully on their own.

The mechanical aspects of addition, subtraction, division, and multiplication and their signs, (+, addition; −, subtraction, ÷, division, ×, multi-plication) will be learned later after children have many activities in real experiences designating those symbols that humankind has designed for abstracting these ideas.

Mathematical Concepts Between Five and Nine Years

The years between five and nine at school typically represent kindergarten, first, second, third, and fourth grades. The depth of perception that children acquire during these years is as impressive as those in the first two years of life except that the content of thought is more sophisticated. Mathematical concepts require clear and analytical thinking and different approaches, from several angles, that have to be considered in solving problems.

Many writers illustrate and provide guides for an understanding of children's mathematical development. The years between early and more advanced stages of childhood involve complicated growth changes.[22] The meanings that children bring to the problems that have to be solved in an academic or an intellectual sense are derived mainly from their own internal frame of reference relative to concepts that may have been experienced with real objects.

Problem Solving

By the time some children are in kindergarten they have had many experiences with the understanding of relationships between things and concepts, things and labels, things and functions. They have been shown by adults or older siblings how things work and what they are called. This means that their first level of mathematics may have been approached. For some children this does not happen until they reach school. It may happen in the kindergarten or first grade for them. First developmental levels for any child exposed to a new field may occur in the first grade or earlier. Books or lessons introduced to children, therefore, have to include an awareness by the adult or publisher of materials, that first level means different things to different people.[23]

Early levels of problem solving involve the consideration of the unknown (solution) when there are one or more several known givens.

$$1 + 1 = ?$$

Children will, of course, see objects that represent this:

One box plus one box equals two boxes.

Gradually they will see it represented by pictures and then by symbols or figures that represent abstractions:

$$1 + 1 = 2$$

Children are given different opportunities to see a rearrangement of figures.

$$2 = 1 + 1$$
$$3 = 1 + 1 + 1$$
$$1 + 1 + 1 = 3$$
$$2 + 1 = 3$$
$$? + ? + ? = 3$$
$$1 + ? + ? = ?$$

By the rearrangement of figures (or objects), children can see how many different ways there are to arrive at an answer.

How many different ways are there to find three? See the above.

Find the quickest way to make three. Try another way. Try another.

It is hoped that children will take leaps following trials that will allow them to feel comfortable about experimenting with figures and ideas.

Under supervision of the teacher the kindergarten children are placing numbers, symbols, and articles that coincide with one another. Three airplane forms cut out of flannel material stick to the flannel board which provides an enjoyable and easily manipulated teaching tool. (Photo by Gerald J. Margolin.)

Even though humankind has devised a system, it does not mean that there are no different or newer ways to try out ideas. For this reason, pupils are supplied with many kinds of materials, equipment (e.g., buttons, toy cars, trains, and plastic tubing to make circular "set" representations of equal and unequal sets) for such experimentation. The more practice they have with reality, numbers of objects placed in piles or boxes or within sets, the more likely it is that pupils will conceptualize abstractions that they will meet in symbolized form.

As the children progress through the grades, first, second, and third, their problem-solving skills should increase, both in depth and facility. Educators realize however, that prior to new problem-solving skills, the use of real materials has to have a priority. The touching, changing, and rearranging injects a rational element into the activities. The pupil is better able to make the transition between concrete reality and abstraction. Pictorial representation helps as a second level understanding in the process toward abstraction of the idea as represented by a figure or operation (plus + or minus −, etc.).

Seeing a picture of objects after the pupils' experiences with real things, makes the concept easier for them to translate from reality to abstraction. It also permits the teacher or parent to notice where a child might be in his/her thinking. The child might need more activities with objects before leaving them to go on with abstractions.

It is wise to take advantage of holidays or celebrations to use objects that are significant at the time. Hallowe'en involves pumpkins. Christmas involves trees, Santa Claus figures and faces. Thanksgiving celebrations highlight turkeys, Pilgrims. The fall season is beautiful with rustic atmospheric impressions and colorful leaves, plus the change of various weather conditions affecting the way people dress and live. Children should note these differences.

Teachers can use these significant associations during appropriate seasons and popular celebrations and create bulletin boards designating the relationships to the themes. Problem solving involves real things and people. The reality of any holiday is symbolized by certain objects plus the way they are decorated. Each society has its significant events. Children learn to associate events with the forms of celebrations or rituals preferred by various groups. Symbolism occurs and reoccurs each year. With each year, the celebration for children involved in holiday observances acquires different meanings.

Problem solving derives, to a great extent, from the particular social context. Problem solving related to Thanksgiving involves preparation for a feast of thankfulness. It also involves the underlying theme of fulfillment by the people who were the first to celebrate the event (as history describes it). The event is not taken lightly, but is significant for a culture (or society).

Children enjoy making representations of turkeys, drawing them, drawing the Pilgrims, the holiday feasts, and the people preparing those dinners.[24] Many solutions for problems arising in the planning and conceptualization of holiday celebrations generate thinking skills and can engender self-confidence in children as a result.

If a family needs to have enough turkey for six people, how much should they prepare? Why? Although this question does not always produce an answer, the children need to figure a way to find one. If they plan to "have some turkey left over," they need to plan differently. The teacher asks questions if the children do not think of the answers themselves. If the children had not thought to include the idea of wanting turkey the day after the celebration, the teacher asks them. Pupils need to be guided toward a more comprehensive way of thinking than might occur without suggestions from the teacher. Imagination is encouraged. Even if the teacher had not expected to include an idea given by a pupil, it should be considered for another situation. It should not be dropped. The teacher must consider different ways to enlarge his/her own thinking so that new ideas, unanticipated in planning by the teacher, can be included when offered by a child.

Children are sometimes suppressed by the teacher's limited awareness whether it be a fact or simply an attempt on the children's part to express something imaginative or funny.[25] Problem solving does not have to exclude a sense of humor. Often the leap from the serious to something silly can produce creative answers, as well as relieve tension of the moment in an extended lesson.

Children enjoy giving answers they think the teacher and pupils do not expect. The teacher might ask, "When we have one rabbit who joins another in a hutch, how many will we have?" One child may say, "We have two." Another might say, "A whole bunch, because they multiply fast!" Another might say, "Two and some babies." Depending on the way the child perceives the question, will the solution to the problem be correct or not.

Children's problem-solving abilities are widely divergent. Their own background with number experiences and juxtaposing one figure with another, along with the mental gymnastic opportunities they may have had with parents or older siblings, have their effects on the skills children have acquired. For a child who has not been around people who state problems in mathematical or number terms the experiences in kindergarten or first grade may be alien and totally without meaning.

For this reason, among others, when children progress through the grades from one, two, three, and four, they represent diffuse levels of achievement as far as problem-solving skills are concerned. The diffuseness is not in them; it is in the record-keeping that can occur in the school and in the classroom. Teachers cannot be sure, in many cases, if a child is capable of manipulating or mastering certain elementary concepts considered to be completed at earlier levels of the child's development. Thus even when children are promoted to the second grade at school, they may not necessarily know what the textbooks say they should already know. The teacher must be sensitive to this knowledge and help children in experiences that will engender mathematical understanding for them.

Children *in the second grade*, typically seven years old, are given problems of much greater difficulty than those in the first grade or in kindergarten. These activities are not offered until the teacher has determined that many children are able to proceed with complex problems.

Some children may still need many opportunities to use materials that can be manipulated. Review is needed, if not only for the children, then also for the teacher in order to observe processes and the way they are handled by the pupils.

The children have typically seen some statement problems:

If I have two (2) candies, and I eat one (1), how many will I have left?

They have learned to transpose from one idea (or level) to another and to make the transition by using figures or objects or number statements and problems. It is wise to give them a surfeit of practice with these transformations.

Problem solving in all grade levels involves a knowledge of many different functions and operations in the mathematical system. Children learn this, as has been said, through real experiences handling real objects, rearranging, adding, subtracting, and so on. They are, in a sense, learning things simultaneously, that is, the operations *and* the manner of identifying which operation is best to use in a given problem format. This choice may become easier with practice, although the types of problems that may be presented to a child can be a challenge. The transferability of knowledge from one to another operational technique does not always hold. Decisions that have to be made by the child in making one choice over another in order to find an answer can be overwhelming at times.

Problem solving continues in all grades, becoming as difficult as the pupils are able to manage. By the time children reach the third and fourth grades, they should be accustomed to doing many kinds of problems (although they may not necessarily be totally successful with them). Their ability to read, to reason, to understand the implications of methods and figures in the mathematical system, combine to support (or interfere with) their rationalizations and justifications for doing a problem in a particular way.[26]

The ability to deal with money becomes crucial in solving problems. How much do I have after I spend 15¢ of my quarter? What can I buy for 10¢? How much of it should I save?

Parents and teachers can use facsimiles of money at home and in the classroom. The size should be comparable to that of real money. Children need many experiences with the equality factor of money forms and sizes. The children who can least afford the loss of money are often cheated out of it because they do not know how to make correct change. People visiting another country, too, have difficulty in money denominations.

Practice, experiences, reasoning processes discussed with a teacher or parent, can help children become excellent problem solvers. This skill is essential to growth of intellectual capacities.

Functions and Operations

As mentioned earlier, the mathematical functions and operations make sense after children use them in appropriate experiences. The actual solution reached by using addition, subtraction, multiplication, or division is accompanied by the symbols of those operations. This will remain with a child if it is done over and over again, and often. Children are not different from adults in that sense. We learn what we experience often. Something that is new requires more time for mastery of a concept.

When children add several sets, for example, they learn that this can be done by a system called *multiplication*.

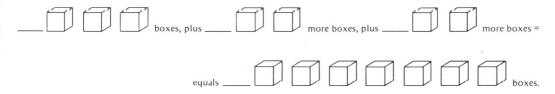

Children can learn to see one number in a circle, one number in each of a second and third circles. They learn that the similarity permits a multiplication process to facilitate the answer they need.

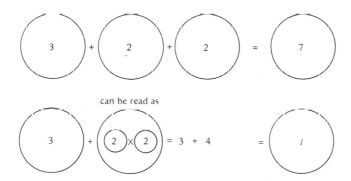

Multiplication involves a certain degree of memorization to facilitate quick computations. It first must be understood for the function it represents.[27]

The teacher may ask the children how many crayons the class of 35 children will need if (s)he wants everyone to have a red, a green, and a black one. The children can be taken through the process. They need to understand why first they have to decide how many crayons each child in the class of 35 will have. Then they have to multiply that number by 35. They will also have to know about place value of numbers. All these topics are introduced to the children, gradually, as appropriate to each problem. The teacher or parent must decide when children are able to understand a problem.

Pupils should never be made to feel embarrassed or incompetent if they cannot find the answer to a problem. This alone can veer them away from trying to do it in the future.

Children will learn how to judge whether multiplication or division is needed in a given problem. They learn how subtraction is needed. Long division is one of the most difficult of functions to understand. Every operation is involved: addition, subtraction, division, multiplication. Children have to learn when each one is appropriate in order to arrive at the correct answer. When they understand the logic of it, however, they can do it.

Simple division begins with one number to be divided by one other number. No carrying process or complicated multiplication or subtraction should be used in the beginning. This is enough to defeat anyone just beginning to learn a new process.

New mathematical systems and their implementation, as well as the former systems, need to be understood by young pupils. Facility with numbers in and of themselves provides children with confidence and pleasure in their own ability to solve problems. Terms different from those used in textbooks many years ago are based on a different contemporary understanding of how mathematics should be taught. Perspectives are also based on an adaptation to a universal system of computation and measurement.

The earlier emphasis on rote learning and on correct single answers led to an emphasis on *only* the answers. Less interest was focused on the means by which an individual reached an answer. Some teachers were conscientious enough to be interested in the way a child arrived at an answer, but it was not typically stressed in relation to an appreciation of the process of any form of learning. The concentration on process as an aspect of learning became more relevant in educational institutions of the 1950s. The reasoning underlying this view is that society changes. Ideas change. If children are taught that only one answer is correct for once and for all times, they may not learn how to adapt processes to different elements. They need to learn that different answers may be correct, that is, answers different from those that are correct in today's views.

Children are taught now to reason, to argue, to pursue different answers. They are also taught to accept an answer as correct if it makes sense within a given mathematical system. They are urged to question authorities. With this same suggestion, comes greater responsibility for one's own answers or behavior. One must rise or fall on the basis of his/her own choice of action.

Proportion, Ratio, and Percentage

Operations that involve proportion, ratio, and percentage demonstrate that totals can be taken apart and referred to, symbolized as parts. Children learn what it means to judge relationships of parts to the totals. They have to have many experiences doing this with real objects. They associate the symbols of proportion, one button to every three people (1 : 3). Similarly, the ratio sign, which is between the figures indicates proportion. Percentages, which represent part of the 100 per cent whole, signify a portion of the total.[28]

Easy ways to show children what 50 per cent represents can occur as real situations provide such an opportunity. Half of something is 50 per cent of it. There will also be workbook opportunities for children to use when they reach later grades. Third and fourth grades use mathematical textbooks, as do the earlier grades. By the time children are eight and nine, however, homework and concentrated periods of independent work by the children are expected.

Educators advise that teachers not rush into workbook activities for pupils. Discussion, active manipulation of materials, and various mathematical operations should occur often. Sometimes children appear to know what they are expected to do. They often do not like to ask the teacher to repeat directions or to admit that they were not listening. Distractions, talking, and thinking of other things have to be considered by the teacher as an interfering influence that is typical in many assembled groups of children at school.

Parents and teachers need to acquire many books that demonstrate gamelike activities based on mathematical principles. The practice that can be gained from performing the activities carries strengths for the much-needed foundations leading toward more complex operations.

When children have had practice, they can do their mental manipulations rapidly. This means that their computations are becoming almost automatic. When they have mastered concepts to that extent they can go on toward complicated problems. What is significant here is that they will enjoy the challenge of doing complicated work rather than turn away from it.

Measuring Areas and Distances

Measuring area, circumference, perimeter, lengths, and widths occur in the advanced grades. Some of these are done on simple levels in the second, third and fourth grades, but they can become very complicated when formula symbols are introduced. When children see the basic premise in all of these, the concepts are not difficult to grasp.

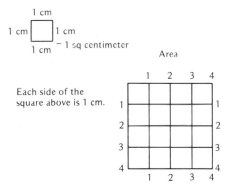

Each side of this square unit is 4 centimeters (4 cm) long.

Area is measured by square unit.

The area of this figure is 16 square centimeters (sq. cm.)

This would *not* be done as a first exercise. Very simple square units would be shown first. They would lead up to a more difficult problem as the one above and more.

This is measured by adding the lengths and sides of a figure.

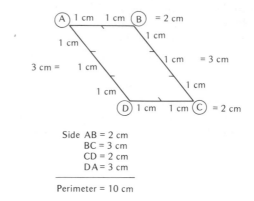

Side AB = 2 cm
BC = 3 cm
CD = 2 cm
DA = 3 cm
_____

Perimeter = 10 cm

This sketch includes many concepts. They should be presented in three parts in separate sketches.

One should show, first, only the centimeters.

The second should show only the ABCD with the centimeters marked out.

The third can show the sketch with all the markings. This again is not the first abstraction that a child would see of the conceptualization of perimeter. It needs to be much easier at the beginning. Consult mathematical books for young children and workbooks for elementary grades for simple sketches and figures leading to advanced ideas.[29]

These measurements can of course by made with inches. It is not difficult for children to understand both centimeters and inches.

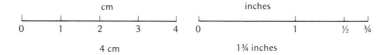

The development and sequences taken prior to leading up to any complicated measuring process are up to the discretion of the teacher. Clear, easy choices must be planned for the children in order to give them the feeling of mastery.

THREE-DIMENSIONAL OBJECTS

Measuring various forms and shapes, such as cones, cylinders, oval (football) entails a recognition first of their differences. Three-dimensional objects have volume (space). Cubic units measure volume. Children can start out by recognizing 1 cubic unit.

= 1 cubic unit

Count the number of cubic units in order to find the volume. (Or compute them.) If you thought 4 was the correct answer, you were correct. Four cubic units is a volume of 4 cubic units.

The topics as they are presented here would not be used directly with children. They are only to represent the kinds of functions and operations in mathematics that children would be expected to do. Much more is required in breaking out each step. Many more times are needed with practice in any given step if children are to master the concepts mentioned here.

Numbers, figures, shapes, sizes, volume, area, and perimeter involve more than familiarity with figures representing counting, enumeration, and the like. An understanding of those concepts also includes a kind of visualization in perceiving an object (e.g., a square, a rectangle, a cube, a hexagon) that requires different ways of thinking than children have ever before encountered. If adults are to be fair to children, they need to place themselves in the child's position and imagine the novitiate helplessness in trying to capture the correct visual perspective. It is totally foreign unless the provisions have been made for activities that have led up to that point in an appropriate manner.

Reading and Problem-Solving Skills in Mathematics

Often when children reach the point of being tested on verbally written problems rather than symbols in mathematics, they have difficulties in understanding what they are expected to do. Simple sentences have to be used during any lesson that permits a sentence to coincide with a series of figures with an operation to be performed.

Children often understand the mathematical concept but do not perceive what the written, verbal problem is requesting. Teachers, therefore, must check to see whether the pupils know what the problem elements are. The children may need help in perceiving the relevant figures that need to be computed.

The speed of reading for a child influences his/her ability to begin a problem. If a child is a slow reader, (s)he needs more time to comprehend the terms of the mathematical problem. If the child needs more help in this in the early stages of approaches to problems of this nature it should be given. The child who needs this support will give it up when (s)he can manage easily without it. There need not be concern that a child will become lazy or dependent with frequent help by the teacher or older child. This quality of having support when needed does not become engrained in the individual's personality. Everyone wants to do things on his/her own power as soon as possible.

Teachers show problems written on the board, or on charts. They discuss a given problem with the children. They ask questions about it. Children read it several times from the board. When these problems are to be solved at their desks, they read them aloud for the class. After hearing them several times and becoming more at ease with what the problems represent, children can much more easily do their work independently. The feelings that accompany ineptness crowd out attitudes that would help children want to approach an understanding of problems.

Practice in reading problems from simple to complex can arise often in the classroom. This practice also should be included in most review lessons. Prior to the start of any new concepts, teachers typically introduce review content to the children. This provides a bridge, a transition from known material to the new. It shows relationships of one idea to another. When this is presented well the children cannot help but understand it.

Teachers often include in spelling lessons words that are used in mathematical problems. Reading is a technique that is used in a variety of subject matter areas. For this reason, the content of those various areas must be included in reading periods. They must become part of a routine. In that way the children may begin to make the needed transfer from one subject matter area to another (imperfectly or not).

Even at the university level and other adult course levels, people have difficulty applying what they have learned from one course to another. They seem to leave behind what they learned (and on which they may have been successfully evaluated in a test, receiving a high grade). They do not transfer information from one content area to a related one that requires past knowledge. Children need to see mathematical symbols as part of their reading and spelling activities. The more they see those words and symbols overlapping in tasks, the more likely it is that pupils may use them as part of a "natural" course of thinking.

Teachers can create games in which children need to read symbols, classifications, and problems. These need to be placed on bulletin boards, too. Captions such as Can You Read This? Can You Answer This Problem? present simple forms of challenges to the pupils. When the children are able to look at those ideas intermittently and in an unhurried manner, they may learn for themselves what the answers are. This can become very satisfying for them.

"Try to do one more problem than you are asked." "Create your own problem for someone else to answer." Either of these requests can be made by the teacher or parent urging the pupil to compete with him/herself. This tends to make the child move forward, testing for greater depth of skills or even as a form of review. Self-testing also leads to an awareness that one can create a problem, know the answer, and perhaps discover that a classmate cannot solve it. Among the goals in these activities are, in any case, that the child realize greater confidence in him/herself, and acquire enough awareness of skills and operations in mathematical problems to encourage freedom and desire to pursue more difficult tasks. These mental manipulations are useful in a variety of situations, both in school and out, in academic situations, and in social ones as well.

SUMMARY

This chapter emphasized the importance of creating favorable attitudes in children toward the discipline of mathematics. The subject can be made less difficult than it often appears in the way it is offered at school. Most children can succeed in one aspect of mathematical activities, at least, and can be urged to continue their efforts toward achieving success in tasks of greater complexity. They can add two pencils or cookies. They can be shown simple readings on the clock prior to learning about the more difficult ones related to the quarter hours or other fractions of time on the clock.

Most researchers indicate that children's awareness and understanding of mathematical concepts need to be interrelated gradually, through experiences with real things in the environment before they can be expected to conceptualize abstract symbols and operations of mathematical import. Teachers can help parents understand how children's manipulation of objects at home, noting position, size, shape, comparison, and the like, can be extremely useful in providing the foundations of understanding at school in academic subjects.

New concepts at school need to be supported by children's knowledge of the past as well as their handling of physically present objects that have the attributes or properties of mathematically related concepts. Both the academic information and research-related data that have been made available, and the practical curriculum-recommended ideas for what children need in order to comprehend logical and sequential concepts, are noted in this chapter. Teachers, themselves, as well as in conference with parents, can utilize the enlightening suggestions that many writers have generated as a result of their studies and investigations on cognitive development.

Children have to be involved in trial-and-error processing as they learn. Teachers and parents must be supportive in those attempts. Memorization of ideas and figures may be important in some cases, as when children have to remember the number names (one, two, and so on) for the counting system. Memorization is also involved when later and more advanced operations in multiplication are learned. But children must also be able to build within themselves (or internalize as part of their *schema*, or their own comprehension framework) relationships between meaning and labels provided for shapes, functional operations, and thought processes in the mental juxtaposing of ideas.

Piaget's research contributed to American educators' conceptual frameworks for the way children develop intellectual thought, language, and an understanding of cause-and-effect processes. Other writers in curriculum and those who are interested in the way children learn at school have provided various interpretations for the way Piaget's work can be implemented with children, and with a simultaneous recognition of what many children are capable of learning at various ages in their early development at home and at school.

The terms used for many-sided objects, measurement of them, and logical sequences that need to be observed when one performs a mathematically sound measurement of something, represent many challenges for children. In some cases this challenge continues throughout life. The authors of many books that present mathematics for children seem to be in agreement that a positive orientation toward operations and functions of mathematics can greatly facilitate children's success with numbers and systems. It is urged that parents and teachers be cognizant and helpful in that regard. Approaching mathematical components in activities can be sectioned into simpler processes first, so that the learner does not become frustrated and want to quit in defeat.

The principles that seem to apply for instructional efforts that occur between adults and children regarding attitudinal understanding of the difficulties that emerge within children as they attempt to learn abstract knowledge apply in mathematical instruction as well. In children's early years it is easier to affect positive attitudes toward abstract knowledge by giving them experiences that are manageable and will lead toward greater complexities than it will be later to help them "unlearn" negative attitudes.

The research of decades past had not provided the information that is available in contemporary society demonstrating young children's capacities for learning prior to their attendance at a preschool or kindergarten. The systems, in a sense, have come down to meet the child's size, recognizing that intelligence is functioning from the moment of birth, at least in terms of the way it can be measured by sophisticated scientific methods. Prior to birth, as well, the development of the embryo and fetus represents amazing human growth.

Although the baby and young child are smaller than the adult, the minds of the young are developing at a remarkable rate. They are learning more through their senses and impressions of the environment than people are aware. Scientists have yet to discover the full capacities of infants. Teachers and parents, therefore, must be open, listening well, and noticing what children's skills and abilities are. Children should be allowed to express themselves without sensing heavy pressures to do so, particularly where academic knowledge is concerned.

Mathematics is an essential skill, not only for effective functioning in society, for self-protection, and for creativity, but for general kinds of enjoyment, as well. The functional aspects and the interpersonal elements of mathematically known skills in an individual can influence self-confidence in a variety of ways. Pursuits in that direction are well worthwhile.

TOPICS FOR DISCUSSION

1. Consider five ways of introducing children into a lesson on addition from simple to complex levels. You choose the grade level.
2. Plan four bulletin boards that can be used effectively with children in the first grade. What concepts will you try to develop?
3. In attempting to give parents an understanding of Piaget's work describing his perspective on stages of children's intellectual and mathematical development, how would you proceed? How would this knowledge help parents to know what kinds of activities to present at home so that children might gain from such experiences?

4. Describe three case studies in which children are being given the benefit of effective mathematical "predevelopmental ideas" at home. (It may be based on children you know or on hypothetical cases.)
5. Devise a list of recommendations for 10 Dos and 10 Don'ts that could be given to new teachers who teach mathematics to young children. This list would help teachers understand why it is important not to say or do certain things with children if children's well-being and success in mathematical activities are of concern.
6. Why would you recommend that teachers not use workbooks with young children? What mistakes do teachers make in this regard?
7. List the skills that many kindergarten children have upon entrance to school. How can teachers capitalize on this knowledge in the children?
8. What skill is needed in children to help them understand problem solving in a mathematical sense? (Is it reading? Is it juxtaposition of ideas in their heads? Is it relating past experiences to real objects? How so?)
9. What kinds of mathematical functions will children in the second and third grades be learning? Are all children ready in the same way for such learning? Why? How does the teacher deal with preparation for complex operations in mathematics?
10. What do children in the fourth grade do related to measuring or assessing size, shape, density, and velocity conponents?
11. Are fractions introduced before children are ready to understand them at school or do children have experiences prior to school attendance that enable them to deal with some of the concepts? Explain your answer.
12. Do you remember your own experiences with mathematical concepts in early years, either before kindergarten or later? Were they instrumental in affecting your attitudes toward mathematics or the instruction of it today?
13. In what stage of development are young children between three and seven as Piaget views their mental development?

NOTES

1. Evelyn Goodenough Pitcher, Miriam G. Lasher, Sylvia G. Feinburg, and Linda Abrams Braun, *Helping Young Children Learn*, 3rd ed. (Columbus, Ohio: Merrill, 1979). See the activities that are recommended (pp. 152–154) for young children's experiences in counting, measuring, weighing, noting thermometer readings, and dates on a calendar.
2. C. Alan Riedesel, *Guiding Discovery in Elementary School Mathematics*, 2nd ed. (Englewood Cliffs, N.J.: Prentice-Hall, 1973), p. 24.
3. Ibid., p. 25.
4. Joseph N. Payne, *Mathematics Learning in Early Childhood*, Thirty-seventh Yearbook, National Council of Teachers of Mathematics (Reston, Va.: The National Council of Teachers of Mathematics, Inc., 1975), p. v.
5. Marilyn Suydam and Fred Weaver, "Research on Learning Mathematics," pp. 44–67 in *Mathematics Learning In Early Childhood*, Thirty-seventh Yearbook, National Council of Teachers of Mathematics (Reston, Va.: The National Council of Teachers of Mathematics, Inc., 1975), p. 45.
6. Ibid.
7. Arthur Coxford and Lawrence Ellerbruch, "Fractional Numbers," pp. 192–203 in *Mathematics Learning in Early Childhood*, Thirty-seventh Yearbook National Council of Teachers of Mathematics (Reston, Va.: The National Council of Teachers of Mathematics, Inc., 1975), p. 192.
8. Children cut pictures out of magazines showing animals. The pictures are pasted on a sheet of construction paper and described as showing sets of two eyes among several animals or birds.
9. Herbert Ginsburg, *Children's Arithmetic: The Learning Process* (New York: Van Nostrand, 1977), p. v. From birth to about six or seven years old, children are spontaneously developing in mathematical skills, at least those related to a knowledge of counting.
10. Leonard M. Kennedy, *Guiding Children to Mathematical Discovery*, (Belmont, Calif.: Wadsworth, 1970), p. 330.

11. Ginsburg, op. cit., p. 9. Children discover that in order to count correctly, they must remember to say certain words in a given sequence or they will be told that they are wrong. They can remember one, two, three, but after that it becomes difficult (when they are first learning) to remember in exact order the number names that follow—up to ten. The rationale for why or how the number names must follow each other is not clear. It is very difficult to count correctly to one hundred until the child learns the underlying system with each new set of tens.

12. Suydam and Weaver, op. cit., p. 49.

13. Edith Robinson, "Geometry," pp. 206–225 in *Mathematics Learning in Early Childhood*, Thirty-seventh Yearbook, National Council of Teachers of Mathematics (Reston, Va.: The National Council of Teachers of Mathematics, Inc., 1975), p. 207.

14. Ibid., pp. 221–222.

15. Lloyd I. Richardson, Jr., Kathy L. Goodman, Nancy Noftsinger Hartman, and Henri C. LePique, *A Mathematics Activity Curriculum for Early Childhood and Special Education* (New York: Macmillan, 1980), pp. 157–179.

16. Richard W. Copeland, *How Children Learn Mathematics*, 2nd ed. (New York: Macmillan, 1974), pp. 80 and 97. Comments on Piaget's principles related to children's difficulties in seriation or placing things in graduating order are highlighted.

17. Jean Piaget, *The Psychology of Intelligence* (Paterson, N.J.: Littlefield, Adams, 1960), 182 pp. Herbert Ginsburg and Sylvia Opper *Piaget's Theory of Intellectual Development*, 2nd ed. (Englewood Cliffs, N.J.: Prentice-Hall, 1979), 253 pp. See Chapter Three, pp. 69–112, of Ginsburg and Opper's work to note discussion on Piaget's views of the child's mental and intellectual development between the ages of two and eleven. Constance Kamii and Rheta De Vries, *Physical Knowledge in Preschool Education: Implications of Piaget's Theory* (Englewood Cliffs, N.J.: Prentice-Hall, 1978), 321 pp. Sueann Robinson Ambron, *Child Development*, 2nd ed. (New York: Holt, 1978), pp. 251–261. These are only a few references that can be consulted; they do not represent all that have treated Piaget's writings.

18. David P. Weikert, Linda Rogers, and Carolyn Adcock, *The Cognitively Oriented Curriculum* (Urbana, Ill.: U. of Illinois, 1971), 182 pp. Copeland, op. cit., Barry J. Wadsworth, *Piaget for the Classroom Teacher* (New York: Longman, 1978).

19. Note Weikert, Rogers, and Adcock, op. cit., pp. 119–168. See also Kennedy, op. cit., p. 333, and Riedesel, op. cit., p. 510.

20. An understanding of these time problems will not typically be mastered at this time, but an introduction to and experiences with such concepts are essential to building a basis for awareness and comprehension.

21. Several writers indicate that young children have a great deal of information about number and addition prior to kindergarten experiences: Ginsburg, op. cit., Suydam and Weaver, op. cit., Richardson and others, op. cit., p. 2, are examples representing other writers.

22. Robert E. Valett, *Developing Cognitive Abilities* (Saint Louis, Mo.: Mosby, 1978); Ginsburg, op. cit.; Glenadine Gibb and Alberta Castaneda, "Experiences for Young Children," pp. 96–124 in *Mathematics Learning in Early Childhood*, Thirty-seventh Yearbook, National Council of Teachers of Mathematics (Reston, Va.: The National Council of Teachers of Mathematics, Inc., 1975), 297 pp.; Kamii and DeVries, op. cit., pp. 38–61.

23. Children may have a difficult time with problem solving, not only because so many attributes and operations need to be considered simultaneously but because they do not have sufficient understanding of the basic, underlying logic that prevails through the problem solution.

24. Joanne Hendrick, *Total Learning for the Whole Child* (St. Louis, Mo.: Mosby, 1980), pp. 233–243. Suggestions for ways to celebrate holidays are given here. Observation of holidays through children's activities are viewed as having significant contributions to children's physical, mental, and social as well as emotional development.

25. Marilyn Burns, *The I Hate Mathematics Book* (Boston: Little, Brown, 1975).

26. Activities may be used as recommended by the following authors: Mary Baratta-Lorton, *Mathematics Their Way* (Menlo Park, Calif.: Addison-Wesley, 1976); Valett, op. cit.; Coxford and Ellerbruch, op. cit.; Robinson, op. cit.; Henry Van Engen and Douglas Grouws, "Relations, Number Sentences, and Other Topics," pp. 252–271 in *Mathematics Learning in Early Childhood*, Thirty-seventh Yearbook National Council of Teachers of Mathemat-

ics (Reston, Va.: The National Council of Teachers of Mathematics, Inc., 1975), 297 pp.; Kennedy, op. cit. pp. 358–372 deals with problem-solving processes; Riedesel, op. cit., pp. 297–326, emphasizes that several approaches are needed in helping children improve their problem-solving abilities; and reviews for the teacher's conceptualization of ways to teach mental skills as children approach practice with skills can be found in Hendrick, op. cit., 212–228.

27. Games are needed to help children remember almost automatically which numbers multiply easily. It is suggested that the teacher review counting with children using counting units of twos, threes, fours, and fives prior to teaching the multiplication process.

28. For helpful activities on proportion, see Coxford and Ellerbruch, op. cit., pp. 192–203; for activities on ratio, proportion, and percent concepts, see Riedesel, op. cit., pp. 423–446. Consult Kamii and DeVries op. cit., pp. 26 and 27 to review an understanding of how children acquire logico-mathematical concepts (as Piaget views the process).

29. Geometric concepts include measurement of perimeter, congruence, area, right angles, and other problem computations related to shape and space. See Coxford and Ellerbruch, op. cit., pp. 192–225; activities related to discrimination of spaces and shapes can be found in Richardson and others, op. cit., pp. 53–60; suggestions for measuring area and noting shapes of many sides, edges, or faces can be found in Kennedy, op. cit., pp. 299–357.

SELECTED REFERENCES

AMBRON, SUEANN ROBINSON. *Child Development*, 2nd ed. N.Y.: Holt, Rinehart and Winston, 1978 524 pp.

BARATTA-LORTON, MARY. *Mathematics Their Way*. Menlo Park, Calif.: Addison-Wesley Publishing Co., Inc., 1976. 398 pp.

BURNS, MARILYN. *The I Hate Mathematics Book*. Boston: Little, Brown and Company, 1975. 127 pp.

COPELAND, RICHARD W. *How Children Learn Mathematics*, 2nd ed. New York: Macmillan Publishing Co., Inc., 1974. 374 pp.

COXFORD, ARTHUR, and LAWRENCE ELLERBRUCH. "Fractional Numbers," pp. 192–203 in *Mathematics Learning in Early Childhood*, Thirty-seventh Yearbook, National Council of Teachers of Mathematics. Reston, Va.: The National Council of Teachers of Mathematics, Inc., 1975. 297 pp.

GIBB, CLENADINE, and ALBERTA CASTANEDA. "Experiences for Young Children" in *Mathematics Learning in Early Childhood*, Thirty-seventh Yearbook, National Council of Teachers of Mathematics. Reston, Va.: The National Council of Teachers of Mathematics, Inc., 1975 297 pp.

GINSBURG, HERBERT. *Children's Arithmetic*. New York: D. Van Nostrand Company, 1977. 197 pp.

———, and SYLVIA OPPER. *Piaget's Theory of Intellectual Development*, 2nd ed. Englewood Cliffs, N.J.: Prentice-Hall, Inc., 1977. 253 pp.

HENDRICK, JOANNE. *Total Learning for the Whole Child*. Saint Louis, Mo.: The C. V. Mosby Company, 1980. 405 pp.

KAMII, CONSTANCE, and RHETA DEVRIES. *Physical Knowledge in Preschool Education*. Englewood Cliffs, N.J.: Prentice-Hall, Inc., 1978. 321 pp.

KENNEDY, LEONARD M. *Guiding Children to Mathematical Discovery*. Belmont, Calif.: Wadsworth Publishing Co., Inc., 1970. 429 pp.

NELSON, DOYAL, and JOAN KIRKPATRICK. "Problem Solving," in *Mathematics Learning in Early Childhood*, Thirty-seventh Yearbook, National Council of Teachers of Mathematics. Reston, Va.: The National Council of Teachers of Mathematics, Inc., 1975. 297 pp.

PAYNE, JOSEPH N. *Mathematics Learning in Early Childhood*, Thirty-seventh Yearbook, National Council of Teachers of Mathematics. Reston, Va.: The National Council of Teachers of Mathematics, Inc., 1975. 297 pp.

PIAGET, JEAN. *The Child's Conception of Physical Causality*, translated by Marjorie Gabain. Paterson, N.J.: Littlefield and Adams and Company, 1960. 309 pp.

————. *The Child's Conception of the World,* translated by Joan and Andrew Tomlinson. Paterson, N.J.: Littlefield, Adams and Company, 1960. 397 pp.

————. *The Psychology of Intelligence.* Paterson, N.J.: Littlefield, Adams and Company, 1960. 182 pp.

PITCHER, EVELYN GOODENOUGH, MIRIAM G. LASHER, SYLVIA G. FEINBURG, and LINDA ABRAMS BRAUN. *Helping Young Children Learn,* 3rd ed. Columbus, Ohio: Charles E. Merrill Publishing Company, 1979. 209 pp.

RICHARDSON, LLOYD I., KATHY L. GOODMAN, NANCY NOFTSINGER HARTMAN, and HENRI C. LEPIQUE. *A Mathematics Activity Curriculum for Early Childhood Education and Special Education.* New York: Macmillan Publishing Co., Inc., 1980. 433 pp.

RIEDESEL, C. ALAN. *Guiding Discovery in Elementary School Mathematics,* 2nd ed. Englewood Cliffs, N.J.: Prentice-Hall, Inc., 1973. 657 pp.

ROBINSON, EDITH. "Geometry," pp. 206–225 in *Mathematics Learning in Early Childhood,* Thirty-seventh Yearbook, National Council of Teachers of Mathematics. Reston, Va.: The National Council of Teachers of Mathematics, Inc., 1975. 297 pp.

SUYDAM, MARILYN, and FRED WEAVER. "Research on Learning Mathematics," pp. 44–67 in *Mathematics Learning in Early Childhood,* Thirty-seventh Yearbook, National Council of Teachers of Mathematics. Reston, Va.: The National Council of Teachers of Mathematics, Inc., 1975. 297 pp.

VALETT, ROBERT E. *Developing Cognitive Abilities.* Saint Louis: The C. V. Mosby Company, 1978. 271 pp.

VAN ENGEN, HENRY, and DOUGLAS GROUWS. "Relations, Number Sentences, and Other Topics," in *Mathematics Learning in Early Childhood.* Thirty-seventh Yearbook, National Council of Teachers of Mathematics. Reston, Va.: The National Council of Teachers of Mathematics, Inc., 1975. 297 pp.

WADSWORTH, BARRY J. *Piaget for the Classroom Teacher.* New York: Longman, Inc., 1978. 303 pp.

WEIKERT, DAVID P., LINDA ROGERS, CAROLYN ADCOCK. *The Cognitive Oriented Curriculum.* Urbana, Ill.: University of Illinois, 1971. 182 pp.

WILLIAMS, ELIZABETH, and HILARY SHUARD. *Elementary Mathematics Today: A Resource for Teachers.* Grades 1–8. Menlo Park, Calif.: Addison-Wesley Publishing Co., Inc., 1970. 462 pp.

Science in
Young Children's Lives

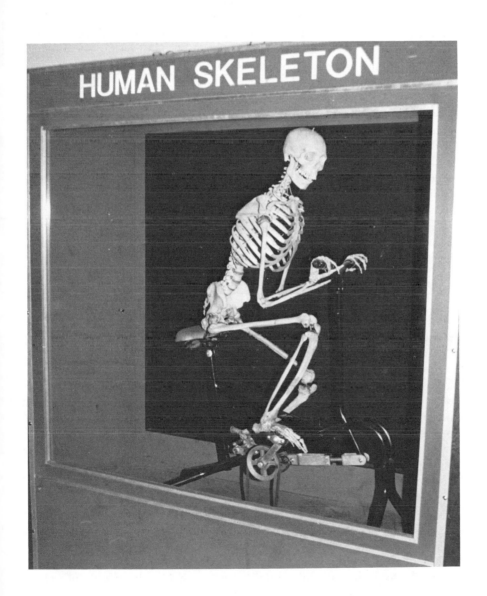

Early Appreciation of Science

Contemporary society learns about scientists from books that provide romantic and exciting accounts of discoveries made by some of the conscientious and driven individuals of past years. Such figures seem far removed from the image of a child who is carefully examining the parts of a flower (maybe while pulling it apart), or observing hard clay as it becomes pulverized by a heavy object crushing it, or noting the colors reflected in a prism. But the polarities that appear to exist between the sophisticated knowledge of a scientist who has contributed to society in some unusual way and the young child who is impelled by something within to scrutinize an object or process diminish when one considers how similar the goals may be for each person. The scientist working toward discovery and the child who is in process of doing the same thing may be manifesting similar behavior toward achievement of a goal, one that will satisfy curiosity and will provide an answer to some internal questions.

Children, at least in very early stages of their development, do not typically verbalize for themselves the ways in which they will seek answers to a problem. But they can, from the age of only a few months, act on the environment in such a way that they discover many attributes about objects, people, and events.

Concepts related to science are involved both at the sophisticated levels of knowledge and at the early levels of inquiry. Similar qualities are called for at all levels—qualities such as careful observation, an understanding of what things can do, how they will act under pressure or touch, and how they will change from one form to another.[1] Steady and careful concentration on how things work can provide an individual with skills related to predictability of events, or how objects can be changed from one form to another through heat, cold, rain, or air pressure. Predictability is an important quality in any scientific endeavor.

The differences between contemporary knowledge related to scientific facts and science as a body of knowledge in the past lie in today's perspectives of science, not only as an accumulation of facts, but also as including testing, experimenting, processing, manipulating, and investigating the properties of things, as well as disciplining one's search by rules of objectivity.[2] If one is not guided by attempts to be impartial toward what one expects to find, before initiating the pursuit, one is not being scientific. The search for truth injects a readiness to see what is there to be found, not clouded by a bias one way or another. When that objectivity is practiced, the experiment performed by one scientist should result in similar results when performed by another, given the information in precise terms of condition, nature, materials, and process of the experiment.

Young children are active and are interested in things around them. They like to push, pull, roll, throw, squeeze, and mash separate objects as they explore throughout the house. Although they are not aware that their behavior is similar to the activities of adults who, in the roles of architect, geologist, scientist, or science educator are investigating and recording the nature of objects as needed by the discipline involved, they are neverthe-less discovering essential knowledge for themselves. Piaget's work that de-scribes children's sensorimotor activities, and the way that knowledge is pursued and acquired through those efforts, has become famous as an ex-planation of his perspective of children's intellectual development.[3]

Among the most crucial aspects in young children's learning to under-stand the environment is a gradual development within themselves of in-formation that they acquire through internal perceptions of what the envi-ronment is like. No one can sense for them what is noted by their own bodily functions. The intricate internal computer composed of the brain and sense receptors in one's body records the effects of an external world of objects, events, people, and motion, or air pressure and the like. As children become more aware of the regularity of some things, such as the way certain foods taste, what happens when mother is ready to nurse the baby, and many other situations, they are acquiring an intellectual frame-work for sorting out objects and events in the world (that is closest to them).

It is suggested that a conceptualization of the way children are perceived to be learning include an awareness that a developmental increase in skills typically does not occur in complete or distinct stages that can be clearly noted from the end (or close) of one stage to the beginning of another.[4] If children's development is viewed as contained within stages, described by specific characteristics within those stages, new scientific facts may not be discovered owing to premature closure and acceptance of a priori knowl-edge. This does not engender viable and critical thinking.

Proceeding from the point of view that children's development in scien-tific thought is as continuing a process, as are other aspects of their devel-opment, it is necessary to mention here how valuable the comments of parents can be in giving children information at their own levels of under-standing even during the ordinary daily events at home. Many categories of scientific phenomena are seen by the child long before those things will be encountered at school.[5] The earth, sun, sky, grass, flowers, air, wind, rain, heat (that cooks food, or that is encountered in high temperatures in the atmosphere), machines (lawn mower, vacuum cleaner, refrigerator, au-tomobiles), the human body, and the functions of touch, smell, taste, vi-sion, hearing, and kinesthetic sensations provide many occasions for the use of scientific terms or descriptions that can direct a child's thinking.

Children's Experiences with Science-Related Concepts

Formalized programs of schools use a variety of approaches to have chil-dren become involved in experimentation, manipulation, examination, and investigation of scientific phenomena.[6] Teachers can attempt to use three types of questions: those that urge the children to ask questions them-selves, those that probe ideas stated by the children, and those that lead to bringing closure (or summarizing understanding) on a given topic or set of ideas.[7]

A program involving process skills has activities that generate many opportunities for children to observe, classify, measure, communicate, infer from what they see, predict what may happen as a result of what they find, using time and space relationships in discovering information, and using numbers with their experiences. The pupils in primary grades who experience this program are learning various processing skills that are highly valued in the scientific orientation toward acquiring knowledge.[8]

Some recommendations for a series of activities that give children an opportunity to acquire some information from less structured plans are given in several brief groups of descriptions.[9] The activities do not require lengthy preparation nor involved, complicated discussion in order that children and teacher may enjoy them. Depending on how complicated or simple a teacher or parent might want a task for children to be, other ideas are available as substructures (or subcomponents) of larger (complicated) ideas. The intent in the instruction of mathematical or systematically oriented disciplines such as science (involving classification, observation skills, chemical and life-generating changes in matter) is to help children understand first the smaller parts of a concept and to simplify the tasks for pupils.[10] When the teacher has a variety of materials at hand it is not difficult to give the children experimental opportunities for tasks that are congruent with their skills.

In terms of the scientific processes that are significant to systematizing knowledge related to the earth, ecology, plants, trees, physical sciences, and biological phenomena, it must be remembered that skills acquired in mathematical activities also contribute to the characteristics of scientific pursuits. Classifying, examining, counting, differentiating among shapes, sizes, and weights, noting capacity or velocity, labeling objects, and other qualities that focus children's attention on arrangement of materials in mathematical tasks can be reviewed and applied to scientific experiences.[11]

Primary grades programs include pupils' involvement with activities of measuring objects, plant growth, people's arms, legs, feet, and so on.[12] Children are involved in many kinds of activities at their levels of enjoyment and learning. The series of materials do not form a structure or sequence for developmental skills. The designers intended that children use the natural orientations of play behavior and become involved in their manipulation of materials provided by the activities. The units do not include behavioral goals. It is expected that teachers will want to involve the pupils in various ways because children are at various levels of understanding the implications of certain tasks.

Children in kindergarten play with light and shadow concepts, they plant seeds, note butterflies, grass, flowers, trees, and bugs. Their activities are classified in terms of indoor and outdoor activities. The same plans govern experiences that will be planned for children in the first, second, and third grades. When the children can be outdoors a number of activities are provided that capitalize on earth-related studies and atmospheric changes.

Another program, (SCIS) The Science Curriculum Improvement Study focuses, on scientific literacy.[13] This series of units includes content in the

Sunshine, Fresh Air, and Water vs. Darkness, and Lack of Air or Water

Plant grows in sunshine and fresh air, and with provision of water.

Plant does not thrive without sunlight, fresh air, and water.

What Plants Need to Grow Properly.

Concept
Illustration
6–1

physical sciences and the biological sciences. Concepts within the lessons are "named, defined, explained, and clarified by the teacher."[14] The teacher motivates the children to become involved and to experiment with the materials. The pupils talk, ask questions, and manipulate objects, liquids, and a variety of things that are often seen in the children's environment.[15] They record what they see by drawing their own concepts of what happened to objects or what they look like.

Even with packaged programs, teachers can adapt their own ideas as they note that the pupils need more practice or review in handling materials and making records, pictorially or graphically, of what they see. Observation from the child's eye, as that perception is made and translated on paper by drawing a picture of what was seen, provides a significant skill in the scientific process.

An experiment with plants can be done. (Note Concept Illustration 6–1 in which two different treatments are given for plants.) The children enjoy seeing the effects of their own work. Not only two plants are involved in the experiment. Several children in teams or partnerships can plan their tasks for comparing the facilitation and inhibiting of growth.

Process, observation, reconstruction of ideas and things, are all a part of children's learning in science. The extent to which some children are able to comprehend ideas or a process relates to the materials they are given, the questions they are asked, and the explanations that adults give them as reasons for the causes or effects of combinations of acts or experiences.[16] Because many kinds of operations or reasoning sequences that occur in children's minds involve a combination of skills, it is recommended that teachers provide repetitious tasks in which the same themes are used. Concepts such as conservation of number, area, or weight may be easy to describe in terms of children's success in understanding (or the lack of it) as perceived by an observer evaluating the children, but the skills themselves are not that clear in the way they occur in the human being.[17]

Because of the uncertainty as to when children are clearly able to master certain concepts, the process approach in science is valued by many educators. A definition of process-centered teaching by some authors proceeds from the spirit of a scientist and one in which the teacher and pupils pursue scientific inquiry together.[18] Among some significant goals in that vein are that time is unimportant (experimentation, classification, comparing, measuring, and the like can be done in an unhurried fashion), answers are not given in the materials (questions to find answers are more important than the answers themselves), self-checking on solutions is encouraged by questions to verify one's results, and a constant usage of measuring, predicting, estimating, comparing, classifying, communicating, inferring from results, and analyzing. Practice in this context also permits children to make mistakes, to try something that does not seem logical, to go off on tangents in the process of searching for data that confirm or deny their questions or hypotheses.[19]

Many educators have faith in the process or inquiry types of approach to learning. Bruner suggests that at least four kinds of elements can occur as a result of teaching that proceeds from the discovery point of view for the child: *Intellectual potency* can develop through the student's own assimilation of skills that facilitate problem solving; intrinsic rewards provide satisfaction in the form of confidence that the pupil may derive from discovering facts and generalizations on his/her own impetus and implementation; the child is able to transfer the knowledge that is gained from knowing how to proceed in a certain design or approach in solving problems and in so doing is strengthening significant skills in the scientific approach; and last, children are expected to remember their own conceptualizations as they proceed in tackling a problem, and in that orientation they can recall more effectively what was done in terms of their own meaning, thus using a discovery approach facilitates the processing of memory.[20]

Some writers suggest that a degree of guidance must be given from the teacher if the discovery method is to be effective. Children need a supporting repertoire of some facts in a subject that needs analysis by them. To pursue inquiry without some previous knowledge seems a somewhat unreasonable expectation of minimally motivated children. This would suggest that the teacher becomes crucial in influencing the way questions are asked of the children and how the lessons are structured (directly or indirectly), and also in determining how much time is allotted for the pupils' participation in pursuing what they do not know.

Teachers, however, are also in a position to be able to give ideas to parents who can provide children with experiences at home with pets, plants, soil, caterpillars, butterflies, air, water, sand, or trips to the beach for enjoyment of the ocean. The teacher indicates to the parent that it is not necessary to instruct children in the formal sense of the word, but rather to encourage and nurture children's interests in the environment.

Teachers can also send home with the children various messages regarding skills of observation that can be practiced by drawing what is seen when presented with a small box of five objects. Showing how one object links into another because of a curved edge can be pictorially represented by a child. "Boxes of homework" that the teacher knows will be enjoyed by the child in the presence of the parent can be developed to send home periodically. In this way, scientific orientation can be encouraged in an easy manner.

Even though a walk around the block may seem routine for children and parents, the things that can be collected, observed, and recorded because of the trip can become valuable scientific resources.[21] Questions about houses that are seen, trees, shrubs, flowers, cars, dogs, window shapes in tall and smaller houses, roof styles, and the like yield classification, number, discrimination of color, size, and shape, addition, subtraction, and several comparative forms of conceptualizing information. The science and mathematical reasoning processes are also involved when children experiment, push, roll objects, dig, and pour various liquids and solid or pulverized matter in the activities of play in a yard or playground.[22]

Developmental Awareness in Biological, Earth, and Physical Sciences

The categories of biological, earth, and physical sciences relate to various topics that are named differently when they are offered to children. Topics in the social sciences, as well, are sometimes renamed when taught to children. Children's experiences with nature, with plants, living things, climate and weather, physical changes in matter and energy, ecological imbalance (or balance), wheels, levers, pulleys, and a variety of topics that are more congruent with children's direct involvement, are typically those planned for the classroom or outside the door of one.[23]

Children's experiences in cooking provide several topics related to science such as classifying of objects (e.g., liquids, solids, powdery substances) noting the form of those objects or ingredients, observing the sequence or order of including the ingredients, becoming aware of the change of matter as it is affected by heat, cold, or room temperature), following directions for a recipe, sensing the tastes (e.g., sour, sweet, salty) and discussing the way things look, feel, taste, smell, and may sound when eaten (e.g., crunched, sipped). Noting and discussing the sounds, smells, and tastes, and talking about how things need to be prepared, organized, and processed prior to eating or mixing them together, provide for children the scientist's orientation toward precision and sensing aspects of environment in a careful manner.[24]

Bacteria are a form of plant life. Food is also a part of plant life. Food affects the growth of human beings, who are also living things as classified in some textbooks or teaching units.

Matter is both living and nonliving. Texts involve units that are part of an overall system based not only on processes but on an organization that coincides with the sciences and with the needs of children's conceptualization or the skills that pupils have at certain grade levels. This is not to say that all pupils in the second grade are ready for the same instruction.

The teacher has to know which pupils can become involved in activities that will not be frustrating to them.

Children can collect leaves, rocks, and small plants and note that plants can be classified as vascular and nonvascular. The rocks and leaves can be saved to examine and also to note which types are found around certain plants. Environmental settings are relevant to the way that things grow. Children may be able to note the liquid that passes through the tubular carriers in the plant. They may experiment with celery, for example, which absorbs food coloring when both are placed in a small container or plastic tumbler of water. The celery changes color. The children have noted, however, prior to the food coloring's presence in the water, the color of the celery, its texture, the stalk, and tubular elements in the celery. They learn through careful observation and recording on paper the cause-and-effect stages. It is difficult to remember as distinctly what happened before certain techniques were implemented, as one might if the recording process were not completed well. This is, in fact, one of the most significant aspects of scientific inquiry—to record effectively exactly what was observed.

Children can learn that nonvascular plants, such as mosses, algae, and fungi of various kinds grow in moist areas. Fungi, for example, include mushrooms, molds, rust, and also smut and mildew.[25] Fungi, which grow on other living plants, are parasitic, and have no vascular structure, but reproduce by means of spores and cannot obtain their own food in the ways that other plants do from sunlight. Children can see the algae that are common in bodies of water.

As children learn how to classify, to some extent, various plants in terms of some attributes or characteristics, they begin to acquire greater depth of information. As indicated earlier, however, they do not absorb abstractions without having firsthand experiences with the things, the plants, and the measuring (or writing and recording materials) that are needed for demonstrating awareness of events or details at the children's levels of development.

A field trip to explore the outdoors may be brief or lengthy.[26] The purposes for the trip must be planned so that children gain knowledge from it. Teachers are reminded that the field trip in itself cannot instruct the children. The implications of what the pupils see and how they relate to scientific information become the major concentration, before, during, and after the trip. Drawing, writing, creating poetry or stories about the trip, can also involve the scientific terminology related to the focus of the field trip.

Typically children see vascular plants such as trees, flowers, ferns, or various grasses that constitute the scenery around a school. These plants acquire food from sunlight, which creates chlorophyll or the green effects in the plant. The nonvascular plants are not able to acquire growth through *photosynthesis*, the process that occurs when the sun's energies and light change the chemical elements in a plant. These ideas can be explained and shown to children through simple experiments recommended in books for young children.[27]

The weather and its changes and how atmospheric changes affect the appearance and temperature of the outdoor environment are intriguing to children. Parents and teachers should take full advantage of opportunities to provide (and to ensure the safety of) the children's firsthand experiences involving the elements of weather.[28] Classification of various phenomena that occur outdoors and participation in activities that are simple enough for children to enjoy (and be somewhat challenged by) can be offered as part of a curriculum or program of tasks.

Several ideas are given for the ways that teachers (or parents) may provide a resource idea and stock of materials that can be effectively used with children in their science participation.[29] Included with information on ways to create an excellent personal resource file as well as a teacher's developmental appreciation and preparation for children's experiences with science in the classroom and outdoors, are tips for approaches to use for observation of various phenomena.

For teachers who have not had an extensive background in science prior to classroom work with young children at school, it is recommended that many resources be acquired, for the teacher's level of understanding as well as the child's. Such information can provide stimulation for the teacher, who may have thought that science was complicated beyond easy mastery (especially at earlier levels of learning that are of interest to young children). The manner in which activities and materials are presented to children in contemporary science education permits the "nonscientific" teacher to at least provide the minimal essentials needed by children for their comprehension at beginning levels.

The simplicity of experiments and the clarity of directions for their implementation can be encouraging for the teacher. When the children ask questions that cannot be answered, the teacher merely suggests that the children and teacher find out ways to solve relevant problems. Since process is important in the way children are expected to learn about science today, the teacher can capitalize on helping children value the accuracy of taking more time in seeking answers rather than to give quick, perhaps impulsive answers that stop the search of inquiry.

The teacher's attitudes toward the children's work affect to a great extent the time spent in activities, the quality of thinking that is expressed in children's discussions of the things observed, and the ways that interest and question-raising are sustained throughout the period and as provoking further anticipation for future activities.[30]

Even the activities and materials planned for rainy days provide a provocative list of surprises that may be achieved by the children who pursue the experiential goals that have been planned in the teacher's concerns for scientific work for children.[31] Plans for approaching the curriculum by selecting the area in science in which the teacher feels most comfortable are recommended as a way of initiating the student's interest and also the teacher's self-confidence about science at the beginning of the school year.[32] The rapport that can be engendered with pupils when successful lessons are enjoyed together is considered to be a contribution to the teacher's willingness to continue efforts toward better science lessons as a means of meeting one's own challenges in working well with children.

Teachers may consult sources of information on the earth sciences and the physical sciences to note how the children may pursue through discovery techniques the currently available data in those fields.[33] The teacher may adapt the recommended lessons and either simplify or modify them to suit the needs of a given classroom of pupils.

Teachers may also need to observe their own patterns of interaction with children in order to note whether they are giving adequate time for children to answer questions.[34] The quality of science instructional programs seems to relate to the time allowed (or encouraged) when pupils are in the process of pursuing answers to questions, and also to the kind of reward system the teacher uses. More students seem to answer when they are given more time to do so, their answers are more reflective, and involve an awareness of other hypotheses and explanations. More time between questions and answers also seems to encourage a greater variety of questions (than does less time) from the teacher.[35] It is also recommended that teachers do less of the structuring and questioning and encourage students to react, respond, and question.

Various programs, then, can be helpful in providing recommendations for materials and techniques for implementing some of the processes that are valued in science. Some authors, however, advise that teachers be critical of programs that are offered to them to use for instruction with children. Analytical and experimental studies still need to be made on various programs that have been devised for children to learn about science. Questions regarding the nature of science, how children can best learn about it, and whether it is teachable persist in the minds of those who are still seeking efficacy in science instruction for children.[36] The philosophy of the teacher is still perceived to be a strong influence in the way children learn about science in the classroom. The teacher who is aware of the physiological, emotional, social, and intellectual differences among pupils is the one who adapts to a great extent the information of the science themes to the children's ability and skills developmental levels.

Because sensory information through vision, hearing, taste, smell, and touch is vital to young children's learning to understand the environment, a unit of study on the self or the body is typically helpful for young children. Teachers often present materials to children that will enable them to measure each other's height, length of arms and legs, feet, and the like. Children enjoy doing illustrations of themselves or members of their families, pets, and others that are significant in their lives. A unit on the self includes periodic contributions to a booklet in which a child has drawn or cut out pictures of things and representative themes that the child prefers. The booklet becomes a small treatise on the child's favorite foods, friends, hobbies, habits, books, and other topics that describe the child.

The children see filmstrips, read books, and hear stories about health, growth, and valid health practices related to body care, nutrition, adequate rest, exercise, and various other aspects of the way human beings grow. Although these units are offered in the categories of social studies or health education as well as science, the areas overlap and the teacher provides lessons in acquiring effective skills for self-care.

Writers suggest various techniques for initiating and sustaining interest in children's awareness of individuality in appearance, tastes, skills, lan-

The eye sees _an object._

The mind considers these questions:

What is its shape?

How heavy is it?

What colors are in it?

What does it remind me of?

Where can I put it in my house or school?

How can it be used?

Is it fragile or strong?

When did it first appear on earth?

Why is it here in the classroom?

Could I have a collection of them?

Is it thin or thick?

Is it dark or light?

Will it shrivel in the sun?

Is it alive?

Would my dog hurt it?

Astute Observation Powers: Vision and Interpretation.

guage patterns, and many other aspects of people's qualities.[37] By having children notice their classmate's hands, eyes, nose, fingers, and associating those body parts with what they are able to do, powers of observation are increased as well as information gained on skin textures, shapes, the mechanical aspects of the hand and fingers, and flexibility of joints of the body.

Children can learn how growth occurs and that living things need proper food, care, and rest in cycles that are appropriate to maintaining wise nurturing. They learn that the human body is an intricate mechanism and needs to be treated carefully. Children have to learn that it is dangerous, for example, to rub their eyes when their hands are sandy or have finger paint on them. For children in the early grades, teachers have to discuss often, in a matter-of-fact manner, how essential it is that children be aware of what goes into their mouths, of the dangers of falling if one runs while holding a sharp object in one's hand, and of a number of other actions that can lead to serious accidents and cause injury to their bodies.

The structure of bones, tissue, and blood in one's body, and how the respiratory system works, can be explained at the children's level of comprehension.[38] The skeleton as seen in graphic representations of animals (or as it can be seen in museums), gives children a vague understanding that something exists beneath one's flesh. Here, again, as was mentioned earlier, the teacher's attitude toward this knowledge can affect a receptive response from the children. The value of one's body and of life itself should be made clear in many ways to children.[39] This attitude also engenders respect for the feelings, physically and mentally (or emotionally), of others when the teacher presents the information effectively.

One writer suggests that the use of puppets can provide attractive and effective science lessons for young children.[40] By using a series of lessons on the topic of one's body, children can learn significant information as the teacher discusses the uniqueness of each person's body, the importance of taking good care of one's body, how each person's senses function (even while being aware of the fact that stimuli affect each individual differently). And by means of a structure of straws and wire that resemble a skeleton, the children can gain an understanding of the skeletal structure as well. Simple activities are also recommended in the same vein of the teacher's interaction with the hand puppet and dialogue with it, in which the children obtain some information about the way the human heart works (and pumps blood, air energy) to maintain the body.

Elementary school science textbooks have more complicated sketches and lesson plans for children in the third and fourth grades in which the human body, respiratory functions, the stream of blood through the system, the functions and structure of the eye, and a number of intricate study components are available. One teacher of children in the fourth grade had them make a diagram of the tongue and note the parts of the tongue that sense sweet, sour, salty, or bitter tastes.[41] Clean cotton swabs were used as each child tasted from various vessels, vinegar, salt, sugar, juice, or water. The diagram that the children used to represent the tongue, and upon which they were able to denote the various taste buds, was made of red burlap or felt. Black felt was used to show which areas coincided with specific taste sensations. Often a teacher may adapt activities that were used in upper grades for children in the earlier grades. It depends mainly on the teacher's ingenuity, the psychological, academic, social, and emotional characteristics and levels of children in a particular class.

Organization of materials for science is a crucial part relating to the success of any lesson. All the materials must be assembled before the children are ready to participate. To leave the children after the beginning of the lesson, even if it is only for a short time, to get something from the cupboard, is to break their concentration.

Teachers must always exercise care and caution, too, when specific objects are used for demonstrating science lessons. Accidents or allergic responses among children (regarding tasting) have to be avoided by anticipating (and remembering) which children may have difficulty with certain lessons. Anything that involves electricity must be carefully planned when a process is implemented in the classroom. Some teachers try to have aides, parents, or an older child present when the science lesson involves heat or other elements that may cause accidents. Children become very eager to get up close to see what is happening. They can, in their eagerness, inadvertently hurt themselves or others.

Resource people who can talk to young children about the special care that needs to be taken of the body should visit the classroom periodically, if only to keep pupils updated on current practices regarding nutrition, inoculation procedures, and other knowledge that children should have in order to protect themselves. They need to be aware that what goes into their bodies (poked into an eye or ears), or is swallowed indiscriminately (without care as to what it might have in it) can do damage to bodily functions. Abuse of drugs or other chemical properties can be discussed at the level of children's understanding regarding their need to protect themselves and maintain an effectively functioning body.

Various unusual and amusing facts about food, and aspects related to how food purchases occur, are available in a number of places, from manufacturers pamphlets on foods to entertaining booklets for children.[42] Supermarkets, health stores, libraries, and shopping mall fairs devoted to good health practices for a community provide excellent sources. Teachers and parents, however, must be selective about what they offer children. Criteria for determining what constitutes healthful food that the body needs for effective nutrition should be explained to children. The milk foods, bread and cereals, vegetables and fruits, and protein groups can be pointed out to children through various charts that companies send to teachers.[43]

Some school systems provide the textbooks that will be used in the classroom. Some schools are allowed to choose among several textbook series that may have been selected by a state committee. In any case, the teacher must have some basic knowledge to know how to involve the children effectively so that pupils know what the scientific process is and how facts can be determined through that process. One book for teachers indicates at higher levels of information what the teacher should know about the human body and how it works, for example, and in several sections following that explanation, describes ideas and activities that can be used with children of various ages.[44] The teacher has to be in search of various materials that can be offered at the level of skills that can be managed by the children. Thus, not only are books that give scientific data in the substantive sense directly to the teacher an important consideration, but also important are those books that can be used directly by the children.[45]

Because the attitudes that are developed with young children in the experiences they have in science are crucial to the way they approach the subject, teachers have to have resource materials organized well in boxes, cartons, or plastic containers, and labeled as to the contents or purposes. Many common household objects, such as straws, wire, lids, plastic containers of many sizes and shapes, spools of thread, paper plates and cups are ready-made materials that are needed for science lessons. Teachers may also want to know, in general, how children's minds work at certain ages and to what extent the children may be able to understand abstractions. References to the works of many writers who interpret Piaget's work and those who implement classroom activities to coincide with some of the developmental stages described by Piaget may be consulted.[46] Generally, then, the teacher must be aware of the nature of children's abilities to abstract information and also must know how to provide activities that will be easy for children to do and at the same time will stretch their minds to some extent—short of the point of extreme frustration.

Young children need many opportunities, as mentioned earlier, to work with real objects and to form generalizations about how those objects function. As they progress in their thinking, they will be able to become aware of internal thought and how they arrived at a solution. They will be able to retrace their sequences of thinking. When individuals are able to abstract and reason about concepts, without having the articles they are thinking about present in the environment, it will be possible for them to transcend the real and mentally manipulate possibilities of thought.

Even though children are able to imagine possibilities and to play with objects that are represented in the children's minds as something else, this is not the same as being able to think in an abstract sense, to reason, and to be aware of how one reached an analysis or end product when thinking about an idea. It is difficult for young children to be aware of contradictory statements that they made (and this may still be true at times for adults). Children do not always remember what they thought in a sequence of reasoning.

Abstract thought that occurs in the formal operational phase, as Piaget terms it, occurs at about fourteen or fifteen. Some writers raise doubts about whether a high per cent of adolescents and adults actually achieve the skills involved in being able to think logically as can the mathematician or scientist.[47] An internal consistency of thinking or analysis, as the scientist is involved in it, does not need an external type of validation, rather it is validated within certain rules of logic. For the human mind to reflect upon itself, is remarkable.

Parents can be helped in understanding that the terms, technology, process, observation codes, and combinations of ideas that are part of the scientific structure and its viewpoints hold the keys to understanding relationships between the environment and the field of science. Children at school are becoming more familiar with the discipline. Often, however, children are blocked in their learning because they have heard that science is difficult. It is not so much difficult to learn about and understand as it is an area that has been maligned, in a sense, by people who have not had adequate preparation in elementary school. These people transmit to their young the notion that science is abstract, dull, and difficult to master.

Even the concept of touching along with tasting, smelling, seeing, and hearing presents topical and easily learned ideas each day. The opportunities for learning about science exist. Adults need to become more familiar with the relationships between those opportunities and the terms or processes that are part of the scientific framework.

Pupils have to have things, the natural and mutable properties of those things in the original state, plus the variations and processes that accompany the original condition, elaborated for them in words, labels, and touch sensations. An extremely important sense of the human body is the one associated with vision. The biological properties of the eyes are one aspect of seeing. Many of the other sensitized elements that affect the way one sees the world of things, people, and events are involved in perceptions. *How* one looks at the world, *what* one sees in it, *how* one judges the things seen (even to *how* one describes the world)—these interpretations relate to the way one processes personal perceptions. Perceptions are in part judgment, emotions, knowledge (that is not purely scientific), and factual receptiveness as well as the way the physical aspects of the body function.

Vision in the biological or physiological sense is one part of the seeing process that is necessary for scientific awareness. Observation is a form of vision with intent to concentrate on what is being seen to the point of being able to describe it later after it is not physically present in the environment. Recalling a visual image is significant in learning. The schooling process builds its curriculum on this skill. It is assumed that everyone who has normal eyesight qill be able to see. The schooling process formalizes the observation and recall internal operation in the human brain.[48]

Art and science are significantly associated in their uses of vision. Although art may represent an internal form of thought or image, science is more dependent on external evidence of a thing, event, person, or place. Both subject matter areas rely heavily, however, on a way of seeing or perceiving. Each, art and science, begins in a sense, with perception of one form or another. The body relates in some way to the external environment. It follows with a representation within the brain. One may then either talk about it or draw or paint it.

Inventions, Processes, and Machines

Children who have grown up in the age of television, missile rockets, walks by astronauts on the moon, and the computerized effects on a myriad of tasks and activities in daily living take for granted that these things exist. As time goes on, however, with the evidence of new machines and intricate mechanisms that become part of a home or business, one can be impressed with the products of the human brain. Because of the number of gadgets or conveniences that seem to appear often, it is also easy to accept and become less overwhelmed by the discoveries made possible by the work of human minds. Children, however, should be encouraged to appreciate the fact that people, not machines, created and developed the ideas that were used for those inventions—and that through them humankind acts on the environment.

The implementation, tools, materials, and processes are available in the province of science, but it is the minds of people who trigger the creation of new machines, computers, and missiles of incredible speed and impact as well as accuracy in the target zones. Children need to know that the power of the human mind makes the difference between effective and non-effective living, either in the world or for the individual. They are able to understand at their levels how certain inventions have become significant for them.

WHEELS

Children enjoy hearing about the invention of the wheel. It is impossible for them to think of life without wheels. Young children do not understand the time aspect of history in its abstractive sense and how long ago the wheel was first invented. They can learn, however, how the wheel affected the solution to a problem of transportation. They can learn how much easier it was to turn a round rather than a square-shaped mode of transportation propelling or carrying a vehicle or slight cart of some kind.[49]

PULLEYS

When children first see a pulley bringing an object from one place to another, or bringing force to a container being conveyed on a pulley-connected belt or rope, they are intrigued.[50] Teachers can make pulleys by obtaining the parts at a hardware store and show children what the major principles of their dynamics are. If the teacher has not had sufficient experience with the development of a pulley, a parent who has done it and is familiar with the mechanics of one can be invited to show the children how to do it. This is an effective way to involve parents and an important way to help parents realize what their own skills are in relation to science for children.

LEVERS

The machine that is operated by a lever may be seen by children in the toys that they have. A switch, turning something on or off, making the machine go faster or slower, also provides a form of control that children are able to observe. Children can cut out of the newspaper or magazines various machines that are operated by a lever. Lifting, lowering, stopping, or accelerating things that people use have to be regulated in some way. Again children can be helped in understanding why levers were invented, how they protect people, and how they provide a way for people to adapt well to the environment, making things that work for human beings.

MICROSCOPES AND TELESCOPES

Microscopes and telescopes were planned to provide more refined observations than could be accomplished by the human eye. The human eye is not as endowed with abilities to make magnified observations as are those two inventions. Children need to know this in order to appreciate why these objects were invented. Again, closely affiliated with the need to invent them is the awareness that a human mind, or several of them, developed objects that allowed humankind to enjoy and to help the world in its various functions. Children need to know that they too can be inventive and that they can plan things or machines to help others.

Children are amazed to see a piece of hair, fingernail, or other object under the microscope and to become aware of bacteria and other forms of life that are not visible to the human eye without the use of a microscope. They should be encouraged to draw what they see. It becomes a reality for them and also provides them with an opportunity to use the scientific principles of observation, record keeping, and reporting.

The telescope and its usefulness in seeing astronomical bodies in the sky can be shown to them in pictures. If it is possible for them to visit a planetarium and to experience the phenomena in seeing the sky through a telescope, this would be excellent for them. Ideas for teaching about the telescope and how it functions can be obtained from local observatory/planetarium agencies and from books dealing with the information that the teacher needs and containing sections for teaching young children in the elementary school.[51]

Young children cannot absorb complexities in inventions. They can hear for the most part, perhaps, that Edison had something to do with electricity, that Bell had something to do with the telephone, that Whitney had something to do with cotton. Libraries have information on these topics at many levels. Precision comes later for young children. More information comes later, too. In the kindergarten and first grade, children are exposed to many ideas and inventions—a name, an item, many years ago—that a person thought of before it became a household product which few people would want to be without.

Some inventors, also artists, medical or anatomical drafters were unusual in their skills or capacities to accomplish many things. Leonardo da Vinci is one such person. His drawings of the human body and his paintings were awe-inspiring. Before the universe became as complicated, diverse, multifaceted, and multipopulated as it is today, many men were able to produce in various fields such as the arts, medicine, and creative inventions. The ability to create encompassed several topical disciplines. In present-day society, however, the sciences have proliferated into many forms, such as auditory sciences, respiratory sciences, visual sciences (related to various aspects of the body). As various fields within science develop and combine with each other, more information is discovered through research. More information makes it necessary to classify, identify, and magnify in deeper perspectives what is known and to allow for new information to be integrated.

Thus, while inventors of the past might have done many things in several fields, one must also be aware that classifications among sciences and other fields were not as prevalent then as they are in contemporary society. There are geniuses today as there were in the past. Children need to realize, however, that all the things that were invented were invented by people. The inventions were not "natural" developments as compared to trees, flowers, animals, and people. People had to think and to create. They had to dream. They had to implement ideas that grew from their own imagination. This is what it is hoped children can learn from teachers at school. Children's minds either create opportunities for them or deny them experiences that they can enjoy and from which they can learn about the world. They may also contribute to that world. Their minds can create things that give pleasure not only to themselves but to many other people.

Science may be an exacting discipline. But it also allows for creation, free thinking, and exploring. The imagination that in itself pulls away from the routine and the constraints of conformity is an excellent means for mental acuity. The apparent contradiction between conformity and imagination focuses on the need for teacher information. Children need to deviate from conformity, logic, and orderly sequential thinking at certain times, and to be allowed them an appreciation for original viewpoints. An orientation toward playfulness, originality, and flights of fancy can encourage a variety of concepts and ideas. Scientists obtain their "leaps" to discovery when they permit intuition and free-form thinking to occur.

One of the skills in teaching requires that a teacher know when to encourage one form of activity over another. Children cannot be creative in spelling the words, *cat*, or *dog*, for example, in whatever way they wish if they are to know how to communicate those words correctly or to understand them in reading. Children can be creative where specificity does not convey a message such as is carried by correct spelling or reading forms.

Machines, which are the creation of necessity and which may arise from the playful spirit of the individual who wants to make life easier in some way, can become the basis for various forms of industrialism. The United States in its technological phases became different from the way it was before manufacturing in mass production numbers occurred. Society is now experienced differently than it was in an age that did not supply materials, goods, and services as productively as has been done in contemporary years. The beginning of factories and widespread accessibility to easier living for some groups in the population influenced new experiences in living for many.

Science, industrialism, and mass production of serviceable goods brought about a new view of scientifically engineered machines. Often the industrial processes were created because of practical concerns for more efficient ways of producing materials or services. Eventually, science, shifted from its theoretical/imaginative orientation to a practical level, and emerged to affect routine or everyday living. It was no longer seen from an esoteric, medically oriented perspective. Children need to be aware even of the development of frozen foods and how food processing was affected by scientific knowledge. Protecting foods from spoiling, from developing growth of bacteria, or from nonsanitary storing or shipping practices are all part of scientific and research studies.

The preparation of milk and cheese, of breads and most things made of flour, involves the studied process of safe edible products. Often the public is advised of cooking practices using foods, liquids, or canned substances that may have been improperly prepared and are consequently unsafe for human consumption. Chemical additives are noted, too, for carcinogenetic qualities. People are warned. They make the choice as to whether they will eat the products that are publicized as cancer-producing.

Machines sort out the improperly processed foods. Even in the packing process, machines designed by people set into motion the scientifically based processing functions that will protect consumers. Again, although children do not comprehend the total conceptualization of machines and processes, they can understand at minimal levels the purposes of such functions and the motivation underlying them.

Designing a bubble machine with a straw and paper cup that has been pierced at the bottom to allow the straw to come through, shows children how simple articles can become an "efficient" device for bubbles. Using a wire clothes hanger pulled to form a diamond-shaped form around which a nylon stocking has been stretched (just the bottom half of the stocking), creates a paddle about the size of a ping-pong racket. This can be used to play with a light-weight styrofoam ball, much like a shuttlecock, which is tapped back and forth among several players. Children enjoy creating. They like what they make if the teachers and others appreciate it too. It is a scientific endeavor, however, to take one form of material and change it in form and function to meet a need.

Children can eventually learn how science is relevant to simple as well as complicated things or machines in the world. They learn that science explains phenomena in the natural and physical environment. It describes patterns of behavior in objects, events, people, and animals. It has the capacity to predict because of a structured inquiry process created by humankind.

If parents are given simple booklets (not because they are unintelligent but because the booklets will expedite time for them when they want to help their children), that can give them examples of scientific phenomena in the every day environment, parents may know when to call children's attention to certain products or machines. Parents need specific data, as do the children. Often the parents want to help but are not sure how to do it.

The names of the processes can be linked into what the parent uses daily and experiences in terms of the processes being described. Food, weather, bathing, and being outdoors involve the processes of change just described. When the parent realizes that the association with the terms and the reality of the examples that can be used for them in children's lives can be easily brought out at home, they may be willing to become involved in the scientific explanatory process with children.

Children are led into thinking about rain or weather conditions, for example. They can see how a pan of water becomes dry after it has been placed near heat. They can discuss why heat absorbs moisture. They can observe after a pan has been placed in darkness or in a cool place how the pan of water appears. The absorption of water is slow.

Pictures must accompany concept development for young children. Pictures help at any age when people are learning new ideas. Besides the pictures, films, film strips, various audio-visual aids and other graphs, posters, actual experiments, and repetition whenever possible on a new concept help children master understanding.

Chemical changes of one form of matter to another are not understood in the symbolic and abstract nature possible at later levels of science learning. Children can easily see, however, that the boiling of water for gelatine powder, becomes different in shape, form, and taste after it undergoes another temperature treatment in the refrigerator where it has been chilled. They can at least see how the hot mixture becomes cold and solid after it has been refrigerated and before it is eaten. The teacher can explain what the children are able to comprehend. Accurate answers are given to questions related to boiling water, cold acting on heat, and changes in form by means of energy.

One of the significant issues related to body equilibrium in contemporary society is stress and its effects on the human body and mind. Mental health has been an issue of study and research in the last twenty years. Sustained stress on the body has deleterious effects. When children do not feel well, they can tell their parents or the teacher and can consequently help themselves to live a better life than they would in ignoring body signals. There is a self-knowledge that comes with the educational process and one which should not be ignored or taken lightly.

Teachers in the primary grades can do a great deal to help the present and future generation live a healthier, happier life by heeding the scientific knowledge of the past decade. Of course, the physical and the life sciences relate intricately to the social sciences. They have to be understood in tandem throughout the growth cycle. Teachers, however, can "dispense" truth, caring, concern, and genuine desires for finding effective solutions with each new group of children they meet.

Science, with its highly technical and sophisticated processes and findings can be brought to the level of children's appreciation. The precision, measurement, tactile, visual, olfactory, kinesthetic, taste, and auditory aspects of scientific processes experienced by children each day can contribute to later understanding at an abstract level. The process is slow, but it is worth the attention given to it.

SUMMARY

This chapter emphasized the need for young children to know about science through well-programmed activities geared toward fostering favorable attitudes toward the discipline. Even though young children are not typically capable of managing abstract thought to the extent that science concepts involve patterns of logic and sequential thought, they are, however, capable of seeing noncomplicated relationships between objects and elements such as heat, energy, cold, light, and darkness.

Between the ages of four and five to about eleven or twelve, children are, as Piaget views it, in the prelogical and concrete reasoning stage of intellectual development. These years coincide with the kindergarten year to the end of the elementary school. During these years, children are learning to reason with things in the immediate environment and can learn to solve problems with those objects present. It is suggested that to give children science lessons that do not include real objects is an error in judgment of the curriculum planner. Children have to act on the items in order to ascertain data from them. Their own internal understanding builds on their manipulation of the objects.

Most writers in science education for children suggest that it is extremely important that teachers help children enjoy experiments and activities in science that have meaning and relevance for pupils. The time that teachers must take to allow for handling of objects, making comments, asking questions, examining materials, writing or illustrating what is seen, classifying, identifying, and observing effectively has to be planned wisely. Some writers are concerned that teachers do not allow sufficient time for children's questions, for curiosity to be aroused, and for touching the objects offered for science orientations.

Various approaches are used with young children in science classrooms. Activities can be adapted to the four-, five-, and six-year-old children to include experiences with weather, heat, cold, and other aspects of activities that involve things that are familiar to the child. Children can measure plants, themselves, and objects in the classroom. As measurement of real objects is a component of science skills, pupils should do this when possible, and the teacher should record (or write) the results on the board.

Observing is one of the essential skills in developing accuracy and reporting correctly in a science experience. Kits of materials that can be measured and classified by the children in terms of color, shape, size, or texture can provide an important review for the pupils. Children may be asked to guess what might happen if a certain object were mixed with others; might it appear lost or outstanding? The teacher encourages children to ask questions. They should be doing more of the talking than the teacher, raising questions, trying to solve problems, and creating different positions and structures with the materials.

In the fourth grade, children are beginning to make inferences and interpreting data leading to hypothetical formulations. They use materials at hand. After investigating various aspects of an experiment, and observing the solution(s), children may formulate ideas, reasons, or hypothetical statements as to why the solution occurred in the way it did.

The biological, the physical, and the earth sciences, as scientists classify them, are translatable to children's experiences in the activities that have meaning for them in the classroom. At early levels of understanding, children can become familiar with their world through interaction with planting seeds, growing plants, classifying and measuring, comparing and inferring from action on things that are familiar to them.

An understanding of various processes involving foods, inventions, and other things that families use can be accomplished by pupils who are shown aspects of operations that contribute to frozen food processes, to pasteurized milk, to various mechanical household objects (electrical mixing machines, cooking utensils) and other unique inventions that were created from ideas of the human mind. Children need to understand that telephones, automobiles, and airplanes were products of creativity applied to scientific means of implementation.

Among the most essential efforts in sciences lessons are those in which the teacher helps the children develop an attitude of willingness to participate in asking questions, in being curious, and in pursuing unusual courses of thought or using imaginative thinking, even, with the need, at other times, to remember scientific rules of investigation. The teacher should not hurry investigative processes for the pupils. They need to develop their own internal framework of understanding before scientific abstractions can mean anything to them. Teachers need to be sensitive to timing and to know when it is appropriate to offer certain activities relative to the skills and abilities of the pupils of a given classroom.

TOPICS FOR DISCUSSION

1. Select three major activities for children in kindergarten that you think are appropriate for (a) a simple level of understanding; (b) a moderate level of understanding; (c) an advanced level of understanding on the topic of pets. Show how these activities would advance children's levels of thinking about a science of animals, birds, fish (whatever pets you have chosen for study).
2. Bring five books to the university classroom in which discussion for children's development in science seems to be clear, relevant, and age-appropriate. Those books may have been written for the teacher or they may be books directed toward children who know how to read well. Indicate why you have selected those books. Why do they present clearly what you think children should know? On what basis does the author (or do the authors) provide a rationale for the readers, thereby showing how a framework for study can be used? A rationale refers to justification for a statement or idea. Although you are aware of this, children are not. They need to have ideas defined, described in several ways, and presented at their level of understanding.
3. Demonstrate ideas to pupils that you think would illuminate principles of air including its properties of weight, space, and mixture properties. (Select three activities to discuss that could be used with children in the first, second, or third grades.)
4. Find six kinds of rocks. Show how you would use them to create a lesson for the children in the third grade (eight-year-olds) and indicate what you would expect them to do as a future project as a result of your lessons.
5. Create a unit on nutrition with children that would show them how their bodies gain energy and vitality from a diet composed of healthful foods. Have them bring picture examples (from newspapers or magazines or supermarket posters) of vegetables, milk foods, proteins, or meats, wheats, breads, or cereals.
6. Write a unit and discuss its implementation for parents who want children to develop a basis at home or in their travels for understanding elementary science concepts related to air, earth, ecology, the wheel, the airplane, or other basic topics of your choice.
7. List the significant qualities that can be learned by children when they develop the characteristics needed to pursue the truth (objectivity) of scientific investigations.
8. Describe the ways that teachers who are not comfortable with pursuing information in science can develop a sense of confidence in themselves. How can they also provide excitement for children they teach so that the study of science can be anticipated eagerly as part of the school day?
9. Why is it important for every child to know something about the qualities and skills required for a search for truth or objectivity? How does it apply to everyday life so that one can protect the self from events or situations that can be deceiving? Why do children need it so that they can receive their fair share of the "good things" in life? Why do teachers need it?
10. Briefly describe the relationships between Piaget's perceived stages of prelogical and concrete intellectual development in children and the nature of activities in science that can be offered to children.

NOTES

1. Louis I. Kuslan and A. Harris Stone, *Teaching Children Science: An Inquiry Approach*, 2nd ed. (Belmont, Calif.: Wadsworth, 1972), p. 55. Even though observation begins in early years, children will begin to sharpen their powers of observation in a systematic way at school if they experience structured opportunities to seek certain identification properties of things with certain principles.

2. William K. Esler, *Teaching Elementary Science* (Belmont, Calif.: Wadsworth, 1973), p. 11.

3. Jean Piaget, *Psychology of Intelligence* (Paterson, N.J.: Littlefield, Adams, 1960), 182 pp. Note also Herbert Ginsburg and Sylvia Opper, *Piaget's Theory of Intellectual Development*, 2nd ed. (Englewood Cliffs, N.J.: Prentice-Hall, 1979); and Constance Kamii and Rheta DeVries, *Physical Knowledge in Preschool Education* Englewood Cliffs, N.J.: Prentice-Hall, 1978).

4. Ronald G. Good, *How Children Learn Science* (New York: Macmillan, 1977), p. 327. Good indicates that stages of development do not exist; rather there are categories that people use in order to communicate their own ideas about a way of perceiving the world. He suggests that students and others, although valuing an idea for its provocative nature, be cautioned against accepting noncritically the conceptualization of stages without being aware of the overall implications of what is being assumed if one agrees with such concepts.

5. Imogene Forte and Joy MacKenzie, *Creative Science Experiences for the Young Child* (Nashville, Tenn.: Incentive Publications, 1973).

6. Esler, op. cit., pp. 31–51, discusses reasons for using the inquiry approach which involves children in solving problems by asking questions. The rational approach represents open-ended questions asked by the teacher, who guides the children toward generalization and solutions; the discovery approach allows the children to manipulate materials, discovering qualities by themselves to some extent; and the experimental approach involves the children in defining data and controlling various elements in experimental situations.

7. Ibid., p. 52.

8. Ibid., p. 107. SAPA (Science: A Process Approach), involves the children more in process than in the acquisition of content. Teachers need to follow the sequential development in this program because the designers of it consider the order of learning to be significant for children's growth in conceptual and processing skills.

9. Doreen J. Croft and Robert D. Hess, *An Activities Handbook for Teachers of Young Children*, 3rd ed. (Boston: Houghton, 1980). See especially the sections on science and on mathematics, cooking, and ecology.

10. Evelyn Goodenough Pitcher, Miriam G. Lasher, Sylvia G. Feinburg, and Linda Abrams Braun, *Helping Young Children Learn*, 3rd ed. (Columbus, Ohio: Merrill, 1979), pp. 166–175. See also, Rosemary Althouse and Cecil Main, *Science Experiences for Young Children: As We Grow* (New York: Teachers College, 1975), 38 pp.

11. Doyal Nelson and Joan Kirkpatrick, "Problem Solving," pp. 70–93 in *Mathematics Learning in Early Childhood*, Thirty-seventh Yearbook, National Council of Teachers of Mathematics (Reston, Va.: The National Council of Teachers of Mathematics, Inc., 1975). Mary Baratta-Lorton, *Mathematics Their Way* (Menlo Park, Calif.: Addison-Wesley, 1976).

12. David P. Butts, *Teaching Science in the Elementary School* (New York: Free Press, a Division of Macmillan, 1973) pp. 79–125. The Elementary Science Study (ESS) emphasizes that children be involved in their own discovery of facts, sequences, and generalizations.

13. Kuslan and Stone, op. cit., pp. 228–254.

14. Ibid., p. 229.

15. Such objects as paper clips, rubber bands, string, squeeze-type plastic bottles, are among those used for experimenting. Children enjoy watching the attraction of a magnet acting upon clips and other metal objects. Objects that are not picked up by the magnet are also handled by children as they experiment with several types of materials.

16. Good, op. cit., p. 109.

17. Ibid. The attainment of operational understanding as Good views the skill, rather than the way an experiment describes it, has been developing prior to the point that a child may be tested for it. He suggests that a variety of scientific skills have been increasing in children before they are perceived to be *in* a "stage" of development. The cluster of abilities required to perform certain tasks do not simply appear suddenly as one total operation or accomplishment on a given day, and consequently warrant a justifiable judgment of the child's arrival at stage containment. The gradual and even inconsistent understanding of concepts that occurs with growth does not allow for full confidence that once a child has given some answers to a problem that child has sufficient comprehension of certain skills to apply his/her new knowledge in other situations as well.

18. Kuslan and Stone, op. cit., pp. 186–187.
19. Ibid., p. 187.
20. Ibid., pp. 188–189.
21. Kenneth W. Kelsey, "A Neighborhood Field Trip," *Science and Children* Vol. 16, No. 7 (April 1979), pp. 14–15.
22. Rita Swedlow, "Problem Solving on the Playground," *Science and Children* Vol. 16, No. 7 (April 1979); pp. 20–21.
23. Mary Yates Hall, *Simple Science Experiences,*, Instructor Handbook Series (Dansville, N.Y.: Instructor Publications, 1972). The topics for experiences are machines and energy, living things, surface of the earth, the sky above, climate and weather, seasonal change, and the child.
24. Oralie McAfee, Evelyn W. Haines, Barbara Bullman Young, and Patricia Maloney Markun. *Cooking and Eating with Children*, Washington, D.C.; Assoc. for Childhood Education International, 1974). See also Croft and Hess, op. cit.; pp. 201–227.
25. Esler, op. cit.; p. 129.
26. Don W. Jurgs, "The Real World Out There," *Science and Children* Vol. 16, No. 7 (April 1979); p. 12.
27. Rosemary Althouse and Cecil Main, Science Experiences for Young Children: *Seeds* (New York: Teachers College, 1975). See also, Hall, op. cit., pp. 18–20. An interesting experiment on the way certain materials can be used in watering one's plants is shown in Elin McCoy, *The Incredible Year-Round Playbook* (New York: Random, 1979), p. 49. An experiment with food coloring and the way it "moves" water is shown on the opposite page (48), indicating the properties of liquids and the way they affect things.
28. Hall, op. cit., pp. 27–41. Croft and Hess, op. cit., pp. 161–198 includes a variety of processes that are affected by ecology, lightning, thunder, rain, and air pressure, among other characteristics or attributes. Good, op. cit., pp. 281–294, presents tasks, approaches, and probing questions that can be used by the teacher, and questions that the children may ask about things and experiences in the outdoor environment.
29. Bess-Gene Holt, *Science With Young Children* (Washington, D.C.: National Assoc. for the Education of Young Children, 1977). Among many ideas for developing a collection of materials, are warnings about things that are not safe for children. A listing of common plants that are poisonous and the symptoms shown in children who taste those plants is included for easy reference.
30. Good, op. cit., pp. 217–243, emphasizes the role of the teacher in guiding the children through stimulating activities. The teacher can facilitate children's thinking effectively if the classroom atmosphere permits individual learning to occur at various levels. Kuslan and Stone, op. cit., pp. 486–505, suggest a variety of ways that teachers may plan for a science program for children of varying abilities.
31. Holt, op. cit., p. 23. The teacher can provide the unexpected by arranging the time and space in the classroom environment to include activities involving surprise, novelty, humor, even by making "scientific" centerpieces of scientific objects at lunch gatherings, and in that way utilize technically related scientific ideas. Such activities can sustain the attitudes (and playful discovery) in science experiences. Pp. 40–43 in Holt.
32. Ronald D. Anderson, Alfred DeVito, Odvard Egil Dyrli, Maurice Kellogg, Leonard Kochendorfer, and James Weigand, *Developing Children's Thinking* (Englewood Cliffs, N.J.: Prentice-Hall, 1970), p. 259.
33. Robert B. Sund, Bill W. Tillery, and Leslie W. Trowbridge, *Elementary Science Discovery Lessons. The Earth Sciences* (Boston: Allyn, 1970). Robert B. Sund, Bill W. Tillery, and Leslie W. Trowbridge, *Elementary Science Discovery Lessons. The Physical Sciences* (Boston: Allyn, 1970).
34. Linda Snyder, "How Effective Are Our Teaching Practices?" *Science and Children* Vol. 16. No. 1 (September 1978), pp. 31–33. Note. p. 32.
35. Ibid., p. 33.
36. Ibid.
37. Holt, op. cit., pp. 86–88.
38. Forte and MacKenzie, op. cit., pp. 127–159.
39. Joanne Hendrick, *Total Learning for the Whole Child* (Saint Louis, Mo.: Mosby, 1980), pp. 37–43.

40. Jean Harlan, *Science Experiences for the Early Childhood Years*, 2nd ed. (Columbus, Ohio: Merrill, 1980), pp. 203–227.
41. Geraldine D. Thompson, "Where Do You Taste?" *Science and Children*, Volume 16, No. 8 (May 1979), p. 25.
42. Marilyn Burns, *Good For Me!* (Boston: Little, Brown, 1978).
43. University and college bookstores have booklets that indicate places for teachers to write for free materials. Dental associations, insurance companies, and medical offices as well, have materials that are useful for teachers. Communities are doing more than was done in past years to provide public health information and are happy to distribute materials to interested people.
44. Glenn O. Blough and Julius Schwartz, *Elementary School Science and How to Teach It*, 5th ed. (New York: Holt, 1974), pp. 346–386.
45. McCoy, op. cit. See also, Pat Blakely, Barbara Haislet, and Judith Hentges, *Free Stuff for Kids* (Wayzata, Minn. Meadowbrook Press, 1979).
46. Ginsburg and Opper, op. cit.; Kamii and DeVries, op. cit.; Good, op. cit., pp. 149–154.
47. Good. op. cit., p. 141.
48. A file box of activities that involve only the five senses is not difficult to develop. Many teachers cut articles from the newspaper or magazines, paste them on 5½" x 8½" cards, and classify them for their own use under each of the senses. They also have headings for animals, pets, insects, weather, plants, time, energy, ecology, and water. Some may want to broaden a section on ecology including ideas for land abuse, energy abuse, relationships between human use of the environment and the effects of those activities and the appearance or effectiveness of the land.
49. Rosemary Althouse and Cecil Main, Science Experiences for Young Children: *Wheels* (New York: Teachers College, 1975), 27 pp.
50. *Messages. Sending and Receiving Them* (A Puffin Book. Penguin Books: Australia Ltd., Melbourne, Australia, 1978), pp. 19–20.
51. Blough and Schwartz, op. cit., pp. 196–217.

SELECTED REFERENCES

ALTHOUSE, ROSEMARY, and CECIL MAIN. Science Experiences for Young Children: *As We Grow; Colors* 47 pp; *Foods* 35 pp; *Pets* 43 pp; *Seeds* 36 pp.; *Wheels* 27 pp. New York: Teachers College Press, Columbia University, 1975.

ANDERSON, RONALD D., ALFRED DEVITO, ODVARD EGIL DYRLI, MAURICE KELLOGG, LEONARD KOCHENDORFER, JAMES WEIGAND. *Developing Children's Thinking Through Science.* Englewood Cliffs, N.J.: Prentice-Hall, Inc., 1970. 370 pp.

BARATTA-LORTON, MARY. *Mathematics Their Way.* Menlo Park, Calif.: Addison-Wesley Publishing Co., Inc., 1976. 398 pp.

BLAKELY, PAT, BARBARA HAISLET, and JUDITH HENTGES. *Free Stuff for Kids.* Wayzata, Minn.: Meadowbrook Press, 1979. 116 pp.

BLOUGH, GLENN O., and JULIUS SCHWARTZ. *Elementary School Science and How to Teach It*, 5th ed. New York: Holt, Rinehart and Winston, 1974. 753 pp.

BURNS, MARILYN. *Good for Me!* Boston: Little, Brown and Company, 1978. 127 pp.

BUTTS, DAVID P. *Teaching Science in the Elementary School.* New York: The Free Press, a Division of Macmillan Publishing Co., Inc., 1973. 199 pp.

CROFT, DOREEN J. and ROBERT D. HESS. *An Activities Handbook for Teachers of Young Children*, 3rd ed. Boston: Houghton Mifflin Company, 1980. 257 pp.

ESLER, WILLIAM K. *Teaching Elementary Science.* Belmont, Calif.: Wadsworth Publishing Co., Inc. 1973. 566 pp.

FORTE, IMOGENE, and JOY MACKENZIE. *Creative Science Experiences for the Young Child.* Nashville, Tenn.: Incentive Publications, Inc., 1973. 161 pp.

GINSBURG, HERBERT, and SYLVIA OPPER. *Piaget's Theory of Intellectual Development*, 2nd ed. Englewood Cliffs, N.J.: Prentice-Hall, Inc., 1979. 253 pp.

GOOD, RONALD G. *How Children Learn Science.* New York: Macmillan Publishing Company, Inc., 1977. 337 pp.

HALL, MARY YATES. *Simple Science Experiences*. Dansville, N.Y.: The Instructor Publications, Inc., 1972. 47 pp.

HARLAN, JEAN. *Science Experiences for the Early Childhood Years*, 2nd ed. Columbus, Ohio: Charles E. Merrill Publishing Company, 1980. 237 pp.

HENDRICK, JOANNE. *Total Learning for the Whole Child*. Saint Louis, Mo.: The C. V. Mosby Company, 1980. 405 pp.

HOLT, BESS-GENE. *Science With Young Children*. Washington, D.C.: National Association for the Education of Young Children, 1977. 134 pp.

JURGS, DON W. "The Real World Out There," *Science and Children,* Vol. 16, No. 7 (April 1979), p. 12.

KAMII, CONSTANCE, and RHETA DEVRIES. *Physical Knowledge in Preschool Education*. Englewood Cliffs, N.J.: Prentice-Hall, Inc., 1978. 321 pp.

KELSEY, KENNETH W. "A Neighborhood Field Trip," *Science and Children* Vol. 16, No. 7 (April 1979), pp. 14–15.

KUSLAN, LOUIS I., and A. HARRIS STONE. *Teaching Children Science: An Inquiry Approach*, 2nd ed. Belmont, Calif.: Wadsworth Publishing Co., Inc., 1972. 533 pp.

McAFEE, ORALIE, EVELEN W. HAINES, BARBARA BULLMAN YOUNG, and PATRICIA MALONEY MARKUN. *Cooking and Eating with Young Children*. Washington, D.C.: Association for Childhood Education International, 1974. 48 pp.

McCOY, ELIN. *The Incredible Year-Round Playbook*. New York: Random House, Inc., 1979. 96 pp.

McPHEE GRIBBLE PUBLISHERS. *Messages. Smells*. A Puffin Book. Penguin Books, Australia, Ltd., 1978. 32 pp. each book.

MAYESKY, MARY, DONALD NEUMAN, and RAYMOND J. WLODKOWSKI. *Crative Activities for Young Children*. Albany, N.Y.: Delmar Publications, 1975. 195 pp.

NELSON, DOYAL, and JOAN KIRKPATRICK. "Problem Solving," pp. 70–93 in *Mathematics Learning in Early Childhood*, Thirty-seventh Yearbook, National Council of Teachers of Mathematics. Reston, Va.: The National Council of Teachers of Mathematics, Inc., 1975. 297 pp.

PIAGET, JEAN. *Psychology of Intelligence*. Paterson, N.J.: Littlefield, Adams and Company, 1960. 182 pp.

PITCHER, EVELYN GOODENOUGH MIRIAM G. LASHER, SYLVIA G. FEINBURG, and LINDA ABRAMS BRAUN. *Helping Young Children Learn*, 3rd ed. Columbus, Ohio: Charles E. Merrill Publishing Company, 1979. 209 pp.

Science and Children. National Science Teachers Association, Washington, D.C.

SNYDER, LINDA. "How Effective Are Our Teaching Practices?" *Science and Children* Vol. 16, No. 1 (September 1978), pp. 31–33.

SUND, ROBERT B., BILL W. TILLERY, and LESLIE W. TROWBRIDGE. Elementary Science Discovery Lessons. *The Earth Sciences*. Boston: Allyn & Bacon, Inc., 1970. 304 pp.

———, ———, and ———. Elementary Science Discovery Lessons. *The Physical Sciences*. Boston: Allyn & Bacon, Inc., 1970. 302 pp.

SWEDLOW, RITA. "Problem Solving on the Playground," *Science and Children* Vol. 16, No. 7 (April 1979), pp. 20–21.

THOMPSON, GERALDINE D. "Where Do You Taste?" *Science and Children*. Vol. 16, No. 8 (May 1979), p. 25.

VICTOR, EDWARD. *Science for the Elementary School*, 4th ed. New York: Macmillan Publishing Co., Inc., 1980. 789 pp.

WILT, JOY, and TERRE WATSON. *Listen!* Waco, Tex.: Creative Resources, 1977. 159 pp.

———. *Look!* Waco, Tex.: Creative Resources, 1978. 152 pp.

———. *Rhythm and Movement*. Waco, Tex.: Creative Resources, 1977. 176 pp.

———. *Taste and Smell!* Waco, Tex.: Creative Resources, 1978. 160 pp.

———. *Touch!* Waco, Tex.: Creative Resources, 1977. 160 pp.

Social Studies and the Social Sciences: Finding Out About One's Society

Self and Society

As some of the most significant ideas in life focus on individuals' perspectives about themselves and others, it is no wonder that society is viewed from the inside out, so to speak. The individual looks out to his/her society and formulates some impressions as to what goes on "out there." What that environment looks like, however, is created to some extent by parents and others who guide children in their period of growing. The crux of how individuals think of themselves is strongly dependent on a given society and its[1] predispositions to reward or to deny certain behaviors in members of that society.

The society in which one lives is affected by a specific history and also a contemporary development indicative of change. All this combines to affect what and how an individual perceives the self, and how that individual relates to the society. As society changes in several ways with every new generation, children and parents undergo experiences that resist or facilitate changes within themselves.

The social sciences at higher educational levels and through the work of scholars and researchers involve studies of society and the dynamics of people's relationships to each other and to various institutions intended to facilitate activities of people in various roles. Institutions such as schools, hospitals, government facilities, or offices in Washington, D.C., for example, and other institutions that regulate people's behavior such as marriage, religious rites and legal processes related to functions that are central to a society's continuity, are a means for providing what people in a society need frequently. Births, deaths, education, and other aspects that affect individual members of a society need to be recorded and implemented in some way. Institutionalized routines or ways of processing what people need provide individuals with a way of organizing their own behavior relative to interacting with other members of society.

Doctors, lawyers, teachers, and others in the professions represent certain roles that define what they are expected to do when they function in those roles. A role represents a cluster of behavior patterns needed to implement one's own activities in relation to other people expecting to be served by a given role. A role-set refers to the dyadic relationship of one role with another. One does not teach unless a pupil or someone receiving the information needs that instruction or guidance. A mother is not in the role of mother unless a child, son, or daughter is involved. While it is true that some people may act maternally or as though the mother role were involved, instincts to act in that manner do not endow the person with the mother role unless someone has chosen to do so. Thus, the role of husband involves a wife, the role of doctor a patient, and so on. These roles regulate people's relationships to each other so that they know, to some extent, what can be expected from each other in the capacities of those roles. It provides a degree of order in people's lives when they have an idea as to what they may be able to expect from people in certain roles. This knowledge of roles also contributes to social order or organization in a society and to some regulation in daily human interaction.

Again, as was true in science lessons with children, the principles of the subject matter are sophisticated in concept, but they must be adapted to the levels of children's understanding. Activities need to be designed for pupils so that they can understand the generalizations, facts, and concepts used by social scientists.

The social sciences from which derives the content used for children's social studies materials include the fields of anthropology, economics, geography, history, political science, psychology, sociology, and—according to some writers—philosophy. From these sciences of society come the facts that are used and applied in children's social studies units. This ensures that, at least to some extent, children will be receiving accurate information about their world as it is written about on paper. How they receive their instruction and how the teacher helps them interpret what is written is another matter. The social sciences and the way they are viewed depend to a great extent on how the adults around the child perceive life, events, human interaction, and the like.

Social studies have been taught in many school systems throughout the United States prior to the contemporary period, though the substance of the topics were only history, geography, and civics (or government, citizenship, etc.). Current recognition of social studies as an area or group of disciplines that are taught in elementary school includes the provinces of the social sciences, anthropology, economics, geography, history, political science, psychology, sociology, and philosophy. The disciplines are studied by writers who create social studies units in a comprehensive sense. Including only two or three disciplines as constituting the social studies would be selling the subject short. The children would miss out on significant information, as would the teacher.

For young children, the social studies content is adapted to topics congruent with their levels of understanding. The principles of each of those subject matter areas are typically abstractions. Young children are not ready for abstract thought, but they can manage relationships to their ideas when the examples and units that they use directly refer to their own daily lives, for the most part.

The society of children can be better understood when they are aware of certain regulations, concepts, ideas, facts, and generalizations that represent humankind's thought patterns regarding the way a society or its members should conduct themselves. Even with change that occurs with every fifteen years or so, children growing with a family or care-givers acquire ideas about how to eat, speak, dress, walk, address others in daily interaction, and a number of other norms that can be observed in a society.

In a society as large as the United States, it is difficult for one individual to experience many aspects of living styles that are known to all the individuals in the United States. Each individual knows best what is experienced directly by that individual. Children experience a small component of society directly with their relatives or care-givers. In the privacy of one's home (even with the world brought in by television, newspapers, or magazines), one learns directly about aspects of life that adults consider important. It is reasonable, therefore, to note that people at an early age in life experience only a small segment of what they will know later about a broader, larger world of events, people, things, and situations.

The next section deals with the ways that children learn about experiences that other people have even while living in the same society but in different parts of the United States. The children's own parental background, orientations toward norms, values, religious practices, beliefs in education, and the like affect their perspectives about their society. Through the social studies, children will discover how many customs occurred in the United States and also how a variety of people feel about certain norms and patterns of behavior. Small groups of people, who interact with each other often, affect each other in the way they act and in what seems to be acceptable as normal behavior. Children, like adults, are affected by what they see in others. People imitate each other's actions. Gradually, habits build on frequent activity and individuals begin to think that their own actions (which are in part a result of the imitation of others) are, in fact, their own personalities. This is true to a point. How one interprets the behavior of others into one's own pattern of behaving is one's personality. That personality, however, can be changed when it comes in contact (given certain exceptions) with new (or different) experiences from those learned in former years.[2]

Social Studies in Kindergarten and the Primary Grades

Children have mixed levels of information on society. Directly or indirectly, formally through stories or books, and informally through spontaneous or normal interaction patterns with their family and friends, children obtain some notions about what their country is like. Teachers too have grown up with various ideas that they accept as society. A definition of society includes an awareness that various people, in similar geographical areas, observe similar customs, rules, ceremonies, and norms for acceptable behavior.[3]

People who interact frequently, who share similar values within a broad range of behavior patterns to implement those values, and who view norms and values in similarly acceptable or routine fashion represent a society. Very few complex societies can act in concerted fashion as though all the people represented a homogeneous group. A society's members are similar to some extent but differ from each other on certain issues. Particularly in a democratic society that encourages freedom of thought, of action, and of conflicting ideas, differences among people within that one American society will be obvious.

Children in kindergarten gain an understanding of society as made up of people from various backgrounds and cultural, racial, and ethnic origins. They also appreciate the fact that different people have different experiences. Some people prefer the mountains, some prefer the sea or the beaches, and some like to go camping for recreational purposes. The variety of people's preferences also contributes to the differential effects of backgrounds, over and above the differential effects of individual heritage.

The kindergarten curriculum includes as one of the first units that children have in the social studies a study of the family. Children can speak from family experiences. They have some knowledge and feelings about where they live, with whom, what they do before and after school or on week ends. Studies of the family use concepts and generalizations taken from sociology, anthropology, economics, geography, and history to some extent.

Some teachers start the children with a unit that compares families' routine schedules, various compositions of families (including how many siblings, adults interacting frequently at home, and one's pets). These units permit the children to appreciate their own families, thereby implementing an important goal. The more information a teacher has on how to provide more ideas to children on how interesting their families are (for what they do, think, believe, or create), the better for the children. Each family is unique and has characteristics that can be appreciated when the discussion on each one is guided properly.

Family—A Social Studies Concept

Children study their own families and the purpose of the family by creating a booklet about themselves.

A Story
About Myself and
My Family

Inside the cover are pages devoted to the following:

Things I like best
People I like to be with
My best friend
My father's work
My mother's work
My sisters/brothers and what they like
I can play a/an ———
My favorite ice cream flavor is
My grandfather's name is
My grandmother's name is
When school is out, I like to

Illustrations and short comments are included as the pupil is able to indicate them.

Booklets on the family are created along with daily information that emerges from lessons planned for family role descriptions (e.g., what fathers do, what mothers do, what younger/older brothers or sisters do in a family). Sociologists describe families in studies at higher educational levels. They define family roles in a division-of-labor sense. They discuss roles and interaction of roles geared toward the implementation of certain purposes or goals. People in groups want to accomplish what is needed to satisfy their purposes. Mothers take care of children as fathers do too in contemporary society. Meals are made, clothes are washed, children are fed and put to bed at appropriate times. Tasks carried out by individual members in a family are part of the roles performed in order to attain certain goals.

Children do not discuss abstractions. They talk about what their parents do, how they earn a living, or where they work. This gives pupils some impressions about the variety of occupations that exist in contemporary society. It also suggests the differences and similarities among a classroom of children in the way their lives are conducted at home.

Family life is in part sociological, in part economic, in part politically based, in part geographic, in part psychological. These areas are part of the social science constructs and research findings in higher education. When these generalizations or facts are presented to children, they are receiving accurate information. It is applied to their own lives. This contributes to knowledge, a capacity to think, and an ability to understand how society and communities work to affect family life.

Even though children in kindergarten may discuss families and different ways of living (in different homes, different sizes, or numbers of people in a family), they nevertheless perceive it differently when they are in the first, second, or third grades. Children's background changes from year to year. They accumulate more information, which applies to more sophisticated data with each new grade level. Their perceptions change as a result of assimilating more knowledge at a more mature level.

One of the unique functions of the social studies is to help children become aware of facts, concepts, principles, and generalizations that have been discovered to be true by social scientists. This effort is planned to avoid the instruction of untruths or inaccuracies about one's society. Even if a great deal is not learned, children can, however, learn *how* to search for, and to select critically and analytically, the data needed to give them the accurate information they need.

Instead of learning about countries and people in a way that gives only the recreational or tourist view about a society,[4] children learn how their own society and people may be similar to people in other countries. Instead of learning about Sweden or Norway in terms of their fiords or fishing industry, children also learn about the people, how they earn a living, how they vote, how they orient themselves in terms of a value system about life, about education, about the arts, and so on. Children learn that people in countries outside the United States are human, have desires, have goals and aspirations, just as American children do. They also learn to identify with others outside their own territory.

Many social studies units involve the study of families in various parts of the world. One of the reasons that units on both the Japanese family and the American one are offered to children is that pupils are able to compare school routines, food patterns, ways of eating (utensils that are used), shopping, and other household-need patterns of adults who provide care for the young, recreational preferences, reading habits, writing, learning, educational processes, technological effects, value orientations, religions, and social amenities of the two countries. Comparing families of two different cultures permits a depth of learning about one's own culture as well as that of others. It also permits pupils to understand why people differ and how the cultural context affects the way one thinks, what one's values are, which people or heroes one admires, what one's aspirations are, and how one perceives family life generally.

The openness of thinking, when one begins to consider in a broader sense, beyond one's immediate context, the life of various families, results in extended learning. The mind has to reflect and judge what information makes most sense. The mind chooses to remember certain things and not others. Even young children are selective in what is significant to them. A skillful teacher, however, strengthens certain facts and helps children articulate them effectively.

The study of families is a major sociological theme in higher education. Many theoretical ideas are emerging from contemporary research on that topic. Nuclear families, communal, and extended families live in terms of different orientations and value systems. The nuclear family refers to one that has a set of parents and offspring living together in one domicile or residence.[5] There are single-parent families (parent and child or children), which are also considered nuclear families living in their own residences without grandparents or relatives bound by biologically derived ties.

Extended families are those in which several generations, children, parents, and the parents' parents (or grandparents of the children) live together in one residence.[6] This may be popular in some cultures. It used to be more common in the United States in preindustrial society when agrarian modes of life were more predominant. Farmers needed large families to help them on their farms and often the older members of the family, such as grandparents or other relatives, would remain in the family compound to contribute to the chores as well as to be provided for by their married children.

Communal families are those in which several adults live together with their offspring. Some of the adults are single and some constitute marital pairs. The need for community and a feeling of belonging affects the desire of some people to live in groups of more than just a few people.

The religiously oriented views toward the family in the United States have become examined by people who think of the trends in the 1960s to 1970s as providing different directives. Women's liberation movements, self-fulfillment, and equal heads of families involving father and mother sharing the parenting tasks have changed child-rearing patterns in the

United States. People's expectations of what marriage should afford in terms of emotional satisfaction for each partner have risen.

In spite of the stress placed on the nuclear family that has to solve economic, social, psychological, and educational problems for itself, and in spite of the accessibility of contraception devices, or abortion, which may contribute to minimizing the number of nuclear families, their desirability seems to be sustained among Americans. The emotional support that can be provided by a family unit, even with its stressful times, seems to be preferred by a number of people in American society.

Young children, in their unit on themselves and their families, would not be discussing technical knowledge or theoretical issues that can be found in sociology or anthropology books dealing with those topics. What children do learn, however, is that there are different types of living styles, that some children will have their grandparents living near their homes or even within their homes. Children need to know that some people prefer, or in certain cases are forced, through circumstances imposed upon them, to live differently than others might expect. This kind of acceptance is valuable.

Ethnocentrism is a perspective that regards one's own patterns of behavior as better than those of others. To be proud of what one is or what one does is one thing. To criticize, reject, or ridicule other people who have not grown up in the same way one has (or are different in some way) is evidence of ethnocentrism. When this is called to a child's attention, it is not difficult to mediate the attitude to some extent and to help a child be aware of needing to expand his/her limited perspective. Each individual takes for granted that his/her own way of being reared is the best or is the only way. When one receives some new information that shows how restricting such a mode of thinking can be, one often begins to reassess his/her thoughts.

Studying a unit on the family provides significant data for children, not only in helping them to value themselves, but also to value the feelings of others for the way their families are structured and functioning. How groups or units of people help each other as part of a small system trying to achieve various goals is also part of the family unit of study. The division of labor as sociologists view it, applies as a principle describing how the family can work together and share certain chores. Principles of economics apply to the family functioning system because the work that one or both of the parents do supports the children and parents, providing food, shelter, and clothing, and meeting medical, recreational, and other needs.

In the first grade, children study community life through learning about workers in their neighborhood, in rural and urban neighborhoods, stores, libraries, farms, and various schools. They also learn some map skills in relation to where people live in the neighborhood, around the school, farther out into the community, and so on. The generalizations, concepts, and facts are drawn from the social sciences. See Concept Illustration 7–1.

At about seven years old, in the second grade, children learn about the work in the community, how food may be processed, clothing, transportation, police work, and hospitals and various agencies that help people in a given community. With each grade level, children are able to bring more

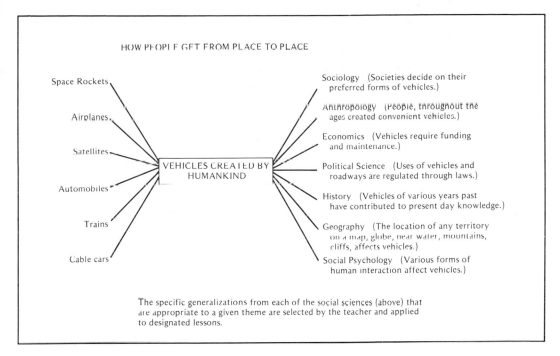

HOW PEOPLE GET FROM PLACE TO PLACE

Space Rockets

Airplanes

Satellites

Automobiles

Trains

Cable cars

VEHICLES CREATED BY HUMANKIND

Sociology (Societies decide on their preferred forms of vehicles.)

Anthropology (People, throughout the ages created convenient vehicles.)

Economics (Vehicles require funding and maintenance.)

Political Science (Uses of vehicles and roadways are regulated through laws.)

History (Vehicles of various years past have contributed to present day knowledge.)

Geography (The location of any territory on a map, globe, near water, mountains, cliffs, affects vehicles.)

Social Psychology (Various forms of human interaction affect vehicles.)

The specific generalizations from each of the social sciences (above) that are appropriate to a given theme are selected by the teacher and applied to designated lessons.

A Social Studies Unit and Relationships to Social Sciences.

Concept Illustration 7–1

knowledge and experiences from their own background and the units acquire more meaning for them even though some of the topics touch on ideas of the neighborhood and how products purchased in the stores are processed from raw materials.

The principle of interdependence among people is emphasized in social studies through various activities that indicate how people buy from each other what another has produced or grown or made. Even though it teaches cooperation in one sense, it also is an example of how people and communities need to depend on each other for a satisfactory existence. The sanitary worker, for example, who picks up the garbage or refuse that has been placed in containers for the workers to dump into a truck, is extremely important to the health of a community or city. If the refuse is permitted to remain in the street it can breed disease. The apearance of it in the streets suggests that people do not care about the environment, and it generally creates negative effects in any neighborhood. The worker picking up the refuse is paid by the community. Each citizen, then, does not have to make a trip to the dump to get rid of garbage. The division of labor in societies provides a means for accomplishing a great deal when people in different occupations or professions facilitate what the community, city, or state needs.

Children learn that not only do individuals work together to facilitate a group goal, but so can communities, states, countries, and the like cooperate with each other. Countries are interdependent in preventing wars. As new councils are formulated for purposes of ameliorating world issues, people can accomplish a great deal for the protection of many individuals of various societies. As children progress through the grades at school, they are able, let us hope, to understand more about mutual services among people and the satisfactions that can result from such forms of cooperation (or division of labor).

In the third grade, children at about eight years old study people of various communities in their own countries as well as those in other countries. They learn more about transportation in the air, at sea, and on the land. They learn how vehicles for transportation derive from scientific principles, and also how their use has involved social interaction between people who have helped each other in creating and developing what is now taken for granted as commonplace transportation.

Children may be able to understand, in varying degrees, how people need to plan ways to improve their own communities, why cities have changed, and what has contributed to the current problems of the city. They can also become aware of local community and city government. Government functions can be understood by children when some government workers come into the classroom and talk to them about what they do. The children themselves may visit a local office and see maps on the wall that exemplify the area in which the local government worker is interested. (Most public utilities offices, such as electricity, gas, and water have excellent maps on the wall designating the areas needing services or having major problems.)

Some children in the third grade, at eight, may be ready for fourth-grade social studies materials. The teacher needs to observe this and provide children with activities and tasks that are commensurate with their level of development. The social studies units having specific components are an excellent means through which children may be challenged to their own limits.

In the fourth grade, at about nine years old, pupils are typically studying the state in which they live, its products, land forms, and other significant aspects. Through this study they become familiar with the economic, sociological, anthropological, ecological (both scientific and sociological), political, geographical, and historical backgrounds of an extended environment that they should know. Depending on how ready the pupils are for studying other countries in depth, the teacher provides units on India, Japan, or other countries on which (s)he has firsthand information, along with books, pictures, and film strips. Visitors from those countries may be brought in, dressed in their native country's costume of earlier years, and of contemporary times if such clothing is significant. The visitors may discuss their own educational background, if it was obtained in another country, habits and patterns of family life, and many other aspects of life in another land— its art, customs, ceremonies, music, and dance.

Teachers who are sensitive to what each pupil can manage conceptually and intellectually (granted, this is not always easy to know or to assess), can enjoy with children the variety of substantive information that exists for social studies instruction. It is easy for a teacher to think that growing up in one's society qualifies one to teach all about it. But there is so much to know in terms of what can be drawn from the social sciences, that it typically requires searching through books and films to find what is appropriate both for the teacher's knowledge in the preparation of a unit and for the children's knowledge through participation in the activities the teacher plans for the unit.

The Teachers' Search for Information and Background

Even though teachers have received, in their undergraduate lower division, courses and information on the social sciences, they have to be taught how to apply the generalizations they have learned to the instruction of given units. This is a separate skill. A teacher must become familiar again with the substantive data of the social sciences before creating and developing a unit of study for children. This involves translating social science information into a format different from the one in which a university student typically learned it.

Teachers have to learn how to recognize which generalizations and which concepts apply appropriately to the social studies content of children's work in any given grade. Each of the social sciences has a complete structure in itself. As major ideas are drawn from each of them, teachers have to use these ideas in the context of something that is familiar to the pupils.

Sociology has this as one of its generalizations: All people have norms or regulations to guide them in their own daily forms of living.

Anthropology includes the following as one of its generalizations: Humankind has created and adapted various forms of technological tools and operations throughout the ages.

Political science includes this generalization, among others: All peoples govern themselves in some way chosen to fit their own mode of life.

Economics discloses this as one among other generalizations: Goods that are scarce (difficult to make, find, or create) will cost more than goods that are in abundance.

Geography has as one among many generalizations: The location on the earth's surface of any territory or country will affect its temperature, quality of life, climate, accessibility to harbors (bodies of water), mountains, plateaus. (Each generalization will specify a single concept or theme related to content that can be useful to children's studies.)

History indicates a generalization: The contemporary society is a reflection of what has gone before and what has been developed or delineated in its past. (Each country has a past that has affected or influenced its life and government, its patterns of living, and the attitudes and beliefs of the present.)

Social psychology suggests this to students: People interact in groups to affect each other. (They do affect each other whether they try to or not; there are results in other people's behavior because of different kinds of interaction.)

Generalizations are based on frequency of behavior observed among people. Social scientists have conducted carefully controlled studies in which certain results (or findings) have emerged.[7] These results permitted the researchers to make statements of predictability that they could depend on regarding people's behavior, the trends of a country, geographical observations, and change in a given society. The universality of the statement, making it scientifically valid, allows a sense of responsibility to be placed in the content area of the social studies. The content area might be, for example, transportation to and from a city, country, or society. Teachers helping children understand these scientific generalizations trust the researchers who have generated such statements based on conclusions drawn from scientific data, not merely personal opinion.

A scientific generalization is different from a personal one such as the stereotypes that children form about people. Such personal views are sometimes retained throughout life. Sometimes they are changed through study and educational information. A personal impression, formulated on the basis of some judgments made through experiences with certain people, is not synonymous with a scientifically discovered generalization (one that has been tested many times by objective observers). The personal point of view typically does not include investigation and scientific modes of verification.

Teachers must learn how to differentiate between personal perspectives with which they have grown up, and which were acceptable within their own family settings, and those that are broadly and differently, more extensively, verified as the scientific judgment of several researchers. The social studies provide an excellent medium for investigating the social world of the teacher and children.

The social sciences have been productive in the last thirty years, yielding information on the social structure and its effects on the way adults think. Psychologists have been focusing on patterns among individuals, in different times and spaces, and their feelings in those situations. Sociologists focus on groups as part of the social structure. They are interested in the reactions of people as members of any given group. The smallest unit of interest is the *dyad*, consisting of two people interacting with each other.

Teachers can do a great deal to help children understand how society works. The social climate changes for many reasons. Children can learn how to look for simple things that affect change.

Children can learn why and how certain trends occur. They can find out how and why things change, how people and events affect those changes. The shortage of energy resources, for a variety of reasons, will have some unique effects on the way people live in the next five or ten years. The children can learn that they are not pawns as members of society. They can contribute to their own social groups to improve them. As young children they learn that to have something become better one must contribute to improvement. It does not merely happen. Something affects change, thereby making life different in some way for people.

Children typically enjoy becoming involved in activities that have some meaning and purpose for their own levels of development. The developmental interactionist approach involves children becoming engaged in the activities around them at school and bringing to those tasks the pupils' own unique cluster of skills and interests. In that sense, the activities planned and provided for the pupils in the classroom are to be handled, manipulated, changed, redirected, and perceived from a variety of perspectives, with the children's being considered extremely important in that investigative approach.

The themes selected for children's study are sometimes decided by the school system. When the school system supplies the text for the teacher, the lessons are followed as designed in the kits or textbooks. In such instances that teachers are given an opportunity to plan and develop their own social studies units, it can be a very satisfying experience, for both the teacher and the pupils. The teacher can assemble two kinds of units, a resource unit and a teaching unit.

A resource unit includes the materials that will be useful for the teacher in providing information, pictures, bibliographical items, and lists of books or other reference in which the materials on the theme chosen by the teacher can be found. The resource unit will have all the information that a teacher can assemble and from which the ideas, concepts, and generalizations that will be used directly with the children will be drawn. The resource unit contains as much information as possible on a theme, along with information related to it.

The *resource unit* is geared toward the understanding of the teacher, who will translate and redesign the information to fit the needs of the pupils in a given classroom. If the teacher were doing a unit on India, for example, all the information on the arts, music, dance, values, population figures, land forms, geographical aspects of the country, historical aspects, food, clothing, religious patterns, and typical daily routines of some of the people in India would be noted, organized, and filed.

The *teaching unit* refers to the unit that will be put together for the children in a specific class. Besides the substantive data on various topics, there would also be examples of activities that the teacher intends to use directly with the children. It becomes a specifically designed program of studies for a class. It uses the resource unit from which to obtain information of depth. A well-organized resource unit is an excellent background and extended source of information close at hand. If the teacher has selected certain books from the resource unit that can be useful to the children, this is convenient in terms of time saved when those books are needed for teaching on a given day.

The teaching unit can be used as a compilation of subunits. When the teacher has it organized so that several subunits can be complete in themselves within the larger teaching unit, the subunits become a very useful form that can serve the children and teacher in several ways. A subunit contains a great deal of information about a topic. It can be completed in a period of a couple of weeks if within those two weeks one hour is spent for three days a week, making a total of six hours spent on a subunit. If children were working on transportation, for example, a subunit would be on the kinds of wheels that are used on many different vehicles. Depending on the ages of the pupils and their levels of interest, the information would represent skimming the surface of knowledge about wheels or it could go into depth on the topic.

Planning a Social Studies Unit

The first concern of the teacher deciding on a social studies unit for instruction would be a consideration of pupils in the classroom. If the person preparing to work with children has not had a classroom of his/her own, it is advisable to decide on a certain age group (fives, sixes, sevens, and so on) or on a grade level in order to envision the general levels of intellectual capacity among the children. The social interests of the children are significant, too. Their hobbies, the objects, events, and people in the environment in which they live, are in some way functional for them. Children are surrounded by certain things and ideas (seen on television, read in books, told to them by parents, older siblings, or others) and they need further meaning in relation to those things.

Young children are not able to understand concepts related to the history of a society in the way that older pupils can. Abstractions that are not related to their own experiences (other than love, justice, and equalitarianism, which, although being abstractions, can be associated with their own lives) should be minimally involved in the classroom at the beginning of a unit. Abstractions can be used in relation to understandings that are more familiar to children. Unfamiliar ideas can be built onto those that have in small part already been met by the children. If an idea were introduced as part of a unit that the pupils understood they would be able, to some extent, to integrate it with their former knowledge the second time they heard about it.

The psychological, sociological, and academic aspects of children's development have to guide the teacher's choice in deciding on the substance of the unit. The teacher has to know, too, that the objects needed for demonstrating ideas should be available in some way. They may be borrowed from individuals or community resources, or they can be visited in a museum, planetarium, aquarium, aviary, or the like. Objects that are used as part of a unit are called *realia*, and refer to things related to the unit that are used in the classroom. An example would be clothing representative of types worn by some people in India (for a unit on India); or for a study on transportation, the tray used to serve people on an airplane would be the real object shown to pupils so that they could see how it relates to a type of service given people on an airplane.

After decisions have been made as to what topics would be appropriate for pupils to study in a social studies unit, the teacher selects one topic that it is feasible to bring to young children's understanding, considering, as well, whether the required materials may be available. Resources that are manageable need to be brought to the classroom, arranged, placed, and matched to appropriate subtopics that will be studied by the children.

Some teachers choose two or three units and prepare materials for them. This affords opportunities to provide an introduction of ideas to the children and to note which one seems to motivate them most. The children's discussion and the interests manifested by them help determine which unit will be taught first during the school year. Preparing three units, however, requires time, energy and skill on the part of the teacher.

After a teacher has done several units throughout a year a file may be kept of them. The units can be updated and supplemented, and extraneous materials may be culled from them, and in this way the teacher retains an up-to-date collection of social studies units.

Most teachers acquire excellent materials throughout the years. A teacher may have a fine collection of selected materials with pictures, photographs, articles, *realia*, book titles (or bibliographies), recordings, filmstrip titles or the film strips themselves if this is possible. In any case, the collection of social studies units with updated materials is an invaluable resource and accomplishment. It is extremely useful for teachers who are serious about doing significant work with pupils on topics of social studies.

Resource Data

In planning the unit for pupils, the teacher begins to collect at the adult level of interest and at the children's level of interest, books, articles, newspaper information, museum brochures or publications, community articles that touch on the topic. For example, the teacher who plans a unit "How People Get from Place to Place" can write to the Smithsonian Institute in Washington, D.C. and to Cape Canaveral or Cape Kennedy to receive information on space, flights to the moon, and so on. One does not have to be a scientist or computer specialist to appreciate or comprehend the missile or rocket operations, at least to a minimal extent. Depth perception of the scientific functions and creation of the rockets is not expected of pupils. First levels of information on those topics provide a beginning basis for understanding. Children learn of the existence of such entities in their lives.

Each institution that has been involved in the development of worldwide flying equipment has public relations brochures written for the general population to understand. Since many of the organizations supported by federal funds have been part of local, state, and federal or governmental agencies, they have an obligation to disseminate their working reports at various levels so that the people within a given government can understand how their tax dollars are spent. Fiscal as well as moral obligations provide documents and brochures that are available upon request from a number of such federal agencies or institutions.

The teacher has to be very resourceful and imaginative, as well as ever curious about the topic. Questions about various ideas within a topic lead to very exciting information that the teacher may never have thought of before while growing up in his/her native country. Community personnel in various jobs are usually pleased (and often flattered) by requests to speak to children in a classroom on topics that are familiar to the professional or resource person, and also to give information on what kind of training was needed for functioning on any given job.

All the resource data are placed together in a large file. Some of the

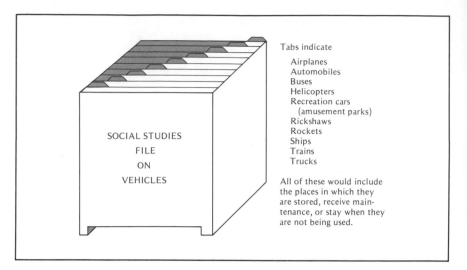

Tabs indicate

   Airplanes
   Automobiles
   Buses
   Helicopters
   Recreation cars
    (amusement parks)
   Rickshaws
   Rockets
   Ships
   Trains
   Trucks

All of these would include
the places in which they
are stored, receive main-
tenance, or stay when they
are not being used.

SOCIAL STUDIES
FILE
ON
VEHICLES

Concept Illustration 7–2

Social Studies File.

things in the file that include pictures will be categorized. Articles and notes on the content of the unit will be classified and separated by dividers that clearly show what is in each section. The more the dividers show what the file contains and how information is organized, the more will the file be used and the easier it will be to use for all involved.

Note Concept Illustration 7–2 to see what categories might be chosen by the teacher prior to writing the unit, "How People Get from Place to Place." The dividers or categories are created, selected, and designed by the person who develops the file. The teacher has some ideas on how the materials will be used. Even though ideas on the history of aviation, for example, may not be immediately appropriate for a social studies unit presented to kindergarten children, directly used as a lesson in itself, the teacher nevertheless saves materials or articles on that topic. When the unit is presented or is upgraded for older children, the history of aviation would then be of greater interest to them.

After the teacher has gathered a great deal of information geared for the comprehension of adults and for children's use, the materials are organized to fit a sequence. If the teacher decides, for example, that children will first learn about the recent walk on the moon and satellites in the air that transmit television pictures across the world, the decision to place those materials first in the sequence will be noted on paper.

Sequence of a Unit

The sequence of a social studies unit refers to an order of logic that the teacher considers psychologically sound for a given classroom of children. The order relates to the children's abilities to comprehend the subject. It is *not* typically the order in the way a subject is written for a book, starting often with the history of an invention or idea. Often in the instructional process, the teacher plans to begin a unit with what is most familiar to children's experiences even though it is mainly what they may see on television or in the newspapers and hear discussed (or not) by their parents.

The order and sequence of any social studies unit involve careful planning on the part of the teacher. For example, the teacher knows that simple concepts have to become the basis for more difficult understandings. The teacher, therefore, would not start out with abstract ideas of missile or airplane suspension or concepts of gravity until clear experiments were demonstrated on those principles.

Sequence is a form of organization based on how children learn. It is based on educational and psychological principles of learning. The teacher knows that children can effectively learn from a presentation of simple to complex concepts as ideas move smoothly from one to the other. Very little of what is taught is random. Although a teacher may capitalize on a teachable moment, capturing children's susceptibility to or interest in new knowledge when something is happening outside the classroom (and distracting the children) to stimulate it, random teaching is not a practice or at least is not organized to be. Organization in terms of the theme is vital in teaching. The teacher can be successful in it when the nature of the pupils is clearly known. The two threads of psychological appropriateness to the students' paths of learning and the substance of the social studies content have to come together to constitute decisions relative to the sequence or order of the unit presentation.[8]

The action that young children need to take on the instructional materials provided for them in the classroom is associated with the ideas of Piaget, of Vygotsky, and of Bruner, as well as other writers who describe work with children.[9] Learning is simply not imposed, it is integrated within a child to become part of what is already known by the child. Consequently, the way children assimilate knowledge to become an integral part of their own intellectual and sense experience frameworks has to be considered by the teacher in the way it contributes to the pupils' understanding of what they are expected to learn.

Children are in the preoperational and concrete operational stages of development (as Piaget uses the terms) when they are in elementary school. As children are developing in their abilities to perceive their worlds by means of symbols and signs, and are beginning to separate objects from names and symbols of such objects, and are learning how to use language in relation to actions and words, they are in phases of their intellectual development in which they will benefit greatly from physical action on objects and from social interaction with peers and in representative play.[10] The social studies provide an excellent opportunity for children to perform in a way that is not alien to their physical and (in varying degrees) their mental development. Individual differences in skills, physical capacities, and mental and intellectual characteristics prevail in the classroom. The teacher must be cognizant of this. For the most part, however, although the teacher is aware of individual differences in readiness to comply with the directions that come with a given activity, the pupils are at least given a fair chance to learn when the teacher is aware that manipulation of objects is needed for their concept development.

In relation to the order or sequence of a unit, the teacher must decide the the boundary lines of the content that will be offered as part of the instructional mode of the unit. This decision relates to how much material the teacher thinks the children may be able to interact with, in a sense, throughout a given period of time, be it four weeks, eight, or twelve.

Scope of a Unit

The scope of a social studies unit typically refers to the inclusion of substance, content, principles, concepts, and facts that will be used in the total process of presenting that unit. Scope can also indicate what will not be included, by giving a brief statement on the intention to exclude inappropriate content that would be premature (or superfluous) for the pupils being taught.

A teacher could state that vehicles of almost every type that humankind has information on may be included in the unit. All the background on the history of each of them however could not be attempted for study. It would be impossible to accomplish. History will be mentioned but not given a great deal of study time. Young children may not be as interested as older ones may be. The teacher must be sensitized, however, to recognize the children who are able to comprehend intellectual abstractions that may be atypical for a given group of pupils, and offer challenges to some.

If the teacher were compiling a unit on the study of the United States, it is obvious that the children would not learn well the facts on *each* of the states in the country. The semester or school year would not permit enough time for such comprehensiveness. Some teachers might include a study of the industrial centers, or of several major concepts of large areas that are significantly known for various contributions to society, and also for those having a unique population assemblage within the United States. These topics may comprise a scope for the unit.

Some teachers may want to study, with the children, the regions of the United States and to classify those regions in terms of manageable concepts for the unit. The scope of a unit contributes to the manner in which it will be organized and presented to the children. Certain aspects of knowledge on a given unit will be excluded for a number of reasons, decided on by the teacher in relation to what is known about the children, their levels of abilities and skills, their interests, and their tendencies to interact effectively with materials provided for them in a given unit.

After the resource data have been compiled, classified, placed into a series of portfolios or a file, the teacher has made some decisions, too, on how the unit will be portioned out in the series of instructional subunits. Ideas are developing as the unit compilation occurs. The scope and sequence of the unit as the teacher envisions who the children will be as participants fall into place in reference to when or in which parts of the unit, the subunits will be introduced. Thus, again, the psychological and the substantive aspects of the unit interact in theme and in relation to a given classroom of pupils.

Format of the Teaching Unit

The teacher has notes prepared to organize the way that the social studies will be presented to the children, as well as the time sequence of the various introductory periods of new materials within the unit. The teacher guides the children in the learning process, but the ideas and principles that will be introduced to them have to be presented so that the children will enjoy the experiences in learning. See photographs on the activities of people in the city and buildings constructed and maintained by them. Chil-

Children see the contrasts of the city even during the activities that occur a few streets away in readiness and preparation for a holiday parade. This street is quiet, has very few cars, is less populated, and the sparse number of people echoes minimal activity. It is relatively unusual to see a downtown street in the early morning of a city uncrowded with cars or people. (Photo by Gerald J. Margolin.)

The child, along with others, is ready to see the parade. The excitement and loneliness in expectation of beautiful and gigantic floats becomes overpowering along with other mixed emotions of joy and elements of fear. (Photo by Gerald J. Margolin.)

The feeling of looking up to and being close to the much-loved characters that are familiar to millions of people provides a memory and appreciation of the parade developers' efforts to bring happier experiences to people, adults and children alike, of the city. (Photo by Gerald J. Margolin.)

Children need the stimulation of a parade. It cannot be appreciated in the same way when it is not seen in person. Even though one's thoughts and feelings are individualistic and private, sharing an unusually colorful parade in the presence of crowds of people, too, can provide an excellent immemorable experience that contributes to young children's educational and emotional development. (Photo by Gerald J. Margolin.)

dren learn from discussions about those themes and concepts. They learn how the minds of human beings have created things and activities that many other people can enjoy

The form of teaching in the kindergarten and primary grades has to be by means of activities that the children do so that they obtain concepts through participation. They cannot be expected to sit and listen to a lecture on the generalizations of principles of the social sciences that describe the various dynamics of a society. They have to be involved in doing something from which they can obtain ideas leading to concepts that are related to a more comprehensive overall view of their work in a social studies unit.

The state (or nature) of teaching many years ago reflected lecture formats as the most effective manner of instruction. Talking at or to children did not work out as well as assumed, however animated and well-motivated the lecturer might be. The mode of teaching that seems today to be more appropriate is the kind of guidance that facilitates learning experiences for children in the classroom, as well as their abilities to apply learning skills outside the classroom. The children do the work and become involved after the teacher plans specific ways to motivate them in wanting to become involved.

The teacher's goals are not to answer questions *for* the pupils. The un-

The color, unusual form, and stylistic head observed by children who attend the parade in New York City provide information about the world that is not always serious but intended to appeal to a variety of tastes artistically and psychologically. (Photo by Gerald J. Margolin.)

derlying idea in instruction is that children learn for themselves through the many experiences or activities that the teacher plans for them. The teacher motivates the children to ask questions that can be pursued by pupils in the search for information available through activities in the classroom. The pupils begin to exercise skills in inquiry and the pursuit of learning so that they realize they can be their own instigators of learnings, that they can discover facts for and by themselves at times, and that they can create unique ideas as well. They begin to appreciate their own minds as sources for their own intellectual guidance.

The teacher *and* the children are searching together for the most effective answers, for the means for attaining the best qualities in the answers to questions. As this mode of delivery is considered an appropriate one for life outside the classroom, it is encouraged. When individuals have to guide themselves effectively in making life's choices, they need to know how to ask the proper questions (related to their own personal goal attainment). The intellectual search in the classroom, therefore, involves asking questions, stating problems clearly, identifying places to find answers, acquiring rational modes of thought, and having enough patience to persist in the search.

Teachers who enjoy helping children learn how to discover their own abilities are, to a great extent, intrigued by this approach. They provide materials, books, pictures, photographs, and activities that motivate and stimulate pursuits toward learning. They are also willing to suspend easy quick answers to some questions and to encourage validation of ideas by the children themselves. The children discover that they can, given certain skills and abilities, create and sustain a world of learning for themselves. Independence in the pursuit of knowledge and problem solving is important in children's development.

The materials used for the study of one area, such as vehicles for transportation, can also be used for ecological studies. Photographs of a city, giving an indication of the number of people that live in it and work in or outside of it, on the river, near it, and the like give children an idea as to how the waste may be managed from those sources. The layout of a city, the design of its buildings, and placement of trees also contribute to the amount of waste or refuse that will be evident on the surface of a city's area. Relationships among water, sky, buildings, crowded areas, heights of buildings, and shade or sunlight in a city all provide excellent learning topics for children.

The social studies content becomes the substance that children write

Sunlight and shade among the buildings of the city prohibit or facilitate the growth of certain plants.

about in *language arts* periods, read about in *reading* instruction periods, become artistically expressive about in the *art* or *music* periods, become rhythmically expressive about in the *art, body rhythms, and movement periods*, become scientifically conversant with and knowledgeable about in the *science* period, mathematically expressive about and adept with in the *mathematics* period. Reading the map and globe, identifying places and people's homes on the map, also provide another set of skills for children. Geographical skills are drawn into the social studies whenever suitable to a conceptual understanding.

The flexibility of social content (which is about people and their own society) as it is integrated into all the various subject matter areas in the elementary or primary grades program is a joy to teachers who are aware of its potential. This binding together of content permits children to understand the substance and generalizations of the social studies through the use of techniques that are central to language arts, reading, art, music, and other expressive forms of a creative nature, science, mathematics, and health education.[11] Pupils are involved in an interrelationship of disciplines and activities all of which are significant to humankind and can be enjoyed at various levels as people are able to become interested in such content.

The teacher writes a plan that designates when certain ideas will be presented, how they will be introduced to the pupils, and what the pupils will do to comprehend the facts, concepts, generalizations. The activities need to be designed as they will be given at certain times on certain days.

The plan for a six-week program includes a judgment for the amount of time that will be allowed for devoted to units in social studies. If a teacher can plan to have social studies three or four times a week, for about 30 or 45 minutes (depending on the age of the children), this means that a six-week period will allow eighteen or twenty-four sessions for teaching at about a half- or three-quarter hour session each time.

Along with the time that the social studies will be instructed must be considered whether any societal holiday (e.g., Easter, Christmas, Thanksgiving) comes within that time. This has to be accounted for, since many children have to observe those holidays and understand why they are celebrated. They typically make something to bring home to their parents or "special" people. These plans have to be included in the program.

Judgments related to individual interests have to be considered in the total format of the teaching plan. This fact suggests that several means of teaching certain concepts have to be included. Two or three levels of activities have to be included so that children who have difficulty understanding an idea or concept at one level can have it shown to them in an activity at a simpler level. For children who need a challenge for higher levels of thinking, activities of a more difficult nature can be prepared. The teacher needs to remember that several activities of varying complexities have to be prepared for children at any of those levels.

Thus while a format for the teaching design will be planned in terms of what will be introduced or reviewed at certain times at certain sessions, the teacher also needs to prepare activities of varying levels of complexity. These activities can be kept in a file classifying those concepts or topics that designate various (simple-to-complex) instructional levels in given topics.

The teacher has a section on objectives for the teaching unit. The pupils will be guided toward finding out certain facts, concepts, and generalizations about the questions on vehicles that have been created to move people from place to place.[12] Objectives are stated within each of the activities. They are also presented in the initiation or introductory phase of the unit.

Objectives are often transmitted to children *not* in a way such as, "Today we are going to find out about———," but "Have you ever wondered *how* airplanes were created?" or "How do you think missiles began in the life of today's society?" "Why?" The teacher has to state and to encourage the children's formulation of questions so that they will want to find answers. Their curiosity should be enhanced and strengthened. The educational process builds itself on questions, problems, conflicts, issues. This is important in everyday life. Answering questions, or at least knowing how to go about the process of doing so, has to be done often without anyone's help. Children learn early at school how important it is to obtain what they need for themselves, rather than always allowing others to solve personal or academic problems for them.

Children also learn that they often have to fend for themselves. They understand that what they want is uniquely their own preference. Although people are similar to each other in many ways (in needing food, air, clothing, recognition, and praise among other things), people are unique in having specific preferences. Children want more or less of what many people want. People differ in the *degree* to which they want certain things, such as their feelings satisfied, needing attention from others, and the like. Some people need more than others a surfeit of a given quality, object, or characteristic, before they can feel satisfied with life (or with themselves).

It is important that in the format of teaching, guidance is accomplished through a variety of activities at different levels of difficulties for children. This diversity introduces skills and attitudes or preferences that will be of interest to every pupil in the class. Teachers must be aware (as many of them are) before they begin the instructional sequence that children are not homogeneous. A total classroom group cannot be given materials and expected to learn in a comprehensive sense all that has been presented to them.

To consider "covering" materials for a given classroom group as though presenting ideas meant an automatic assimilation of them by the children, is a fallacy. Such a concept assumes that all children are equally ready to assimilate materials. This is not true as many teachers know. Since it is *not* the case that a classroom at the third-grade level has children who are all ready to learn in the same manner and can assimilate a given idea or concept, in the same way and to the same extent many different activities have to be prepared to present several levels (simple to complex) of the same concept.

The format of the teaching unit includes at the end of it a section on how the teacher will evaluate the children's progress in learning. The bases for this evaluation include not only how effective a given unit plan was, but also a consideration of whether the content was treated appropriate to the children who participated in the unit or teaching plan.

Implementing and Initiating a Unit

The social studies unit begins with the teacher's awareness that all children may not be interested simultaneously in the same aspects of the total unit. They will, however, be involved in certain elements of the unit. For example, a child who may not enjoy analyzing ideas may not be interested in *why* a rocket can go to the moon, but (s)he may be intrigued with the way it evolved and the way it happened on a given day.

Starting out with the social studies unit complete with pictures, activities, objectives, designs, and other related brochures and data, the teacher, as an individual who is well prepared to guide children, exudes an enthusiasm, a readiness to move, and a willingness to note clues of interest and skills among the pupils.

The first day of the presentation, the teacher typically takes great care and pleasure in arranging the room to reflect the social studies content. This arrangement of the environment, or the teaching atmosphere of the pupils, is extremely important for several reasons.

The teaching/learning environment

- Stimulates the children to move through curiosity about what is seen
- Motivates questions for answering in the learning activity process.
- Provides a common set of interests among pupils and the teacher.
- Instills enthusiasm for finding answers to solutions posed in activities.
- Heightens focus and attention in learning.
- Provides a strong base from which to draw ideas that will be used in activities.
- Provides a colorful atmosphere (pictures, objects, realia related to the unit).
- Germinates ideas for learning beyond the immediate articles shown.
- Through visual attractiveness of materials lures learners to activities.
- Emphasizes, elaborates, enlightens, clarifies, and extends for the pupil's own initiative the subject matter to be approached.
- Focuses on individual differences, interests, and aptitudes as children are encouraged to design their own questions about subject matter in the unit.

After the teacher has placed the materials in the learning/teaching environment, the children are permitted to walk around the room viewing these materials with intent to learn about them. The teacher notices and listens to the children as they look at the materials on walls, tables, displays, on record players or film-strip machines. Notes are taken on a pad as the teacher observes what the children do, how they handle the materials, what they say to each other, and the comments that they make. A comment such as, "I saw this once when my parents took me to see ———. I wonder how it works. Push it here. No, try it there," give the teacher ideas as to what might be of interest when the children become involved in lessons which will be offered to them and are related to specific content areas. The children's comments are clues that let the teacher know what their interest levels are. They allow the teacher to capitalize on the motivation engendered by seeing the materials close at hand. A diver's suit, for example, usually draws a crowd of children around it when it is displayed in the classroom. The suit is used in the process of moving from one place to another in the sea. One can recognize that the teacher has to be an entrepreneur in acquiring teaching materials that will excite children in the process and pursuit of learning.

Objectives for the unit are developed with the children. The teacher has some ideas that can lead toward an articulation of objectives that may be accomplished through the activities in the unit. Sometimes objectives arise in a study trip made to a local facility, whether it be an airport, bus terminal, or whatever the teacher (with the children) considers is relevant to the social studies unit and its goals.[13]

Film strips or films provide information that can spark children's interests and questions about social studies concepts. A significant resource person or several persons who know about the content of the social studies and a subunit of it can be invited to the classroom to tell the children about a given area or topic. The content of a subunit can be made clearer when an individual in the community comes to school to discuss it with children.

Objectives for learning about the subject matter are discussed. Why is it important to know about the materials in the room, which have been selected by the teacher on the basis of what is known about educational processes and development? Children begin to identify with the teachers the reasons for the validity of such study.

A word about the subjectivity involved in the teacher's selection for children's study. The selection is not done entirely on a personal or selfish basis. The teacher includes among the criteria considered for teaching a specific unit, at least what is important for children's development and an ability to function effectively in their own current and future societies. As they need to learn *how* to pursue learning and the processes that yield effective learning skills, pupils will be exposed to process, design, means of, and paths of pursuit and in achieving results.

When the teacher selects a unit and is implementing it with the pupils, the decisions have been based not only on what the teacher thinks the student will gain in significant information, but also what motivates the teacher's interest. When both the teacher and pupils are excited about the content, everyone stands to gain. The teacher is pleased when the children benefit from plans that originated from the him/her. The children gain because they learn and also because they simultaneously receive the approval of the teacher, who enjoys the subject matter as do the children.

Even though children should not be motivated only to gain the approval of the teacher, their doing so does have its implicit and beneficial psychological effects on instruction. Teachers need to know that children benefit from effective decisions designed for teaching. Positive reinforcement of the teacher's goals for children does exert renewed energies for the teacher who needs to know that (s)he is successful in helping children learn.

The teacher considers the time blocks for each session and plans objectives that can be introduced in each one. Even though review time is taken and the children are led from one known idea to a new one, the time block can accommodate what the teacher knows the children can realistically accomplish.

Social studies units allow a building and development of broad units of knowledge. This is essential to learning and to acquiring perceptual depth in a discipline. Studies do not close off at the completion of lessons as though the ideas were completed entities isolated from other parts of the social studies. This connectedness of subject matter evolves or comes about because the social studies interrelate with several subject areas. The concepts and generalizations of each of the social sciences yield endless facts that children can learn in relation to the theme of a social studies unit.

If children finish a lesson before an allotted time or a period having a few minutes left before having to leave the classroom, the teacher can start another related concept without its seeming inappropriate to the studies that will go on the next day. The children can begin thinking about another aspect of a subunit because the interrelationships are many and require various paths of thought to the solution of problems. The social studies content is an excellent source for continuity in topics and pupils' interests.

The Culmination of a Unit

Depending on the time that seems appropriate to spend on any given unit, the teacher plans for activities that will draw the unit to when the children seem to have obtained most of what they could from participation in the unit.[14] When the children have worked on a unit for about six weeks, for example, they may have accumulated information in the form of booklets, papers they have written individually, pamphlets that have been illustrated and detailed through their knowledge, science experiments that were performed and recorded on paper, and they may have produced exemplary art and music products. They have learned, perhaps, many different techniques, operations, and functions relative to the nature of various vehicles of transportation. They may also have learned about designers, engineers, and scientists who had something to do with the creation of vehicles used in contemporary society.

The teacher indicates that after a certain day they will have to go on to another social studies unit. At such a point they have to bring together all they know about the unit, or all that is significant about it that can be summed up, and demonstrate in some way what has been learned. Often the children and the teacher decide that they would like to present what they know to parents, teachers, and to children in the school. Several ideas can be used to summarize what was learned from doing the unit.

Children sometimes prepare posters or write individual papers or booklets on a given topic within the social studies unit. They like to display these in the classroom and even in the front office of the school. Sometimes the principal of the school likes to see these outside the classroom, placed in the corridors of an entry way to the school.

Often children make a mural depicting part of their learning efforts. A mural that represents a stream of progression of vehicles throughout history is an exciting product giving evidence of the fact that children understood what was being done in their social studies. Some airport terminals display the efforts of children who have visited the airport terminal and who illustrate their impressions of the facilities.

By the time the social studies unit reaches it culmination, the students will have encountered the need for many skills and abilities in other fields relating to their social studies work.

LANGUAGE ARTS AND READING

The stories written (fiction or nonfiction) by the children are displayed. Pupils disclose their knowledge of the social studies theme. They write poetry. They read their products to the class. All this may later become part of a program for parents or other classes in the school. The program on social studies is typically very successful. Children enjoy seeing their schoolmates present a program about which they (the participants) are also knowledgeable. When children have been studying a theme for six weeks they have become familiar with it.

The pupils are given many opportunities to read what they have written. They may also want to read something that they used during their studies of the unit. Reading materials are presented often. When children demonstrate to an audience how they have secured their information on the social studies unit, they have practiced sufficiently to read easily. This opportunity can be used to help the shy child present him/herself well to a group of people. Such an experience is significant in a child's development. It can do a great deal toward giving the child another improved point of view about him/herself.

MATHEMATICS

The mathematical concept is used often in the idea of vehicles that people have created for their own use. The engineering design, the wheels, the propulsion, the air ducts, the gasoline, the chassis size and shape, all relate to the purposefulness and success of the vehicle. Children learn about angles, shapes, and forces of air or energy as they create impact on a vehicle. This can be done easily at any grade level. The teacher who knows the material well can simplify it in terms of what the pupils can comprehend. Many illustrations can be obtained from reliable sources (from engineers or vehicle designers themselves in the community) to show children how mathematical principles and design affect the function of any vehicles used by humankind.

SCIENCE

Children are using many scientific concepts in the social studies unit. They often show at the end of a program of studies, the experiments that dem-

Creating a block building that will accommodate various vehicles, toys or accessories involves thought, judgment, experimentation. (Photo by Gerald J. Margolin.)

onstrate how the air vacuum created by the path of an airplane in the air affects the fuselage of the airplane. The shape of the plane (consider the Concorde or the DC10, for example, and the differences between them) influences the speed. The tensile strength of the materials that go into the construction of the airplane affects the speed as well as air pressures that push against the plane in a certain way.

Investigations, scientific experiments, and graphs made as a result of the findings in any experiment are described and shown to an audience observing the pupils' culmination of a social studies unit. The objectivity, controlled sequence and techniques of the scientific pursuit are explained to the audience of children, teachers, or parents or all of them.

GRAPHIC ARTS, MUSIC, AND MOTION

Evidence of children's knowledge of the arts such as music, painting, drawing, and aesthetic movement in rhythmic representation or dance are displayed in the pictures, illustrations, songs, or movement presentations related to the social studies unit. Children enjoy showing their work that represents what they have learned and placed into an aesthetic context to be enjoyed by others viewing it. Posters or murals and individual booklets demonstrate individual and groups' expressions that emerge from ideas stimulated through and from the social studies theme.

HEALTH, PHYSICAL EDUCATION, AND NUTRITION

Health, physical education, and nutrition are sometimes included in the science period of work at school. In some cases, teachers represent it to children in a separate category. It (all of physical education, health, nutrition) requires a scientific perspective. It involves a study of human anatomy and how the body receives and acts upon food, and is affected by exercise and environmental elements. Mental health is an extremely significant component in this regard. The body is affected by mental functions and perceptions. Physical, medical, and digestive functions are influenced by mental outlook and interpretations. These can be reflected in culmination activities indicating differences between and similarities of various cultures, people, their eating habits, exercise, recreation and the like.

Physical education departments treat this area comprehensively. Elementary grades and primary levels have to bring it in whenever possible. Health is paramount in children's learning. It sustains their interest, capacity, and endurance. Whether it is treated in the category of science or of physical education, it needs constant emphasis, especially for young children who are developing philosophical orientations. Activities, then, for a culminating social studies unit should include selected games that capture the spirit of the unit (whether the games are preferences of a people who were studied, or are symbolic of a theme such as transportation).

Evaluating the Unit

The culmination, summary, and presentation of activities relating to any social studies unit is typically a memorable event if it is planned properly. Every child can participate effectively and successfully in it. The child's participation depends on the skills of the teacher in being perceptive and sensitive to what children can do well and to what the audience will appropriately respond to, making the participants feel proud of themselves.

The teacher uses the children's presentations to evaluate how well the children understand what was offered as a social studies unit. The evaluation reflects the teacher's work as much as it does the children's. A serious teacher makes notes for future use on how (s)he would improve the unit and the manner of presentation to another class. (This, however, is not shared with the audiences, who enjoy the culminating event as a form of entertainment and sharing of intellectual searching.)

The juxtaposition of buildings, bridges, water that accommodates transportation and shipping activities, and a hotel plaza as well as the United Nations building in New York City, all reflect the many ways that humankind answers its needs. Transportation, communication, and vehicles that have been created by the work and inventiveness of individuals and groups of people are evidence of humankind's ingenuity and desires to make life meaningful. Children can learn about the fact that this panorama of the city does not just happen. Many minds at work—the work of people and machines accomplished such an array of functional roads, bridges, and buildings. (Photo by Gerald J. Margolin.)

Expanding Interests in the Social Studies

Even though the teacher selects a social studies unit on acquiring information on vehicles that have been used to carry people from one place to another, the pupils are receiving other kinds of information that should be leading them to other areas of interest. Branching out from studies on the chassis and power forms that bring people from one place to another, students become interested in who accomplished these inventions. They become interested in the societal context in which these achievements were completed and recognized.

The era or societal context (life in society) of the steam engine was a different one from the time that produced the motor engine of the car. The paddle-wheel of the riverboat introduced another concept of propulsion of water power.

Children's minds do not classify items of information in air-tight containers blocking ideas off one from the other. Although this sometimes happens in interpersonal relationships, as psychologists suggest, that people shut out from their minds, conflicting personal knowledge if it interferes with getting what they want, the relevant information that becomes a curiosity to children when they study a social studies unit can flow into another set of interests for study.

The teacher tries to keep in mind that children will have opportunities, if they are guided to study other things outside of school. Many books and pamphlets or articles need to be presented in class if the children are to veer off in another direction during or after they have spent time studying a specific theme.

The *social studies* represent social sciences involved in finding out the many ways that humankind relates to the environment and either adapts or changes it. Social scientists are interested in the ways that groups interrelate. They want to know how people interact. They want to know why people vote as they do, what is important to them. Social scientists are interested in values that orient people in doing what they do.

Political science involves studies in governmental structures and legislative mandates, judicial systems, and people's voting patterns, all of which provide information that is useful for the social studies. Some children may be vitally interested in this aspect of their social studies work.

Anthropology and the tools or inventions that have supplemented people's desires and purposes throughout the years, and patterns of appropriating what was necessary for one's survival, leave an imprint on different groups in different ages of history. Some children may be intrigued by this. Such study can start in elementary school, not at the highest abstract levels, but as its earlier elementary principles, which are comprehensible to children.

Sociology, a study of people and how they influence or are affected by a particular societal concept at any given time in history, is a stimulating subject or science that children enjoy. They need the terms, facts, and generalizations that come within their levels of understanding the social studies unit. They are able to move on toward more difficult concepts when these ideas or materials are available in the classroom environment and they may go to them when they desire. Greater depth of study in an area happens best when the pupil takes the initiative. Materials, books, and various aids must be available, however, if children are to recognize these as something that is manageable for them.

Economics, which deals with financial aspects of society, goods, services, and their availability to people at different levels of the income stratifications in a country, state, city, or county, is a challenging area of study. Every student needs to have at least a superficial understanding of it because each student spends or saves money depending on decisions made in relation to acquiring or dispersing money or property.

Children can have simple mathematical problems shown to them, it is true. They also need to know something about theories of economics. If gems, services, or articles are scarce, they are going to be costly. When fruits or vegetables are plentiful they are less expensive than when they are not (because of drought, or nonseasonal growth). Children must learn this in order to know how to buy food, clothing, services. They can be helped in understanding the rationale underlying any purchasing power.

The neighborhood grocer and the supermarket manager or owner differ in many ways. They differ in terms of what they can offer in quality, quantity, or reasonable services. Children can understand this. If they want to patronize the smaller store, they have to know the choices they are making or from among which choices they are deciding what to do.

Economics often relates to the presence of depression, inflationary practices, unusual buying practices, interest rates, loans and other trends relating to money gains or losses. Elementary ideas can be introduced to children in social studies units. They, of course are also present when mathematics is studied. The theories underlying economic findings, however, must be introduced. Children remember the reasoning when it is sensible and related to a real experience or at least one that is simulated for them.

The interrelationships among the social sciences make it difficult to know where one category stops and another begins. This is not crucial, however, to the pursuit of studying them. The classification in itself refers to the sciences as humankind perceives them and as they are an influence on the way people live. Humanism is interwoven throughout the theme of the social sciences. For young children, the social studies are an excellent focal point to help them become familiar with what they will be encountering again in the junior high and high school years.

Many other unit choices are possible among social studies. There are excellent ones that include principles and generalizations that can challenge children of all ages. Some of them are too difficult for certain age levels. The social studies unit that is more theoretical than it is practical in its examples and experiences for children will not be effective. Children will find it too difficult. The teacher has to be aware of what the children can assimilate.

Teachers often invite resource people into the classroom to discuss occupations or professions that they represent. Pilots, engineers, artists, writers of children's books, gourmet cooks, newspaper reporters, travel agents, librarians, and many other people who are in the community are asked to speak to the children. Before they come, pupils are expected to think of questions that they would like to ask the speaker.

Some of the questions include these: "What exactly do you do in your job?" "How did you have to prepare or train for it?" "Why do you like it?" "What is your typical day like?" As the person speaks the children will think of more questions.

Sociological concerns are related to studies of professions and occupations in any society. This aspect of children's learning about people who have various interests and who are paid for working at those interests reveal a form of sociology. Of course, the study of occupations also gives children an understanding of what goes on behind the scenes in any job service or in the creation of a product. They discover that "things are not always what they seem." They begin to realize how much time and energy go into the preparation and organization of a product—not easy to do.

Children's interests should always be expanded beyond the present classroom study. Books, articles, and other items pique their curiosity. The teacher has to remember that children are in the classroom for only part of a day. Although schooling is important of itself, it is also a device for stimulating the initiative of pupils to continue asking questions and seeking answers beyond those posed by the teacher in school. The American culture depends greatly on the originality of its citizens. Schooling sometimes teaches children to conform, to follow directions, to wait for the teacher to instruct what is expected, but there is a balancing element that has to be presented. Children have to be encouraged, at the same time that they are learning to follow directions, to also reach beyond the present or specifically obvious materials. Their doing so is, in part dependent on the qualities of idealism, of wondering, and of questioning. The ability to be dissatisfied, somewhat critical, and hopeful of more than what is given, goes far in extending children's studies and intellectual capacities.

Growth occurs at all levels. It will not occur, however, if children are taught to think that final answers prevail once an individual has heard some. After children realize that they have discovered many answers to a specific social studies unit themselves, they also have to realize the scientific orientation, which is that people do the best with what is available right now as correct answers to questions. People must be aware, however, that tomorrow or the next day or the one after they may uncover new ideas that can refute the old or supplement them at least. The scientific perspective of the physical or life sciences is sustained in the social sciences as well. This is what pupils can learn in the social studies unit, that although, within a given frame of reference, the ideas of today are correct, they may be differently perceived or explained tomorrow or in the next five or ten years. This does not invalidate the work or serious efforts today to continue to function in the pursuit of excellence or accuracy.

A degree of flexibility, of a willingness to provide evidence for what we know, and a willingness to engage in the see-saw effects of argument of right or wrong, sensible or foolish, provide the stuff for intellectual probing. The teacher's attitude in bringing the pupils to that point of enjoying discussions of two or more points of view on a topic or concept becomes the mirror for the children. The teacher has to take care that this fresh-minded and spiritual approach to seek academic truth is well fed. The children benefit as well as the teacher.

Teaching Decision Making Through the Social Studies

Besides involving children in decision making when they have to read in science or mathematics, they can be effectively responsible in it when they are involved in the social studies. Because society is a topic of their concern, they read about it and learn how people operate in their own society to affect social policy.

Children learn about voting, about a government for the people, by the people, and of the people. Society is much the same. No single person can make up a society. It requires collectivities of people, of individuals. People decide how to govern themselves; they decide on certain rules that are compatible with their values or beliefs and patterns of living.

When children first meet as a classroom group, the teacher typically asks them to create rules that seem fair for them in their daily routines. Some teachers will watch for situations that can be used to stimulate questions and reasons for rule making. The necessity for ideas that will help children refrain from getting in each other's way or from misusing materials, that will allow everyone a fair chance to do what (s)he would like at appropriate times in the school day, become obvious when something that caused conflict occurs.

The pupils, with the guidance of the teacher, learn how to decide which modes of conduct would be better for a particular class. The teacher may have ideas to recommend, but the children are guided in making their own decisions that will serve their own group well. Sometimes, even when the teacher anticipates some problems in the decisions they have made to govern themselves, (s)he lets them put those decisions into practice. If they do not involve a safety hazard, and merely introduce inconsistencies or difficulties, the children find out by putting the rule into effect how it works. If it needs to be amended or rescinded they can do so. They learn in that manner, to some extent, how society works.

By taking responsibility for their own behavior through the creation of rules intended to be fair to everyone, children learn how decisions are made. They learn that if they make the rules, they have to abide by them. They learn, too, that rules cannot be made capriciously. If they were, nothing would be accomplished. People would not be able to trust each other and have confidence in the intentions and hopes of individuals.

The teacher uses examples that will allow children to see a decision through to its ultimate realization. If everyone can take paintbrushes out of the cupboard and use them whenever it pleases him/her, what will happen to the number of paintbrushes on hand for use? If they can be used whenever one wishes and merely kept or placed in the sink when the individual is finished with them, what happens to the supply on hand for everybody? Teachers have to help children anticipate problems so that suggestions for group behavior can be created by the children and the teacher. The teacher's will is not imposed on the children. The teacher senses a valid opportunity to help children learn to make decisions that will affect them and improve their quality of classroom life.

Decision making for young children is done on simple levels related to which should be done first, get a drink or go to the bathroom. On what do these decisions depend? They depend on consciously stated options related to the anticipated best outcomes. For the decisions related to several possibilities leading to new choices for children, more time is needed to explain what may happen if any one of the choices is followed.

The experimentation used in science gives clues. The problem is defined. Possible ways of solving the problem are offered. Reasons for choosing any one of the options are given as a rationale for following any one of them. This accustoms children to the habit of thinking of several alternatives for any decision before they make one. This perspective can strengthen mental health habits. It can help children realize that more than one answer can solve the conflict. The greater the facility for finding solutions, the better the chance children have for choosing what they will like.

Democratic frameworks are based on the assumption that each individual's voice will be heard or counted. The basis for helping children realize how important their own views are emerges from the fact that they live in a country that employs voting to allow people to register their feelings or perceptions. Individual citizenship rests on education. It is assumed that people will find out for themselves why and how they should vote a certain way. It is assumed that they are sensible and want to have their views counted among others in society.

This view is different from that of governments which want to hold the power of rule within the body of a few men who formulate a group that "speaks" with one voice. This arrangement would not necessitate the people's knowing anything except to fearfully obey any ruler or ruling body in power at any given time. This view is also predicated on the thinking that people held to the rule of a supreme governmental power are inferior. It assumes that they need not have the intelligence to question or to analyze what is happening to them.

The democratic society is based on the assumption that the leaders represent the ideals and goals of the people; therefore it must assume an informed group in its citizenry. In any idealized plan for a people, it must also be considered that the plan will not always be perfectly implemented. Ideals are goals toward which people strive. They are not always reached. It is significant and important, however, that people continue to strive for the ideas that are viable to a society.

Children learn, too, that what works well for one people may not work well for another. They are committed to their own country's goals, for the most part. It does not mean that they cannot be critical, wanting to improve their country. This, too, is a function of the democratic framework, an admirable and courageous perspective.

The goals of American people stem from an ethic that has been with this society ever since it began; the effort toward improvement for everyone's well-being goes on in several ways. Television and radio, plus other communicative media, have facilitated the immediate awareness of an American public concerned about what happens to others less fortunate than themselves. This value impels many individuals to offer help or money to people they do not know but who have been identified as victims in a situation over which they had not control.[15]

The process of helping one's self, or others, is strongly related to making effective decisions. Judgment, wisdom, and choices depend on how an individual interprets the opportunities at hand. Very often an individual victimizes him/herself because of not being able to create new opportunities. This limiting perspective makes the difference between an individual who simply follows directions blindly, without thinking of ways to alter them, and an individual who recommends new choices that haven't been considered up to this point. Children must be encouraged constantly to create new alternatives for themselves and for others in order to further their well-being in contemporary society.

Contemporary society, with its myriad of books telling people how to take the responsibility for their own fates, is testimony to the fact that somewhere in past educational practices children were not taught to think of worthwhile ideas that could help them become more discerning and effective people. There has to be a degree of self-satisfaction along with the satisfaction one receives from helping others. One receives impressions of self-worth from the way others treat him/her. A mutuality of exchange that is satisfying has to occur. This is not easy throughout a life cycle.

The educational process is strategic in the decision-making role. Families can also provide children with the reasoning that underlies consideration of the best anticipated outcome. Children hear the way parents make decisions about purchasing something, about moving, about renting or purchasing a place to live. This kind of discussion, often carried on at the dinner table, is sometimes referred to as the hidden curriculum in the middle-class home. It has the elements of reasoning, of justifying one's position in terms of given facts, emergencies, or whatever in order to win an argument. Children at school have to learn how to reason, how to state a perspective based on acceptable facts, all of which are part of the ability to be logical and to persuade others of an interpretation for a solution to a problem.

Democracy, routines in life, life-saving choices, consideration for others, a society's well-being, improved conditions, peaceful world status—all of these relate to effective decision making on both an individual and a group basis. The collectivity in any society and various subgroups, affects the destiny of its individual members. Children learn this in real life, whether it be in the kindergarten, first, second, or third grade. Their teachers are aware of what has meaning to them relative to home or school life. They know how to approach them in affecting the ways and means of making effective choices.

Often, when an election year approaches, teachers use this as a means of helping children learn how to present both (or more) points of view of different political parties. They learn to criticize aspects of all. They mention advantages and disadvantages of all. They become analytical in efforts to understand the issues. Just as is true of advertising, political platforms are intended to persuade people that the best means will be employed for the people, and that consequently they should vote for or buy a represented product, or support an individual or platform.

Debates are appropriate when children are able to prepare facts and arguments on each side, pro and con, of certain issues. Young children, five or six years old cannot implement a debate as successfully, of course, as can older children. Sustaining the thought, the original argument, being consistent in taking a position and knowing how to answer the refuting or defending statements require mental agility that can develop after a few years in school. Debates are done well in high schools. The underlying ideas, however, should be approached in elementary school.

Since teachers are expected to have the wisdom and perception for arranging activities that children can accomplish with success, they are also expected to understand and to know children well. The perceptive teacher does not burden children with ideas that are known to be too difficult or frustrating. The skill of knowing how to approach new ideas so that at least the gifted children can gain from them, while at the same time not extending these ideas for the whole class to the point of losing their interest, is priceless. This kind of teacher is well aware at all times what is affecting the pupils. This kind of teacher, too, gains great satisfaction from teaching.

After making decisions, teachers often check with the children in order to determine whether the decision making was effective. A discussion arises. Could it have been improved? If so, how? How has it helped? Children need to be self-analytical as well.

Decision making and problem solving are skills that children need to acquire at various levels of their abilities. Social studies often introduce ideas that may be anywhere from very familiar to unfamiliar to the pupils. Various authors suggest ways to stimulate problem solving and learning how to make decisions, not only in the scientific process of inquiry but also in an interpersonal sense.[16]

Interpersonal relationships are an excellent topic of discussion in the context of social studies units. They are examples of the products of many people interacting effectively with each other toward the realization of a common goal.

Critical observation of one's environment stimulates discussion among groups. Disagreement does not mean dislike of one another. An excellent medium or focus as a topic for discussion can be provided through the observations made by children of television programs. They should be taught to be critical and nonaccepting.[17]

Parents can be very helpful to children if they can help them respond thoughtfully and reflectively to what they see, hear, read, and observe around them in the behavior of people in the environment. Being selective in what one chooses to accept is in part a way of acquiring a philosophy for a way of conducting one's life. Being appreciative of another person's point of view does not mean that one has to agree with it and be guided by it for one's own course of action.

Children can learn how to disagree through scientific modes of discourse. They can learn, too, how to stand their own ground when they are convinced by a given point of view. They can also learn that it can help them when they seek further information on an idea to read about it or to ask a resource person some questions about it.

The habits and guidance that can be generated through studies of social import and the products of humankind of the past or present are worthwhile when put to work by a skillful teacher. Many books on the instruction of scientice, of mathematics, and of social studies place a high emphasis on the role of the teacher in guiding pupils so that they will profit by their experiences at school. Social studies patterns and ideas underlie many perspectives that many teachers value. In that sense alone the subject of matter can be taught with conviction and the materials of the classroom can be arranged to tempt pupils' interests and modes of inquiry.

Children can be taught an independence in the pursuit of inquiry as well a confidence in their choices based on objectivity and dependable data. When children are critical enough to protect themselves from accepting false information, the teacher who has worked with them may take pride in such an accomplishment. Parents, too, who urge their children to search for facts, suspecting easy answers, are doing a service for their children's best interests.

SUMMARY

This chapter was concerned with the means and manner of creating social studies units. It involved the processes for acquiring facts, concepts, and generalizations used in teaching social studies units.

Although social studies at the elementary levels are abstract forms of subject matter, the teacher can become skillful in bringing the meaning to real relationships in a child's life. The teacher realizes that the generalizations of the social studies are drawn from the social sciences. Researchers at higher educational levels conduct research, investigations, and surveys that yield data upon which trust can be placed for instruction.

Many years ago, educators used to acquire social studies information from other than social scientists. Minimal knowledge was given on how a country governed itself, what its people thought, how its people earned their livings, what their children did, what their educational systems were like. In contemporary social studies programs, children are receiving better information about other people and countries. They are able to compare and to identify with other societies. This is not done to consider one superior to the other. It is done to have understanding occur in regard to the ways that people are similar and different.

Humans values stem from their own society and from families that transmit cherished goals for human behavior. Certain attitudes and characteristics make parents proud of their children and make their children proud of themselves. This is a complicated dynamic affecting years of person-to-person interaction. The social studies provide a crucial role in the curriculum of the school.

Not only do children learn about interpersonal behavior through the social studies unit that is taught well, they also learn about social values as reflective of their society. They learn why and how democratic behavior is significant in the American culture. They learn how some other societies function differently. They learn what their own responsibility is relevant to contributing to the well-being of their own society.

Pupils learn how humankind has both changed and adapted to the physical environment. They learn how inventions, imagination, creativity, or initiative function to build an exciting and progressive society. Each person may benefit from the thinking of enlightened minds. People with illuminating minds can help the condition of people less fortunate than they are. Children learn what compassion means. They learn how it feels to become aware of victimized individuals in their own society. The educational process via the social studies does a great deal toward helping children learn how to empathize with others.

Any social studies unit can be developed in the same manner. The teacher acquires information at the adult-oriented level and at the pupils' level. The bulk of data in the form of booklets, newspaper articles, books, notes, pictures, graphs, and any other *realia* that can illustrate concepts of the unit are brought together, filed effectively, and reread to create the teaching unit for the pupils at a given grade level. Any teacher can become adept at this process. It is very satisfying and exciting.

TOPICS FOR DISCUSSION

1. Why are the social studies important in the kindergarten and primary grades? What do they contribute to children's development and learning? How is the teacher instrumental in these directions?
2. How does the teacher acquire information needed for a specific social studies unit? What affects the decision to select a particular theme or topic to use with the children?
3. After observing a social studies unit being taught in the kindergarten, discuss its major objectives, what you think the children gained from it, and how you think it might have been improved. You may want to observe the social studies unit while it is being instructed for three sessions if the teacher will permit it.
4. Develop a mini-unit of three major generalizations on the topic that you think would be appropriate for children in the first grade. Consult several books to obtain information on both adult-oriented data and child-oriented data. Books for children should be brought to class for the discussion. Five books will be sufficient to demonstrate your point indicating that you are aware of what is important for children to read. In cases where children are not able to read the level of book you have brought, indicate that you would read it to them if you were the teacher.
5. What characteristic would guide you in deciding on a topic for young children? What elements in the children and what elements in the social studies unit would affect your choices in creating activities for children? You may focus on a given age group or grade level.
6. Has the educational system changed in the past twenty years regarding social studies, what is included in them, and how units should be written? Describe and explain.
7. How has the understanding about children's personality development changed the way teachers guide them in decision-making processes? Why is this view appropriate today? Does society change from year to year or from decade to decade? How so? How can teachers help children modify their thinking to fit changes in society?
8. Look at three different courses of study in social studies (any school district in the city, state, or country) and indicate the differences or similarities among them. Note the references they used. Comment on the objectives they have indicated are important to their units.
9. What would be an ideal social studies unit for children in a second grade that you would want to teach? Give the objectives for the unit as children would learn from it, the major content areas or generalizations that they would study, and the general outcomes of the unit when they were finished. Could the processes you use during their studies help them in their life outside of school? If so, why and how?

NOTES

1. Knowledge of what a society values is transmitted to the young by parents and other adults. It is difficult to reconcile the feelings of constraints that are sensed by individuals in relation to what they think "society" wants when those constraints were actually implemented by the children's own close care-givers or people that they see frequently.
2. When prisoners or hostages are incarcerated in some way and kept from their typical life

patterns of behavior, and forced to behave as their captors enforce them, these personalities change.

3. Norman Goodman and Gary T. Marx, *Society Today*, 3rd ed. (New York: Random, 1978), p. 560. Goodman and Marx define society as "A relatively large, relatively autonomous collection of people who have a common heritage that is transmitted from generation to generation and who interact with one another in socially structured relationships."

4. Look at curriculum guides of years past and note how different the social studies units were from those that are presented today.

5. Leonard Broom and Philip Selznick, *Sociology: A Text with Adapted Readings*, 6th ed. (New York: Harper, 1977), pp 303 and 304. Most nuclear families, consisting of "a conjugal pair and their offspring" are involved with "sexual, reproductive, economic, and educational" aspects of the vital functions in a society. There are a few exceptions to kinship systems using the nuclear family as a type and which do not also perform educational or economical functions.

6. Ibid., p. 305. One form of extended family is one in which "three generations live together under the same roof or in a family compound. Several married siblings, their spouses and offspring, and the grandparents together form a residential, economic, and educational unit."

7. John U. Michaelis, *Social Studies for Children in a Democracy*, 6th ed. (Englewood Cliffs, N.J.: Prentice-Hall, 1976), p. 19. Michaelis refers to facts as specific items of information. Concepts are abstractions that apply to a class or group of objects "having some qualities in common." "Generalizations are statements of broad applicability that indicate relationships between concepts." They are presented as main or major ideas, principles, laws, and other broad conclusions.

8. Ibid., Chapter 4. "Relating Instruction to Growth Characteristics and Individual Differences," pp. 111–143.

9. Loren Weybright, "Young Children Growing Through Action," pp. 18–31 in *Social Studies in Early Childhood: An Interactionist Point of View*, edited by Alicia Pagano (Washington, D.C.: National Council for the Social Studies, 1978).

10. Ibid., p. 25.

11. Michaelis, op. cit., pp. 299–443, provides excellent ideas for integrating various types of subject matter offered at different times of the day into the substantive learnings of the social studies.

12. Even the toys that young children or their younger siblings use can be mentioned (e.g., pull-toys, carts, wagons, musical revolving cylinders that are pulled along the ground).

13. Lavona A. Hanna, Gladys L. Potter, and Robert W. Reynolds, *Dynamic Elementary Social Studies*, 3rd ed. (New York: Holt, 1973), pp. 92–108. Several ideas are offered for ways that units can be initiated.

14. Ibid., pp. 117–118.

15. Sociologists who have studied the values of American society indicate that the philanthropic orientation is a strong one among Americans, who contribute money to people in various forms of distress (flood victims, victims of unfair treatment by someone or an agency, a sick child or adult who needs money).

16. Hanna, Potter, and Reynolds, op. cit., pp. 148–184. See also, Michaelis, op. cit., pp. 178–218, and John R. Lee, *Teaching Social Studies in the Elementary School* (New York: Free Press, a Division of Macmillan, 1974), pp. 60–72.

17. Luberta Mays and Alicia L. Pagano, "Children and Media," pp. 70–81, in *Social Studies in Early Childhood: An Interactionist Point of View* (Washington, D.C.: National Council for the Social Studies, 1978).

SELECTED REFERENCES

BRANDWEIN, PAUL F. The Social Sciences. Concepts and Values. Series for the Elementary School. New York: Harcourt Brace Jovanovich, Inc., 1970.

BROOM, LEONARD, and PHILIP SELZNICK. *Sociology: A Text with Adapted Readings*, 6th ed. New York: Harper & Row, Publishers, Inc., 1977. 619 pp.

DURKIN, MARY C., ALICE DUVALL, and ALICE McMASTER. *The Taba Social Studies Curriculum*. Menlo Park, Calif.: Addison-Wesley Publishing Co., Inc., 1969. Units for each grade in an elementary school (six in all). 3rd ed.

GOODMAN, NORMAN, and GARY T. MARX. *Society Today*, 3rd ed. New York: Random House, Inc., 1978. 592 pp.

HANNA, LAVONE A., GLADYS L. POTTER, and ROBERT W. REYNOLDS. *Dynamic Elementary Social Studies*, 3rd ed. New York: Holt, Rinehart and Winston, 1973. 484 pp.

JAROLIMEK, JOHN. *Social Studies in Elementary Education*, 5th ed. New York: Macmillan Publishing Co., Inc., 1977. 369 pp.

LEE, JOHN R. *Teaching Social Studies in the Elementary School*. New York: The Free Press, a Division of the Macmillan Publishing Company, Inc., 1974. 367 pp.

MAYS, LUBERTA, and ALICIA L. PAGANO. "Children and Media," pp. 70–81, *Social Studies in Early Childhood: An Interactionist Point of View*, edited by Alicia Pagano. Washington, D.C.: National Council for the Social Studies. 95 pp.

MICHAELIS, JOHN U. *Social Studies for Children in a Democracy*, 6th ed. Englewood Cliffs, N.J.: Prentice-Hall, Inc., 1976. 516 pp.

PERROT, PAUL N. "Children, Museums and Changing Societies: The Growing Interdependence of Cultures," *Children Today*, Vol. 9, No. 1 (January–February 1980), pp. 17–21.

SENESH, LAWRENCE. *Our Working Families*. Teacher's Resource Guide. Chicago, Ill.: Science Research Associates Inc., 1973. 288 pp.

TRUNDLE, ROMA. *Peoples of the World*. London: Usborne Publishing, Ltd., 1978. 32 pp.

WALSH, HUBER M. *Introducing the Young Child to the Social World*. New York: Macmillan Publishing Co., Inc., 1980. 283 pp.

WEYBRIGHT, LOREN. "Young Children Growing Through Action," pp. 18–31 in *Social Studies in Early Childhood: An Interactionist Point of View*, edited by Alicia L. Pagano. Washington, D.C.: National Council for the Social Studies, 1978. 95 pp.

The Arts: Their Potential in Children's Development

Few other areas of subject matter that children are exposed to at school carry the generativity needed to lure individuals into expressing themselves that the arts carry. The frameworks of the arts fields encourage uniqueness and originality. These fields prize individuality and a recognition of new ideas. The schools can encourage such expression. Teachers need support for the courses of action that are helpful in removing some of the constraints that children sense in the expressive areas of work at school.

It stands to reason that children are not born with constraints to the extent that they may sense them when they arrive at school. Few individuals would fare well if no constraints were imposed as a functioning member of society. Rules for learning and governing one's self vary to some extent. Constraints where self-expression in the aesthetically created frameworks are concerned, however, are different from the usual face-to-face morally oriented constraints that people sense in the course of human interaction.

This chapter compresses, in the interests of space limitations, the topics of art, music, and rhythms/movement that young children experience at school. The children have experiences at home, too, and in other non-school contexts. Their knowledge of the arts and self-expression in them represents a range of differences in terms of experiences they might have had, an understanding of the arts, and what those fields mean to them in the sense of self-expression or as satisfying intellectual or aesthetic acts.

Painting, Drawing, Collága, Puppetry, and Clay Modeling

Young children who attend kindergarten have typically had some experiences in self-expression with a crayon, a pencil, a ball-point pen or a marker. The kind and number of experiences that children have had in this category vary greatly from child to child, as do other activities in school subjects. Limited experiences with those media are the result of a limited income of parents, in some cases, or of a lack of people in the environment who can give the children opportunities to draw, paint, write, and the like.

One child whose parents have given him many opportunities to draw, paint, and express himself in a variety of ways created the birth announcement that his family mailed to friends when the youngest child was born. See an illustration of it on page 362. Noah was eight years old when he drew the announcement.

Five-year-old children in kindergarten need media that are manageable for them. They enjoy experiences with painting at an easel on which newsprint has been attached, using large brushes and containers of paint that are easily accessible to them. They need facilities that permit them some

Noah's drawing was used as the family's birth announcement of Sarah's arrival.

freedom of movement. Teachers need to encourage them to put on paper what they wish to do. Some teachers show children how to avoid the dripping of watery paint mixtures if the children seem to want help. Typically, however, the teacher may avoid giving too many directions when the children start painting. Too much direction can distract and inhibit some children who are worried about following directions properly.

One writer indicates that art is a way of learning, not a subject like other subjects.[1] Teachers use art as a tool involving children in the process of learning and in that sense they are not teaching art, per se.

During the preschool years, children's art takes on the appearance of scribblings, followed at later stages of development by "circular, ovoid, and sticklike representations of people and things."[2] Various forms occur repeatedly in the early elementary grades, gradually acquiring greater detail as the child wishes to express it.

Children's impressions of what they see, and consequently draw when given the opportunity, vary in terms of chronological age and frequency of experiences with various media in arts. The child attempts to organize to some extent the perceptual imagery as it relates to his/her retinal imagery.[3] The child's perceptions are different from adults'.

Teachers are urged to give children reasons to create so that when they are involved in working with an art form they may have identified the process as their own. Unless children are oriented toward purposeful activity when they are involved in art, they are not, as Feldman sees it, becoming effectively involved.[4] He also advises that child art be recognized as an inevitable aspect of the children's normal development, that children's creation of imagery is natural in the context of their needs rather than the needs of others, that children must not be entrapped into creating art in order to have educators or others use the product to diagnose or assess a developmental stage of the children, that curricula have to be designed so that art is one among several objectives rather than the only one, and that people should not consider that intelligence can be trained by urging children to create images that conform with preconceived conceptual or established norms.[5]

Children in contemporary society have had to accelerate perceptual imagery interpretations owing to the television, movies, and other electronic media in the environment. Life, travel, and means of obtaining meaning from experiences have become upbeat, quick, and oversimplified. It is suggested that teachers help children learn how to criticize art products, how to reflect, and how to take more time to make decisions of their own.

Art is seen more as a part of reality than it has been in years past.[6] Viewers of the art form are perceived as part of the organization of a product in art. The instability of art forms is assumed to be more popular today

Bulletin boards in the classroom contain the contributions of the children. It is their art work that enhances their own classroom. (Photo by Gerald J. Margolin.)

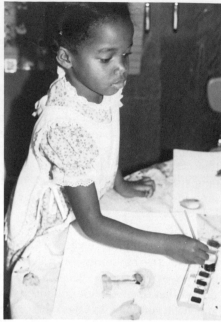
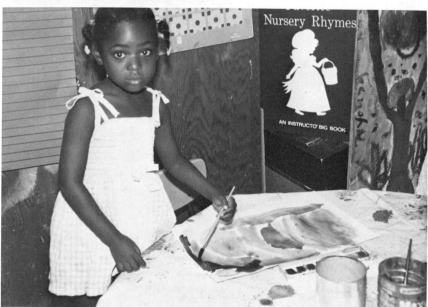

Kindergarten children take their work seriously as they look at the blank page
before them and begin to paint. They appreciate the admiration and attention
given to them by the kindergarten teacher. (Photo by Gerald J. Margolin.)

than before, because the participation of the observer is expected to be more satisfactory with such art. But even if art forms in contemporary society have changed, children need purpose.

Children's work at school takes on an apparent artificiality when the pupils themselves do not have a purpose for their product or work toward that end. Planning of the teacher has to be done with the children so that together they decide how to proceed. The children's major interests in creating a product are uppermost in the teacher's mind, preorganization for the lesson is done by the teacher, but the motivation and specifics for the children's directions in their work have to be cooperatively planned.

The interdependence of creating art and responding to it is essential to an art program.[7] The enrichment of an individual's feelings can be made visible through art. It also contributes to a way of looking at the world. One's perceptions are affected by the way one interprets the world. Several individuals may see something and yet interpret it differently when describing it to another. Art is boundaryless in this sense that it can become an instrumental large and personalized part of any individual's life.

Children can be encouraged in tendencies to express themselves. They may in their early years at school want someone to help them draw or paint, thinking that their work has to look like something other than their own expression. Their own work represents elements of the environment or perceptions that have significance for them. A child thinking of an elephant, for example that was seen at the zoo, may draw large ears, a trunk, heavy legs and a narrow body. Depending on what the child was impressed with at any given time, the drawing will represent those images of thought. An emphasis on a body part reflects the child's perceptual emphasis, not the actual retinal images on the eye.

Painting is one medium that will attract children if it is presented to them as something that everybody can do. When children choose to take up the paintbrush after it has been dipped into the tempera (a water soluble mixture of paint), and to see what the movement of the paint-tipped brush does to the paper, they are intrigued. Children need time to explore handling the materials, to see what they can do. In a sense, the artistic approach is like the scientific creative approach, which involves playful changes in the materials and placement of them. Testing, manipulating, trying an idea out one way, then another, in a relaxed manner allow the child to sense the kinesthetic aspects of controlling the paint and the brush.

The teacher's comments of appreciation about the shape of the line, the characteristics of it (e.g., bold, fine, concentrated, exciting and jagged) and the colors or color blends encourage the child to try at more products.

Art is a way of seeing life and events. Whatever the medium used in expressing an idea, it represents an individual's perceptions and interpretations. Drawing, whether with a pencil, charcoal, crayon, cray-pa, or other materials, allows a visual development of an idea in an unusual way. The medium affects the qualities and textures expressed in an image.

Drawing involves three types of seeing: first, an ability to judge shapes, relationships, and proportions; second, an ability to recognize or to organize the potential for drawing a subject; and third, an ability to interpret the lines of the drawing itself.[8] The kind of seeing that is involved in the act of

Five-year-old Children's Drawings of Themselves and of Their Families. The placement of the hands relative to the length of arms, position and appearance of fingers, expression on the faces, hair styles, action suggested by the direction of legs of the figures, all suggest individual differences among children as they express ideas about the people they know.

drawing is closer to perceptions of the eye, less with the "interpretive actions of the brain."[9] This observation suggests that an individual needs to have time and practice to become engaged in the process of drawing. Habits of seeing or of focusing on lines in the way that a map is read for preciseness and direction are different from the seeing that is involved in perceiving an object for a basis of drawing.

Children develop symbols to represent things or people in the products they draw. As they have more practice, those symbols are replaced by more naturalistic depictions."[10] A box represents a body, lines from the top represent arms and other oddly placed forms manifest an idea or representation in the child's mind. Adults who start drawing begin in a similar manner. Older habits of seeing or drawing can change with more opportunities to draw and to visualize proportions and shapes.

It is essential that a teacher of young children be aware of the children's need to express ideas and to have time to do so. What children's work looks like when they are finished with it is less important than their thinking, reflective activity, and judgment during the process of drawing. When children have placed on paper some of their own "marks," they have learned to bring together an external world with an inner one. Children are seeing their environment in another form, in another way, and in another mode of perceptiveness, given a specific instrument that is used to note that world around them.

From the earliest years to elementary school, adults "must tread carefully within the realm of art" of children.[11] Children need time, space, an appropriate place, and ample materials for self-expression in art forms. After children experience a scribbling stage, they move to making shapes at about three or four years old. Drawing or painting designs follow the shape-making stage, which gradually becomes a pictorial stage for some children at about four or five. Kindergarten teachers see these changes in children's drawings from one stage to another. It is recommended, however, that children be allowed to develop ideas themselves and that they grow into each stage, not be forced into each one.

In teachers' desires to teach, it often becomes difficult for them just to stand back and appreciate the child's unique efforts and ideas. Lines and circles as well as relationships of shapes to each other demonstrate the child's attempts to structure parts that formulate a total entity. Even if the teacher does not understand what the child is seeing or thinking about, the child is involved in an important process of making sense out of a thought. This process mediates an internal and external bond between the child and the environment.

The child needs minimal help from the teacher other than quietly standing by implicitly showing that the child can continue with what is happening to a drawing or painting. Respect for the child's work is necessary in the same way that one respects the feelings of an individual who is explaining them to a teacher.

The teacher can introduce new materials by making them or buying them. Many books give ideas for recipes that stimulate finger paint, molding or sculpturing media, and various forms of collage materials.[12] The materials must be safe, nontoxic and noncaustic. Children must be protected

Slotted plexi-glass has a quality and texture to it that lends itself to certain forms and varying designs that go beyond other materials that kindergarten children have been given to use in art periods. (Photo by Gerald J. Margolin.)

from harshness in media. They often put their hands to their eyes, nose, or other body parts. Media that are used for art must be considered in several ways before the teacher uses them. Are they water soluble? Are they nonpoisonous? Can they hurt the children if fingers are placed into the mouth, eyes, or nose while the children are involved in their work?

A variety of media brings interest into children's work as well as giving them the opportunities for knowing what various textures can do when one manipulates them in certain or personal ways. Materials, feathers, velvets, and sandpaper offer a variety of sensations and opportunities for design.

Collage, which involves cutting and placing paper, various textures, and objects on a background, is not a difficult activity for young children. They learn to control several textures simultaneously and to place shapes, lines, or string forms in various ways on a large sheet of construction paper or heavier cardboard. The characteristics of the paper or objects that are to be pasted on a background determine to some extent the kind of paste that will be used or strength of the background paper (or cardboard) that will be used to hold the shapes in place for an extended period of time without crumbling or tearing. The teacher has to anticipate wrinkling, ripping, or crumbling effects that can happen when children manipulate their work. Whenever possible, the media should be strong enough to endure mishandling, unintended for the most part, by the children.

Children enjoy handling things that have various textural surfaces. Roughness, smoothness, ridged surfaces, deep-piled fabrics' surfaces and the many things that are touched in the environment reveal different characteristics. Often people like a certain fabric because of the way it feels to them. Suedes, silks, dotted swiss, celanese, or cotton twill offer different sensations to the touch.

Collage is a form of three-dimensional art involving the type of material selected, the shapes and placement of them, and the general composition in space and design. An unusual use of space, form, and materials combined represent a total entity. This activity encourages "play" with materials, which is excellent for learning about shapes, textures and the nature of various art materials. Children need time for this. Sometimes children bring magazines that have pictures of things or scenery that interest them. They may use these to depict an idea or theme.

Teachers can collect in several large boxes objects and materials that can be used as trimming for cards that children will make at various holiday times of the year. Collage ideas, or paper assemblages, or three-dimensional products involve a range of sizes of materials and shapes. Even the smallest piece of lace extending from a fold that represents a hat becomes a focal point in the total composition. Effectiveness of selection and placement depends on the way the child wishes to represent an idea.

Creativity in children can be expressed when permitted. Teachers are expected, as art educators view it, to allow children to acquire skills in art as they experience activities at school, and to allow children to "gain insight into and identify with the nature of creative, artistic acts."[13] Collage can be used to create valentines and mother's day cards, and to develop bulletin board ideas and posters for any of the holidays. The teacher can also motivate the children by bringing a variety of books and ideas or photographs to school in which scenic or object representation can be sensed by the children. Ideas can be obtained, for example, when a teacher shows children a book such as *Windows*,[14] in which the psychological impressions of looking through a window (from the inside out, or from the outside in) can be bound with the materials or objects that can be seen.

Similar ideas can be used by the children when the teacher brings in objects that are typically carried in one's pockets. The subject of pockets as holders of objects, hands, fingers hooking on to them, and a variety of ideas stimulate children's activity as they start on an unusual self-expressive product.

The teacher usually stimulates ideas in children by asking them what they think about something, how it feels to them, what it makes them think of or why. These questions arouse visual impressions and kinesthetic ones, as well, at times. The children can be asked questions that arouse a sense of smell, taste, or sound. Imagery arousing the different senses results in a stronger sensation than only one sense may provide. Some teachers use music with art activities in order to create feeling tones.

Animation controlled by children is created through the use of puppets developed by children. Simple hand or fist puppets, paper bag puppets, finger people papier maché heads with material/fabric bodies and clothing, stimulate ideas as the children speak for the characters that have been created.[15] Puppets become very real to children—and even to adults. Focusing on a puppet and its conversation is similar to watching an individual speak in an animated manner.

Various types of finger, stick, or stringed puppets or marionettes can be made when children at various age levels and developmental abilities are considered. Frustrating activities defeat the purposes of art for a child. Planning a puppet for conveying a message that has been planned with the children provides purpose for the pupils and presents a means through which artistic efforts can be made. Reasons for the creation of art products should emerge from the children.

Messages that can be conveyed by the puppets can be singular ones much like those that are performed by "talking dolls." Children can think of greetings or short poems that they would like to present through the movements of a puppet. Some teachers plan with the children a brief playlet that has grown out of content that has been learned in social studies and present a short dialogue planned by the children's working knowledge of a given set of topics.

The teacher takes the clues from the children's comments and questions, and guides ideas that emerge from the content originating from the pupils' statements. The teacher is helping the children externalize their ideas. Mind images become transformed into expressions that can be heard and enjoyed by other children. In these instances, teachers become artistic translators of children's ideas.

One writer recommends that poetry be used with children's puppets.[16] Animated dolls that seem to jump out of the child's (or the teacher's) pocket attract the children's attention. Spontaneous action during a poetry reading (or dialogue between characters) enriches the experiences. Children can plan to make a character that appeals to them and seems to make a story come alive.

Even though teachers may have inhibitions about their own artistic tendencies, they have to encourage children to express theirs. Most books that are used at university levels to prepare teachers to work with children in the areas of art education, include sufficient information to provide teachers with a sense of direction. That direction typically includes allowing the children to move actively with their materials. It permits the children to mix, mess, and move art media within their own province, so to speak. Children learn that they may not misuse materials by throwing them or using them in ways that annoy other children. Young children sometimes become so comfortable with their finger painting that they begin doing it on the faces, arms, or legs of their classmates. Materials for any activity need to be used appropriately to the purpose of the activity.

Scraps of materials or boxes and empty plastic bottles or other containers can make interesting puppets.[17] Cereal boxes, large and small, as well as tiny gift boxes, present ideas for the creation of puppets. Children's imaginations often go into high gear with the impetus provided by discussions of shape, form, and colors or fabrics that can be used for puppet development.

Creativity with puppet design, production of playlets to accompany one's puppet, or the creation of poetry and dialogue that animate the words that come from the child who planned the production can become, in the planning process, silly and hysterical at times. Creation of new ideas, leaps of imagination, and a "What-Would-Happen-If" orientation lead to funny statements.[18] This possibility has to be capitalized on, enjoyed with the children, and encouraged in the vein of humor.

Children may enjoy animating the various types of alphabet symbols that exist throughout the world.[19] Shapes and symbols are a form of approach to other products in art. Again, experiences in art lead not only to understanding one's own thoughts; they lead to understanding what other people think as well. The symbolism used by various peoples in the world gives children an appreciation of relationships between thought and symbols.

Unusual sources of ideas for the teacher or the pupils can be seen in compilations of work representing early efforts of well-known people.[20] The work of people such as Hemingway, Churchill, Beethoven, Picasso, and H. G. Wells, to name a few, are represented in a collection of drawings, poetry, music, and other art forms. Some children (or the teacher) may be able to identify with the writers, artists, historians, or notable personalities and their experiences in childhood and adolescent years.

Various types of clay permit children mold and shape them into rolled "worms," bulky animal forms, and the like. Children enjoy the quality of clay that allow them to push, pound, join together, place lumps on top of one another, and generally poke it in the way it will yield to the touch. The permanent medium of ceramic clay is used when the school can afford it, and when there is a kiln available (or nearby) to bake the product so that it lasts. A child's artistic animal created in kindergarten or the first grade is a priceless treasure indeed. Parents typically appreciate having it.

Children can mold objects out of plasticene, sand and water, play dough, and ceramic clay when the teacher can help them use it successfully. It is recommended that children work the clay on a cloth-covered board about 6 inches square. This allows the children to move the work, apply pieces to it when they want to attach something, and also to remove it for study or exhibiting it.[21]

Doweling, tongue depressors, and various utensils can be used when the children have had some experience manipulating clay with their hands. Children can learn how to keep their clay in workable condition by using water and by storing it properly in a covered damp container. Clay can be made usable, after it has become hardened through exposure to the air, by adding water and kneading it into the clay to remove air bubbles.[22]

Children enjoy creating various textures on the surfaces of their clay products. Brush strokes, or ceramic clay mixed with water and pushed through a fine sieve can become hair that can be placed on an animal art form. Experimenting with the clay and letting one's imagination guide one's hands can result in very satisfying art forms.

It is suggested that no singular technique is known to be the best one for modeling with clay. Children in kindergarten may be given a lump of clay that is about half a pound; children in the first grade can manage about the same and slightly more than the half pound.[23] By the time children are in the second grade they may have had experiences with heavier masses of clay. Pupils in higher grades can typically manage about a two-pound piece.

Until a child has completed his/her work, it can be kept moist by covering it with a damp cloth and enclosing it in a plastic or rubber airtight form, or bag. When a child's heavy clay object is finally intended to dry, it may do so when left on a shelf (away from the handling of others in the classroom). It can be touched with water and a brush in order to protect pieces attached to the clay product from falling off prior to the total drying of the form.[24]

Sculptors do their original planning in clay forms at times because it is possible to think in terms of what an object will look like when it is made of clay.[25] Because it can be squeezed, sliced and stretched out flat and rolled or folded and cut, and because it can be joined together by large or small pieces, clay affords kinesthetic and artistic experiences that children value. After children have had experiences with clay, they become more perceptive about appearances of vessels, animals, and other objects that involve manipulation, artistic placement of pieces or joining parts to each other. They have to concentrate and observe lines, angles, volume, shapes, and thicknesses of objects. This promotes excellent observation skills.

Again, art is a way of viewing and experiencing one's world. Even though children may not have a sophisticated vocabulary to describe what they have felt (in terms of feelings or emotions), touched, pushed, scraped, and skillfully joined together, they are able to tell someone when something was difficult to do. They can, when looking at someone else's work, empathize with another person's efforts that resulted in a skillfully or artistically created product. They have some ideas about the difficulties involved in making something well.

Flat pieces of clay can be assembled much like a collage form. As children manipulate their work, roll it out into flat surfaces or sheets of thickness that can be placed, or curled, or wound into each other in a way that they can manage, a clay assemblage or collage product results, much to the pupils' excitement and pleasure.

If teachers can take the children on a field trip to a museum or art gallery that has a sculpture collection on exhibit, this can stimulate children even more toward the expression of ideas using clay as a medium. The teacher also encourages the children to follow their own unique thoughts when they want to model with clay. Pictures, photographs, colors, shapes, various and interesting line placements in an art form shown to the children, continue to affect ideas that have been unexpressed. The teacher's appreciation of differences among the children's work emphasizes to the children that each of their products has something that is important to the teacher.

The teacher needs to have periodic stimulation of new ideas in order to transmit the endless number of possibilities that are available to children. They accept questions raised by the teacher to arouse imagery in their own minds and follow through with those images in their products. A file of ideas representing objects that are familiar to children, as well as ideas that seem humorous, unusual in color or shape and size, should be compiled and organized by the teacher. Scenic representations, food, animals, houses, pathways to a distant point, stars, and a number of other subjects can be the source of initiating a child's efforts in implementing an idea.

Children may also want to start a collection of things that remind them of sculptured objects. Clay toys, buttons, boxes made of clay, clay animals, and other items that seem to have the qualities or characteristics of clay can be saved in lined containers to protect the pieces from breaking.

The experiences that children have in the classroom with various art media will affect their attitudes toward and feelings about the media. They will notice when they are in stores (or museums), the qualities of various art forms. If they have had experience with them, they can comment on the tactile nature of them and the various "quirks" of the medium that work against or with one's hands. A language about art and its qualities develops.

Through language much like that which architects use, children can begin to learn about the characteristics of materials and how one may refer to them. *Tension strength, durability, flexibility, frame, pitch, level, arch, post-and-beam* (a single beam is supported by two vertical posts that can be made of wood, stone, marble, etc.), *gable roofs,* and *dormer windows* are terms of the various elements of buildings that characterize the language of those who are working with or creating such buildings. The language associates itself with a way of seeing or perceiving something that will be created or has already been created. Children can be involved in learning terms that are not difficult and that fit easily into a discussion of what is being seen at a given time.

Learning to see so that conceptual forms are recognized is part of a child's education. Although the terms applied to ideas need not limit what children are able to imagine, they can help pupils begin to refer to things that are known to mature or sophisticated artisans or architects. Teachers are in an effective position to encourage the use of correct terms that are part of the fields of art.

Developmental Vision in the Arts

The eye can be described in an anatomical sense. Biologists, physicians, opthamologists, and opticians describe their perspectives of the eye in various ways. Diagrams in medical books, or in books used by people in related fields preparing to work in certain professions, can depict through sketches what the general properties of the eyes are in their physical appearance. Surgery on the eyes involves the manipulation or changes of various parts of the eyes.

Visual therapy can affect changes in the way an individual perceives objects and events. The mind coordinates images acting on the retina of the eye. Psychological impressions that coincide with what is seen, interpreted, or recorded are integrated with vision.[26] People can be urged to change the way they view objects in the environment. How one sees, what one sees, and how one is psychologically impressed with what one sees are as much a psychological event as a physiological one.

The notion of a vision therapy, or a perspective that can help people view life and their eye-messages differently than they might without the new information about seeing, is accepted and applied by many teachers. It is helping them to orient children's perspectives and vision codes so that less restriction occurs in the interpretation of the perceived object, scene, or individual.

Edwards, as one among several others who has been interested in the right hemisphere of the brain as it processes information received and related to various abilities manifested by people, has used her findings to advise teachers. The major hemisphere, the left side, deals mainly with language, logic, certain mathematical or sequential concepts. Right-handed people use that part of their brain to process reading, writing, and computing tasks.

An approach toward stimulating the coding of information from the right hemisphere of the brain while suspending the judgmental critical impressions related to the left side of the brain, is facilitated through certain techniques.[27] Drawing the object while looking at it placed upside-down, an individual is more likely to note the light and shadowed areas, spaces (negative and positive), and to pay less attention to the name of the object or its function.

When an individual sees an object in other than its usual way, the visual perception has to adjust in a variety of ways, and thus it can be viewed in terms of other characteristics or elements. Edwards suggests that it is easier to draw an article that is not familiar in form because the individual does not feel obligated to name it or recognize it. (S)He is thus allowed greater freedom for drawing the article in terms of shapes, parts, spaces, and the like. Noting the lines, direction and proportion, an individual who has not used drawing skills, which in part are processed in a right hemispheric mode, can typically do well on this upside-down mode of object placement.

Researchers who are concerned about hemispheric laterality and the use of mainly one side of the brain, indicate that the school curriculum is short-changing pupils.[28] Limiting the direction of learning by thinking mainly of logic, reasoning, writing, or reading prevents pupils from becoming aware of other modes of processing what they see in the environment.

Educators are becoming more aware of releasing constrictions or limitations that have been unwittingly imposed on children. Pupils who have teachers that have been exposed to newer techniques involving the encouragement of children's ideas, energies and skills may benefit from the way that they may learn. Approaching drawing and visual interpretation in unusual ways can influence a new readiness to respond differently to one's environment. Further, it heightens other areas of the mind to perceive differently and to reconstruct former habits to accommodate new visual images and psychological interpretations of them. The excitement of seeing what one had missed up to a given point is stimulating. It provides new perspectives, much like suddenly allowing sunlight to stream into a room that has been dark for a long time.

Edwards recommends that children be permitted to draw something by turning the object upside down. If they are drawing a picture while looking at someone's photograph, the photograph should be turned upside down. If they draw a shoe, it should be placed before them upside down. She indicates that when an object is drawn upside down, the person who is accustomed to hesitating to draw at all, may be willing to pursue the task by seeing parts that eventually compose the whole. The minimized ability of the left side of the brain to interpret an upside-down object, allows the right side to continue with its form of perception.

The contemporary generation of teachers are in the midst of changing and applying recent information yielded from contemporary research, and of unlearning in a sense what they have already learned in teacher education institutions in past years. Teachers' attitudes toward children's creativity are more respectful than they used to be. Respect for children's ideas and an understanding of the use of new materials take time to engage in— time both for the pupils and for the activities that need to be created and used.

As young children begin various attempts to create art when they are provided with materials at school, there will be times that comments may be made about their work. Teachers may ask children if they want to talk about what they have done. They may talk about ideas they had while they were working in a given medium. They may describe sections or colors and strokes of the product they have drawn or modeled. The teacher should not ask, "What is it?" This can sometimes arouse an uncomfortable feeling in the child who then realizes that perhaps it should have looked like something in reality.

When teachers talk to children about their work, they can use words that describe the elements of art as adults know them. A line, for example, is used in a certain way to represent an idea. A narrow long line going in the horizontal direction represents an image that might be carried to another area or space, and end in a large block or circle. Children can comment on a bold, heavy, strong line, or a thin, fragile, and delicate line.

The use of space presents an image; it may be used to balance ideas presented in a background. Children's attention can be called to open spaces and how they affect an impression. (These ideas are not usually pointed out until the children have had some experiences doing what they enjoy when brushing paint on newsprint or creating drawings with craypas or crayons or pastel chalk.)

Various colors, from intense to gentle or light, give the children an idea about the messages that color sometimes gives. They learn how to mix colors. They often show bold and jagged deep red and orange lines to represent a fire. This association with color, ideas, images, and the like is not intended to impose or restrict ideas or imagination. The use of terms that are part of the arts can be started whenever teachers talk to children about their work. The terms do not prescribe content or color or space in the children's use of any of them in their efforts. The terms help the children when they are talking about what they have done or what they like in the work of others.

The process of children's work is significant. Attention has to be given to how they are working. When time, space, and materials (needed for science experimentation) are available in the classroom the environment becomes encouraging for testing, mixing, and rearranging ideas. Children are affected by the teacher who suggests various ideas and says, "How else can it be done?" "What are some other interesting ways of placing these things?" When a variety of recommendations is valued, the children sense an open-mindedness in artistic pursuits. They realize that there are more than just one way to create a picture or model something out of clay, that they can draw something in different colors, use space differently, and enjoy the use of various lengths and widths of lines.

Terminology used in order to develop a visual sense and deeper interpretation of line, color, shape, space, and balance is used after the fact, so to speak. Terms are introduced after children have experimented with their own ideas. Naming things, as indicated earlier, can interfere with depicting positive and negative spaces, light and dark areas, airy and heavy images.

Art has forms of rhythm to it. Rhythm involves a repetition of something in an art form,. A series of trees or fenceposts establish a rhythmic pattern in an expression of art.[29] An order or regularity in space as in music lends a rhythm that can be pleasing to the eye or ear attending to a product of art. An alternating type of rhythm adds another element to the rhythmic pattern.[30] Cars winding down a road can be shown next to flowers on the side of the road, lending another visual element to the rhythm in the picture. Sometimes artists use a progressive type rhythm which involves repetition, but also a consistent change accomplished by shape, size, or color of the periodic introduction of change.

Proportion estimation involves relative judgment. Young children have difficulty estimating relationships of things or parts of things to each other in size, length, height, or color. They need many experiences to decide how something appears smaller when it is placed next to some objects that are much larger. They typically think that if something has been labeled larger at one time, it keeps that label for other times, regardless of how it looks when it is placed next to much larger objects. (When a child sees an airplane on the ground and is walking toward it, the airplane looks large. When it is in the sky in the horizon, it appears as a tiny dot, barely perceptible. The child knows that it is large. This is why it appears large when children draw it over a house meant to be in the foreground.)

Judgment of size and shape involves experiences with things close at hand. After the child has mental images of certain objects at different times and places in the environment, several images of varying sizes can be accommodated. Even for adults who have never flown in an airplane and who are accustomed to seeing the sun at a distant point in the sky, or seeing clouds overhead, it is an interesting and perceptively changing experience to see the clouds below, under the airplane, or to fly through clouds. Seeing the sun rise when one flies in an airplane too, and watching the sun flood across an expanse of the sky line, involve a change of understanding relative to one's position in the observation of a sunrise and its relationship to space and height.

As many artists indicate, art is a way of life, a way of seeing and perceiving that can enrich one's experiences. It is a way of externalizing images that are seen from within. It is a way of looking grandly out at the world in one's unique way. The world can become sweet through modeling with special recipes or one that depicts, one's fondest ideas through candy clay, (consisting of margarine, corn syrup, salt, vanilla and choices of food coloring mixed with a pound of powdered sugar).[31]

It is suggested too, that children's ability to understand ideas not be underestimated.[32] Fine works of art can be shown to children and various points of interest can be discussed by them and the teacher. Attractive displays of the children's work, too, show that their work is as respected as are the products of well-known artists.

As teachers and parents provide examples of various objects that reflect balance, interesting line, or use of color, space, and rhythm, children learn a new language in the aesthetic vein. They learn that certain words represent certain concepts in art. This gives them another dimension to have in describing or characterizing what they see around them.

Art, science, and reading involve the recognition of space relationships, configuration of objects as they interrelate on paper or in reality as part of a scene. Powers of observation need to be sharpened whenever possible. When children learn this at an early age, they are at an advantage, not only for themselves but in relation to others who are also concerned for the protection and well-being of children.

Musical Development and Appreciation

From the earliest years, children hear music or rhythmic beats of some kind. Intra-uterine sounds are a mixture of the swishing or muted sounds of water moving in a rhythmic cadence. One of the sensations that an individual experiences early in life is the heartbeat. It influences to some extent the pace, timing, and dynamics of an individual's movement.

Young children hear music in the environment from radios, television, their own musical rattles, music boxes, or the humming of people near them. They often move to music when they see others do it. By the time they attend school, they have heard many sounds; some have heard instruments and can name or even play a piano to some extent. Musical toys are more available now than they used to be and are made in less expensive materials.

Depending on the skills of the teacher, will children have more or less in music experiences at school. The ideas from the teacher's background flow easily to the children. When a teacher is not at ease with music and has a block against it, the children will not receive as much in that classroom as they might from a teacher who is more comfortable with music instruction.

Because many recordings are available that can be used with children, the teacher need not delete music from children's school experiences. Musicians can be brought into the classroom. Often some of the children's parents are talented and can provide experiences that the teacher may not be able to give. If possible, children should be taken to a city's musical center or a symphony orchestra in a municipal concert hall. They should be given the opportunity to see and hear music at its finest.

Using recordings of classical music that represent moods or stories for children's appreciation provides a beginning that can sensitize the ear to melody, pitch, dynamics, rhythm, loud, soft, fast, slow, and other elements of musical treatment. If parents have recordings they would like to present to the children, the lesson can be discussed with the teacher before the parent brings favorite and appropriate records to school.

Children are intrigued with musical instruments when they can see them and touch them. An amateur or professional musician can bring much pleasure to the children by playing for them and letting them touch the musical instruments after explaining how they work.

Some schools provide orchestral beginnings for children. This provision depends on financial support, on the size of the orchestra (or band in later grades), and on the neighborhood itself from which support for an orchestra may be obtained. Very young children would not be playing in an orchestra. They would be an enthusiastic audience to an orchestra playing music that would appropriately appeal through the quick, unusual sounds and imaginative themes of brief selections. Children can recognize humor in music when stories are told through the whimpering sounds of an instrument or the wailing of a horn or instruments that imitate a hearty laugh.

Rhythm bands can be developed in kindergarten or first grade. The instruments can be purchased so that different components for the band can be represented. Finger cymbals, tone blocks, tone bells (xylophone), shakers, and other forms of instruments can be purchased in specific amounts. An entire set, if too expensive, is not needed. It can be acquired gradually when more money is available or if the school has an event in which some money is raised to buy more instruments. Rhythm band instruments for young children, however, are not as expensive as the musical instruments in adult orchestras.

Generally, when the teacher is aware of several components of a program in music for children, recordings, instruments, songs, and other forms through which music can be offered, they are collected and provided for children. A variety of recordings can be presented to children so that they can become familiar with famous selections as well as more recent and less well-known music. At certain holidays, for example, children hear songs or orchestral pieces that are typical for Christmas, Thanksgiving, Valentine's Day, and others. They become familiar with a country's national anthem by learning to sing it. Exposure to ideas, sounds, symbols, and the dynamics of music is the major means of bringing musical awareness to pupils in the classroom.

Singing, Listening to Music, Instruments

Some of the first songs children hear in kindergarten relate to greeting songs of "Good Morning to You!" or nursery rhymes, "Jack and Jill, Went up the Hill," or when the season is appropriate (or not at times), "Jingle Bells." Singing short songs is one of the mainstays of a nursery school, kindergarten, of play group. Acting out fingerplays (through making motions with the hands and fingers to supplement the word and message of the song) is often done. Sometimes the whole body is involved in movement as suggested by "Jack Be Nimble," when Jack jumps over the candlestick. Children enjoy waiting for that part of the song and doing what is described. They also enjoy the action that accompanies a song about the Jack-in-the-Box when Jack jumps out and surprises people. The build-up in music, tempo, and words gives pupils a sensitivity toward climax in an artistic form.

Children learn to sing a song when they hear it repeatedly. When the teacher wishes to introduce a new song to pupils, (s)he may discuss ideas related to the song, such as why someone wrote it and what it suggests in mood, and may even hold up pictures or props that can enrich imagery related to the musical expression. Some teachers use a recording for teaching a song. The children listen to it, sing along with it, and the teacher turns down the recording in volume as the children know the song better and come through stronger in using the words of the song.

The instruction of songs should be pleasant. As the teacher sings the song, the children are asked to join in wherever they can. Some teachers note the difficult parts of the song for the children and emphasize those parts so that the children may practice them. The entire song is sung again so that the children become accustomed to hearing it sung correctly. Teachers use their hands to indicate whether the melody goes higher or lower while the children sing. These provide easy clues for the children so that talking is minimized during a song that the children are trying to learn.

Teachers need to remember that an attitude is learned by children who are watching the teacher sing. The atmosphere that is pleasant is more inviting and conducive to song than one that is reprimanding and foreboding. Children do not have to sing songs perfectly. They will learn what they can and should be encouraged to persist in that expectation.

Some teachers use a flannel board with musical notes that are placed on it as new levels of a song are introduced. They use figures of animals appropriate to a song to show a sequence of melody. The imagination of the teacher brings the children's interest to high levels. The teacher who becomes "caught up" in the mood of the song is very significant to the way children can learn. The children seem to be swept along with the mood, melody, and rhythm when the teacher knows where they can be encouraged to perform effectively. A box of props with surprises in it holds the children's attention. Novelty can have a creative effect in the children's development of their own songs as well. This is encouraged whenever possible.

Children can be encouraged to create songs as they listen to the sounds of ordinary household items, outdoor sounds, and the rhythm of people's walks. They can listen to their own rhythm as they walk across the room. They can clap to their own rhythmic beat. Listening relates to musical expression; making one's own music affects increasing facilities or one's capacities to become more proficient in musical expression.

Mothers can experience children's enjoyment with music by learning with them. Some parents sing to their children from the moment of birth. Lullabies and soothing, simple songs attract the attention of babies. The human voice has great appeal for them. Children can remember what they hear repeatedly and imitate often. Adults have retained songs of earliest childhood years.

Young children's spontaneity is complementary to many types of songs. Their interest in participating can be drawn upon. When they are urged, however, to perfect a skill or are stopped often to be corrected for something they are doing (or not doing) it can destroy in part the major purpose of enjoying a lesson. When teachers are overly concerned about perfection of some kind, and premature emphasis on a few points occurs often during early introduction to a song, it can affect the children so that they will not want to persist in listening or learning at that time. If the children become tired, the teacher should end the lesson, not as a reprimand, but because the teacher recognizes waning interest or capacities to respond well.

The first, second, third, and fourth grades at school involve songs that are more difficult to learn. Greater numbers of skills are needed for the children's participation. The teacher who is not comfortable teaching songs may invite a music consultant to the classroom, a parent, as mentioned earlier, or bring in a recording that has the desired songs. Teachers often use a capable student to lead the others in the class. A program that organizes themes for singing is planned to include many styles of songs that are often those selected by students. Contemporary, jazz, classical, folk songs, multicultural recreational songs, and dancing songs contribute to the children's repertoire so that they can develop various tastes and appreciation for differences in music.

Most books on music for children include music from many lands or cultures.[33] The universality of the arts has been recognized for years since humankind recorded them in any form on paper or audio-track. Multicultural songs are part of the American culture in its most natural sense.

Note Concept Illustration 8–1 for suggestions on how to teach a difficult song for children. Although attention is not typically given for each line, it can be when a particular phrasing is difficult. For the most part, the teacher needs to keep in mind that songs should be considered in terms of auditory and perceptual wholeness. Years ago, the emphasis on the end product used to take the attention away from the process of learning as the teacher thought of it in the classroom. Contemporary emphasis on early learning of the arts reflects concern for children's enjoyment of the process as well as the pleasure they receive from the final product.

1. Discuss the values of the song; why it was written; who enjoys hearing it; why it was selected for the children.

2. Show some pictures related to the theme of the song; have children comment on what they see.

3. Tell the children to listen for a particular idea while you sing the song.

4. Ask them what part of it has the focused material. Can they repeat it in song?

5. Sing the song again. Slow down in a difficult part so that they can detect distinct phrases or notes.

6. Have them sing the first two phrases.

7. Repeat it again yourself.

8. Add phrases that they have not sung, until the song is complete.

9. You sing a few phrases, then they sing them again. Both you and they have repeated the phrases to the end of the song.

10. The theme underlying this effort is to have them listen in a way that seems natural, not pressured. It is as though both of you, the teacher and the class, are pursuing the joy of song.

11. Use appropriate and attractive props as needed to focus the children's attention.

12. Be as creative as possible to engage individual pupils in participation.

Concept Illustration 8–1

Teaching a Song to Children: Enjoyment in Learning.

Listening effectively is a crucial skill in academic learning as well as in the process of interpersonal relationships. No human being is capable of taking in and processing everything in his/her environment. The human brain is selective in what it hears and interprets. The teacher can stop, show the class how to listen attentively, and discuss what was heard in order to help them learn how to listen in a discriminating or sensitive manner. The power of concentration contributes to significant listening skills.

Some of the vital elements that children need to know about listening are these:

1. Concentrate on only the present stimulus, or what is presented.
2. Look for certain elements such as sound, pitch, tonal quality, dynamics, the highs and lows, changes from one melody to another.
3. Note similarities or repetitious themes (or music phrases) in the presentation.
4. Identify the beat in relation to a waltz, march, folk dance.
5. Identify a message or feeling that the composer was giving.
6. Imagine a scene that would symbolize the music being heard.
7. What would people be doing in that scene and what would the background be?
8. Have you heard other arrangements presented for music that sounded like this?
9. What activities that people do would this arrangement accompany?

10. How many different themes are there in the musical arrangement?
11. Does this give you an idea for something that you would like to compose?
12. Note the loud and soft dynamics.
13. Does this arrangement sound modern? Why or why not?
14. Is it necessary to concentrate solely on what you are listening to?
15. Is the quality of the transmitted sound what it should be in terms of presenting the arrangement to its best advantage?
16. Does all music reflect a mood of the composers of certain songs? Are the composers happy, sad?
17. Identify your own mood in relation to the music.
18. Why does concentrated listening help us in learning effectively?
19. How does music give us a sense of timing, beat, rhythm? Where do we get clues?
20. Are there certain rules or guidelines that influence the creation of music?

To hear something and subsequently decide or analyze what was heard is part of the act of listening. To attend with purposes of remembering or responding to something is more like listening. When someone asks a question and wants a specific answer in order to know what to do next, one listens differently from the way one would when someone is talking about another subject. Listening with intent to remember is a focused type of attending. It helps in learning. If children can be taught to listen attentively because they might otherwise miss something important, this will serve them well in most other school subjects they need to learn.

One writer recommends that children can have opportunities to exercise listening skills by hearing lullabies or soothing music played on the record player.[34] They are also given activities in which they can answer questions about the theme of a recording. They can be asked what the music makes them think of and how it makes them feel or what it makes them want to do. Discriminating among various moods, rhythms, sounds, and patterns of sound can help children learn to use effective thought with hearing.

Some teachers ask the children to show by raising their hands during the playing of a recording when the music is high in sound and when it is low, when it accelerates or when it decelerates. This sensitizes the children to listen for something. Focused listening helps the children perceive related ideas as well as learning how to attend selectively to something in the environment.

Listening to music has been varied in recent years with the addition of electronic and technological media and technical skills. Although music is a beautiful medium, it can be misused at times to influence people who are not aware that this intent is part of an advertiser's focus. Critical listening is an important skill to develop. Commercial songs are catchy and easy to remember. If one has heard them often, it is sometimes difficult to erase them from one's mind. Repetition is a powerful means of influencing people. It can be used to the advantage of a learner or to his/her disadvantage. Children will be taught to listen critically when they discuss subject matter of the social studies. They will learn to detect influential words that are intended to persuade people to do something that may not be in their best interests. Skills for listening that are learned through music may transfer to reflective listening needed for learning academic knowledge as well as protecting one's self from accepting information that is not true, accurate, or helpful in the pursuit of an argument.

A sophisticated listener knows how to obtain from what is heard the answers, facts, or data that will apply to something that is significant for that individual. Knowing how to listen effectively can make the difference between being successful or not when one is attempting to advance a perspective or refine an argument in an intellectual sense. Young children can be sensitized to listening for certain words that may be intended to mislead people or to influence them in unfair ways.

The differences among sounds that depict jungle animals, fairyland characters, jack-rabbits, giants, and other mythological or real entities provide opportune moments for critical listening. Children are often asked to move like a heavy-footed giant, a tiny nymph, or a snake. The imagery that this arouses in their minds is externalized by their actions on the cleared space of a classroom floor.

Listening can be stimulated when children have their own rhythm instruments and enjoy the experience of playing as a group. Recommendations for selected purchases of instruments, as well as helping children learn how to make them, are presented by several writers.[35]

Bells, rhythm sticks, tone blocks, tambourines, finger cymbals, a zylophone, shakers of various kinds, or maracas, drums, and claves, are only some of the instruments that children can enjoy. Scraping sounds, soft resonant ones, and staccato-type striking sounds are appropriate for various selections that are offered to children.

Some teachers use a guitar or autoharp to play simple melodies or chords that accompany children with the band. The teacher uses judgment in knowing when to stop by asking the children to listen as well as play their own instrument. Playing together in a group involves different listening than the times that children listen only to one person and are not absorbed in processes of performing themselves.

Some advocates of early learning of music for children are evident in the writings of those who originated methods that are used by some teachers in contemporary society.[36] Eurhythmics involves the synchronization of one's movement to music or sound. The child's body becomes the instrument of interpretation. The children respond to changes in music, stopping for silence, moving on their toes when a light mode of music is heard, and stepping more heavily when the music suggests it.[37] This method, originated in the early part of the 1900s is known as the Dalcroze method having been created by Émile Jacques-Dalcroze. Whereas the Dalcroze method began with the use of a piano to urge children's responses to music, Zoltan Kodaly, a Hungarian musician, created songs and games to encourage the children to use their voices to make music.[38] Orff-Schulwerfe methods, introduced by Carl Orff, emphasized rhythm with young children, and he created rhythm instruments that he felt would help children understand musical elements.[39] For those who are interested in obtaining more information on Orff methods or instruments and the introduction of unusual fragmented melodic themes, it is possible to obtain them by writing to several sources.[40]

It is interesting that the Suzuki method designed by Dr. Shinichi Suzuki in Japan involves parents who must first learn to play the violin.[41] The pupils imitate the parent, who encourages the children for their efforts as early as the children's third, fourth, or fifth year of life. After the children have physical exercises that prepare them to move, stoop, bend, and balance on one leg while holding a violin that is proportionate to their size, they are given lessons that involve replication of songs or melodies played by the parent or on recordings and are gradually taught to read music.

Imitation of the teacher is significant to early patterns of learning how to play the violin in terms of the Suzuki method.[42] Rote learning (i.e., exact memorization) is the relevant thread. Large groups of young children play certain selections of music together, exemplifying the controlled learning that is integrated into the discipline of this method. Typically, in the United States, educators do not think of young children under five performing in large groups, acting in concert and exact timing cadences with each other. American children are perceived as unique individuals that can cooperate, but that should not be subordinated to total group action. The cultural framework of any country affects the educational orientation of young children. This orientation is often reflected in the variety of ways that children can learn throughout the world. When educators transfer patterns of learning from one country to another, the societal context must be considered as well. A certain kind of learning technique may not be congruent with a given philosophy in another country trying to adopt a pattern of learning. Differences between what children *are able* to do and what is *exposed to them* for achieving demonstrate the fact that the human being is capable of many skills and abilities. How those skills and abilities are developed, and whether they are encouraged or not for development, depend to a great extent on what a given culture values.

Instruments for children's use can be made by teachers and parents, and by the children themselves.[43] Several precautions must be taken in those projects.

Making Instruments

1. Instrument making must include the safety precaution of using only containers that cannot splinter, crack, or spill in an explosive manner.
2. Seal the container with masking tape and paint over it to secure the contents of the container well.
3. The children may want to paste a picture from a magazine over the container. This would have to be covered in order to seal it well. Nontoxic materials only should be used for spraying.
4. Help the children make instruments that will have endurance. The children become very upset and anxious when things break. The flexibility of materials produces a tendency toward easy breakage. Children are not aware of this and attribute breakage to their own lack of wisdom, in a self punishing sense.

5. Help children determine what things should be used to fill a box; some sounds are transmitted better than others by using different materials for fillers in the boxes.

6. Remember that children are to have an enjoyable time with music; perfection is inappropriate as a concept in that context. Emotions reflect a wide range of "acceptable expression." Children need to learn how to enjoy the flow of feelings. Music is one of the arts that encourages this natural spontaneity.

7. Store the instruments in a safe place. Explain to the children that they will be used at appropriate times together.

8. Remove distracting elements in the environment when the children play in their rhythms orchestra.

9. Permit each child to be the leader at given times.

10. Keep a record of which children were given special opportunities and at which times, so that all pupils are given recognition for leadership skills.

Rhythms, Movement, and Aesthetic Expression

The joy of moving is emergent at birth and even before it. Children not only like to see movement; they themselves like to initiate it. At times, in fact, it is difficult for them to sit quietly. Movement is a more natural part of one's body function than is standing or sitting still when one has energy.

After children hear instructions, directions, and exactly what they are expected to do, they sometimes react to this precision by pulling back. They fear making a mistake. It therefore seems safer to them not to try at all. The period in a primary grades program in which work with rhythms is introduced can be an excellent time for coordinating ideas with movement.

Children can discuss with the teacher what their favorite animals, birds, or reptiles might be. The children can, with the help of music, instruments, or recordings replicate from their own memories the movement of their preferred ideas or creations. This is an activity that stimulates memory and imagination; it represents muscular movement coordination with psychological and cognitive impressions.

Rhythms can revitalize thought and creativity. They provide another way of interpreting one's world. This is a crucial element in learning and in an advancement of ideas at various levels of learning.

As there are few guidelines for the way a child will direct his/her own movements, rhythms involve immediately and directly the child's most intuitive thinking with skills, talents, and cognition. The activity becomes an immediate translation of an intellectualized and noted vision recorded in the brain into physiological properties as well as kinesthetic movement. It is both private and public.

The teacher can have the children describe in color and form what they

The kindergarten teacher can, when the idea is developed properly with children, show them the life cycle of a butterfly. The class can do a significant lesson in rhythms depicting the changes of the butterfly from its earliest forms to its mature stages. This idea of change contributes to excellent opportunities for rhythms expression. The teacher has to guide it with care. (Photo by Gerald J. Margolin.)

are depicting or feeling. This gives depth to the experience. One of the most significant and viable forms of helping children develop reading, language arts skills, and scientific and mathematical elements is to help them describe reality in terms of their own perceptions. Description facilitates the desire to be exact and to convey a higher quality message. Reality, interpretation, individual and distinctive perspectives, affect children's progress at school when they are taught how to use those qualities.

Spatial relationships are involved in movement and rhythms. This fact has not been emphasized in school programs to the extent that it might be. Writers indicate that more attention is needed in the instruction given to children and their knowledge of space, imagery, and other forms of affective sensory perceptions. Two languages seem to guide views of reality.[44] One language is governed by grammar, logic, syntax, and analysis; the other is guided by imagery, metaphor, synthetic impressions, but not by analysis.

The forms of rhythms that can be expressed by children can be described by such words as, "trotting, tripping, stamping, tossing, circling, skating, banging, grasping, rocking, creeping, sliding, tumbling, whirling."[45] Children enjoy walking, running, skipping, and galloping to music or to the steady beat of clapping hands.

After children have been on a field trip to a store, bakery, or dairy, they

Accessories, hats, various kinds of clothing change one's feelings especially when one sees the expressive and strong reactions of one's kindergarten classmates. Often a "home-type" corner that has chairs, a stove, materials for dressing up when playing mother, father, or other role stimulates activity and creative ideas. (Photo by Gerald J. Margolin.)

can act out in rhythms what they saw in the processes of product creation. Their bodies put into motion an intellectual theme. The rhythms, however, allow them to show individual perceptions that are accepted as learning, feeling, and recognizing objects in the process. The children can guess what pupils are showing when they move objects from a floor to a counter, or when they imitate the motion of a swirling mixture in a large container.

Props are helpful in rhythmic expression. Scarves, wands, feathers, belts, jewelry, and hats that are either donated or created in the classroom serve effectively to influence the atmospheric tone. Children need very little assistance (considering the excellence of their final products) to give them the impetus needed for imagining or for creating a mood, dramatic effect, or inspiring act. Children use scarves as headgear, as skirts, as fairy tale themes, as jump ropes, or as masks. They become pirates, fairy princesses, or queens and kings. Scarves and props become different things to each child with new ideas.

Some children will readily dance when the teacher requests it; others will wait, uncertain as to what is expected and will just watch. Rhythms can play a significant part in the kindergarten program, however. Self-management of one's movement and control in responding to music or rhythmic beats of various kinds, is a source of self-confidence. Children typically enjoy classroom dancing and movement as long as the teacher does not expect perfection. (Photo by Gerald J. Margolin.)

Recommendations for Encouraging Rhythms Experiences
1. Create a place in the classroom that has props in good condition for children's use whenever it is planned.
2. Select excellent recordings that encourage children's movement to music that stimulates and inspires moods of different kinds.
3. Identify groups of children who are to show their ideas to others.
4. Recognize each child's efforts in order to stimulate vitality and continued participation in rhythmic expression.
5. Ask children what they are thinking when they are moving; tell them you almost had that feeling too when you watched them.
6. Indicate your sensitivity and understanding of the children's efforts.
7. Be sure to explain to parents why these "free" imagery-evoking experiences are important to children's development.

8. Ask them to show how they think the rain looks when it comes down.
9. Have them show how they think a bowl of cereal looks when someone is eating it.
10. Have them pretend they are at a party, showing what they are doing.
11. Have the children use lower-level space (sliding across the floor like reptiles, alligators, snails).
12. Ask the pupils to use middle space levels (relative to their own-bodies).
13. Ask them to use higher space levels (head and shoulders and reaching above).
14. Imagination and safety guide limitations in thinking and rhythmic ideas.

Some children may be taking ballet or other dance lessons outside of school. Their instruction in specific movements and names for steps can be used as part of their experiences in rhythms. They should not, however, transcend the freedom intended in the rhythmic expression that comes from associating images with muscular coordination. The ingenuity that provides impetus and motion in an originally conceived idea is important to preserve, sustain, and further encourage. Children will not know they have the skills unless they are told.

When children create a playlet, or when they act out a story they have heard, they can use imagination as well as procreation, in a sense. They can add to what they heard in the story. This is artistic license. For the benefit of art, the individual expresses ideas that are beyond reality or other people's perceptions of it.

Scientists urge teachers to encourage children's imaginative expression. They say that somewhere out in the schools now are children or perhaps one child who will discover a cure for diseases not yet conquered. Urging intellectual expression through media that facilitate imaginative products can translate to cognitive ideas needed in science, mathematics, and other forms of intellectual "playfulness."

Ideas are recommended for initiating movement by calling children's attention to the way their fingers move, and how they pinch, snap, pat, pinch, or rub.[46] It is recommended that for boys who may feel self-conscious about moving to music, marches may be played as a warm-up activity[47] until they respond to images in their own mind to demonstrate with other children.

Playing a recording that describes a story or incident provides a beginning set of ideas. The children can respond in movement (after the recording is turned off) as they demonstrate their interpretation of the story just heard. Teachers may have the children remember a trip to the ocean, to the mountains, or fishing with someone and allow that to follow with rhythmic expression of those ideas.

Sometimes teachers suggest a nature walk in rhythms. Groups of children show the rest of the class what they see and hear on their nature walk in the woods or in the fields or in the city block. The movement of their bodies gives clues regarding the objects, people, or events they notice during their walk. Sounds may be imitated; tall houses may be outlined, tiny birds in the trees may be simulated in whatever the way the children imagine and express interpretations of the environment.

Children can move as they think toys would do, such as a spinning top, a car, an airplane, a clown, a rag doll, a bold crayon on paper and a variety of objects. As teachers allow children to externalize ideas and indicate that each person's ideas are valuable as unique products, children will not copy as often as they might otherwise do the actions of classmates.

Children can also move to the rhythm and themes of poetry on the topics of trees, flowers, airplanes, ships, bubble gum, food, swimming, and the like. The social studies content (e.g., vehicles, people, communities) provides subtopics that arouse imagery and opportunities to express it in movement.

Art, Music, Rhythms, and Social Studies Units

When children are studying about a people, a country, or a theme, the arts appropriately constitute a part of their study and can be used effectively as focal points. This can be done either during a social studies period or when art or rhythms are offered. Segments of activity, such as those showing a boat unloading products at the dock in the harbor, or a truck carrying lettuce, cattle, or a tank of oil, provide another way for cognitive and imaginative ideas to be expressed.

Sometimes, the children like to act out people going to a store, buying groceries, bringing them home to a family, and showing the attitudes of the individuals involved. The social studies content of people from various lands typically provides impressions that children use when the teacher has props on hand representing a variety of countries or vehicles used in those countries. Musical instruments, clothing, headdresses, shoes, capes, coats, and other reminders can trigger ideas.

Songs of people from other countries can be obtained in music books. Cultures have songs of celebration, of mourning or sadness, work songs, and patriotic ones. The instruments used for musical expression in various cultures, too, become part of a music program related to social studies content.

When children plan a mural they can act it out so that they have some idea as to where they will place objects on a background. They discuss a general plan, focus on specific content, then show a background that serves as a contrast to people and vehicles in the foreground.

With older children, acting out the trip on the *Mayflower*, arriving at Plymouth Rock in the new country, which was to become part of what are now the United States, and later preparing for the celebration of Thanksgiving are recommended as enjoyable and profitable learning experiences.[48] Ideas of other countries can also be obtained by consulting books that show the activities, festivals, games, foods, and customs of children and adults in those countries.[49]

Some children might become so intrigued with multicultural knowledge that they may read in areas of anthropology and sociology. This information does not suggest that pupils should emulate people of other countries. Learning about these ideas means that an understanding can be gained of other people's customs or habits. The knowledge provides examples of the values chosen by various people who understandably have feelings and ambitions reflecting their cultural goals. It broadens children's perceptions of underlying behavior or motives that affect people's choices in what they say or do.

Children can learn to understand and appreciate that other people reared differently from those in their own native country find it comfortable to observe what was learned as they grew up in that country. They learn not to deride another culture's forms or religious practices, art or recreation. To do so, reflects limited judgment and betrays a lack of awareness of the fact that people have different values and motives that orient their behavior.

Puppet shows provide an excellent means through which social studies ideas can be depicted. The clothing of the puppets is made by the children, who have studied facts specifically related to styles and fabrics. Craft shops often have parts of dolls or puppets that can be used to implement the children's ideas. Puppets can become as elaborate as the children can make them; however, pupils can still convey an effective message through a simply styled puppet. Children study the aspects of the puppet's appearance that enrich the ideas that they want to present through the puppet's activity in song, dance, discussion, or other artistic expression prompted by the presentation. What the puppets do is as influential in effect on the audience as is their appearance.

Children are encouraged to be original in their work. Their ideas and the implementation of them as they carry through to completion the plans they make on specific projects should be appreciated. The process of their work is as important as the product. Creative expression can flow easily when the children have an appreciative teacher.

Kindergarten children can make murals representing transportation, the community, or space missiles on the ground or in the air. After they have had a social studies unit on any of the topics related to vehicles or community, they have enough information to show a specific part of their studies. The teacher asks them what they would like to show. They select, after discussion, a scene that includes what they are able to talk about and translate into an artistic form on paper.

Some children as a group can decide that they would like to plan and develop the background of the mural. (This may include making clouds, trees, houses in the distance, depending on how much can be appropriately shown without overpowering the major ideas in the foreground.) When the children are able to talk about what they would like to show, they typically have impressions as to how they will do it. Sometimes children like to draw or paint separate objects that can be superimposed on the mural background, giving a three-dimensional effect, or taking on the appearance of collage.

In kindergarten, the teacher needs to guide the discussion of the children and encourage them to move at their own pace. Murals can sometimes be completed within a week. They do not require as much time as one might think. Butcher paper or very wide paper of about 36 inches or more that is about three or four times as long or more provides ample space for a scene that can "hold" the children's composite ideas. After the children's work is completed, the mural must be kept in a safe place while it dries if paint or paste has been used. After it is sufficiently dry, it may be rolled up, though not tightly. The medium used will affect the way it can be stored or carried.

The rhythm of words can be discovered by the children as the teacher asks them to move to certain words that they like. Often children clap to the rhythmic pronunciation of words. The language arts period can be used periodically to express relationships between words and rhythms. Even the elements of wind, rain, and thunder suggest rhythm. Children are encouraged to listen to the various beats or emphases in words.[50] When only the children's bodies are involved in movement without the use of props, many activities can be introduced, with minimal planning in some cases. Extemporaneous opportunities to involve the children in listening and clapping or moving to a rhythmic wind, a word, or phrase are significant for the teacher. Often there are waiting moments or gaps of time between the end of one activity and the beginning of another (or the time that children are preparing to leave the classroom for home or assembly). When teachers have ideas that can interest the children to implement as well as review cognitive and artistic imagery coordinated with movement or rhythms, they show skills that can serve both the children and the teachers.

Processes of scientific orientations, such as changes of matter from one form to another, are topics that are amenable to rhythmic movement and expression. Churning butter, for example, presents unique opportunities to show change from liquid to creamy, to more solid consistencies of form. Even very young children are able to show the movement of rotating brushes that wash the locomotive when it is going through the soaping and rinsing stages. Gears moving, cogs bending, machines and levers extending armatures in various ways can be interpreted by children who have seen films, studied pictures, and discussed the processes. Film actors often have acting exercises that involve them in acting out the characteristics of a piece of chalk, or an eraser that has fallen from the ledge of a chalkboard to the floor. Turning the inanimate to the animate, through a visual and physical coordination of ideas, gives the imagination an opportunity to exercise itself. The spatial organization and coding processes that are done in the right hemisphere of the brain may be more involved in the pupil's interpretations of space and ideas.

The social studies content relates to science, mathematics, health education, language development (and rhythms of language, speech, and various forms of poetry), reading, and the art forms. Expressive activities can concentrate on various topics of social studies. As the children have been studying (in detail at times) various subtopics of the social studies, they have the topics fairly well represented in a cognitive sense. The rhythms period is one among others that can allow children to draw mental pictures with the mood and movement of their bodies.

The arts, in children's expression of them, are not to be used as measuring devices to determine what children's cognitive understandings are about social studies topics. The expression that children are permitted in using the social studies content is merely another way for them to externalize what they know. Their impressions represent points of view. Individualization of perspectives must be emphasized. Every child does not need to agree on how someone feels about something. The child who expresses an impression honestly is showing authentic evidence of feeling or thinking. The situation is different from that of conforming with mathematical terms or with the operations of addition, subtraction, and the like. In the expressive arts children do not all need to find the same answer in order to be considered as having a correct one.

The use of expression in the arts at school is in part an answer to the educators' principles that children be treated as unique individuals. Translating subject matter of the social studies into content that is considered in an artistic sense answers to the idea that, when more than one of the five senses are used in an individual's responsiveness to new or review learning, that individual is more likely to retain the ideas and to internalize them to fit his/her own intellectual and aesthetic framework of thought.

SUMMARY

This chapter offered only an impressionistic discussion on the importance of self-expression in the early grades at school. Considering the data available on the subject and the richness of sources on creative activities, more courses and in-service, as well as preservice, programs are needed to disseminate this direction for the curriculum in primary grades.

Research and writings on the modes of processing of the right and the left hemispheres of the brain indicate that not enough work in the schools is geared toward a mode of processing that involves spatial orientation and symbolic totalities different from reading from left to right, following logical sequential thought, and configurative perspectives. The literature on per ception, psychological perspectives, and modes of seeing reality as they are internally processed indicates that the right side of the brain has been relatively ignored in the school process.

Cognitive techniques have been the major concern of the school curriculum. The affective, aesthetic, spatially oriented hemisphere of the brain where, for many people, the artistic, musical, and metaphorically perceived elements are processed, has been considered less relevant in learning. Oddly enough, the scientist who discovers contributions that save many people's lives finds clues in giant or quantum leaps *from* "logic" or accepted reality to some extent. When the researcher tries something in an experiment that appears to be ridiculous or is highly imaginative and subject to ridicule at the start, this attempt is perceived as part of a processing mode that occurs in the right hemisphere, the so-called less logically directed or restrictive side of the brain.

Teachers were encouraged throughout this chapter to help children develop skills in art, music, rhythms, and forms of creativity related to those areas. Most of all, creativity and originality are supported through the teacher's recommendation that children do things that are different from each other. They are urged not to copy their work based on other children's products. When the teacher makes a conscious effort to recognize individual elements in the pupils' aesthetic work, they are willing to continue such effort.

Children can learn to value their own ideas when the teacher and other children tell them in what way they are unique, or how they reflect interesting perspectives in color, in movement, in shape, in music. Creativity may contribute to richness of thought and ideas learned in cognitive terms of the social studies, science, mathematics, and the like. Although one does not *cause* the other, it can work in a manner supplementary to the other.

The emphases in the arts at school is more on the process in which the children are involved rather than on the end product. Children discover that everyone sees events in a different way. People prefer different colors, different foods, different music. Preferences that arise in artistic impressions are different from products that are expected from children in the disciplines of an exacting nature and which function within a broader conceptual framework or system of logic, analysis, measurement, and accuracy.

Children can learn a great deal about interpersonal relationships when they present and discuss their ideas about a mural, a theme for rhythmic interpretation, decisions about a puppet show that the total class will put on, and general feelings about artistic endeavors. They find out how children feel about objects, colors, ideas, and friendships. Aesthetic expression, in its expansive view of the ranges of ideas and feelings that people may have, opens many pathways for children's appreciation for people and for the differences that can be enjoyed among them.

Most of the expressive modes mentioned in this chapter stem from natural functions in people (interpreting the world of color, shape, and form, through song, rhythmic movement, and the like) which happen without being intended. What the schools can do is to capitalize on natural tendencies to move, to respond to music, to see shapes and differences, and encourage the potential to be developed further in children.

When adults (who experienced a childhood in which no drawing or limited drawing was done) begin to draw they typically do work that looks similar to a child's early attempts in art. Learning to see the environment in a different way, however, helps the adult visualize and perceive objects and people in a way that may clearly reflect the physical appearance of what is observed. Because the participation in aesthetics affects people in different ways when they decide to become involved, the developmental levels rather than grades or stages of involvement are considered. Individuals may start "seeing" their surroundings and people in different ways at any time of life. Their own efforts in practicing and becoming more deeply involved gradually affects their own development and depth in the accomplishment of their own goals. Developmental levels of achievement represent early stages (whether they are efforts of five-year-old children or of fifteen-year-olds), as well as later stages that can be attained at sixteen or at thirty. The work reflects more the focal point of observation rather than the age of the participant. A child in the fourth grade, for example, may in early attempts do work that looks like the first attempts of any individual regardless of age. Understanding in art may continue to deepen throughout a lifetime.

TOPICS FOR DISCUSSION

1. Give ten reasons why creative expression is an important aspect of teaching in the kindergarten and primary grades.
2. How does the mode of processing on the right hemisphere of the brain affect the human being? Why?
3. State three different activities that can be taught in music and which relate to the social studies content. Describe how you would teach them.
4. Suggest five songs that could be taught to children in the kindergarten and primary grades that would be related to a social studies unit of your choosing. What motivating props would you select for each of the songs?
5. What materials would you use for kindergarten children in their period for painting (in small groups of four, not the entire class simultaneously)? How would you prepare the paint? What kind of brushes would you use?
6. What would you say to children in the first grade to motivate them in creating a brief play using puppets? What kind of puppets would you recommend for their activity? Name five books that would provide information in this regard. What do they recommend in terms of preparation, materials, modes of planning, and the like?
7. What kind of rhythm instruments do children enjoy using? How do you obtain these instruments? Can pupils create their own? What are some of the safeguards that need to be considered?
8. Should people be guided by the critical interpretation of newspaper analysts' views of the world? How can people formulate their own impressions relating to their own view of reality? What things in people's backgrounds shape their perceptions of what reality is? How can children be helped in an honest view of the world stated as they may perceive it?
9. How do creative experiences affect children's individualized impressions and their modes of giving accurate interpretations in terms of their own personal perceptions? Can teachers create atmospheres that encourage or facilitate honest answers? How so? How can some moods of the environment detract from a child's desire to express personal views?
10. Do you think that creativity is inborn? Do people have limited capacities in that direction? Can you support your impressions with citations of studies on the question? Opinions are legitimate in certain contexts. Do not be embarrassed if you do not find data that indicate support of your impressions. Hunches, intuition, and ideas that are yet unsupported by research findings are part of creativity and can guide new research efforts.
11. Can people be taught how to perceive? Is their reality subjective or objective?
12. Why do people's interpretations differ from one another's on things that are seen in the environment? How does this relate to impressions of a movie or a painting?
13. How can the teacher have ready for frequent usage by the children, boxes of materials for colláge? Why do children seem to enjoy cutting and pasting these assemblages?

NOTES

1. Edmund Burke Feldman, *Becoming Human Through Art* (Englewood Cliffs, N.J.: Prentice-Hall, 1970), p. 137.

2. Ibid., p. 143.
3. Ibid., p. 156.
4. Ibid., p. 158. One of the most serious errors in creating an art curriculum "emerges in *the isolation of the child's image-making from the social and human matrix of artistic creation.*" Italics are Feldman's.
5. Ibid.
6. Ibid., p. 166.
7. Laura H. Chapman, *Approaches to Art Education* (New York: Harcourt, 1978), p. v.
8. Seymour Simmons III and Marc S. A. Winer, *Drawing. The Creative Process* (Englewood Cliffs, N.J.: Prentice-Hall, 1977), pp. 2–3.
9. Ibid., p. 2.
10. Ibid., p. 3.
11. Olive R. Francks, "Scribbles? Yes, They *Are* Art!" *Young Children,* Vol. 34, No. 5 (July 1979), pp. 14–22.
12. Doreen J. Croft and Robert D. Hess, *An Activities Handbook for Teachers of Young Children,* 3rd ed. (Boston: Houghton, 1972), pp. 5–27. See also, Robert Kohls, *Your Art Idea Book* (Dansville, N.Y.: The Instructor Publications, 1973). Ideas for making one's own media are found in parts throughout the book.
13. Charles D. Gaitskell and Al Hurwitz, *Children and Their Art,* 2nd ed. (New York: Harcourt, 1970), p. 41.
14. Gordon Beck, and others, Photography. *Windows.* Text by Val Clery. (New York: Penguin, 1978)
15. Gaitskell and Hurwitz, op. cit., pp. 301–312.
16. Aida Cannarsa Snow, *Growing with Children Through Art,* (New York: Van Nostrand, Reinhold, 1968), p. 47.
17. Kohls, op. cit., pp. 25–26.
18. Mary Mayesky, Donald Neuman, and Raymond J. Wlodkowski, *Creative Activities for Young Children* (Albany, N.Y.: Delmar, 1975), p. 7.
19. Leonard Everett Fisher, *Alphabet Art. Thirteen ABCs From Around the World* (New York: Four Winds Press, 1978).
20. Tuli Kupferberg and Sylvia Topp, *First Glance. Childhood Creations of the Famous* (Maplewood, N.J.: Hammond, 1978).
21. Chapman, op. cit., p. 286.
22. Gaitskell and Hurwitz, op. cit., pp. 241–242.
23. Ibid., p. 243.
24. Ibid., p. 244.
25. Feldman, op. cit., p. 311.
26. Dr. Richard Pozil, an optometrist of Los Angeles, Calif., works with children and vision in a developmentally oriented sense. He recommended, in conversation with me, the book by Betty Edwards, *Drawing on the Right Side of the Brain* (Los Angeles: J. P. Tarcher, Distributed by St. Martin's, New York, 1979).
27. Edwards, ibid., pp. 50–55.
28. Michael S. Gazzaniga, "Review of the Split Brain," *U.C.L.A. Educator,* Vol. 17, No. 2 (Spring 1975), pp. 9–12. Gazzaniga indicates (p. 11) that a child who is more talented in processing data (or things seen in the environment) in a visual-spatial sense can become, when forced to solve problems using a verbal articulatory mode at school, hostile toward both the teacher and the learning process.
29. Feldman, op. cit., p. 267.
30. Ibid., p. 269.
31. Barbara Herberholz, *Early Childhood Art* (Dubuque, Iowa: Brown, 1974), pp. 100–104.
32. Ibid., p. 39.
33. William R. Sur, Adeline McCall, William R. Fisher, and Mary R. Tolbert. *This Is Music for Today,* Book 1, Boston: Allyn and Bacon, Inc., 1971. 192 pp.; and Adeline McCall, *This Is Music for Today,* Kindergarten and Nursery School. Boston: Allyn and Bacon, Inc., 1971. 160 pp.
34. M. C. Weller Pugmire, *Experiences in Music for Young Children* (Albany, N.Y.: Delmar, 1977), p. 97. It is suggested that the background music of some movies (recorded on records or cassettes) can be appropriate for use in creating a quiet or relaxing mood for the children's rest period.

35. Ibid., pp. 145–149. Kathleen M. Bayless and Marjorie E. Ramsey, *Music. A Way of Life for the Young Child* (St. Louis, Mo.: Mosby, 1978), pp. 38–51. See also, John Hawkinson and Martha Faulhaber, *Rhythms, Music and Instruments to Make* (Chicago: Whitman, 1975).
36. Bayless and Ramsey, op. cit., pp. 171–172.
37. Ibid., p. 171.
38. Ibid., 171–172.
39. Ibid., p. 172.
40. M. Hohner, Inc., Andrews Road, Hicksville, N.Y., or Rhythm Band Incorporated at 407–409 Throckmorton Street, Fort Worth, Tex. 76102 and Lyons Band Instrument Company, 688 Industrial Drive, Elmhurst, Ill. 60126. More information on the quality of music found in the Orff methods can be found in referring to Robert Evans Nye and Vernice Trousdale Nye, *Music in the Elementary School*, 3rd ed. (Englewood Cliffs, N.J.: Prentice-Hall, 1970), pp. 373–374.
41. Bayless and Ramsey, op. cit., p. 172. Parents are expected to know how to play the violin after several months of instruction before the child is expected to become involved in learning how to play the violin in any formalized sense.
42. Dorothy T. McDonald, *Music in Our Lives: The Early Years* (Washington, D.C.: National Assoc. for the Education of Young Children, 1979), p. 44.
43. Hawkinson and Faulhaber, op. cit., 96 pp.; Bayless and Ramsey, op. cit., pp. 44–51; Martha Faulhaber and Janet Underhill, *Music: Invent Your Own* (Chicago: Whitman, 1974). Timbre and melody of voices are discussed as aspects of creating music.
44. Paul Watzlawick, *The Language of Change* (New York: Basic, 1978), pp. 14–17.
45. Nye and Nye, op. cit., p. 186.
46. Pugmire, op. cit., p. 102.
47. Ibid.
48. John U. Michaelis, *Social Studies for Children in a Democracy*, 6th ed. (Englewood Cliffs, N.J.: Prentice-Hall, 1976), p. 305.
49. Roma Trundle, *Peoples of the World* (London: Usborne Publishing Ltd., 1978), 32 pp.; and Ann Cole, Carolyn Haas, Elizabeth Heller, and Betty Weinberger, *Children Are Children Are Children* (Boston: Little, Brown, 1978).
50. William R. Sur, Mary R. Tolbert, William R. Fisher, and Adeline McCall, *This Is Music Today*, Book 2, Teacher's Edition (Boston: Allyn, 1971), p. 45.

SELECTED REFERENCES

BAYLESS, KATHLEEN M., and MARJORIE E. RAMSEY. *Music. A Way of Life for the Young Child.* St. Louis, Mo.: The C. V. Mosby Company, 1978. 206 pp.

BECK, GORDON, and others, photography. *Windows.* Text by Val Clery. New York: Penguin Books, 1978. 159 pp.

CHAPMAN, LAURA H. *Approaches to Art Education.* New York: Harcourt Brace Jovanovich, Inc., 1978. 444 pp.

CHERRY, CLARE. *Creative Art for the Developing Child.* Belmont, Calif.: Fearon Publishers, Inc., 1972. 186 pp.

COLE, ANN, CAROLYN HAAS, ELIZABETH HELLER, and BETTY WEINBERGER. *Children Are Children Are Children.* Boston: Little, Brown and Company, 1978. 212 pp.

CROFT, DOREEN, J., and ROBERT D. HESS. *An Activities Handbook for Teachers of Young Children*, 3rd ed. Boston: Houghton Mifflin Company, 1980. 257 pp.

EDWARDS, BETTY. *Drawing on the Right Side of the Brain.* Los Angeles, Calif.: J. P. Tarcher, Inc., Distributed by St. Martin's Press, New York, 1979. 207 pp.

FAULHABER, MARTHA, and JANET UNDERHILL. *Music: Invent Your Own.* Chicago: Albert Whitman and Company, 1974. 48 pp.

FELDMAN, EDMUND BURKE. *Becoming Human Through Art.* Englewood Cliffs, N.J.: Prentice-Hall, Inc., 1970. 389 pp.

FISHER, LEONARD EVERETT. *Alphabet Art. Thirteen ABCs from Around the World.* New York: Four Winds Press, 1978. 64 pp.

FLEMMING, BONNIE MACK, DARLENE SOFTLEY HAMILTON, and JoANNE DEAL HICKS. *Resources for Creative Teaching in Early Childhood Education.* New York: Harcourt Brace Jovanovich, Inc., 1977. 634 pp.

FRANCKS, OLIVE R. "Scribbles? Yes, They *Are* Art!" *Young Children*, Vol. 34, No. 5 (July 1979), pp. 14–22.

GAITSKELL, CHARLES D., and AL HURWITZ. *Children and Their Art*, 2nd ed. New York: Harcourt Brace Jovanovich, Inc., 1970. 507 pp.

GAZZANIGA, MICHAEL S. "Review of the Split Brain," *U.C.L.A. Educator*, Vol. 17, No. 2 (Spring 1975), pp. 9–12.

HAWKINSON, JOHN, and MARTHA FAULHABER. *Rhythms, Music, and Instruments to Make.* Chicago: Albert Whitman and Company, 1975. 96 pp.

Herberholz, Barbara. *Early Childhood Art.* Dubuque, Iowa: William C. Brown Company, Publishers, 1974. 174 pp.

KOHLS, ROBERT. *Your Art Idea Book.* Dansville, N.Y.: The Instructor Publications, Inc., 1973. 48 pp.

KUPFERBERG, TULI, and SYLVIA TOPP. *First Glance. Childhood Creations of the Famous.* Maplewood, N.J.: Hammond Incorporated, 1978. 192 pp.

LAMENT, MARYLEE McMURRAY. *Music in Elementary Education.* New York: Macmillan Publishing Co., Inc., 1976. 320 pp.

LOWENFELD, VIKTOR, and W. LAMBERT BRITTAIN. *Creative and Mental Growth*, 6th ed. New York: Macmillan Publishing Co., Inc., 1975. 430 pp.

McDONALD, DOROTHY T. *Music in Our Lives: The Early Years.* Washington, D.C.: National Association for the Education of Young Children, 1979. 68 pp.

MARKOW, JACK, *Drawing Funny Pictures.* New York: Grossett & Dunlap, Inc., 1969. 48 pp.

MAYESKY, MARY, DONALD NEUMAN, and RAYMOND J. WLODKOWSKI. *Creative Activities for Young Children.* Albany, N.Y., Delmar Publishers, 1975. 185 pp.

MICHAELIS, JOHN U. *Social Studies for Children in a Democracy*, 6th ed. Englewood Cliffs, N.J., Prentice-Hall, Inc., 1976. 516 pp.

MOORE, ELAINE, and JERRI GREENLEE. *Ideas for Learning Centers.* Belmont, Calif.: Lear Siegler, Inc./Fearon Publishers, 1974. 128 pp.

NYE, ROBERT EVANS, and VERNICE TROUSDALE NYE. *Music in the Elementary School* Englewood Cliffs, N.J.: Prentice-Hall, Inc., 1970. 660 pp.

PUGMIRE, M. C. WELLER. *Experiences in Music for Young Children.* Albany, N.Y.: Delmar Publishers, 1977. 272 pp.

SIMMONS, SEYMOUR, III and MARC S. A. WINER. *Drawing. The Creative Process* (Englewood Cliffs, N.J.: Prentice Hall, Inc., 1977). 272 pp.

SNOW, AIDA CANNARSA. *Growing with Children Through Art.* New York: Van Nostrand Reinhold Company, 1968. 150 pp.

SUR, WILLIAM R., ADELINE McCALL, WILLIAM R. FISHER, and MARY R. TOLBERT. This Is Music for Today, Book 1. Boston: Allyn & Bacon, Inc., 1971. 192 pp.

———, MARY R. TOLBERT, WILLIAM R. FISHER, and ADELINE McCALL. This Is Music for Today, Book 2. Boston: Allyn & Bacon, Inc., 1971. 194 pp.

THOMAS, JENNIE. *Helping Children Draw.* Dansville, N.Y.: The Instructor Publications, Inc., 1973. 48 pp.

TRUNDLE, ROMA. *Peoples of the World.* London: Usborne Publishing Ltd., 1978. 32 pp.

WATZLAWICK, PAUL. *The Language of Change.* New York: Basic Book, Inc., Publishers, 1978. pp. 14–17.

INDEX